Microsoft®
Windows® XP
Illustrated Complete

Steven M. Johnson

THOMSON
™
COURSE TECHNOLOGY

Australia • Canada • Mexico • Singapore • Spain • United Kingdom • United States

Microsoft ® Windows ® XP—Illustrated Complete
Steven M. Johnson

Managing Editor:
Nicole Jones Pinard

Senior Product Manager:
Emily Heberlein

Associate Product Manager:
Christina Kling Garrett

Editorial Assistant:
Elizabeth M. Harris

Production Editor:
Karen Jacot

Developmental Editor:
Jennifer T. Campbell

Composition House:
GEX Publishing Services

QA Manuscript Reviewers:
Christian Kunciw, Harris Bierhoff,
Chris Scriver, Shawn Day

Text Designer:
Joseph Lee, Black Fish Design

For permission to use material from this text or product, contact us by
Tel (800) 730-2214
Fax (800) 730-2215
www.thomsonrights.com

Disclaimer
Course Technology reserves the right to revise this publication and make changes from time to time in its content without notice.

Trademarks
Some of the product names and company names used in this book have been used for identification purposes only and may be trademarks or registered trademarks of their respective manufacturers and sellers.

Microsoft and the Office logo are either registered trademarks or trademarks of Microsoft Corporation in the United States and/or other countries. Course Technology is an independent entity from Microsoft Corporation and not affiliated with Microsoft in any manner.

Credits
Some of the images and videos used in this book are the property of Atlas Image [or Atlas Image mosaic] obtained as part of the Two Micron All Sky Survey (2MASS), a joint project of the University of Massachusetts and the Infrared Processing and Analysis Center/California Institute of Technology, funded by the National Aeronautics and Space Administration (NASA) and the National Science Foundation; and media was also created by STScI under contract for NASA.

ISBN 0-619-05702-5

The Illustrated Series Vision

Teaching and writing about computer applications can be extremely rewarding and challenging. How do we engage students and keep their interest? How do we teach them skills that they can easily apply on the job? As we set out to write this book, our goals were to develop a textbook that:

▶ works for a beginning student

▶ provides varied, flexible and meaningful exercises and projects to reinforce the skills

▶ serves as a reference tool

▶ makes your job as an educator easier, by providing resources above and beyond the textbook to help you teach your course

Our popular, streamlined format is based on advice from instructional designers and customers. This flexible design presents each lesson on a two-page spread, with step-by-step instructions on the left, and screen illustrations on the right. This signature style, coupled with high-caliber content, provides a comprehensive introduction to Microsoft Windows XP — it is a teaching package for the instructor and a learning experience for the student.

ACKNOWLEDGMENTS

Once again, it has been a wonderful experience working with the talented and professional people at Course Technology. I would like to especially thank Jennifer Campbell for making this book easier to read, understand, and follow. I would also like to thank the manuscript reviewers, Rebekah May and Tracy Miller, for their helpful feedback during the writing process. And, most importantly, I would like to thank my wife, Holly, and three children, JP, Brett, and Hannah, for their support and encouragement during the project.

Steven Johnson

Preface

Welcome to *Microsoft Windows XP—Illustrated Complete*. This highly visual text offers users an introduction to Windows XP, covering both the Home and Professional versions. It also serves as an excellent reference for future use.

▶ Organization and Coverage

This text contains sixteen units, which cover basic through advanced Windows XP software skills. Students learn how to work with Windows programs, manage files and folders, customize Windows using the Control Panel, maintain their computers, explore the Internet with Microsoft Internet Explorer, and exchange mail and news using Outlook Express. Students also learn to manage shared files, backup and administer their computer, and work with Windows media and Movie Maker. A comprehensive appendix covers the new features of Windows XP and differences between the Home and Professional versions, as well as how to install Windows XP.

▶ About this Approach

What makes the Illustrated approach so effective at teaching software skills? It's quite simple. Each skill is presented on two facing pages, with the step-by-step instructions on the left page, and large screen illustrations on the right. Students can focus on a single skill without having to turn the page. This unique design makes information extremely accessible and easy to absorb, and provides a great reference for after the course is over. This hands-on approach also makes it ideal for both self-paced and instructor-led classes.

Each lesson, or "information display," contains the following elements shown in the sample two-page spread to the right.

Easy-to-follow introductions to every lesson focus on a single concept to help students get the point quickly.

Each 2-page spread focuses on a single skill or concept.

Paintbrush icons introduce the real-world case study used throughout the book.

Unit D Windows XP

Using Personal Folders

Windows makes it easy to manage the personal and business files and folders you work with everyday with a set of personal folders. My Documents is a personal folder, which contains additional personal folders, such as My Pictures, My Music, and My Videos. Depending on previous installation, devices installed or other users, your personal folders might differ. The contents of your personal folders are private, unless you decide to share the contents with others who use your computer. Windows creates personal folders for everyone on your computer to make sure the contents of personal folders remain private. Each personal folder is identified by the user's name. For example, if John Casey and an associate Shawn Brooks use the same computer, there are two sets of personal folders, one named John Casey's Documents and another named Shawn Brooks' Documents. When John logs on to the computer, his personal folders appear as My Documents and Shawn's appear as Shawn Brooks' Documents, but John cannot access them. John wants to open his personal folders and find out more about their functionality.

Steps

1. **Click the Start button on the taskbar, then click My Documents**
   The My Documents window opens, as shown in Figure D-17.

   QuickTip
   To open the My Pictures folder from the Start Menu, click the Start button, then click My Pictures.

2. **Double-click the My Pictures folder**
   The My Pictures window opens, displaying the contents of the folder as thumbnails. A thumbnail is a miniature image of the contents of a file; thumbnails are often used to quickly browse through multiple images. If the folder doesn't contain images, Windows inserts icons instead of thumbnails.

3. **Double-click the Sample Pictures folder**
   The Sample Pictures window opens, displaying the contents of the picture folder as a filmstrip, as shown in Figure D-18. Filmstrip is a special view, located on the Views button or View menu, available only for folders with many pictures.

   QuickTip
   To rotate pictures in Filmstrip view, click the Rotate Clockwise button or the Rotate Counterclockwise button.

4. **Click the Next Image (Right Arrow) button until the last image in the Sample Pictures folder appears in the filmstrip**

5. **Click the Back button on the Standard Buttons toolbar twice to display the My Documents folder**

6. **Double-click the My Videos folder**
   The My Videos folder opens, displaying the contents of the folder as thumbnails. For videos, the first frame appears in the thumbnail.

TABLE D-1: Picture tasks in the My Pictures folder

picture task	description
View as a slide show	Displays a full screen version of each picture in the folder for five seconds; click buttons on the Slide Show toolbar to start, pause, and stop the show
Order prints online	Opens the Online Print Ordering Wizard, which helps you order prints of your digital photographs over the Internet
Print this picture or Print the selected pictures	Opens the Photo Printing Wizard, which helps you format and print photographs from a digital camera or scanner
Set as desktop background	Sets the selected picture as the desktop background
Show for pictures online	Opens the Windows XP Pictures Online Web site in your Web browser, where you can find and download pictures over the Internet

▶ WINDOWS XP D-14 **CUSTOMIZING FILE AND FOLDER MANAGEMENT**

Hints as well as troubleshooting advice, right where you need them — next to the step itself.

Tables provide quickly accessible summaries of key terms, toolbar buttons, or keyboard alternatives connected with the lesson material. Students can refer easily to this information when working on their own projects at a later time.

Clear step-by-step directions explain how to complete the specific task. What students will type is in green.

Every lesson features large-size, full-color illustrations, bringing the lesson concepts to life.

FIGURE D-17: My Documents folder

General file and folder task links

Personal folders; yours might differ

FIGURE D-18: Sample Pictures folder

Picture specific task links

Buttons to display and modify pictures

Filmstrip view

Pictures in filmstrip

CLUES TO USE

Using the Shared Documents folder

Shared folders are related to your personal folders on a shared computer. They provide a place for you to make files, pictures, and music available to everyone who uses your computer. Your personal folders: My Documents, My Pictures, My Music, and My Videos each have a shared counterpart: Shared Documents, Shared Pictures, etc., in which you can copy files and folders to share with others. To share files and folders on your computer, click the Start button on the taskbar, click My Documents, click the file or folder you want to share, then drag the file or folder to Shared Documents in the left pane under Other Places. To share pictures and music on your computer, open My Documents, double-click the My Pictures or My Music folder, click the file or folder you want to share, click Move this file or Move this folder to open the Move Items dialog box, click the Shared Documents folder, click Shared Pictures or Shared Music, then click Move.

CUSTOMIZING FILE AND FOLDER MANAGEMENT WINDOWS XP D-15 ◀

Clues to Use boxes provide concise information that either expands on one component of the major lesson skill or describes an independent task that is in some way related to the major lesson skill.

► **What kinds of assignments are included in the book? At what level of difficulty?**

The lesson assignments use Wired Coffee, a fictional coffee company, as the case study. The assignments on the blue pages at the end of each unit increase in difficulty. Project files and case studies, with international examples, provide a great variety of interesting and relevant business applications for skills. Assignments include:

• **Concepts Reviews** include multiple choice, matching, and screen identification questions.

• **Skills Reviews** provide additional hands-on, step-by-step reinforcement.

• **Independent Challenges** are case projects requiring critical thinking and application of the skills learned in the unit. The Independent Challenges increase in difficulty, with the first Independent Challenge in each unit being the easiest (most step-by-step with detailed instructions). Independent Challenges 2-4 become increasingly open-ended, requiring more independent thinking and problem solving.

• **Visual Workshops** show a completed file and require that the file be created without any step-by-step guidance, involving problem solving and an independent application of the unit skills.

► **What online learning options are available to accompany this book?**

Options for this title include a testbank in MyCourse 2.0, WebCT and Blackboard ready formats to make assessment using one of these platforms easy to manage. Visit www.course.com for more information on our online learning materials.

Instructor Resources

The Instructor's Resource Kit (IRK) CD is Course Technology's way of putting the resources and information needed to teach and learn effectively into your hands. All the components are available on the IRK, and many of the resources can be downloaded from www.course.com.

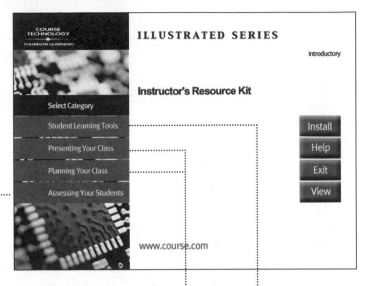

ASSESSING YOUR STUDENTS

Solution Files
Solution Files are Project Files completed with comprehensive sample answers. Use these files to evaluate your students' work. Or, distribute them electronically or in hard copy so students can verify their own work.

ExamView
ExamView is a powerful testing software package that allows you to create and administer printed, computer (LAN-based), and Internet exams. ExamView includes hundreds of questions that correspond to the topics covered in this text, enabling students to generate detailed study guides that include page references for further review. The computer-based and Internet testing components allow students to take exams at their computers, and also save you time by grading each exam automatically.

PRESENTING YOUR CLASS

Figure Files
Figure Files contain all the figures from the book in .bmp format. Use the figure files to create transparency masters or in a PowerPoint presentation.

PowerPoint Presentations
Each unit has a corresponding PowerPoint presentation that you can use in lecture, distribute to your students, or customize to suit your course.

STUDENT TOOLS

Project Files and Project Files List
To complete some of the units in this book, your students will need **Project Files**. Put them on a file server for students to copy. The Project Files are available on the Instructor's Resource Kit CD-ROM, the Review Pack, and can also be downloaded from www.course.com.

Instruct students to use the **Project Files List** at the end of the book. This list gives instructions on copying and organizing files.

PLANNING YOUR CLASS

Instructor's Manual
Available as an electronic file, the Instructor's Manual is quality-assurance tested and includes unit overviews, detailed lecture topics for each unit with teaching tips, comprehensive sample solutions to all lessons and end-of-unit material, and extra Independent Challenges. The Instructor's Manual is available on the Instructor's Resource Kit CD-ROM, or you can download it from www.course.com.

Sample Syllabus
Prepare and customize your course easily using this sample course outline (available on the Instructor's Resource Kit CD-ROM).

Brief Contents

Contents

Windows XP

Contents

Contents

Unit K: Sharing Information among Programs   K-1

Unit L: Working with Windows Media   L-1

Contents

Read This Before You Begin

Differences Between Microsoft® Windows® XP Home and Professional

This book is written for Microsoft Windows XP Home and Professional Editions. The Home Edition is a subset of the Professional Edition. In other words, the Home Edition contains all the same features contained in the Professional Edition. However, the Professional Edition contains additional features geared toward the business world that are not included in the Home Edition. When there are differences between the two versions of the software, steps or features written for a specific Windows XP edition are indicated with the name of the edition. (See "Identify Differences between Windows XP Home and Professional" in the appendix for more information.)

Windows XP Software

Windows XP ships in three editions, including Home Edition for consumers, Professional Edition for business and power users, and a 64-bit version for Intel Itanium processor-based systems, called Windows XP 64-bit Edition.

Installing/Upgrading: Windows 98, 98 SE, and Me users can upgrade to Windows XP Home Edition or Professional. Windows 2000 Professional and Windows NT 4.0 Workstation users can upgrade to Windows Professional, but not to Home Edition. Windows 95 and Windows NT 3.51, or earlier, are not supported for upgrading, so you will need to buy a full version of Windows XP if you wish to upgrade.

Uninstalling: Windows 98, 98 SE, and Me users can uninstall Windows XP if the upgrade doesn't work out for some reason. This capability is not available to Windows NT 4.0 and Windows 2000 upgraders.

Windows XP Settings

Each time you start Windows XP, the operating system remembers previous settings, such as the Control Panel options. When you start Windows XP, your initial screen might look different than the ones in this book. For the purposes of this book, make sure the following settings in Windows XP are in place before you start each unit.

- Change folder option settings to match the steps and screens in the book. Click the Start button on the taskbar, click My Documents, click Tools on the menu bar, then click Folder Options. In the Folder Options dialog box, set the following settings, then click OK:
- On the General tab, click the Open each folder in the same window option button.
- On the General tab, click the Double-click to open an item (single-click to select) option button.
- On the View tab, click Restore Defaults, click the Hide file extensions for known file types check box to deselect it in the Advanced settings list box to make sure you can see the three letter DOS filename extensions on your computer.
- For Home edition users, Backup is not available to install using Add or Remove Programs. To install the software, insert the Windows XP Home installation CD, open My Computer and navigate to the folder where the software is located (CD *driveletter*:\VALUEADD\MSFT\ NTBACKUP), double-click the file named Ntbackup.msi to start the setup wizard, follow the installation instructions, then click Finish to complete the process.
- In addition to the programs installed during the typical Windows installation, the following Windows programs should also be installed: Clipboard Viewer, Character Map, Paint, and Backup. If a program is not available, use the Add or Remove Programs icon in the Control Panel to install the program. (See "Adding a Program" in Unit F for more information and specific instructions.)
- Turn Status Bar Off for Control Panel. Click the Start button on the taskbar, click Control Panel, click View on the menu bar, then click Status Bar to uncheck the option.
- Turn off AutoArrange icons on desktop. Right-click a blank area on the desktop, point to Arrange Icons By, then click Auto Arrange to uncheck the option.
- Reset toolbars. Click the Start button on the taskbar, click My Computer, click View on the menu bar, point to Toolbars, click Customize, click Reset, then click Close.

Project Files

To complete the lessons and end-of-unit material in this book, students need to obtain the necessary project files. Please refer to the instructions on the inside cover for various methods of getting these files. Once obtained, the user selects where to store the files, such as to the hard disk drive, network server, floppy disk, or Zip disk. Depending on where you store the files, you might need to relink any external files, such as a video clip, associated with a project file when prompted as you open it. If students use a 1.44 MB floppy disk, they might not have enough space to store all the solutions files on the disk. If so, use another floppy disk.

Using Copies: For Units C, D, and J that work with managing folders and files using My Computer and Windows Explorer, make sure students use a *copy* of the Project Files instead of the originals. Using a copy of the Project Files will allow students to work through the lessons again.

Restore Settings: In order to work through the lessons in this book, students need to change operating system and program settings. The lessons make every attempt to restore the operating system and program settings, but please be aware that your initial settings might be different than the ones in this book.

To Use Print Screen

To complete many of the lessons and end-of-unit material in this book, students need to take a snap shot of the screen and print it out. To take a snap shot of the screen and print it, complete the following instructions: Press [Print Screen] (also appears as [PrtScrn] or [Print Scrn]) to place the entire screen on the Clipboard or press [Alt][Print Screen] to place the active window on the Clipboard. Click the Start button on the taskbar, point to All Programs, point to Accessories, then click Paint to open Microsoft Paint, a graphics program. In Paint, click Edit on the menu bar, click Paste to paste the screen into Paint, then click Yes to paste the large image, if necessary. Click the Text button (contains the letter A) on the Toolbox, click a blank area in the work area, then type your name to identify your print out. Click File on the menu bar, click Page Setup, change 100% normal size to 50% in the Scaling area, then click OK. Click File on the menu bar, click Print, then click Print in the Print dialog box.

Getting
Started with Windows XP

Objectives

- ► **Start Windows and view the desktop**
- ► **Use the mouse**
- ► **Get started with the Windows desktop**
- ► **Manage windows**
- ► **Use menus, toolbars, and panes**
- ► **Use scroll bars**
- ► **Use dialog boxes**
- ► **Use Windows Help and Support**
- ► **Turn off the computer**

Microsoft Windows XP Home and Professional is an **operating system**, a computer program that controls the basic operation of your computer and the programs you run on it. **Programs**, also known as **applications**, are task-oriented software you use to accomplish specific tasks, such as word processing, managing files on your computer, and performing calculations. When you work with Windows XP, you will notice **icons**, which are small pictures on your screen intended to be meaningful symbols of the items they represent. You will also notice **windows** (thus the name of the operating system), rectangular frames on your screen that can contain several icons, the contents of a file, or other usable data. A **file** is a collection of information (such as a letter or list of addresses) that has a unique name, distinguishing it from other files. This use of icons and windows is called a **graphical user interface** (**GUI**, pronounced "gooey"), meaning that you interact ("interface") with the computer through the use of graphics: icons and other meaningful words, symbols, and windows. ➤ In this unit, you will be introduced to basic Windows skills.

Windows XP

Starting Windows and Viewing the Desktop

When you first start Windows XP, you see the Windows desktop, as shown in Figure A-1, or a logon screen (a way to identify yourself on the computer) depending on your installation. See Table A-1 for a description of your computer start-up type. The **desktop** is an on-screen version of an actual desk, containing windows, icons, files, and programs, which you can use to access, store, organize, modify, share, and explore information, such as a letter, a list of addresses, or the news, whether it resides on your computer, a network, or the Internet. The **Internet** is a worldwide collection of computers linked together to share information, while a **network** is a local area one. The desktop is sometimes called **active** because it allows you to access the Internet and view Internet content directly from it. The bar at the bottom of your screen is called the **taskbar**; it allows you to start programs and switch among currently running programs. (At the moment, none are running; the computer is idle.) At the left end of the taskbar is the **Start button**, which you use to start programs, find and open files, access the Windows Help and Support Center, and much more. At the right end of the taskbar is the **notification area**, which displays the time, date, and program related icons. If icons in the notification area are not used for awhile, an arrow appears to hide the icons and reduce clutter. You can click the arrow to display and hide the icons. When you use a hidden icon, it reappears in the notification area. If you upgraded your computer to Windows XP from a previous version of Windows, your desktop might contain additional desktop icons and toolbars, such as the **Quick Launch toolbar**, which contains buttons you use to quickly start your Internet browser and media player and show the desktop. ➤ Windows XP automatically starts when you turn on your computer. If Windows is not currently running, follow the steps below to start it now.

Steps

1. **Turn on your computer**
   Windows automatically starts and displays the desktop, as shown in Figure A-1, or a logon screen (either the Welcome screen or Network dialog box) asking you to select or enter a user name and password to identify yourself on the computer, before showing the desktop. If the desktop appears (meaning you are using a nonshared computer), continue to Step 3, otherwise, continue to Step 2 to log on.

Trouble?

If you are new to using the mouse, read through the next topic "Using the Mouse."

2. **In the Welcome screen (on a shared computer), click your user name, type your password, then press [Enter], or in the Network dialog box (on a networked computer), press and hold [Ctrl] and [Alt] with one hand, then press [Del] with the other to display the Windows Security dialog box, in the User name text box type your username if necessary, type your password in the Password text box, then click OK**
   Only bullets appear as you type the password. This helps to prevent other people from learning your password. Once the password is accepted, the Windows desktop appears on your screen, as shown in Figure A-1.

QuickTip

To run the Windows XP tour, click the Start button on the taskbar, point to All Programs, point to Accessories, then click Tour Windows XP.

3. **If a ScreenTip appears, click the Close button in the ScreenTip**
   A **ScreenTip** is informational help that appears when you need it. When you start Windows XP for the first time, a ScreenTip pointing to the Windows XP Tour icon on the taskbar appears, asking if you want to take a tour of Windows XP. The ScreenTip closes, and the Windows XP Tour icon is removed from the notification area on the taskbar.

FIGURE A-1: Windows XP desktop

Mouse pointer

Recycle Bin icon;
your desktop
may contain
additional icons

Start button

Windows
desktop;
your back-
ground
might be
different

Recycle Bin

start   9:53 PM

Taskbar

Arrow indicates
hidden icons

Notification area

TABLE A-1: Starting a computer with Windows XP

what you see at start up	means you have a
desktop	nonshared (single user) computer; no user name and password required
Welcome screen	shared (multiple users) computer; user name and password required
Network dialog box	networked (connected to a computer on a network) computer; user name and password required

CLUES TO USE

Using and changing a password

Passwords are used to maintain security on a shared or networked computer. Windows uses encryption, which is the process of logically scrambling data, to keep your password secure on your computer. When choosing a password, remember that the Windows password program is case-sensitive, which means the program makes a distinction between uppercase and lowercase letters. Your password should be at least seven characters long, which is optimal for encryption. It should include, if possible, combinations of capital letters, lowercase letters, and non-alphabetic characters (numbers and symbols). Never write down your password on paper or let someone look over your shoulder as you log on to the computer. Always be sure to log off or shut down when you walk away from your computer. You specify a user name and password when you install Windows XP or open User Accounts in the Control Panel on a shared computer, or an instructor or technical support person (the person in charge of your network) assigns you a user name and password on a networked computer. To change your password on a networked computer with Windows XP Professional, press [Ctrl][Alt][Del] after you start Windows to open the Windows Security dialog box, click Change Password, type the old password in the Old Password text box, type the new password in the New Password and Confirm New Password text boxes, then click OK. If you have forgotten your password, the Forgotten Password Wizard allows you to create a password reset disk that you can use to recover user account information (user name and password) and personalized computer settings. To create a reset disk, click Change Password in the Windows Security dialog box, click Backup, click Next, then follow the wizard instructions. To change your password or create a password reset disk on a shared computer, click User Accounts in the Control Panel, then follow the instructions provided.

Using the Mouse

A **mouse** is a handheld input device you roll across a flat surface (such as a desk or a mouse pad) to position the **mouse pointer**, the small symbol that indicates the pointer's relative position on the desktop. When you move the mouse, the mouse pointer on the screen moves in the same direction. The shape of the mouse pointer changes to indicate different activities. Table A-2 shows some common mouse pointer shapes. Once you move the mouse pointer to a desired position on the screen, you use the **mouse buttons**, shown in Figure A-2, to "tell" your computer what you want it to do. Table A-3 describes the basic mouse techniques you use frequently when working in Windows. Now you will try using the mouse to become familiar with these navigational skills.

1. **Place your hand on the mouse, locate the mouse pointer ⬚ on the desktop, then move the mouse back and forth across your desk**
   As you move the mouse, the mouse pointer moves correspondingly.

Trouble?

Your icon may differ.

2. **Move the mouse to position the mouse pointer over the Recycle Bin icon 🗑 in the lower-right corner of the desktop**
   Positioning the mouse pointer over an icon or over any specific item on the screen is called **pointing**. If pointing to the icon highlights it, you are not using default Windows XP settings. Consult your instructor or technical support person. This book assumes you are using Windows default double-click mouse settings.

3. **Press and release the left mouse button**
   The act of pressing a mouse button once and releasing it is called **clicking**. The icon is now highlighted, or shaded differently than the other icons on the desktop. The act of clicking an item, such as an icon, indicates that you have **selected** it to perform some future operation on it. To perform any type of operation on an icon, such as moving it, you must first select it.

4. **Point to 🗑, press and hold down the left mouse button, move the mouse to the center of the desktop, then release the mouse button**
   The icon moves with the mouse pointer. This is called **dragging**, which you use to move Windows elements. If the icon jumps a little when you release the mouse, the desktop is set to automatically align icons with an invisible grid. To turn off the automatic alignment with the grid, right-click a blank area of the desktop, point to Arrange Icons By, then click Align to Grid to deselect it. If you are still having trouble, right-click the desktop again, point to Arrange Icons By, then click AutoArrange to deselect it.

QuickTip

When a step tells you to "click," it means, by default, to left-click. The step says "right-click" if you are to click with the right mouse button.

5. **Point to 🗑, then press and release the right mouse button**
   Clicking the right mouse button is known as **right-clicking**. Right-clicking an item on the desktop displays a **shortcut menu**, shown in Figure A-3. This menu displays the commands most commonly used for the item you clicked; the available commands differ for every item.

6. **Click anywhere outside the menu to close the shortcut menu**
   Clicking outside the menu in a blank area, or pressing [Esc], closes the shortcut menu without performing a command.

QuickTip

To quickly rearrange icons on the desktop, right-click a blank area of the desktop, point to Arrange Icons By, then click the appropriate option.

7. **Move 🗑 back to its original position in the lower-right corner of the desktop using the pointing and dragging skills you just learned**

8. **Point to 🗑, then click the left mouse button twice quickly**
   The Recycle Bin window opens, containing file icons, which you want to delete. Clicking the mouse button twice is known as **double-clicking**, and it allows you to open the window, program, or file that an icon represents. Leave the desktop as it is and move on to the next lesson.

y

▶ WINDOWS XP A-4   **GETTING STARTED WITH WINDOWS XP**

FIGURE A-2: Typical mouse

Right mouse button

Left mouse button

Mouse; your mouse may be different

FIGURE A-3: Shortcut menu

Selected icon

Shortcut menu

TABLE A-2: Common mouse pointer shapes

shape	used to
▹	Select items, choose commands, start programs, and work with programs
I	Position the mouse pointer for editing or inserting text; called the insertion point or cursor
▹⧖	Indicate Windows is busy processing a command
↔ or ↕	Position the mouse pointer on the edge of a window to change its size
ᕐᕂ	Position the mouse pointer to select and open Web-based content

TABLE A-3: Basic mouse techniques

task	what to do
Pointing	Move the mouse to position it over an item on the desktop
Clicking	Press and release the left mouse button
Double-clicking	Press and release the left mouse button twice quickly
Dragging	Point to an item, press and hold the left mouse button, move the mouse to a new location, then release the mouse button
Right-clicking	Point to an item, then press and release the right mouse button

Using the mouse with the Web style

When you use the standard Windows operating system, you click an item to select it, then double-click the item to open it. However, when using the Internet, you point to an item to select it and single-click the item to open it. Because Windows XP integrates use of the Internet with its other functions, it allows you to choose whether you want to extend the way you click on the Internet to the rest of your computer work by single-clicking (known as the Internet or Web style) icons to open them, or by double-clicking (known as the Classic style). To change from one style to the other, click the Start button on the taskbar, click Control Panel, click Switch to Classic View (if necessary), double-click Folder Options, click the Single-click to open an item (point to select), or Double-click to open an item (single-click to select) option button, then click OK. Windows XP is set by default to double-click, and the steps in this book assume you are using Windows Classic style.

Getting Started with the Windows Desktop

The key to getting started with the Windows desktop is learning how to use the Start button on the taskbar. Clicking the Start button on the taskbar displays the **Start menu**, a list of commands that allows you to start a program, open a document, change a Windows setting, find a file, or display support information. Table A-4 describes the available commands on this menu that are installed with Windows XP. As you become more familiar with Windows, you might want to customize the Start menu to include additional items that you use most often and change Windows settings in the Control Panel to customize your Windows desktop. You will begin by viewing the Start menu and opening the **Control Panel**, a window containing various programs that allow you to specify how your computer looks and performs.

Steps

QuickTip

To remove a program from the pinned items list, right-click the program on the Start menu, then click Unpin from Start menu, or Remove from This List.

1. Click the **Start button** on the taskbar

The Start menu opens, as shown in Figure A-4. You use commands on the Start menu to start programs or change Windows system settings. The top of the Start menu indicates who is currently using the computer. The left column of the Start menu is separated into two lists: pinned items above the separator line and most frequently used items below. The **pinned** items remain on the Start menu, like a push pin holds paper on a bulletin board. The most frequently used items change as you use programs: Windows keeps track of which programs you use and displays them on the Start menu for easy access. The right column of the Start menu provides easy access to folders, Windows settings, help information, and search functionality. An arrow next to a menu item indicates a **cascading menu**, or **submenu**, which is a list of commands for that menu item. Pointing at the arrow displays a submenu from which you can choose additional commands.

QuickTip

To move an item on the Start menu, click the Start button, then drag it to a new location. A black horizontal bar indicates the new location.

2. Click **Control Panel** on the Start menu

The Control Panel opens, containing categories or icons for various programs that allow you to specify how your computer looks and performs. The Control Panel appears in Category view, which groups program items together to reduce the clutter, or in Classic View, which displays program items individually. Leave the Control Panel open for now, and continue to the next lesson.

Changing the display to Windows classic settings

The Windows XP enhanced user interface provides a new look for the desktop. If you prefer the desktop display of Windows 98 or Windows Me, you can change the display to **Windows Classic**. With the Windows Classic display, you can take advantage of the new Windows XP functionality, yet work in an environment with which you are more familiar. To change the desktop display, right-click a blank area of the desktop, then click Properties on the shortcut menu. The Display Properties dialog box opens, displaying the Themes tab. A **theme** is a desktop background and a set of sounds, icons, and other Windows elements. On the Themes tab, click the Theme list arrow, click Windows Classic, then click

OK. To add desktop Windows Classic icons (My Documents, My Computer, My Network Places, and Internet Explorer) to the desktop, click the Desktop tab in the Display Properties dialog box, click Customize Desktop, click the check boxes with the icons you want to display, then click OK twice. To change the Start menu to Windows Classic, right-click the Start button on the taskbar, click Properties, click the Classic Start menu option button, then click OK. To show folders in Windows Classic View without the left pane of Common tasks, open My Computer, click Tools on the menu bar, click Folder Options, click the General tab if necessary, click the Use Windows classic folders option button, then click OK.

Windows XP

FIGURE A-4: Start menu

Open Recycle Bin
window

Current user

Pinned items

Most frequently
used items; your list
might be different

Arrow indicates
submenu

Your Start menu
commands might
differ depending on
your Windows XP
version

TABLE A-4: Start menu commands

Icon	command	description
	Internet	Starts your Internet browser; by default, Internet Explorer
	E-mail	Starts your e-mail program; by default, Outlook Express
	All Programs	Opens all the programs included on the Start menu
	My Documents	Opens the My Documents folder, where you store and manage files
	My Recent Documents	Opens a list of the most recently opened and saved documents
	My Pictures	Opens the My Pictures folder, where you store and manage photos, images, and graphic files
	My Music	Opens the My Music folder, where you store and manage sound and audio files
	My Computer	Opens the My Computer window, where you access information about disk drives, and other hardware devices
	Control Panel	Provides options to customize the appearance and functionality of the computer
	Printers and Faxes	Displays installed printers and fax printers and a wizard to help you install additional devices; available only with Windows XP Professional
	Printers and Other Hardware	Displays installed printers and other hardware and a wizard to help you install other devices; available only with Windows XP Home
	Help and Support	Displays Windows Help topics, tutorials, troubleshooting, support options, and tools
	Search	Allows you to locate programs, files, folders, or computers on your computer network, or find information or people on the Internet
	Run	Opens a program or file based on a location and filename that you type or select
	Log Off	Allows you to log off the system and log on as a different user
	Turn Off Computer	Provides options to turn off the computer, restart the computer, or set the computer in hibernate mode

Windows XP

Managing Windows

One of the powerful things about the Windows operating system is that you can open more than one window or program at once. This means, however, that the desktop can get cluttered with many open windows for the various programs you are using. You can identify a window by its name on the **title bar** at the top of the window. To organize your desktop, you must sometimes change the size of a window or move it to a different location. Each window, no matter what it contains, is surrounded by a border that you can use to move or resize the window. Each window has three buttons in the upper-right corner that allow you to resize it. Table A-5 shows the different mouse pointer shapes that appear when resizing windows. Now you will try moving and resizing the Control Panel window.

1. Click the **Recycle Bin button** on the taskbar or click anywhere in the Recycle Bin window
   The Recycle Bin window moves in front of the Control Panel window. The Recycle Bin window is now **active**, which means that any actions you perform take place in this window. At times, you might want to hide a window so that it isn't visible on the desktop but is still open.

QuickTip

You can press [D] or click the Show Desktop button on the Quick Launch toolbar to minimize all open windows and programs and see the desktop.

2. Click the **Minimize button** in the upper-right corner of the Recycle Bin window
   The window no longer appears on the desktop, but you can still see a button named Recycle Bin on the taskbar. When you **minimize** a window, you do not close it but merely reduce it to a button on the taskbar so that you can work more easily in other windows. The button on the taskbar reminds you that the program is still running.

3. Position the mouse pointer on the lower-right corner of the Control Panel window until the pointer changes to , then drag the corner up and to the left until your screen resembles Figure A-5
   The window is now resized. You can resize windows by dragging any corner, not just the lower-left. You can also drag any border to make the window taller, shorter, wider, or narrower.

4. Point to the **title bar** on the Control Panel
   When a window is active, the title bar color changes from gray to blue. You can move any window to a new location on the desktop by dragging the window's title bar.

QuickTip

To arrange all open windows, right-click a blank area on the taskbar, then click the appropriate option.

5. With the mouse pointer over any spot on the title bar, click the **left mouse button**, then drag the window to center it on the desktop
   The window is relocated. This action is similar to dragging an icon to a new location.

6. Click the **Maximize button** in the upper-right corner of the Control Panel
   When you **maximize** a window, it fills the entire screen.

QuickTip

You can double-click the title bar of a window to switch between maximizing and restoring the size of a window.

7. Click the **Restore Down button** in the upper-right corner of the Control Panel
   The **Restore Down button** returns a window to its previous size. The Restore button appears only when a window is maximized.

8. Click the **Recycle Bin button** on the taskbar
   The Recycle Bin window is now the size it was before you minimized it and is now active. When you finish using a window, you can close it with the Close button.

9. Click the **Close button** in the upper-right corner of the Recycle Bin window
   The Recycle Bin window closes. You will learn more about the Recycle Bin in later lessons.

FIGURE A-5: Resized Control Panel window

Title bar

Your window may be in a different view

Active window

Close button

Sizing buttons

Drag here to size both height and width

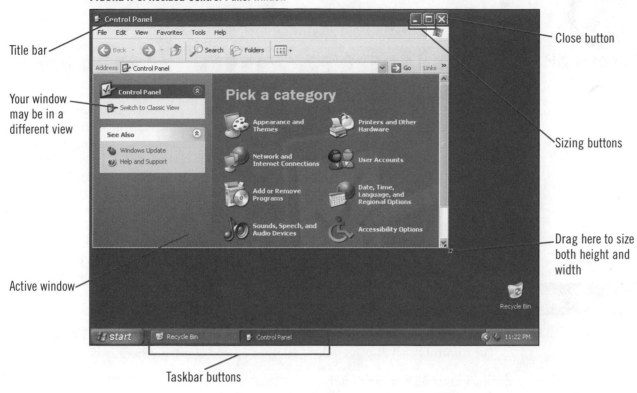

Taskbar buttons

TABLE A-5: Mouse pointer shapes that appear when resizing windows

mouse pointer shape	use to
↔	Drag the right or left edge of a window to change its width
↕	Drag the top or bottom edge of a window to change its height
↘ or ↗	Drag any corner of a window to change its size proportionally

CLUES TO USE

Moving and resizing the taskbar

In addition to windows, you can also resize and move other elements on the desktop, such as the taskbar, using the methods in this lesson. With Windows XP, the taskbar is locked by default, so it cannot be accidentally resized or moved. Before you can resize or move the taskbar, you need to unlock it. To unlock the taskbar, right-click a blank area on the taskbar, then click Lock the Taskbar on the shortcut menu to deselect the option. You can move the taskbar by dragging it to any edge (right, left, top, or bottom) of the desktop. You can also change the size of the taskbar by dragging its edge with the pointer ↕.

Using Menus, Toolbars, and Panes

A **menu** is a list of commands that you use to accomplish certain tasks, such as when you used the Start menu to open the Control Panel. A **command** is a directive that provides access to a program's features. Each Windows program has its own set of menus, which are on the menu bar along the top of the program window. The **menu bar** organizes commands into groups of related operations. Each group is listed under the name of the menu, such as File or Help. To access the commands in a menu, you click the name of the menu. If a command on a menu includes a keyboard reference, known as a **keyboard shortcut**, you can perform the action by pressing the first key, then pressing the second key to perform the command quickly. See Table A-6 for examples of items on a typical menu. You can also carry out some of the most frequently used commands on a menu by clicking a button on a toolbar. A **toolbar** contains buttons that are convenient shortcuts for menu commands. A **pane** is a frame within a window where you can quickly access commands and navigation controls. ➤ You can use menus, toolbar buttons, and commands in a pane to change how the Control Panel window's contents appear.

1. **Click Switch to Classic View in the left pane of the Control Panel, if necessary**
   The Control Panel displays individual icons instead of categories.

2. **Click View on the menu bar**
   On a menu, a **check mark** identifies a currently selected feature, meaning that the feature is **enabled**, or turned on. To **disable**, or turn off the feature, you click the command again to remove the check mark. A **bullet mark** also indicates that an option is enabled. To disable a command with a bullet mark next to it, however, you must select another command (within the menu section, separated by gray lines) in its place. In the next step, you select a command.

3. **Click Status Bar to enable it, if necessary, then click View on the menu bar**
   The View menu appears, displaying the View commands, as shown in Figure A-6. The status bar appears at the bottom of the Control Panel window.

4. **Click List on the View menu**
   When you click a menu name, a general description of the commands available on that menu appears in the status bar. The icons are now smaller than they were before, taking less room in the window.

5. **Position the pointer over the Views button [▦]▾ on the Control Panel toolbar**
   When you position the mouse pointer over a button, the name of the button appears as a ScreenTip. Use the ScreenTip feature to explore a button on the toolbar. The toolbar at the top of the window includes buttons for the commands that you use most frequently while you work with the Control Panel. Some toolbar buttons appear with an arrow, which indicates the button contains several choices. You click the button arrow to display the choices.

6. **Click [▦]▾ on the Control Panel toolbar, then click Details**
   The Details view includes a description of each Control Panel program. In the next lesson, you will use scroll bars in the Control Panel to view and read the description of each Control Panel program.

FIGURE A-6: View menu in the Control Panel

Menu bar

Check mark

Bullet

Arrow indicates submenu

Toolbar

Commands on menu

Pane

Description of menu in status bar

TABLE A-6: Typical items on a menu

item	description	example
Dimmed command	A menu command that is not currently available	Object
Ellipsis	Indicates that a dialog box will open that allows you to select from several options	Find...
Triangle	Indicates that a cascading menu will open containing an additional list of commands	▶
Keyboard shortcut	An alternative to using the mouse for executing a command	Ctrl+Z
Underlined letter	Indicates the letter to press while holding down the [Alt] key for a keyboard shortcut; underline only appears on menu when you press and hold [Alt]	Clear

CLUES TO USE

Unlocking and customizing toolbars

Most toolbars in Windows XP are locked, so they cannot be accidentally moved. If you want to move the toolbars around, click View on the menu bar, point to Toolbars, click Lock the Toolbars to remove the check mark and unlock the toolbars, then drag the dotted left toolbar edge. You can also change the buttons on a toolbar to customize it to the way you work by clicking View on the menu bar, pointing to Toolbars, then clicking Customize. In the Customize Toolbar dialog box, select buttons in the left pane, then click Add to add buttons to the current toolbar. Select buttons in the right pane, then click Remove to delete buttons. At the bottom of the dialog box, you can select options to change the button size or include button text.

Using Scroll Bars

When you cannot see all of the items available in a window, scroll bars appear on the right and/or bottom edges of the window. **Scroll bars** allow you to display the additional contents of the window. Figure A-7 shows components of the scroll bars. The vertical scroll bar moves your view up and down through a window; the horizontal scroll bar moves your view from left to right. There are several ways you can use the scroll bars. When you need to scroll only a short distance, you can use the scroll arrows. When you need to scroll more quickly, you can click in the scroll bar above or below the **scroll box** to move the view up or down one window's height. Dragging the scroll box moves you even more quickly to a new part of the window. See Table A-7 for a summary of the different ways to use scroll bars. ◄━━━ You can use the scroll bars to view and read the description of each Control Panel program. When no scroll bars appear in a window, it means that all the information fits completely in the window.

1. If ellipses (…) appear at the end of comments in the Control Panel, position the pointer to the right edge of the **Comments header** until it changes to ╋, then double-click the edge to expand the comment text

   The column expands the description of each Control Panel program and a horizontal scroll bar appears.

2. In the Control Panel, click the **down scroll arrow** in the vertical scroll bar

   See Figure A-7. Clicking the down scroll arrow moves the view down one line. Clicking the up arrow moves the view up one line at a time.

3. Click the **up scroll arrow** in the vertical scroll bar

   The view moves up one line.

4. Click anywhere in the area below the scroll box in the vertical scroll bar

   The contents of the window scroll down in a larger increment.

5. Click the area above the scroll box in the vertical scroll bar

   The contents of the window scroll back up. To move in even greater increments, you can drag the scroll box to a new position.

6. Drag the **scroll box** in the horizontal scroll bar to the middle of the bar

   The scroll box indicates your relative position within the window, in this case, the halfway point. The size of the scroll bar indicates the amount of information available to scroll. A small scroll box indicates a lot of information, while a large scroll box indicates a small amount. After reading the Control Panel program descriptions, you restore the Control Panel to its original display.

7. Click the **Views button** ▦▾ on the Control Panel toolbar, then click **Icons**

8. Click **View** on the menu bar, then click **Status Bar** to deselect it, if necessary

   The status bar is removed from the bottom of the Control Panel. In the next lesson, you will open a Control Panel program to learn how to work with dialog boxes.

FIGURE A-7: Scroll bars in Control Panel

Up scroll arrow

Vertical scroll bar

Horizontal scroll bar

Scroll box

Down scroll arrow

TABLE A-7: Using scroll bars in a window

to	do this
Move down one line	Click the down arrow at the bottom of the vertical scroll bar
Move up one line	Click the up arrow at the top of the vertical scroll bar
Move down one window's height	Click in the area below the scroll box in the vertical scroll bar
Move up one window's height	Click in the area above the scroll box in the vertical scroll bar
Move up or down a greater distance in the window	Drag the scroll box in the vertical scroll bar
Move a short distance side to side in a window	Click the left or right arrows in the horizontal scroll bar
Move to the right one window's width	Click in the area to the right of the scroll box in the horizontal scroll bar
Move to the left one window's width	Click in the area to the left of the scroll box in the horizontal scroll bar
Move left or right a greater distance in the window	Drag the scroll box in the horizontal scroll bar

CLUES TO USE

Accessibility for special needs

If you have difficulty using a mouse or typing, have slightly impaired vision, or are deaf or hard of hearing, you can adjust the appearance and behavior of Windows XP to make your computer easier for you to use. The Accessibility Wizard helps you configure Windows for your vision, hearing, and mobility needs. The Accessibility Wizard also enables you to save your settings in a file that you can use on another computer. To open the Accessibility Wizard, click the Start button on the taskbar, point to All Programs, point to Accessories, point to Accessibility, click Accessibility Wizard, then follow the steps in the wizard. You can also double-click the Accessibility Options icon in the Control Panel to adjust the way your keyboard, display, and mouse function to suit various vision and motor abilities. Some of the accessibility tools available include StickyKeys, which enables simultaneous keystrokes while pressing one key at a time; FilterKeys, which adjusts the response of your keyboard; ToggleKeys, which emits sounds when you press certain locking keys; SoundSentry, which provides visual warnings for system sounds; ShowSounds, which instructs programs to provide captions; High Contrast, which improves screen contrast; and MouseKeys, which enables the keyboard to perform mouse functions.

Using Dialog Boxes

A **dialog box** is a window that opens when you choose a menu command that is followed by an ellipsis (. . .). The **ellipsis** indicates that you must supply more information before the program can carry out the command you selected. Dialog boxes open in other situations as well, such as when you open a program in the Control Panel. In a dialog box, you specify the options you want using a variety of elements. See Figure A-8 and Table A-8 for some of the typical elements of a dialog box. ▄▃▀ Practice using a dialog box to control your mouse settings.

Steps

Trouble?

If your dialog box differs from Figure A-9, read through Steps 2-4 and do not perform any actions, then continue with Step 5.

1. **In the Control Panel, scroll if necessary to locate the Mouse icon 🖱, then double-click 🖱**
   The Mouse Properties dialog box opens, as shown in Figure A-9. The options in this dialog box allow you to control the configuration of the mouse buttons, select the types of pointers that appear, choose the speed of the mouse movement on the screen, and specify what type of mouse you are using. **Tabs** at the top of the dialog box separate these options into related categories. The tabs in the dialog box vary depending on the mouse installed on the computer.

2. **Click the Buttons tab, if necessary**
   This tab has two or more sections. The first section, Button configuration, has options you can select to make the mouse easier to use for a right-handed or left-handed person. The second section, Double-click speed, has a slider for you to set how fast the mouse pointer responds to double-clicking. The slider lets you specify the degree to which the option is in effect. The other sections vary depending on the Windows version and mouse installed on the computer. Next, you experiment with the double-click speed options.

3. **In the Double-click speed section, drag the slider halfway to the right**
   You set the mouse pointer to respond to a fast double-click. You can test the double-click speed in the Test area to make sure it is comfortable for you to use on a regular basis.

4. **Double-click the Test area to the right of the slider until the graphical icon moves**
   As you double-click the test area, the folder icon opens or closes.

5. **Click the other tabs in the Mouse Properties dialog box, and examine the available options in each category**
   Now you need to select a command button to carry out the options you selected. The two most common command buttons are OK and Cancel. Clicking OK accepts your changes and closes the dialog box; clicking Cancel leaves the original settings intact and closes the dialog box. The third command button in this dialog box is Apply. Clicking the Apply button verifies the changes you've made and keeps the dialog box open so that you can select additional options. Because you might share this computer with others, it's important to restore the dialog box options to their original settings.

6. **Click Cancel to leave the original settings intact and close the dialog box**

7. **Click Switch to Category View in the left pane of the Control Panel, then click the Close button in the Control Panel to close the window**

FIGURE A-8: Dialog box elements

Check box

Option button

Text box

Up and down arrows

Command buttons

FIGURE A-9: Mouse Properties dialog box

Tabs; yours might
be different

Slider

Test area

TABLE A-8: Typical items in a dialog box

item	description
Check box	A square box that turns an option on when the box is checked and off when the box is blank
Command button	A rectangular button with the name of the command on it; it carries out a command in a dialog box
List box	A box containing a list of items; to choose an item, click the list arrow, then click the desired item
Option button	A small circle that selects a single dialog box option (you cannot check more than one option button in a list)
Up and down arrows	A box with two arrows and a text box; allows you to scroll through and choose from numerical increments or type a number
Slider	A shape that you drag to set the degree to which an option is in effect
Tab	A place where related options are organized
Text box	A box in which you type text

Windows XP

Using Windows Help and Support

When you have a question about how to do something in Windows XP, you can usually find the answer with a few clicks of your mouse. The Microsoft Help and Support Center is a complete resource of information, training, and support to help you learn and use Windows XP. **Help and Support** is like a book stored on your computer with additional links to the Internet, complete with a search feature, an index, and a table of contents to make finding information easier. If you have an Internet connection, you can get online help from a support professional at Microsoft or from other users on the Windows newsgroup (an electronic form where people share information), or invite a friend with Windows XP to chat with you, view your screen, and work on your computer to provide remote support. If you are new to Windows XP, you can also take a multimedia tour from the Help and Support Center. ▰▰▰ Now you will use the Help and Support Center to learn more about Windows XP.

QuickTip

To get help on a specific program, you can click Help on the program's menu bar.

1. Click the **Start button** on the taskbar, then click **Help and Support**
The Help and Support Center window opens with a list of help and support categories, as shown in Figure A-10.

2. In the Search text box, type **using windows**, then press **[Enter]**
A search pane opens, displaying results from the search in three areas: Suggested Topics, Full-text Search Matches, and Microsoft Knowledge Base (available only when connected to the Internet). A list of tasks, overviews, articles and tutorials appear under Suggested Topics. To switch between result areas, click the gray title with the area name.

QuickTip

To print a help topic, click the Print button 🖨 on the Help Topic toolbar.

3. In the results area under Overviews, Articles, and Tutorials, click **What's new for Help and Support**, then click the **Expand indicator** ⊞ next to **Online Help** in the right pane
The Help topic appears in the right pane, as shown in Figure A-11. **Panes** divide a window into two or more sections. When you point to a Help category, the mouse changes to the hand pointer 🖑, and the Help category text becomes underlined or bolded to indicate that more information is available by clicking. A single click opens the Help category or topic. This is similar to the way selecting on the Internet works. Read the help information on Windows online help.

4. Click the **Home button** 🏠 on the Help toolbar
The main Help and Support window appears. Now you will display a search pane with more topics.

QuickTip

To find topics from a list of subjects, click the Index button 📖 on the Help toolbar, type a keyword in the text box, then press [Enter], or scroll down the list, then double-click a topic.

5. Under Pick a Help topic, click **Windows basics**, click **Tips for using Help** under Windows basics, then click **Get more out of Help and Support Center** in the right pane
The help topic appears. You can move back and forth between Help topics you have already visited by clicking the Back button ◐ Back ▾ and the Forward button ◑ ▾ on the Help toolbar.

6. Click the **Add to Favorites button** ⭐ on the Help Topic toolbar, then click **OK** if you get a warning box
The Help topic appears in the right pane.

7. Click the **Favorites button** ⭐ on the Help toolbar to display a list of favorites, double-click **Get more out of Help and Support Center** in the list, then click **Remove** below the list to remove the topic

8. Click the **Close button** in the Help and Support Center window
The Help and Support window closes.

FIGURE A-10: **Microsoft Help and Support Center window**

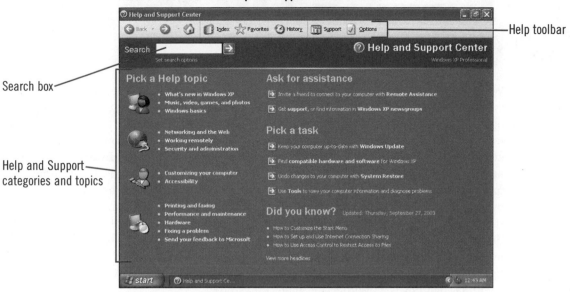

Help toolbar

Search box

Help and Support categories and topics

FIGURE A-11: **Help topic**

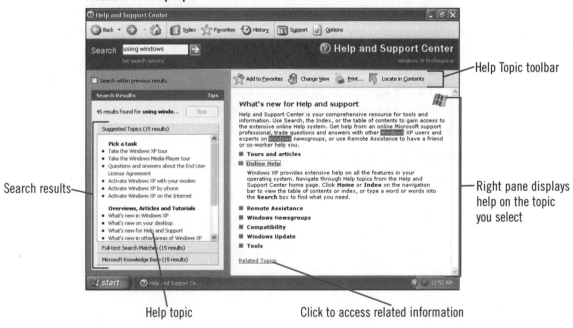

Help Topic toolbar

Search results

Right pane displays help on the topic you select

Help topic

Click to access related information

Getting Help while you work

You can also access context-sensitive help, help specifically related to what you are doing, using a variety of methods, such as pointing to or right-clicking an object. To receive help in a dialog box, click the Help button ? in the upper-right corner of the dialog box. The mouse pointer changes to 🖑?. Click on the item in the dialog box for which you need additional information. A shortcut window opens, providing a brief explanation of the selected feature. You can also right-click an item in a dialog box, then click What's This? to display the explanation. In addition, when you click the right mouse button in a Help topic window, you can choose commands to copy and print the contents of the topic. Help windows always appear on top of the currently active window, so you can see Help topics while you work.

Turning Off the Computer

When you finish working on your computer, you need to make sure to turn off, or **shut down**, your computer properly. This involves several steps: saving and closing all open files, closing all open windows, exiting all running programs, shutting down Windows itself, and, finally, turning off the computer. Shutting down your computer makes sure Windows and all its related programs are properly closed; this avoids potential problems starting and working with Windows in the future. If you turn off the computer by pushing the power switch while Windows or other programs are running, you could lose important data. Once you close all files, windows, and programs, you choose the Turn off computer command from the Start menu. If a program is still open, it will prompt you to save the file and close the program before continuing the shutting down process. The Turn off computer dialog box opens offering several options, as shown in Figure A-12. See Table A-9 for a description of each option. Depending on your Windows settings, your shut down options might be different. ━━━━ To shut down, you will close all your open files, windows, and programs, then exit Windows.

1. If you have any open windows or programs, click the **Close button** in the upper-right corner of each window

2. Click the **Start button** on the taskbar, then click **Turn off computer** ⓞ
   The Turn Off Computer dialog box opens as shown in Figure A-12. In this dialog box, you have several options for turning off your computer.

3. If you are working in a lab, click **Cancel** to return to the Windows desktop; if you are working on your own machine or if your instructor tells you to shut down Windows, click **Turn Off** to exit Windows and shut down your computer

4. If you see the message "It's now safe to turn off your computer," turn off your computer and monitor
   Some computers power off automatically, so you may not see this message.

TABLE A-9: Shut down options

shut down option	function	when to use it
Turn Off	Prepares the computer to be turned off	When you finish working with Windows and you want to shut off your computer
Restart	Restarts the computer and reloads Windows	When you want to restart the computer and begin working with Windows again (when your programs may have frozen or stopped working)
Hibernate	Saves your session to disk so that you can safely turn off power; restores your session the next time you start Windows	When you want to stop working with Windows for a while and start working again later; available when the Power Options setting (in the Control Panel) is turned on
Stand By	Maintains your session, keeping the computer running on low power	When you want to stop working with Windows for a few moments and conserve power (ideal for a laptop or portable computer); available when a power scheme is selected in Power Options (in the Control Panel)

FIGURE A-12: Turn off computer dialog box

 Working on a computer for multiple users

Many users may use the same computer, in which case each user has his or her own Windows identity, allowing them to keep their files completely private, and customize the operating system with their own preferences. Windows manages these separate identities by giving each user a unique user name and password. You set up user accounts during Windows XP installation or by using User Accounts in the Control Panel, as shown in Figure A-13. When Windows starts, a Welcome screen appears, displaying user accounts. When a user selects an account and types a password (if necessary), Windows starts with that user's configuration settings and network permissions. To quickly change users on the same computer, you choose the Log Off command from the Start menu. On a shared computer, click Log Off to save your current settings and log off, or click Switch User to quickly switch between users without having to save your current settings. On a network computer, press [Ctrl][Alt][Del], type your user name and password, then click OK.

FIGURE A-13

Practice

► Concepts Review

Label each of the elements of the screen shown in Figure A-14.

FIGURE A-14

1. Which element do you click to display hidden icons on the taskbar?
2. Which element(s) do you click to resize and close windows?
3. Which element points to the window's pane?
4. Which element points to the notification area?
5. Which element(s) do you click to open and activate a program that is running?
6. Which element points to a toolbar?

Match each term with the statement that describes its function.

7. Recycle Bin   a. Where the name of the program and file appear
8. Sizing buttons   b. Where deleted files are placed
9. Start button   c. Displays the Start button and buttons for currently open programs and windows
10. Taskbar   d. Allows you to minimize, maximize, and restore windows
11. Title bar   e. The item you click first to start a program
12. Mouse   f. Used to point at screen elements and make selections

Select the best answers from the following lists of choices.

13. **Moving an item to a new location on the desktop is called:**
    a. Dragging.
    b. Restoring.
    c. Pointing.
    d. Clicking.

14. **The Maximize button is used to:**
    a. Scroll slowly through a window.
    b. Reduce a window to a button on the taskbar.
    c. Return a window to its original size.
    d. Expand a window to fill the entire screen.

15. **The Minimize button is used to:**
    a. Scroll slowly through a window.
    b. Reduce a window to a button on the taskbar.
    c. Return a window to its original size.
    d. Expand a window to fill the entire screen.

16. **The Menu bar provides access to a program's functions through:**
    a. Commands.
    b. Dialog box elements.
    c. Toolbar buttons.
    d. Scroll buttons.

17. **An ellipsis after a menu command indicates:**
    a. Another menu will display.
    b. A keyboard shortcut to that command.
    c. The menu command is not currently available.
    d. A dialog box will open.

18. **Which is not a method for getting Help?**
    a. Clicking Help on a program's menu bar
    b. Right-clicking in a dialog box, then using the Help pointer to point to what you need help with
    c. Clicking the Start button on the taskbar, then clicking Help and Support
    d. Clicking the question mark button in a dialog box

▶ Skills Review

1. **Start Windows and view the Windows desktop.**
   a. Start Windows and log on, if necessary.
   b. Identify and write down as many desktop items as you can, without referring to the lesson.
   c. Compare your results with Figure A-1.
2. **Use the mouse.**
   a. Move the mouse on your desk, and watch how the mouse pointer moves across the screen.
   b. Point at an icon on the desktop.
   c. Click the icon once. Notice the icon's highlighted title.
   d. Press and hold down the mouse button, then drag the icon to the opposite side of the desktop. (*Hint:* release the mouse button when you finish dragging.)
   e. Drag the icon back to the original location.
   f. Double-click the Recycle Bin icon.
3. **Get started with the Windows XP desktop.**
   a. Click the Start menu on the taskbar.
   b. Click Control Panel.
4. **Manage windows.**
   a. Click the Recycle Bin button on the taskbar.
   b. Click the Minimize button.

   c. Position the mouse pointer on any corner of the Control Panel window and drag to make the window smaller.

   d. Point to the title bar on the Control Panel window, then drag the window to the center of the desktop.

   e. Click the Maximize button.

   f. Click the Restore button.

   g. Click the Recycle Bin button on the taskbar.

   h. Click the Close button on the Recycle Bin window.

5. Use menus, toolbars, and panes.

   a. In the Control Panel, click Switch to Classic View if necessary.

   b. Click View on the menu bar, then click Thumbnails.

   c. Click View on the menu bar, then click Tiles.

   d. Click the Views button on the toolbar, then click Details.

6. Use scroll bars.

   a. In the Control Panel, click the vertical scroll box.

   b. Click the vertical up scroll arrow.

   c. Drag the horizontal scroll box to the right-side of the scroll bar (if visible).

   d. Click the Views button on the toolbar, then click Icons.

   e. Click Switch to Category View.

7. Use dialog boxes.

   a. In the Control Panel, click Appearance and Themes.

   b. Click Change the computer's theme.

   c. Click the Theme list arrow, then click Windows Classic.

   d. Click Apply (but don't click OK yet).

   e. Click the Theme list arrow, then click Windows XP to restore the former theme.

   f. Click OK, then click the Control Panel Close button.

8. Get Windows Help and Support.

   a. Click the Start button on the taskbar, then click Help and Support.

   b. In the Search text box, type **dialog boxes**, then press [Enter].

   c. In the Search Results pane, click Get Help in a dialog box, then read the Help topic in the right pane.

   d. Click Related Topics, click Change views in Help and Support Center, then read the Help topic.

   e. Click the Help window Close button.

9. Turn off the computer.

   a. Click the Start button on the taskbar, then click Turn Off Computer.

   b. If you are not working in a lab or if your lab manager approves of shutting down the computer, click Turn Off. Otherwise, click Cancel.

▶ Independent Challenge 1

Windows XP provides extensive online help and support. At anytime, you can select Help and Support from the Start menu and get the assistance you need. Use the Help and Support options to learn about the topics listed below.

   a. Start the Help and Support Center, then locate and read the help information on the following topics: What's new in Windows XP, Windows keyboard shortcuts overview, Accessibility options overview, and Support overview.

   b. If you have a printer connected to your computer, print one or more Help topics.

   c. Close the Help and Support window.

▶ Independent Challenge 2

You are a student in a Windows XP course and want to review basic Windows XP skills. Use the Help and Support Center to find information on Windows XP tour, then take the tour from the Help and Support Center.

   a. Start the Help and Support Center, then locate and read the help information on the Windows XP tour.
   b. If you have a printer connected to your computer, print one or more Help topics.
   c. Start the Windows XP tour from within the Help and Support Center.
   d. Take the Windows XP tour, then click the Exit Tour button on the lower-right corner of the tour window to return to the Help and Support Center.
   e. Close the Help and Support window.

▶ Independent Challenge 3

You can customize many Windows features to suit your needs and preferences. One way you do this is to change the appearance of the taskbar on the desktop.

   a. Position the mouse pointer over the top border of the taskbar. When the pointer changes shape, drag up to increase the size of the taskbar. (*Hint*: If the pointer does not change, right-click the task bar, then deselect Lock the Taskbar.)
   b. Position the mouse pointer over a blank area of the taskbar, then drag to the top of the screen to move the taskbar.
   c. Open the Control Panel, click Switch to Classic View if necessary, then double-click Taskbar and Start Menu. On the Taskbar tab, click the Show the clock check box to deselect the option, click Apply, then observe the effect on the taskbar.
   d. Print the screen. (Press [Print Screen] to make a copy of the screen, open Paint, click Edit on the menu bar, click Paste to paste the screen into Paint, then click Yes to paste the large image, if necessary. Click the Text button on the Toolbox, click a blank area in the Paint work area, then type your name. Click File on the menu bar, click Page Setup, change 100% normal size to 50% in the scaling area, then click OK. Click File on the Menu bar, click Print, then click Print in the Print dialog box.)
   e. Restore the taskbar to its original setting, size, and location on the screen.
   f. Switch the Control Panel back to Category view and close the Control Panel window.

Independent Challenge 4

You accepted a new job in London, England. After moving into your new home and unpacking your boxes, you decide to set up your computer. Once you set up and turn on the computer, you decide to change the date and time settings to reflect London's time zone.

   a. Open the Control Panel, click Switch to Classic View if necessary, then double-click the Date and Time icon.
   b. Click the Time Zone tab, then click the Time Zone list arrow.
   c. Select Greenwich Mean Time: Dublin, Edinburgh, Lisbon, London from the list (scroll if necessary).
   d. Click the Date & Time tab, change the month and year to September 2003, then click Apply.
   e. Print the screen. (See Independent Challenge 3, Step d for screen printing instructions.)
   f. Restore the original date and time zone settings, then click OK.
   g. Close the Control Panel window.

▶ Visual Workshop

Re-create the screen shown in Figure A-15, which shows the Windows desktop with the Recycle Bin and the Control Panel open. Print the screen. (See Independent Challenge 3, Step d for screen printing instructions.)

FIGURE A-15

Working
with Windows Programs

Objectives

► **Start a program**
► **Open and save a WordPad document**
► **Edit text in WordPad**
► **Format text in WordPad**
► **Create a graphic in Paint**
► **Copy data between programs**
► **Print a document**
► **Play a video or sound clip**
► **Create a movie**

Now that you know how to work with common Windows graphical elements, you're ready to work with programs. A program is software you use to accomplish specific tasks, such as word processing and managing files on your computer. Windows comes with several **accessories**: built-in programs that, while not as feature-rich as many programs sold separately, are extremely useful for completing basic tasks. In this unit, you work with some of these accessories. John Casey owns Wired Coffee Company, a growing company that uses Windows XP. John needs to prepare a new coffee menu, so he plans to use two Windows accessories, WordPad and Paint, to create it. He also wants to use two other multimedia accessories, Windows Media Player and Windows Movie Maker, to play video and sound clips and work with a movie on his computer.

Starting a Program

A **Windows program** is software designed to run on computers using the Windows operating system. The most common way to start a Windows program is to use the Start menu, which provides easy access to programs installed on your computer. Clicking the Start button on the taskbar displays the Start menu, which lists common and recently used programs and the All Programs submenu, with additional programs on the left side. In this lesson, you will start a Windows accessory called **WordPad**, a word processing program that comes with Windows. As you look for WordPad on the Accessories submenu, you might notice an accessory called **Notepad**. The accessory names are similar, and both programs work with text. Notepad is a text-only editor, in which you can enter and edit text only with basic document formatting. WordPad is a word processing program, in which you can create and edit documents with complex formatting and graphics. With both programs, you can open only one document per open program window at a time. John wants to use WordPad to prepare the text of his new coffee menu, so he needs to start this program.

1. Click the **Start button** on the taskbar
   The Start menu opens.

2. Point to **All Programs** on the Start menu
   The All Programs submenu opens, listing the programs and submenus for programs installed on your computer. WordPad is in the submenu called Accessories.

3. Point to **Accessories** on the All Programs submenu
   The Accessories submenu opens, as shown in Figure B-1, containing several programs to help you complete common tasks. You want to start WordPad.

4. Click **WordPad** on the Accessories submenu
   Your mouse pointer changes momentarily to ⌛, indicating that Windows is starting the WordPad program. The WordPad window then appears on your desktop, as shown in Figure B-2. The WordPad window includes two toolbars, called the Toolbar and Format Bar, as well as a ruler, a work area, and a status bar. A blinking line, known as the **insertion point**, appears in the work area of the WordPad window, indicating where new text will appear. The WordPad program button appears in the taskbar and is highlighted, indicating that WordPad is now open and running.

5. Click the **Maximize button** in the WordPad window, if necessary
   WordPad expands to fill the screen. In the next lesson you will open and save a document in WordPad.

Creating documents in other languages

You can install multiple languages on your computer, such as Hebrew, Arabic, Japanese, French, Spanish, German, and many others. You can choose which language you want to use when you create a document, then Windows makes the characters for that language available. You can create documents in more than one language using WordPad or Notepad. To install additional languages, open the Control Panel in Classic View, double-click Regional and Language Options, click the Languages tab, click Details to open the Text Services and Input Languages dialog box, click Add to open the Add Input language dialog box, click the Input language list arrow, click the language you want to add, then click OK. Under Preferences, click Language Bar, click the check boxes to turn off advanced text services and turn on options to display the Language Bar on the desktop and language icons (the first two letters of the current input language, such as EN for English) in the notification area of the taskbar, then close the remaining dialog boxes. To compose a document that uses more than one language, click the language icon on the Language Bar or taskbar, click the language you want to use in the list that opens, then type your message. The language setting remains in place until you change it or shutdown your computer. Any recipient of multilanguage documents must also have the same languages installed on their computer to read and edit the documents.

FIGURE B-1: Starting WordPad using the Start menu

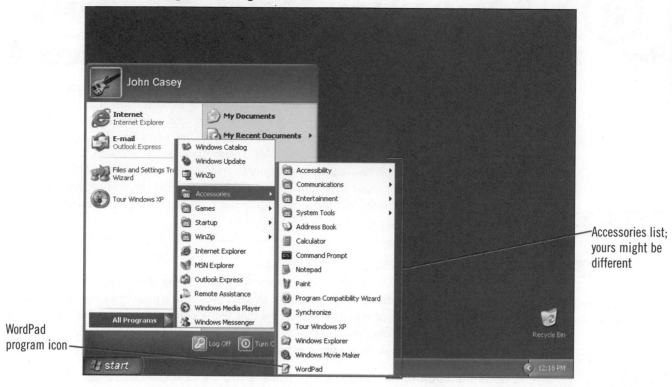

Accessories list; yours might be different

WordPad program icon

FIGURE B-2: Windows desktop with the WordPad window open

Title bar with document name

Menu bar

Toolbar

Insertion point

WordPad program button

Status bar

Format bar

Ruler

Work area

Windows XP

Opening and Saving a WordPad Document

A **document** is a file you create using a word processing program, such as a letter, memo, or resume. When you start WordPad, a blank document appears in the work area, known as the **document window**. You can enter information to create a new document and save the result in a file, or you can open an existing file and save the document with changes. Until you save a document it is stored in the computer's **Random Access Memory** (**RAM**), temporary storage whose contents are erased when you turn off the computer. To store a document permanently, you save it as a file, a collection of information that has a unique name and location. ✎ Rather than typing the menu from scratch, John opens an existing document that contains text of the coffee menu and saves it with a new name before making any changes to it.

Trouble?

In this book, files are displayed with file extensions. Your display may differ.

1. **Click the Open button 📂 on the Toolbar**
   The Open dialog box opens, where you locate and choose a file to open. Icons in the **Places bar**, on the left side of the dialog box, are used to navigate to common locations or recently used files and folders. The Files of type text box shows that the document is of type Rich Text Format (.rtf), the default for WordPad. **Rich Text Format** is a standard text format that includes formatting and provides flexibility when working with other programs.

Trouble?

If you are not sure how to locate your Project Files, contact your instructor or technical support person.

2. **Click the Look in list arrow, then click the drive and folder where your Project Files are located**
   A list of files and folders appears in the file list, as shown in Figure B-3. The files shown are determined by the option chosen in the Files of type list. You can select a file from the file list or type the name of the file in the File name text box. When you type a name in the File name text box, **AutoComplete** suggests possible matches with previous filename entries. You can continue to type or click the File name list arrow, then click a matching filename from the list.

3. **If no filenames appear in the file list, click the Files of type list arrow, then click Rich Text Format (*.rtf)**

4. **In the file list, click Win B-1 to select the file, then click Open**
   The Win B-1 file opens a menu for the coffee company. To prevent accidental changes to the original, you save the document in another file with a new name. This makes a copy of it so that you can change the new document and leave the original file unaltered.

QuickTip

Windows saves all your documents in and opens them from the My Documents folder on your desktop unless you choose a different location.

5. **Click File on the menu bar, then click Save As**
   The Save As dialog box opens, as shown in Figure B-4, which you can use to save an existing document with a new name and in a different folder or drive.

6. **If necessary, select the filename Win B-1 by dragging the mouse pointer over it**
   You must select text before you can modify it. When you select text, any action you take affects it.

QuickTip

When a document is open, click the New button 🗋 on the Toolbar to create a blank new document.

7. **Type Coffee Menu to replace the selected text**
   When you start typing, the text you type replaces the selected text in the File name text box.

8. **Click Save**
   You saved the file with a new name in the same folder and drive as the Win B-1 file. The original file, called Win B-1, closes automatically, and the new filename, Coffee Menu, appears in the title bar of the WordPad window.

FIGURE B-3: Open dialog box

Places bar

Look in list arrow

File list; extensions might not appear

AutoComplete suggests possible matches with previous filenames as you type

FIGURE B-4: Save As dialog box

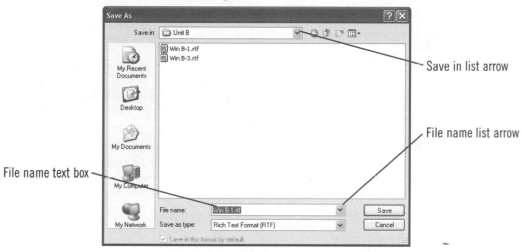

Save in list arrow

File name list arrow

File name text box

CLUES TO USE

File extensions

The program Windows uses to open a document depends on a three-letter extension to the document's filename, called a **file extension**. You might have never seen a document's file extension because your system might be set up to hide it. The file extension for simple text files is ".txt" (pronounced "dot t-x-t"), and many graphic files have the extension ".bmp". This means that the full name for a text file named Memo is Memo.txt. If you double-click a document whose filename ends with the three-letter extension ".txt," Windows automatically opens the document with Notepad, a text only editor. If you want to display or change file extension settings, click the Start button on the taskbar, click My Documents, click Tools on the menu bar, then click Folder Options. If you want to display file extensions in dialog boxes and windows, click the View tab in the Folder Options dialog box, then click the Hide extensions for known file types check box to deselect it in the Advanced settings list box. If you want to change the program Windows automatically starts with a given file extension, click the File Types tab in the Folder Options dialog box to see the list of the file extensions Windows recognizes and the programs associated with each of them, and make changes as appropriate.

Editing Text in WordPad

One of the advantages of using a word processing program is that you can **edit** a document, or change the contents without re-creating it. In the WordPad work area, the mouse pointer changes to the I-beam pointer, which you can use to reposition the insertion point (called **navigating**) and insert, delete, or select text. Table B-1 describes several methods for selecting text in a document. You can also move whole sections of a document from one place to another using the Cut and Paste commands or the drag-and-drop method. The **drag-and-drop** method allows you to simply drag text from one location to another, while the Cut and Paste commands require several steps. When selected text is cut from a document, Windows removes it from the document and places it on the **Clipboard**, a temporary storage place where it remains available to be pasted elsewhere. When you want to move a section of a document a short distance (within the same screen), the drag-and-drop method works best, while the Cut and Paste commands are better when dragging for a longer distance, or for text you want to insert in more than one location. John wants to add a greeting, modify the price of coffee, change the order of menu items so that they are alphabetical, and move text in the Coffee Menu document.

Steps

1. Press [↓] three times
The insertion point appears at the beginning of the blank line just above the text "Specialty Coffee."

2. Type Welcome to the taste tantalizing coffee selections offered to you by Wired Coffee Company. You will find a variety of specialty coffees, including Single Origin, Blends, Dark Roasts, and Decaffeinated., then press [Enter]
WordPad keeps the text on multiple lines together in the same paragraph, using **word wrap**. The text wraps to the edge of the window or to the right side of the ruler depending on your word wrap settings. When you press [Enter], you create a new paragraph. After inserting new text, you want to edit some existing text. To correct a mistake or to change text, you press [Backspace] to delete the character to the left of the insertion point until you delete the text, then retype the text.

3. In the price of the Breakfast Blend (Decaf) coffee, click to the right of the last digit, press [Backspace] twice, then type 00
The number changes from "12.95" to "12.00." Now you want to rearrange the list so that the coffees are listed in alphabetical order. To do this, you first must select the text you want to move.

4. Position the pointer in the margin to the left of the first character in the line "Espresso Dark Roast," the pointer changes to ◿ shown in Figure B-5, then double-click
Double-clicking selects the entire paragraph, which in this case is only one line.

QuickTip
To view the Clipboard, click the Start button on the taskbar, point to All Programs, point to Accessories, point to System Tools, then click Clipboard Viewer.

5. Click the Cut button ✂ on the Toolbar
The selected text is cut from the document and placed on the Clipboard.

6. Click I to the left of the first character in the line that begins with Ethiopian Harrar, then click the Paste button 📋 on the Toolbar
The selection you paste is inserted at the location of the insertion point. The coffee list is now in alphabetical order.

7. Double-click the word "gourmet" in the bottom paragraph to select it, then drag the selection to the left of the word "bean"
As you drag the pointer, the pointer changes from ▷ to ▷ and the insertion point moves, indicating where the selection is placed in the document.

8. Click the Save button 💾 on the Toolbar
You saved the changes made to the Coffee Menu document.

FIGURE B-5: Editing a WordPad document

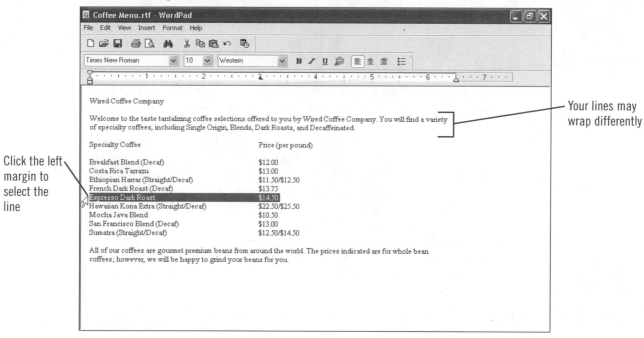

Click the left margin to select the line

Your lines may wrap differently

TABLE B-1: Methods for selecting text

to select	do this
A single word	Double-click the word
A single line	Click the left margin to the left of the first character in the line
A single paragraph	Triple-click a word within the paragraph or double-click the left margin to the left of the first character in the paragraph
Any part of a document	Drag the mouse to select the text you want to select
A large selection	Click at the beginning of the text you want to select, then press and hold [Shift] while you click at the end of the text you want to select
The entire document	Triple-click the left margin

CLUES TO USE

Setting paragraph tabs

Tabs set how text or numerical data aligns in relation to the edges of the document. A **tab stop** is a predefined stopping point along the document's typing line. Default tab stops are set every half-inch on the ruler, but you can set multiple tabs per paragraph at any location. Each paragraph in a document contains its own set of tab stops. The default tab stops do not appear on the ruler, but the manual tab stops ⌐ you set do appear. To display the tab stops for a paragraph on the ruler, click any word in the paragraph. To set a tab stop, click the ruler where you want to set it or use the Tabs command on the Format menu to open the Paragraph dialog box, from which you can set tabs. Once you place a tab stop, you can drag the tab stop to position it where you want. To delete a tab stop, drag it off the ruler. If you want to add or adjust tab stops in multiple paragraphs, simply select the paragraphs first.

Formatting Text in WordPad

You can change the **format**, or the appearance, of the text and graphics in a document so that the document is easier to read or more attractive. Formatting text is a quick and powerful way to add emphasis, such as bold, italics, underline, or color, to parts of a document. For special emphasis, you can combine formats, such as bold and italics. In addition, you can change the font style and size. A **font** is a set of characters with the same typeface or design, such as Arial or Times New Roman, that you can increase or decrease in size. Font size is measured in points; one **point** is 1/72 of an inch high. You can make almost all formatting changes in WordPad using the Format Bar, which appears below the Toolbar in the WordPad window. Table B-2 provides examples of each button on the Format Bar. You can determine the current formatting for text in a document by placing the insertion point anywhere in the text, then looking at the button settings on the Format Bar. ▶ John wants to make the Coffee Menu document more attractive and prominent by centering the title, bolding it, and increasing its size.

Steps

QuickTip

To insert a special character, such as a trademark, click the Start button on the taskbar, point to All Programs, point to Accessories, point to System Tools, then click Character Map. Click a character, click Select, click Copy, place the insertion point in your document, then click the Paste button on the Toolbar.

1. Select the text **Wired Coffee Company** at the top of the document
   Once you select the text you want to format, you can select formatting options on the Format Bar, such as the Center, Bold, or Italic buttons, to apply to the text.

2. Click the **Center button** ☰ on the Format Bar
   The title is now centered and the Center button is selected ("turned on"), while the Left Align button is deselected ("turned off"). Related buttons, such as Left Align, Center, and Right Align, on a toolbar act like options in a dialog box—only one button can be turned on and used at a time; click one to turn it on, and the other related ones turn off.

3. Click the **Bold button** **B** on the Format Bar
   The selected material appears in boldface. If you didn't like the way boldface looked, you would click the button again. Some buttons act as **toggle** switches—click once to turn the format feature on, click again to turn it off. The Bold, Italic, Underline, and Bullets buttons are examples of toggle buttons.

QuickTip

To change the font type, size, style, and color at once, click Format on the menu bar, click Font, make selections in the Font dialog box, then click OK.

4. Click the **Italic button** / on the Format Bar
   Bold and italics are both applied to the selected text. Italicizing does not provide the effect that you want, so you change it back to its previous look.

5. Click the **Undo button** ↰ on the Toolbar
   The **undo** command reverses the last change made, such as typing new text, deleting text, and formatting text. Undo cannot reverse all commands (such as scrolling or saving a document), but it is a quick way to reverse most editing and formatting changes.

Trouble?

If a capital O symbol appears next to a font name in the Fonts list, it is an OpenType font, which appears the same on both your printer and screen. Select it whenever possible.

6. Click the **Font list arrow** `Times New Roman ▾` on the Format Bar, then click **Arial**
   The font, or typeface, of the text changes to Arial.

7. Click the **Font Size list arrow** `10 ▾` on the Format Bar, then click **14**
   The selected text changes in size to 14 point.

8. Click the **Color button** 🎨 on the Format Bar, then click **Blue**
   The selected text changes in color from Black to Blue.

9. Click anywhere in the document to deselect the text, then click the **Save button** 💾 on the Toolbar
   Figure B-6 shows the changes made to the Coffee Menu document. Leave WordPad open for now, and continue to the next lesson.

FIGURE B-6: Formatted WordPad document

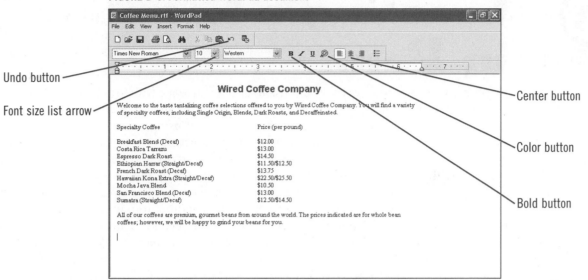

Undo button

Font size list arrow

Center button

Color button

Bold button

TABLE B-2: Format Bar buttons and list arrows

button or list arrow	name	function	example
Arial	Font	Select a font	Arial
10	Font Size	Select a font size	14 point
Western	Font Script	Select a language type	Western
B	Bold	Apply boldface style	**Bold**
I	Italic	Apply italic style	*Italic*
U	Underline	Apply underline style	Underline
Color	Color	Apply or change color	Color
Align Left	Align Left	Align paragraph to the left margin	Align left
Center	Center	Align paragraph to the center between left and right margin	Center
Align Right	Align Right	Align paragraph to the right margin	Align right
Bullets	Bullets	Create a bulleted list	• Bullet

CLUES TO USE

Setting paragraph indents

When you indent a paragraph, you move its edge in from the left or right margin. You can indent the entire left or right edge of a paragraph or just the first line. The markers on the ruler control the indentation of the current paragraph. The left side of the ruler has three markers. The top triangle, called the first-line indent marker ▽, controls where the first line of the paragraph begins. The bottom triangle, called the hanging indent marker △, controls where the remaining lines of the paragraph begin. The small square under the bottom triangle, called the left indent marker ☐, allows you to move the first-line indent marker and the left indent marker simultaneously. When you move the left indent marker, the distance between the hanging indent and the first line indent remains the same. The triangle on the right side of the ruler, called the right indent marker △, controls where the right edge of the paragraph ends. You can also set paragraph indents using the Paragraph command on the Format menu, making your changes in the Paragraph dialog box, then clicking OK.

Creating a Graphic in Paint

Paint is a Windows accessory you can use to create and work with graphics or pictures. Paint is designed to create and edit bitmap (.bmp) files, but you can also open and save pictures created in or for other graphics programs and the Internet using several common file formats, such as .tiff, .gif, or .jpeg. A **bitmap** file is a map of a picture created from small dots or bits, black, white, or colored. You can find buttons, known as **tools**, for drawing and manipulating pictures in the Paint Toolbox, located along the left edge of the window, and described in Table B-3. Tools in the Toolbox act like options in a dialog box—only one tool can be turned on and used at a time. A tool remains turned on until another tool in the Toolbox is selected. In addition, you can use commands on the Image menu, such as rotate, stretch, and invert colors, to further modify pictures in Paint. You can open more than one Windows program at a time, called **multitasking**, so while WordPad is still running, you can open Paint and work on drawings and pictures. John has already created a logo for his coffee company. Now he wants to review the logo and revise it before using it in his promotional materials.

Steps

1. Click the **Start button** on the taskbar, point to **All Programs**, point to **Accessories**, click **Paint**, then click the **Maximize button** in the Paint window, if necessary
The Paint window opens and is maximized in front of the WordPad window.

2. Click **File** on the menu bar, click **Open**, click the **Look in list arrow**, then navigate to the drive and folder where your Project Files are located
A list of all the picture files in the selected folder appears.

> **QuickTip**
> Windows organizes all your picture files in and opens them from the My Pictures folder located, by default, in the My Documents folder to provide a consistent place to store all your pictures.

3. In the file list, click **Win B-2**, then click **Open**
The file named Win B-2 opens in the Paint window, shown in Figure B-7. If you cannot see the logo on your screen, use the scroll buttons to adjust your view. You decide the logo could use some final modifications. Before you make any changes, you want to save this file with a more meaningful name so your changes don't affect the original file.

4. Click **File** on the menu bar, click **Save As**, then save the file as **Wired Coffee Logo** to the drive and folder where your Project Files are located
As you type the new name of the file, Windows automatically determines the file type and changes the format in the Save as type list. In this case, the format changes to 256 Color Bitmap. You want to add a rounded border around the logo.

> **QuickTip**
> Press and hold [Shift] while you drag a drawing tool to create a proportional drawing, such as a square or circle.

5. Click the **Rounded Rectangle tool** in the Toolbox, then click the third color from the left in the second row of the color box
The Rounded Rectangle tool is active, and color fill options appear below the Toolbox. The Foreground color (top color box) on the right side of the Paint Color box changes to red, while the Background color (bottom color box) remains white. The Foreground color is for lines, text, or brush strokes, while the Background color is for filling in a shape. You right-click a color in the Paint Color box to change the foreground color.

6. Move the pointer into the Paint work area
When you move the mouse pointer into the work area, it changes to ┼, indicating that you are ready to draw a rounded rectangle.

> **Trouble?**
> If your rounded rectangle doesn't match Figure B-8, click the Eraser/Color tool in the Toolbox, drag to erase the rounded rectangle, then repeat Step 7.

7. Beginning above and to the left of the logo, drag ┼ so that a rounded rectangle surrounds the image, then release the mouse button when the pointer is below and to the right of the image, as shown in Figure B-8
You like this new look. The logo is complete but you need to save it.

8. Click **File** on the menu bar, then click **Save**
Now you can use the logo in your other documents.

FIGURE B-7: Company logo in Paint

Paint Toolbox

Rounded
Rectangle tool

Logo

Work area

Color box

FIGURE B-8: Company logo with rounded rectangle

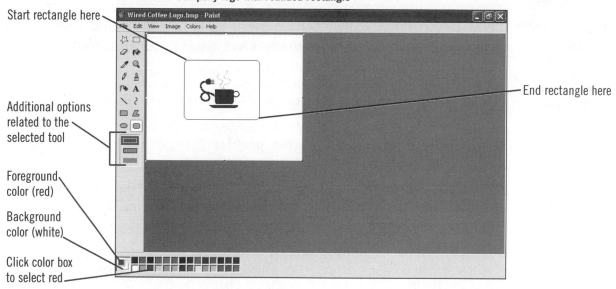

Start rectangle here

End rectangle here

Additional options
related to the
selected tool

Foreground
color (red)

Background
color (white)

Click color box
to select red

TABLE B-3: Tools in the Paint Toolbox

tool	used to	tool	used to
Free-Form Select	Select a free-form or irregular shape	Airbrush	Create dispersed lines and patterns
Select	Select a square or rectangular shape	Text	Enter text in drawings
Eraser/Color Eraser	Erase or color part of a drawing	Line	Draw a straight line
Fill With Color	Fill a closed shape with the current color or texture	Curve	Draw a free-form line
Pick Color	Pick up a color from the picture for drawing	Rectangle	Draw a rectangle or square shape
Magnifier	Magnify part of an image	Polygon	Draw a polygon or irregular shape from connected straight-line segments
Pencil	Draw a freehand line	Ellipse	Draw an oval or circle
Brush	Draw a brush stroke using a brush with the selected size and shape	Rounded Rectangle	Draw a rectangle or square with rounded corners

Copying Data Between Programs

One of the most useful features Windows offers is the ability to use data created in one file in another file, even if the two files were created in different Windows programs. To work with more than one program or file at a time, you simply need to open them on your desktop. A **program button** on the taskbar represents any window that is open on the desktop. When you want to switch from one open window to another, click the correct program button on the taskbar. If you **tile**, or arrange open windows on the desktop so that they are visible, you can switch among them simply by clicking in the window in which you want to work. Just as you worked with the Cut and Paste commands to rearrange text in WordPad, you can use the same commands to move and copy data between two different files. Table B-4 reviews the Cut, Copy, and Paste commands and their associated keyboard shortcuts. ━━━ John wants to add the company logo, which he created with Paint, to the Coffee Menu document, which he created with WordPad. First he switches to Paint and copies the logo. Then he switches to WordPad, determines exactly where he wants to place the logo, and pastes the Paint logo into the WordPad document.

Trouble?

If your windows don't appear tiled, click the program button on the taskbar for each program, ensure that both windows are maximized, then repeat Step 1.

1. Make sure both WordPad and Paint are open and that there are no other program windows open, place the mouse pointer on an empty area of the taskbar, **right-click**, then click **Tile Windows Vertically** on the shortcut menu

   The windows (Paint and WordPad) are next to one another vertically, as shown in Figure B-9, so you can maneuver quickly between them while working.

2. Click the **Paint program button** on the taskbar, or click anywhere in the Paint window

   The Paint program becomes the **active program**. The title bar text changes from gray to white, and the Close button changes from purple to red.

3. Click the **Select button** ⌐⌐⌐ in the Toolbox, then drag around the coffee logo to select it

   Dragging with the Select tool selects an object in Paint for cutting, copying, or performing other modifications.

4. Click **Edit** on the Paint menu bar, then click **Copy**

   When an item is copied, a copy of it is placed in the Clipboard to be pasted in another location, but the item also remains in its original place in the file.

5. Click the first line of the WordPad document

   The WordPad program becomes active, and the insertion point is on the WordPad page, where you want the logo to appear. If you cannot see enough of the page, use the scroll buttons to adjust your view.

6. Click the **Paste button** 📋 on the WordPad toolbar

   The logo is pasted into the document, as shown in Figure B-9.

7. Click the **Maximize button** in the WordPad window, click the **Center button** ≡ on the Format Bar, then click below the logo to deselect it

   The logo is centered in the document.

8. Click Ⅰ at the bottom of the document, type your name, then click the **Save button** 💾 on the WordPad toolbar

   The document is complete and ready for you to print.

9. Click the **Paint program button** on the taskbar, then click the **Close button** in the Paint window

FIGURE B-9: Logo copied from one program to another

Logo selected in Paint document

Resize handle

WordPad and Paint windows tiled vertically

Logo pasted in WordPad document

Program buttons for WordPad and Paint

TABLE B-4: Overview of cutting, copying, and pasting

function	toolbar button	keyboard shortcut	drag-and-drop method
Cut: Removes selected information from a file and places it on the Clipboard	✂	[Ctrl][X]	Press and hold **[Shift]** as you drag selected text to move text without using the clipboard
Copy: Places a copy of selected information on the Clipboard, leaving the file intact	📋	[Ctrl][C]	Press and hold **[Ctrl]** as you drag selected text to copy text without using the clipboard
Paste: Inserts whatever is currently on the Clipboard into another location (within the same file or in a different file)	📋	[Ctrl][V]	Release the left mouse button when you have moved text to the location you want

CLUES TO USE

Switching between files

When you open many file and program windows, the taskbar groups related files together under one program button to reduce the clutter on the taskbar and save space. For example, if you have five windows open, and two of them are Paint files, the two Paint file buttons on the taskbar are grouped together into one button named *2 Paint*. When you click the *2 Paint* button on the taskbar, a menu appears listing the open Paint files, from which you can choose the file you want to view, as shown in Figure B-10. The taskbar only groups file buttons together if the taskbar is overcrowded with windows. If you have only two Paint windows opens, the Paint file buttons will not group together. To open more than one Paint window, you need to start two versions of the program using the Start menu.

FIGURE B-10: Program buttons grouped on taskbar

Printing a Document

Printing a document creates a **printout** or hard copy, a paper document that you can share with others or review as a work in progress. Most Windows programs have a print option that you access through the Print dialog box and a Print button on the Toolbar. Although your printing options vary from program to program, the process works similarly in all of them. It is a good idea to use the **Print Preview** feature to look at the layout and formatting of a document before you print it. You might catch a mistake, find that the document fits on more pages than you wanted, or notice formatting that you want to do differently. Making changes before you print saves paper. ⬤➤ John decides to preview the coffee menu before printing the document. Satisfied with the result, John prints the Coffee Menu document.

Steps

1. In the WordPad window, click the **Print Preview button** 🔍 on the Toolbar
   A reduced but proportionate image of the page appears in the Preview window, shown in Figure B-11.

2. Move the pointer over the logo, the pointer changes to 🔍, then click the screen
   The preview image of the page appears larger, and is easier to see. The space outside the dotted rectangle (not usable for text and graphics) is adjustable and determined by margin settings in the Page Setup dialog box. The **margin** is the space between the text and the edge of the document. The margin is too large, so you are not yet ready to print.

   QuickTip

   To zoom out from the zoom in position, click the print preview area or click Zoom Out in Print Preview.

3. Click **Close** on the Print Preview toolbar
   The Preview window closes, and you return to the Coffee Menu document.

4. Click **File** on the menu bar, then click **Page Setup**
   The Page Setup dialog box opens. In this dialog box, you can change the margin setting to decrease or increase the area outside the dotted rectangle. You can control the length of a line by setting the left and right margins and the length of a page by setting the top and bottom margins. You can also change other printing options here, for example paper size, page orientation, and printer source, such as a paper bin or envelope feeder. Page orientation allows you to select **Portrait** (in which the page is taller than it is wide) or **Landscape** (in which the page is wider than it is tall).

5. In the Page Setup dialog box, select the number in the Left text box, type **1**, select the number in the Right text box, type **1**, then click **OK**
   The document appears with new page margins. You should verify that you like the new margins before printing.

6. Click 🔍
   The page margins are smaller.

7. Click **Print** on the Print Preview toolbar
   The Print dialog box opens, as shown in Figure B-12, showing various options available for printing. Check to make sure the correct printer is specified. If you need to change printers, select a printer. When you are finished, accept all of the settings.

8. In the Print dialog box, click **Print**
   The WordPad document prints. While a document prints, a printer icon 🖨 appears in the status area of the taskbar. You can point to the printer icon to get status information. To close a program and any of its currently open files, click Exit from the File menu or click the Close button in the upper-right corner of the program window.

   QuickTip

   To print a document quickly, click the Print button 🖨 on the Toolbar. To open the Print dialog box from the WordPad window, click File on the menu bar, then click Print.

9. Click the **Close button** in the WordPad window
   If you made any changes to the open file and did not save them, you will be prompted to save your changes before the program closes.

FIGURE B-11: WordPad document in Print Preview

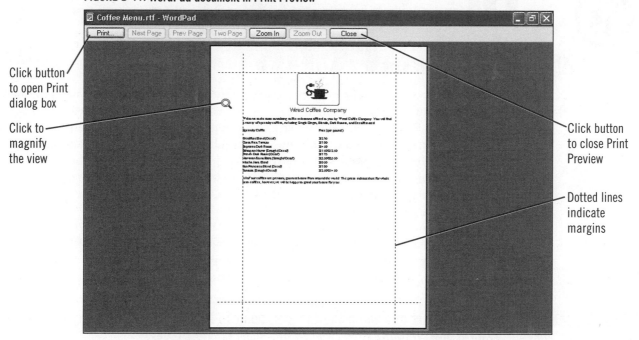

Click button to open Print dialog box

Click to magnify the view

Click button to close Print Preview

Dotted lines indicate margins

FIGURE B-12: Print dialog box

Printer information

Double-click icon to add a printer

Selected printer; your name and location might be different

Click button to change printer properties

In a multiple page document, set which pages to print in the text box

Installing a printer

A new printer is one of the most common hardware devices that computer users install. Windows makes installing a printer quick and easy with the Add Printer Wizard. The Add Printer Wizard asks you a series of questions to help you set up either a local or network printer, install printer software, establish a connection, assign a name to the printer, and print a test page to make sure that the printer works properly. You can start the Add Printer Wizard from a Print dialog box in a program by double-clicking the Add Printer icon in the Select Printer box, or from the Control Panel by double-clicking the Printers and Faxes icon, then clicking Add a printer in the left pane under Printer Tasks. In the left pane of the Printers and Faxes window, you can also click Troubleshoot printing to help you fix a problem, or click Get help with printing to display printer information from the Help and Support Center or a Microsoft Product Support Services Web site.

Playing a Video or Sound Clip

Windows XP comes with a built-in accessory called **Windows Media Player**, which you can use to play video, sound, and mixed-media files. You can use it to play movies, music, sounds, and other multimedia files from your computer, a CD, a local network, or the Internet. The Windows Media Player delivers high-quality continuous video, live broadcasts, sound, and music playback, known as **streaming media**. You can also copy individual music tracks or entire CDs to your computer and create your own jukebox or playlist of media. With the Windows Media Player, you can modify the media, control the settings, and change the player's appearance, or **skin**. Windows XP comes with Windows Media Player version 8. To make sure you are using the most recent version of Windows Media Player, click Help on the Windows Media Player menu bar, then click Check for Player Upgrade or click Windows Update on the All Programs submenu on the Start menu. You must have an open connection to the Internet to perform this check. John experiments using the Media Player to play a sample video and a sound.

Steps

Trouble?

If the Windows Media Player window doesn't match Figure B-13, press [Ctrl][1] to display the screen in full mode, press [Ctrl][M] to show the menu bar, then click the Show Taskbar button, if necessary.

1. Click the **Start button** on the taskbar, point to **All Programs**, point to **Accessories**, point to **Entertainment**, then click **Windows Media Player**
   The Windows Media Player opens in skin mode, in which the appearance varies, or full mode, which displays a Taskbar with tabs along the left side of the window and player controls that look and function similar to those on a CD player. The Windows Media Player opens to the Media Guide by default. If you are connected to the Internet, the WindowsMedia.com Web site appears, displaying current videos, music, and other entertainment. Otherwise, an information page appears.

2. Click **File** on the menu bar, click **Open**, click the **Look in list arrow**, then navigate to the drive and folder where your Project Files are located
   A list of all the media files in the selected folder appears in the Open dialog box.

3. Click **Coffee Cup**, then click **Open**
   The Coffee Cup video clip appears in the Now Playing tab and plays once, as shown in Figure B-13.

QuickTip

To play a music CD, insert the CD in the disc drive and wait for the Windows Media Player to start playing the CD. Double-click a track to play that track.

4. Click **File** on the menu bar, click **Open**, click the **Look in list arrow**, navigate to the drive and folder where your Project Files are located if necessary, click **AM Coffee**, then click **Open**
   The Coffee Cup video clip is closed and the AM Coffee sound clip appears in the Now Playing tab and plays once.

5. Click **Play** on the menu bar, then click **Repeat**
   You set the option to play the media clip continuously, or to **loop**.

6. Click the **Play button**
   When you play a sound in the Now Playing tab, a visual effect, known as a **visualization**, appears, displaying splashes of color and geometric shapes that change with the beat of the sound, as shown in Figure B-14.

QuickTip

To select a specific visualization, click the Select visualization or album art button , then click the visualization you want.

7. Click the **Previous Visualization button** or the **Next Visualization button** to change the visual effect as the sound plays, then click the **Stop button** after the audio repeats several times
   A new visual effect appears as the sound plays.

8. Click **Play** on the menu bar, click **Repeat** to turn off the option, then click the **Close button** in the Windows Media Player window

FIGURE B-13: Playing a video clip in Windows Media Player

Click button to show or hide menu bar

Full mode

Taskbar

Play button

Stop button

Playlist; your name might be different

Media clip name and length

Click button to show or hide Taskbar

FIGURE B-14: Playing an audio clip in Windows Media Player

Visualization

Visualization name; yours might be different

Media clip name and length

Volume slider

Playing media from the Internet

You can play media available on the Internet, such as videos, live broadcasts, and music tracks. You can stream the media directly from the Web site or by downloading the media file to your computer. When you stream the media, the video or music starts playing while the file is transmitted to you over the Internet. The streaming media is not stored on your computer. To stream media from the Internet, locate the Web site that contains the media you want to play using the Media Guide or Radio Tuner, click the link to the media, wait for Windows Media Player to start and the first data to be transmitted to a temporary memory storage area called the **buffer**, then listen to and watch the multimedia. When you download a media file, you wait for the entire file to be transferred to your computer. To download a file, use the Media Guide or a Web browser to locate the media you want to download from the Internet, click the download link to open the File Download dialog box, click the Save this file to disk option, click OK to open the Save As dialog box, specify the location in which you want to save the file, click Save, wait for the file download, then click Close.

Unit B

Windows XP

Creating a Movie

Windows comes with a multimedia accessory called **Windows Movie Maker,** which allows you to create movies from a variety of sources. You can create a digital movie using a digital video camera or digital Web camera or use a video capture card or other device to convert images from an analog video camera, videotape, or TV. Clips are organized in a **collection** for use in movie projects. To create a movie, you assemble the clips from a collection in one of two views, storyboard or timeline, then rearrange and crop parts of the movie. Storyboard view shows the order of video clips, and timeline view shows the duration of clips. You can also add a fade-in or -out transition between clips, and add audio, music, or narration. When you finish your movie, Movie Maker can compress the file. ✎ John creates a movie from an existing collection.

Steps 1 2 3 4

1. Click the **Start button** on the taskbar, point to **All Programs,** point to **Accessories,** click **Windows Movie Maker,** then click **Exit,** if necessary, to close the tour
   The Movie Maker window opens.

QuickTip

To create a collection, select a folder in the Collections pane, click the New Collection button 📁, name the collection, then import existing media clips or click the Record button 📷 to create a video.

2. Click **File** on the menu bar, click **Import** to open the Select the File to Import dialog box, click the **Look in list arrow,** navigate to the drive and folder where your Project Files are located, click **Coffee Cup,** then click **Open**
   Movie Maker creates a collection called Coffee Cup, which inludes the Coffee Cup video.

3. Click **File** on the menu bar, click **Import** to open the Select the File to Import dialog box, click the **Look in list arrow,** navigate to the drive and folder where your Project Files are located if necessary, click **AM Coffee,** then click **Open**
   The AM Coffee sound is added to the Coffee Cup collection, as shown in Figure B-15.

QuickTip

To adjust the length of a media clip, select the clip, then drag the End Trim handle ◢ in the Timeline. If a clip is not in the correct position, drag it in the Timeline to reposition it or click it and press [Delete].

4. Drag the **Clip 1** video clip icon onto frame 1 of the storyboard
   When you drag the video clip onto the storyboard, an insertion point appears in frame 1.

5. Click the **Timeline button** ⊞ above the storyboard, then drag **AM Coffee** in the collection to the beginning of the audio track below the video clip
   When you drag the sound, an insertion point appears in the audio track to indicate where to place it. The sound appears at the beginning of the audio track with a blue border around it, indicating it is currently selected, as shown in Figure B-16.

QuickTip

To play an individual media clip, select the clip in the Timeline or Storyboard, then click the Play button ▶ on the playback controls.

6. Click **Play** on the menu bar, then click **Play Entire Storyboard/Timeline**
   As the movie plays, the movie time progresses, and a marker moves across the Seek Bar.

7. Click the **Save Project button** 🖫 on the Toolbar to open the Save Project dialog box, click the **Look in list arrow,** navigate to the drive and folder where your Project Files are located, select the text in the File name text box, type **Coffee Meltdown,** then click **Save**
   The movie is saved in a form Movie Maker can recognize.

8. Click the **Save Movie button** 🖳 on the Toolbar to open the Save Movie dialog box, type **Coffee Meltdown** in the Title box, then type *Your Name* in the Author text box
   The Save Movie dialog box asks you to select playback quality settings and enter display information. The playback quality set affects the file size and the download time.

Trouble?

If a warning box appears asking to backup the collection, click No.

9. Click **OK,** click the **Save in list arrow** in the Save As dialog box, navigate to the drive and folder where your Project Files are located if necessary, click **Save,** click **Yes** to watch the movie, then close Windows Media Player and Windows Movie Maker
   The video is saved in the Windows Media Video Files (.wmv) format, and Windows Media Player plays the video.

FIGURE B-15: Adding a video to a movie in Windows Movie Maker

Video clip icon

Coffee Cup collection

Contents of the Coffee Cup collection

Timeline button

Frame 1

Audio clip icon

Preview of selected media clip

Storyboard

FIGURE B-16: Adding a sound to a movie in Windows Movie Maker

Save Project button

Media clip duration; drag End Trim handle to adjust length

Storyboard button

Save Movie button

Seek Bar

Playback controls for selected media clip

Video track in timeline

Audio track in timeline; selected media clip

Using copyrighted materials

When creating movies, documents, or other work on your computer where you are compiling elements from different sources, you have to consider whose property you are using. Videos, images, text, and sounds that you have created on your computer or with a digital camera, film camera, or sound recorder are your property to use as you want. However, media from other sources, including magazines, books, and the Internet are the intellectual property of others and may be copyrighted and have limitations placed on their use. Permission for you to use the material may be granted by the copyright holder. Sometimes permission is received just by asking, and other times you may be required to pay a fee. It is your legal and ethical responsibility to use only images that belong to you or that you have permission to use. Once you receive permission, you can use a scanner to transfer images to your computer or download videos, images, and sounds from the Internet.

Practice

► Concepts Review

Label each of the elements of the screen shown in Figure B-17.

FIGURE B-17

1. Which element points to a selected logo in Paint?
2. Which element points to the selected logo in WordPad?
3. Which element points to the original logo?
4. Which element points to the copied logo?
5. Which element points to a grouped program button?
6. Which element points to a nongrouped program button?

Match each term with the statement that describes its function.

7. **Accessories**
8. **Filename**
9. **Select**
10. **Cut**
11. **Copy**

a. Removes selected text or an image from its current location
b. Copies selected text or an image from its current location
c. A set of characters you assign to a collection of information
d. A collection of programs that come built-in with Windows and enable you to perform certain tasks
e. What you must first do to existing text before you can format, move, or copy it

Select the best answers from the following lists of choices.

12. What program command makes a copy of a file?
- **a.** Copy
- **b.** Duplicate
- **c.** Save As
- **d.** Save

13. When WordPad automatically moves words to the next line, it is called:
- **a.** Margin.
- **b.** Word wrap.
- **c.** Tab.
- **d.** Format insert.

14. Which of the following is not a way to select text?
- **a.** Drag over the text
- **b.** Click the left margin in a line of text
- **c.** Click File on the menu bar, then click Select
- **d.** Double-click a word

15. What is the name of the Windows location that stores cut or copied information?
- **a.** Start menu
- **b.** Hard drive
- **c.** Paint
- **d.** Clipboard

16. Which of the following controls the size of the empty border around a document?
- **a.** Paper Size
- **b.** Paper Source
- **c.** Orientation
- **d.** Margins

Skills Review

1. Open and save a WordPad document.
- **a.** Start WordPad.
- **b.** Open the WordPad file named **Win B-3** from the drive and folder where your Project Files are located.
- **c.** Save the file as **Choose Coffee** to the drive and folder where your Project Files are located.

2. Edit text in a WordPad document.
- **a.** Change the spelling of the word "neuances" to "nuances" in the last paragraph.
- **b.** Insert a space between the characters "r" and "a" in the word "ora" in the last line of the first paragraph.
- **c.** Delete the word "heavy" in the last line of the first paragraph, then replace it with "medium."
- **d.** Move the first paragraph and its title to one line below the second paragraph and title.

3. Format text in WordPad.
- **a.** Select all the text in the file named **Choose Coffee**.
- **b.** Change the text font to Garamond (or another available font), then change its size to 12 point.
- **c.** Center the text "Wired Coffee," then change it to 16 point boldface.
- **d.** Underline the text "How to Choose a Coffee" and "How to Taste the Difference," and change both to 14 point font size and blue color.
- **e.** Click anywhere in the WordPad window outside of the selected text, then save the document.

4. Use Paint.
- **a.** Start Paint, then open the file **Win B-2** from the drive and folder where your Project Files are located.
- **b.** Save this file as **Wired Coffee Logo 2** to the drive and folder where your Project Files are located.
- **c.** Draw a green circle around the logo.
- **d.** Use the Undo command or Eraser/Color tool as necessary if the circle doesn't fit around the logo.
- **e.** Save the file.

5. Copy data between programs.

   a. Tile the WordPad and Paint windows vertically. (*Hint:* Maximize both windows first.)

   b. Select the logo in the Paint window, then copy it to the Clipboard.

   c. In WordPad, place the insertion point at the beginning of the document, then maximize WordPad.

   d. Paste the logo in the blank line, then center it.

   e. Save the Choose Coffee file. Close the Wired Coffee Logo 2 file, then close Paint.

6. Print a document.

   a. Add your name to the bottom of the document, then print the Choose Coffee file.

   b. Close all open documents, then close WordPad.

7. Play a video clip or sound.

   a. Start Windows Media Player.

   b. Open the Better Coffee sound from the drive and folder where your Project Files are located.

   c. Play the sound, change the visualization, then close Windows Media Player.

8. Create a movie.

   a. Start Windows Movie Maker.

   b. Import the Coffee Cup video and the Better Coffee sound from the drive and folder where your Project Files are located.

   c. Drag the video clip to frame 1, then drag the sound clip to the audio track.

   d. Drag another copy of the video clip after the first one, drag the End Trim handle to reduce the size of the video clip to end with the audio track, then play the movie.

   e. Save the project as **Coffee Time**, give the movie file the same name, save it with medium quality, then close Windows Movie Maker.

▶ Independent Challenge 1

You own an international bookstore, and you need to create a bestsellers list of international books that you can give to customers. Use WordPad to create a new document that lists the top 10 bestselling international books in your stock. In the document include the name of your bookstore and its street address, city, state, zip code, and phone number, and for each book, the author's name (last name first), title, and publication date. You will make up this information.

   a. Start WordPad. Enter the heading (the name of the bookstore, address, city, state, zip code, and phone number), pressing [Enter] after the name, address, and zip code.

   b. Center the heading information and add color to the heading text.

   c. Enter the title **Bestsellers List**, center it, then change the font size to 18 point.

   d. Enter the information for at least 10 books, using [Tab] to create columns for the author's name, the title, and the publication date. Be sure that the columns line up with one another.

   e. Italicize the title of each book, then format the last and first names of each author with boldface.

   f. Add your name to the bottom of the document.

   g. Save the list as **Bestsellers List** to the drive and folder where your Project Files are located.

   h. Print the document, then close WordPad.

▶ Independent Challenge 2

Your parents are celebrating their twenty-fifth wedding anniversary. Using WordPad, you want to create an invitation to a party for them. Using Paint, you then want to paste a map of the party location onto the invitation.

a. Start WordPad, then type the information for the invitation, which includes the invitation title, your parents' names; date, time, and location of the party; directions; your name and phone number; and the date to respond by.

b. Change the title text to 18 point, boldface, center align, then add color.

c. Change the rest of the text to 14 point Times New Roman.

d. Save the WordPad document as **Invitation** to the drive and folder where your Project Files are located.

e. Start Paint, then open the file **Invitation Map** from the drive and folder where your Project Files are located.

f. Copy the map to the Clipboard.

g. Place the insertion point above the instructions in the invitation, then paste the map into the WordPad document.

h. Add your name to the bottom of the document.

i. Save the document, preview the document, make any necessary changes, then print the document.

j. Close WordPad and Paint.

▶ Independent Challenge 3

As vice president of Things-That-Fly, a kite and juggling store, you need to design a new type of logo, consisting of three simple circles, each colored differently. You use Paint to design the logo, then you paste the logo into a WordPad document.

a. Start Paint, then create a small circle, using the [Shift] key and the Ellipse tool.

b. Select the circle using the Select tool, then copy the circle.

c. Paste the circle from the Clipboard in the Paint window, then use the mouse to drag the second circle below and a bit to the right of the first.

d. Paste the circle again, then use the mouse to drag the third circle below and a bit to the left of the first.

e. For each circle, use the Fill With Color tool in the Toolbox, select the color in the Color box you want the circle to be, then click inside the circle you want to fill with that color.

f. Using the Select tool, select the completed logo, then copy it.

g. Save the Paint file as **Stationery Logo** to the drive and folder where your Project Files are located.

h. Open WordPad, place the insertion point on the first line, then center it.

i. Paste the logo in the document, deselect the logo, press [Enter] twice, then type **Things-That-Fly**.

j. Change the text to 18 point boldface, then add several colors that coordinate with the logo.

k. Add your name to the bottom of the document.

l. Save the WordPad document as **Stationery** to the drive and folder where your Project Files are located.

m. Preview the document, make any changes, print the document, then close WordPad and Paint.

▶ Independent Challenge 4

As creative director at Digital Arts, a music company, you need to find sample sounds for a demo CD. You use Windows Media Player to open sound files located on your computer or the Internet (if available) and play them. You also use the Media Library in Windows Media Player to keep track of the sounds you like best.

a. Open Windows Media Player.

b. Open all the sound files in the Media folder (in the Windows folder) on your computer, or play sounds on the Internet using the Media Guide. (*Hint:* You can use the Search Computer For Media command on the Tools menu to help you find the sounds.)

c. Play each sound file. Close the Windows Media Player.

► Visual Workshop

Re-create the screen shown in Figure B-18, which displays the Windows desktop with more than one program window open. You can use the file **Win B-2** for the coffee cup logo (Save it as **A Cup of Coffee** to the drive and folder where your Project Files are located) and the file **Wired Coffee Logo**. Create a new WordPad document, save it as **Good Time Coffee Club** to the drive and folder where your Project Files are located, and enter the text shown in the figure. Print the screen. (Press [Print Screen] to make a copy of the screen, open Paint, click Edit on the menu bar, click Paste to paste the screen into Paint, then click Yes to paste the large image, if necessary. Click the Text button on the Toolbox, click an empty space in the Paint work area, then type your name. Click File on the menu bar, click Page Setup, change 100% normal size to 50% in the scaling area, then click OK. Click File on the menu bar, click Print, then click Print.)

FIGURE B-18

Managing
Files and Folders

Objectives

► **Understand file management**
► **Open and view My Computer**
► **View files and folders**
► **View the Folders list**
► **Create and rename files and folders**
► **Search for files and folders**
► **Copy and move files and folders**
► **Delete and restore files and folders**
► **Create a shortcut to a file or folder**

File management is organizing and keeping track of files and folders. A **folder** is a container for storing programs and files, similar to a folder in a file cabinet. Windows XP provides you with two file management programs: **My Computer** and **Windows Explorer**. My Computer and Windows Explorer allow you to work with more than one computer, folder, or file at once by using a split window with two **panes**, or frames, to accommodate comparison of information from two different locations. Windows Explorer displays the split window by default, while in My Computer, you need to click a button to display the split window.

In this unit, John Casey, the owner of Wired Coffee Company, reviews the files on his computer and learns about how to keep them organized and also to prepare for the upcoming Wired Coffee Spring Catalog. John keeps the Project Files for this unit on a floppy disk, but yours might be in a different location; if you are not sure how to locate your Project Files, contact your instructor or technical support person.

Understanding File Management

Managing files and folders enables you to quickly locate any file that you created and need to use again. Working with poorly managed files is like looking for a needle in a haystack—it is frustrating and time-consuming to search through several irrelevant, misnamed, and out-of-date files to find the one you want. Windows allows you to organize folders and files in a file hierarchy, imitating the way you store paper documents in real folders. Just as a filing cabinet contains several folders, each containing a set of related documents and several dividers grouping related folders together, a **file hierarchy** allows you to place files in folders, then place folders in other folders, so that your files are neat and organized. Figure C-1 shows the Wired Coffee folder hierarchy, with the files and folders that John uses in his business. At the top of the hierarchy is the name of the folder, Wired Coffee. This folder contains several files and folders, and each folder contains related files and folders.

Details

As you examine the figure, note that file management can help you to do the following:

► **Organize files and folders in a file hierarchy so that information is easy to locate and use**
John stores all of his correspondence files in a folder called Letters. Within that folder are two more folders. One named Business Letters holds all business correspondence. The other, Personal Letters, holds all of John's personal correspondence.

► **Save files in a folder with an appropriate name for easy identification**
John has a folder named Sales in which he stores all information about sales for the current year. He also places files related to accounting information in this folder.

► **Create a new folder so you can reorganize information**
Now that John does more advertising for Wired Coffee Company, he wants to create a new folder to store files related to these marketing efforts.

► **Delete files and folders that you no longer need**
John deletes files when he's sure he will not use them again, to free disk space and keep his disk organized and uncluttered.

► **Find a file when you cannot remember where you stored it**
John knows he created a letter to a supplier earlier this week, but now that he is ready to revise the letter, he cannot find it. Using the Search command, he can find that letter quickly and revise it in no time.

► **Create shortcuts to files and folders**
John created a file within a folder, within another folder to keep it organized with other related files. When he wants to access the file, he has to open several folders, which can take several steps. To save him time in accessing the files, folders, and programs he uses most frequently, John can create shortcuts, or links, in any location, such as the desktop or Start menu, to gain instant access to them. All John needs to do is double-click the shortcut icon to open the file or a program, or view the contents of a folder.

FIGURE C-1: How John uses Windows to organize his files

Windows XP

Opening and Viewing My Computer

The keys to organizing files and folders effectively within a hierarchy are to store related items together and to name folders informatively. Proper hierarchy and relevant names allow you to get a good idea of what's on your system just by looking at the higher-levels of your file hierarchy; you don't have to examine every individual file or memorize a coding system. Drives and folders are represented by icons. Table C-1 lists the typical drives on a computer and how you use them. Each drive is assigned a drive letter, denoted with parenthesis and a colon, such as Local Disk (C:), to help make it easier to identify. Typically, the floppy is drive A, the hard (also known as local) disk is drive C, and the CD is drive D. If your computer includes additional drives, they are assigned letters by your computer in alphabetical order. Like most other windows, the My Computer window contains a toolbar, a status bar (which might not be activated) providing information about the contents of the window, a menu bar, and a list of contents. ▄▄▄▄ The file hierarchy on John's disk contains several folders and files organized by topic. He will use My Computer to review this organization and see if it needs changes.

Steps

Trouble?

If your Project Files are located on a floppy disk, make a copy of the disk before you use it. See your instructor or technical support person for assistance.

1. Click the Start button on the taskbar, then click My Computer

The My Computer window opens, displaying the contents of your computer, including all disk drives and common folders, as shown in Figure C-2. Since computers differ, your My Computer window probably looks different.

2. Click the Maximize button in the My Computer window, if necessary

Now you can see the entire toolbar and the contents of the window as you work.

3. Click the drive where your Project Files are located

The left pane in the Details section displays details about the selected drive and other related management tasks. In this example, details about the 3½ Floppy (A:) disk drive appear. If you select a hard disk drive, the left pane in the Details section displays additional information, including free space and total disk size.

4. Double-click the drive and folder where your Project Files are located

You can see the folders contained on the disk drive. When you open a disk drive or folder, the Address bar changes to indicate the new location. In this example, the Address bar changed from My Computer to disk drive A (A:\), and the title bar for the My Computer window changed to 3½ Floppy (A:). To see what the folders stored on the disk drive contain, you need to open them.

5. Double-click the Wired Coffee folder

You can see the files and folders that the Wired Coffee folder contains. Different types of icons represent files created using different applications. You want to see what files the Sales folder contains.

6. Double-click the Sales folder

You can now see the files that the Sales folder contains. You created these files using WordPad and saved them in the Sales folder.

Opening a document with a different program

Most documents on your desktop are associated with a specific program. For example, if you double-click a document whose filename ends with the three-letter extension ".txt," Windows XP automatically opens the document with Notepad, a text only editor. There are situations, though, when you need to open a document with a program other than the one Windows chooses, or when you want to choose a different default program.

For example, you might want to open a text document in WordPad rather than Notepad so that you can add formatting and graphics. To do this, right-click the document icon you want to open, point to Open With, then click the application you want to use to open the document, or click Choose Program to access more program options. Once you open a text file using WordPad, this option is automatically added to the Open With menu.

FIGURE C-2: My Computer window

Standard Buttons toolbar

Left pane; common tasks related to drives and folders

Floppy disk drive

Files, folders, drives, and devices; your list might differ

Zip disk drive   Hard disk drive   CD-ROM drive

TABLE C-1: Typical disk drives on a computer

icon	type	description
	Local	A hard magnetic disk on which you can store large amounts of data. The disk is faster to access than a floppy disk and typically not removable from the computer
	Floppy	A soft magnetic removable disk that comes in two sizes: 5 ¼-inch (the common size for computers through the early 1990s), which stores up to 1.2 MB (megabytes) of data, and 3 ½-inch, which stores up to 1.44 MB of data. Floppy disks are slower to access than a hard disk, but are portable and much less expensive
	Zip	A soft magnetic removable disk on which you can store 100 MB to 500 MB of computer data. Zip drives are not standard on all computers
	Compact Disc-Read-Only Memory (CD-ROM)	An optical disk on which you can stamp, or burn, up to 1 GB (typical size is 650 MB) of data in only one session. The disc cannot be erased or burned again with additional new data
	Compact Disc-Recordable (CD-R)	A type of CD-ROM on which you can burn up to 1 GB of data in multiple sessions. The disc can be burned again with additional new data, but cannot be erased
	Compact Disc-Rewritable (CD-RW)	A type of CD-ROM on which you can read, write, and erase data, just like a floppy or hard disk
	Digital Video Disc (DVD)	A type of CD-ROM that holds a minimum of 4.7 GB, enough for a full-length movie

Viewing Files and Folders

Once you have opened more than one folder, buttons on the Standard Buttons toolbar help you move quickly between folders in My Computer. When you open a folder, Windows XP keeps track of where you have been. To go back or forward to a folder you already visited, click the Back or Forward button. To go to a folder you visited two or more locations ago, click the Back or Forward list arrow to display a menu of places you visited. To move up one step in the hierarchy, you can click the Up button. When you view a folder in the My Computer window, you can use the Views button on the Standard Buttons toolbar to change the way you view file and folder icons. Table C-2 lists the Standard Buttons toolbar buttons. John moves between folders and changes the way he views folders and files, depending upon the information he needs.

1. **Click the Up button** 📁 **on the Standard Buttons toolbar**
   The Wired Coffee folder and its contents appear in the Wired Coffee window, as shown in Figure C-3. Each time you click the Up button, you move up one step in the folder hierarchy. In this example, the descending hierarchy is 3 ½ Floppy (A:) to Wired Coffee folder to Sales folder. You moved up one step from the Sales folder to the Wired Coffee folder.

2. **Click** 📁 **again**
   You should now see the Wired Coffee folder. Instead of double-clicking the Wired Coffee folder icon again to reopen the folder, you can click the Back button on the Standard Buttons toolbar to go back to the previous folder you visited, which, in this case, is Wired Coffee.

3. **Click the Back button** ⬅ Back ▾ **on the Standard Buttons toolbar**
   The Wired Coffee folder and its contents appear in the My Computer window. You want to open other folders.

4. **Double-click the Advertising folder**
   The Advertising window appears, displaying its contents. You want to go back to the Sales folder. You can click the Back list arrow to display a menu, then select the Sales folder.

5. **Click the Back list arrow** ⬅ Back ▾ **on the toolbar**
   The Back list arrow, shown in Figure C-4, displays the folders you visited recently. You can click the Forward button on the Standard Buttons toolbar to return to the folder that you visited recently, in this case, the Wired Coffee folder.

6. **Click Sales, then click the Forward button** ➡ ▾ **on the Standard Buttons toolbar**
   The Wired Coffee window appears, displaying the contents of the folder. You want to switch the view to Details view.

7. **Click the Views button** ⊞ ▾ **on the Standard Buttons toolbar, then click Details**
   The display changes to Details view, which shows the name, size of the object, type of file, and date on which each folder or file was last modified, as shown in Figure C-5.

8. **Click** ⊞ ▾**, then click Tiles**
   The display changes to Tiles view, which displays summary information (file name, file type, and size) next to each icon. Instead of using the toolbar for navigating between folders and drives, you can use the **Address bar**, which makes it easy to open items on the desktop and the drives and in the folders and system folders on your computer.

9. **Click the Address list arrow on the Address bar, then click My Computer**
   The My Computer window appears, displaying drives and common folders.

FIGURE C-3: Viewing files and folders in Tiles view

Back button

Up button

Click Address list arrow to change drive or folder location

Tiles view

FIGURE C-4: Moving between folders

Back list arrow

FIGURE C-5: Viewing files and folders in Details view

Views button   File size   File or folder type   Last modification date of file in folder

TABLE C-2: My Computer toolbar buttons

button	name	function
Back ▾	Back	Moves to the previous location you visited
▸ ▾	Forward	Moves forward to the previous location you visited
⬆	Up	Moves up one level in the file hierarchy
🔍	Search	Lets you search for folders or files
📁	Folders	Displays a list of folders on your computer
⊞ ▾	Views	Displays the contents of My Computer using different views

Viewing the Folders List

Windows XP offers another useful feature for managing files and folders, called the **Folders list** (also known as the **Folders Explorer bar**), which displays the file hierarchy of the drives and folders on your computer. At the top of the file hierarchy is the desktop, followed by My Documents, My Computer, My Network Places, then other drives and their folders. The Folders Explorer bar splits the window into two panes, or frames, as shown in Figure C-6, which allows you to view information from two different locations. The left pane of the Folders Explorer bar displays all drives and folders on the computer, and the right pane displays the contents of the selected drive or folder. This arrangement enables you to view the file hierarchy of your computer and the contents of a folder simultaneously. Using the Expand indicator ⊞ and Collapse indicator ⊟ to the left of an icon in the Folders Explorer bar allows you to display different levels of the drives and folders on your computer without opening and displaying the contents of each folder. With its split window, the Folders Explorer bar makes it easy to copy, move, delete, and rename files and folders. You can move back and forth to the last drive or folder you opened using the Back and Forward buttons on the Standard Buttons toolbar just as you did in the My Computer window. If you are working in My Computer, you can click the Folders button on the Standard Buttons toolbar to display the Folders Explorer bar. Windows Explorer displays the Folders Explorer bar in a split window by default. ⟶ John wants to open the Letters folder without opening and displaying the contents of each folder in the file hierarchy.

Steps

1. Click the **Folders button** 📁 on the Standard Buttons toolbar

The Folders Explorer bar opens, displaying the contents of your computer's hard drive. Note that the contents of your Folders Explorer bar will vary, depending on the programs and files installed on your computer and on where Windows is installed on your hard disk or network.

2. Click the **Expand indicator** ⊞ next to the drive icon where your Project Files are located in the Folders Explorer bar

The drive where your Project Files are located expands the folder structure for the drive under the icon in the Folders Explorer bar, as shown in Figure C-6. ⊞ changes to the Collapse indicator ⊟, indicating all the folders on the drive or folder are displayed. Because you did not click the floppy drive icon, the right pane displays My Computer as it did before. You decide to display the folders on the floppy disk drive.

3. Click the drive icon where your Project Files are located in the Folders Explorer bar

When you click a drive or folder in the Folders Explorer bar, the contents of that drive or folder appear in the right pane. In this case, the 3½ Floppy (A:) opens.

4. Click ⊞ next to the folder where your Project Files are located in the Folders Explorer bar, then click ⊞ next to the Wired Coffee folder in the Folders Explorer bar

The folders in the Wired Coffee folder expand and appear in the Folders Explorer bar. Because you did not click the Wired Coffee folder icon, the right pane still displays the contents of the 3½ Floppy (A:). You can open a folder or a document in the right pane of the window.

5. Click the **Letters folder** in the Folders Explorer bar

The right pane shows the contents of the Letters folder and the Folders Explorer bar shows the folders in the expanded Letters folder. When you double-click a drive or folder in the right pane, the right pane of the window shows the contents of that item. When you double-click a document, the program associated with the document starts and opens the document.

6. Double-click the **Business Letters folder** in the right pane

The Business Letters folder opens, as shown in Figure C-7. The right pane shows the contents of the Business Letters folder.

FIGURE C-6: Folders on the 3½ floppy disk drive

Address bar ——

Folders Explorer bar —

Project Disk folders;
yours may differ

Selected folder;
contents appear
in the right pane

Contents of My
Computer in the
right pane

FIGURE C-7: Business Letters folder

Open folder icon
indicates the folder
is open and its
contents appear in
the right pane

Contents of
Business
Letters folder

Viewing files using the History list

Windows keeps a list of your most recently used files, folders, and network computers in the History folder. Instead of navigating through a long list of folders to open a recently used file, you can use the History Explorer bar to find it quickly. To display the History Explorer bar on the left side of the screen, click View on the menu bar, point to Explorer bar, then click History. You can view the History Explorer bar in several ways: by date, by site, by most visited, and by order visited today. In the History Explorer bar, click the Views button, then click the view you want. To open a file, double-click the file name in the History Explorer bar. When you double-click a file, the program associated with the file starts and opens the file.

Creating and Renaming Files and Folders

Windows XP

Creating a new folder can help you organize and keep track of files and other folders. In order to create a folder, you select the location where you want the new folder, then create the folder, then lastly, name the folder. You should name each folder meaningfully, so that just by reading the folder's name you know its contents. After you name a folder or file, you can rename it at any time. You can change the way individual files and folders are sorted by using other Arrange Icons options on the View menu, as described in Table C-2. ➤ John wants to create a set of new folders to hold the files for the Wired Coffee Spring Catalog. Then, he renames a file.

1. **Click the Wired Coffee folder in the Folders Explorer bar**
   Next, you will create a new folder in the Wired Coffee folder.

2. **Click File on the menu bar, point to New, then click Folder**
   A new folder, temporarily named New Folder, appears highlighted with a rectangle around the title in the right pane of Windows Explorer, as shown in Figure C-8. To enter a new folder name, you simply type the new name. You name the new folder Spring Catalog.

Trouble?

If nothing happens when you type the name, click the folder, click the name "New Folder" so that a rectangle surrounds it and the insertion point is inside, then repeat Step 3.

3. **Type Spring Catalog, then press [Enter]**
   The Spring Catalog folder appears in both panes. When you create a new folder, the icon for the new folder is placed at the end of the list of files and folders. You can rearrange, or sort, the icons in the folder to make them easier to find.

4. **Click View on the menu bar, point to Arrange Icons by, then click Name to select it if necessary**
   The folder and file icons in the Wired Coffee folder are sorted by name in alphabetical order (folders first, then files) and automatically aligned with the other icons. You want to create folders within the Spring Catalog folder.

5. **In the right pane, double-click the Spring Catalog folder**
   Nothing appears in the right pane because the folder is empty; no new files or folders have been created or moved here.

6. **Right-click anywhere in the right pane, point to New on the shortcut menu, click Folder, type Catalog Pages as the new folder name, then press [Enter]**
   The folder is now named Catalog Pages. Notice that the Expand indicator ⊞ appears next to the Spring Catalog folder in the left pane, indicating that this folder contains other folders or files.

7. **Click the Back button** ⬅ Back ▾ **on the Standard Buttons toolbar**
   The Wired Coffee folder is displayed. Now you will rename a file.

QuickTip

To quickly change a file or folder name, select the icon, click the name, then type a new name.

8. **Right-click the To Do List file in the right pane, then click Rename on the shortcut menu, as shown in Figure C-9**
   The file appears highlighted, in the right pane. When the text is highlighted, you can click in the title to place the insertion point and make changes to part of the filename.

Trouble?

If a warning box appears, click No, then retype the file name, typing ".rtf" at the end of the filename.

9. **Type Important, then press [Enter]**
   The file is renamed Important. You can use the same procedure to rename a folder.

FIGURE C-8: Creating a new folder

New folder appears in both panes

FIGURE C-9: Renaming a file using the right-click method

To Do List file

Expand or Collapse indicators reveal that the folder contains other folders

Click command to rename file

TABLE C-2: Options for arranging files and folders

option	arranges files and folders
Name	Alphabetically
Size	By size, with the largest folder or file listed first
Type	By type, such as all documents created using the WordPad program
Modified	Chronologically by their last modification date, with the latest modification date listed last
Show in Groups	In letter groups by alphabetical order
Auto Arrange	Automatically in orderly rows and columns
Align to Grid	Automatically in rows and columns by invisible grid points

Searching for Files and Folders

Sometimes remembering precisely where you stored a file is difficult. Windows provides a Search Companion to help you find files or folders. The Search Companion opens in the Search Explorer bar and gives you the option to find files or folders by name, location, size, type, and the creation or last modification date. You can also narrow your search by selecting categories, listed in the Search Companion. The Search Companion is also accessible from the Start menu to help you locate files and folders when you are not using My Computer or Windows Explorer. John wants to find a file he created several months ago with a preliminary outline for the Spring Catalog. He cannot remember the exact title of the file or where he stored it, so he needs to do a search.

1. **Click the Search button $\mathcal{P}$ on the Standard Buttons toolbar**

   The Search Companion Explorer bar opens on the left side of the screen with an animated search character. The default character is a dog. Since you remember part of the name, but not the location, of the file you need, you will use the All files and folders option.

2. **In the Search Companion Explorer bar, click All files and folders**

   A list of search options appear in the Search Explorer bar, as shown in Figure C-10. You can enter search information to find folders and files by all or part of the file name, a word or phrase in the file, a specific drive or folder location, a modified date, a size range, or additional advanced criteria.

3. **Type catalog in the All or part of the file name text box**

   You can supply the full name of the folder or file you want to find or only the part you know for sure. If, for example, you were unsure as to whether you saved the file as Spring Catalog or Catalog Outline, you could type Catalog, since you're sure of that part of the name. If you didn't know the name of the file, but did know some text contained in the file, you could enter the text in the A word or phrase in the file text box. Before you start the search, you need to indicate where you want the program to search. By default, the search will occur in the currently open folder, but you can choose any location.

4. **Click the Look in list arrow, then click the Wired Coffee folder if necessary**

   Now that you have defined the location, you are ready to do the search.

5. **Click Search**

   The Search program finds all the files and folders in the Wired Coffee folder, switches from the current folder view to Details view, and lists those files and folders whose names contain the word "catalog" in the right pane. The list contains the full names, locations, sizes, types, and the creation or last modification dates of the folders or files.

6. **Position the pointer between the In Folder column indicator button and the Size column indicator button, the pointer changes to ⟷, then drag to the right to display the location of the file if necessary, as shown in Figure C-11.**

   At this point, you can either double-click the file to start the associated program and open the file, or you can note the file's location and close the Search Explorer bar. You decide to note the file's location and return to viewing folders.

7. **In the Search Companion Explorer bar, click Yes, finished searching to complete the search and close the Search Companion Explorer bar**

8. **Click the Folders button 📁 on the Standard Buttons toolbar to open the Folders Explorer bar**

FIGURE C-10: Search Explorer bar with All files and folders option

Click button to begin the search process

Enter name or partial name of the file you are looking for here

Enter text contained in the file here

Specify file location here

Click arrows to access additional search criteria

Click button to start search

FIGURE C-11: Results of search for "catalog"

Drag to resize column size

Additional search options with the results

Folders and files that match your search in Details view

Your location might differ

Performing an advanced search

You can also perform an advanced search that uses criteria beyond just the name or partial name of the file. If you do not know what the name or content of the file is, but can recall the type of file (such as a WordPad document), click All Files and Folders, click More Advanced Options, then select a file type using the Type of file list arrow and other location specific or case sensitive options. When you click Search, Windows searches for and displays all the files for the type you specify. In some cases, this can take a long time, although probably less time than re-creating the missing files would take.

Copying and Moving Files and Folders

Sometimes you will need to move a file from one folder to another, or copy a file from one folder to another, leaving it in the first location and placing a copy of it in the second. You can move or copy a file or folder using a variety of methods. If the file or folder and the location where you want to move it are visible in a window or on the desktop, you can simply drag the item from one location to the other. Moving a file or folder on the same disk relocates it; whereas dragging it from one disk to another copies it so that it appears in both locations. To make sure that you move or copy an item properly, right-click the file or folder, drag the item to the destination location, then choose the appropriate command from the shortcut menu. When the destination folder or drive is not visible, you can use the Cut, Copy, and Paste commands on the Edit menu or the buttons on the Standard Buttons toolbar. John plans to use and revise the text from the Mail Order Catalog file, currently located in the Advertising folder, which is in the Spring Catalog folder. The Mail Order Catalog file is no longer needed in the Advertising folder, so John moves it from the Advertising folder to the Catalog Pages folder to keep related files together. He also wants to make a copy of the Wired Coffee Logo file and place it in the Spring Catalog folder.

1. **Click the Expand indicator ⊞ next to the Spring Catalog folder in the Folders Explorer bar**
   The Spring Catalog folder expands, displaying the folder it contains. The right pane shows the results of the search. When moving or copying files or folders, make sure the files or folders you want to move or copy appear in the right pane. To move the Mail Order Catalog file, you drag it from the right pane to the Catalog Pages folder in the Folders Explorer bar.

2. **Drag the Mail Order Catalog file in the right pane from the list of search results across the vertical line separating the two panes to the Catalog Pages folder as shown in Figure C-12, then release the mouse button**
   Once you release the mouse button, the Mail Order Catalog file is relocated to the Catalog Pages folder. If you decide that you don't want the file moved, you could move it back easily using the Undo command on the Edit menu. Now you copy the Wired Coffee Logo file in the Advertising folder to the Spring Catalog folder.

3. **Click the Advertising folder in the Folders Explorer bar**
   Notice that the Mail Order Catalog file is no longer stored in the Advertising folder.

4. **Point to the Wired Coffee Logo file, press and hold the right mouse button, drag the file across the vertical line separating the two panes to the Spring Catalog folder, then release the mouse button**
   As shown in Figure C-13, a shortcut menu appears, offering a choice of options. Another way to copy or move the file to a new location is by right-clicking a file in the right pane, then clicking the appropriate option on the shortcut menu.

5. **Click Copy Here on the shortcut menu**
   The original Wired Coffee Logo file remains in the Advertising folder, and a copy of the file is in the Spring Catalog folder.

6. **Click the Spring Catalog folder in the Folders Explorer bar**
   A copy of the Wired Coffee Logo file appears in the Advertising folder.

7. **Click the Catalog Pages folder in the Folders Explorer bar**
   The folder opens and the Mail Order Catalog file appears in the right pane.

8. **Click the Advertising folder in the Folders Explorer bar, then click the Folders button 🗀 on the Standard Buttons toolbar to close the Folders Explorer bar**

FIGURE C-12: Moving a file from one folder to another

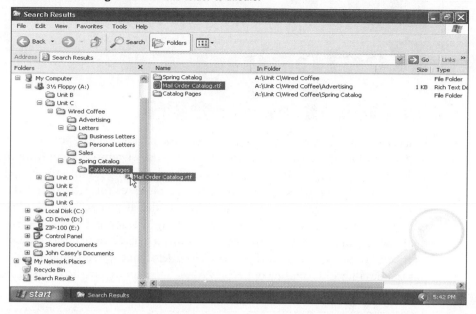

FIGURE C-13: Copying a file from one location to another

Copied file will appear here

Click command to move the file

Click command to copy the file

Sending files and folders

When you right-click most objects on the desktop or in My Computer or Windows Explorer, the Send To command, located on the shortcut menu, lets you send, or move, a file or folder to a new location on your computer. For example, you can send a file or folder to a floppy disk to make a quick backup copy of the file or folder, to a mail recipient as an electronic message, or to the desktop to create a shortcut. You can also use the Send To command to move a file or folder from one folder to another. To send a file or folder, right-click the file or folder you want to send, point to Send To on the shortcut menu, then click the destination you want.

Deleting and Restoring Files and Folders

When you organize the contents of a folder, disk, or the desktop, you might find files and folders that you no longer need. You can **delete** these items, or remove them from the disk. If you delete a file or folder from the desktop or from the hard disk, it goes into the Recycle Bin. The **Recycle Bin**, located on your desktop, is a temporary storage area for deleted files. The Recycle Bin stores all the items you delete from your hard disk, so that if you accidentally delete an item, you can remove it from the Recycle Bin to restore it. If the deletion is a recent operation, you can also use the Undo command on the Edit menu to restore a deleted file or folder. Be aware that if you delete a file from your floppy disk, it is permanently deleted, not stored in the Recycle Bin. Table C-3 summarizes deleting and restoring options. ➤ John is not sure how the Recycle Bin works, so he deletes a file, then restores it to find out.

Steps

1. Click the **Restore Down button** in the Advertising window, then resize and move the window so that you can see the Recycle Bin icon on the desktop
   Because you cannot restore files deleted from a floppy disk, you start by moving a file from the drive where your Project Files are located to the desktop.

2. Point to the **Ad Campaign file** in the right pane, press and hold the **right mouse button**, drag it to the desktop, then click **Move Here** on the shortcut menu
   You moved the Ad Campaign file to the desktop, as shown in Figure C-14.

3. Drag the **Ad Campaign file** from the desktop to the Recycle Bin
   The Recycle Bin icon should now look like it contains paper 🗑.

4. Double-click the **Recycle Bin icon** on the desktop
   The Recycle Bin window opens, containing the Ad Campaign file and any other deleted files. Like most other windows, the Recycle Bin window has a menu bar, a toolbar, and a status bar. Your deleted files remain in the Recycle Bin until you empty it, permanently removing the contents of the Recycle Bin from your hard disk. Because you still need this file, you decide to restore it.

5. Select the **Ad Campaign file** in the Recycle Bin window, as shown in Figure C-15, then click **Restore this item** in the left pane under Recycle Bin Tasks
   You restored the file back to its previous location on the desktop. It is intact and identical to the form it was in before you deleted it.

6. Click the **Close button** in the Recycle Bin window
   The Recycle Bin window closes, and the desktop appears with the Ad Campaign file and the Advertising window open.

7. In the Advertising window, click **Edit** on the menu bar, then click **Undo Move**
   The Ad Campaign file is moved back to the Advertising folder and no longer appears on the desktop.

Trouble?

If a message box appears, click Yes to confirm the deletion.

QuickTip

To empty the Recycle Bin, click Empty the Recycle Bin in the left pane under Recycle Bin Tasks, or right-click the Recycle Bin icon on the desktop, then click Empty Recycle Bin.

FIGURE C-14: Selecting a file to drag to the Recycle Bin

— Selected file moved from the Advertising folder to the desktop

— Drag the selected icon here to delete the file

FIGURE C-15: Deleted file from the Advertising folder in the Recycle Bin

Click link to empty the Recycle Bin and permanently delete the file

Click link to restore the selected file

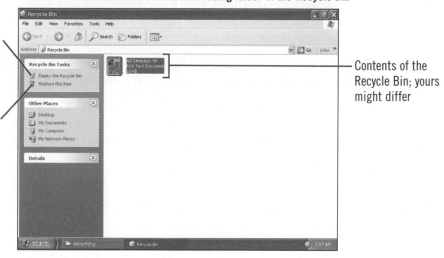

— Contents of the Recycle Bin; yours might differ

TABLE C-3: Deleting and restoring files

ways to delete a file or folder	ways to restore a file or folder from the Recycle Bin
Select the file or folder, click File on the menu bar, then click Delete	Select the file or folder, click File on the menu bar, then click Restore
Select the file or folder, then press [Delete]	Click Edit on the menu bar, then click Undo
Right-click the file or folder, then click Delete	Right-click the file or folder, then click Restore
Drag the file or folder to the Recycle Bin	Drag the file or folder from the Recycle Bin to any location

Recycle Bin properties

You can adjust several Recycle Bin settings by using the Properties option on the Recycle Bin shortcut menu. For example, if you do not want to place files in the Recycle Bin when you delete them, but, rather, want to delete them immediately, right-click the Recycle Bin, click Properties, then click the Do not move files to the Recycle Bin check box to select it.

Also, if you find that the Recycle Bin is full and cannot accept any more files, you can increase the amount of disk space allotted to the Recycle Bin by moving the Maximum size of Recycle Bin slider to the right. The percentage shown represents how much space the contents of the Recycle Bin takes on the drive.

Windows XP

Creating a Shortcut to a File or Folder

It could take you a while to access a file or folder buried several levels down in a file hierarchy. You can create shortcuts to the items you use frequently. A **shortcut** is a link that you can place in any location to gain instant access to a particular file, folder, or program on your hard disk or on a network just by double-clicking. The actual file, folder, or program remains stored in its original location, and you place an icon representing the shortcut in a convenient location, such as a folder or the desktop. ◀───── John is always updating a file that lists special ads. Rather than having to take steps to start WordPad and then open the file, he places a shortcut to this file on the desktop.

Steps 1 2 3 4

1. **In the Advertising folder, right-click the Special Ads file, then click Create Shortcut**
   An icon with a small arrow for a shortcut to the Special Ads now appears in the Advertising window. Compare your screen with Figure C-16. All shortcuts are named the same as the files to which they link, but with the words "Shortcut to" in front of the original name. You want to place the shortcut on the desktop for easy file access.

2. **Position ▷ over the Shortcut to Special Ads file in the Advertising folder, press and hold the right mouse button, drag it from the Advertising folder to an empty area of the desktop, then click Move Here on the shortcut menu**
   The shortcut appears on the desktop, as shown in Figure C-17. You can place a shortcut anywhere on the desktop. You should test the shortcut.

Trouble?

Depending on your file association settings, another word processing program might open instead of WordPad.

3. **Double-click the Shortcut to Special Ads icon on the desktop**
   The Special Ads document opens in WordPad.

4. **Click the Close button in the WordPad window**
   The logo file and the WordPad program close. The Special Ads shortcut remains on the desktop until you delete it, so you can use it again and again.

5. **Right-click the Shortcut to Special Ads icon**
   A shortcut menu opens that offers several file management commands. The commands on your shortcut menu might differ, depending on the item you right-click, or the Windows features installed on your computer.

6. **Click Delete on the shortcut menu, then click Yes to confirm the deletion to the Recycle Bin**
   You delete the shortcut from the desktop and place it in the Recycle Bin, where it remains until you empty the Recycle Bin or restore the shortcut. When you delete a shortcut, you remove only the shortcut. The original file remains intact in its original location.

7. **Click the Close button in the Advertising window**

FIGURE C-16: Creating a shortcut

Original file ───

Your list of files
might differ

Shortcut icons
include a small
arrow

FIGURE C-17: Shortcut moved to a new location

Relocated shortcut
on the desktop

Placing shortcuts on the Start menu and the taskbar

You can place shortcuts to frequently-used files, folders, and programs on the Start menu or on a toolbar on the taskbar. To do this, simply drag the shortcut file, folder, or program to the Start button, wait until the Start menu opens, drag to the All Programs submenu, wait until the submenu opens, then drag the shortcut to the appropriate place on the menu. You can also drag a shortcut to a toolbar on the taskbar using the same method. When you release the mouse, the item appears on the menu or toolbar.

Practice

► Concepts Review

Label each of the elements of the screen shown in Figure C-18.

FIGURE C-18

1. Which element do you click to display folder contents in the right pane?
2. Which element is ready to be deleted or restored?
3. Which element do you click to expand a folder?
4. Which element holds items to be deleted or restored?
5. Which element do you click to collapse a folder?
6. Which element is copied?
7. Which element is a shortcut?

Match each term with the statement that describes its function.

8. **My Computer**   a. A display of drives and folders on the computer
9. **Folders list**   b. A file and folder management tool
10. **File**   c. A storage container for deleted files
11. **Recycle Bin**   d. A storage container for files and folders
12. **Folder**   e. A collection of information that has a unique name

Select the best answer from the following list of choices.

13. My Computer is used to:
  a. Delete files.
  b. Add folders.
  c. Manage files and folders.
  d. All of the above.

14. Which of the following is NOT a valid search criterion for a file using the Search program?
  a. Date modified
  b. Date opened
  c. Name
  d. Location

15. Which of the following is a method for copying a file or folder:
  a. Press [Ctrl], then drag the folder or file.
  b. Drag the folder or file on the same disk drive.
  c. Double-click the folder or file.
  d. Left-click the folder or file, then click Copy.

16. Which of the following locations is NOT a valid place from which to delete a file and send it to the Recycle Bin?
  a. Floppy disk
  b. My Documents folder
  c. Hard drive
  d. My Computer

17. What graphical element appears on a shortcut icon?
  a. pencil
  b. chain link
  c. pointer
  d. arrow

▶ Skills Review

1. Open and view My Computer.
  a. Insert your disk where your Project Files are located in the appropriate disk drive if necessary.
  b. Open and maximize My Computer.
  c. Navigate to the Wired Coffee folder on the drive and folder where your Project Files are located.
  d. Double-click the Letters folder, then double-click the Personal Letters folder.

2. View folders and files.
  a. Click the Views list arrow, then click List. Click the Up button on the Standard Buttons toolbar twice.
  b. Click the Back button on the Standard Buttons toolbar, then open the Business Letters folder.
  c. Click the Back list arrow on the Standard Buttons toolbar, then click Personal Letters.
  d. Click the Forward button on the Standard Buttons toolbar.
  e. Click View on the menu bar, then click Details. Click View on the menu bar, then click Tiles.

3. View the Folders list.
  a. Click the Folders button on the Standard Buttons toolbar.
  b. Click the Expand indicator next to the drive icon where your Project Files are located in the Folders Explorer bar.
  c. Click the drive icon where your Project Files are located in the Folders Explorer bar.
  d. Click the Expand indicator next to the drive and folder icons where your Project Files are located in the Folders Explorer bar, then click the Wired Coffee folder in the Folders Explorer bar.
  e. Double-click the Sales folder in the right pane to open it.

4. Create and rename files and folders.
  a. In the Sales folder, right-click a blank area of the window, point to New, then click Folder.
  b. Name the folder **Sales & Marketing**, then press [Enter].
  c. Rename the Sales & Marketing folder to **Marketing**, then press [Enter]. Arrange the icons by name.

5. Search for files and folders.

    a. Open the Search Companion Explorer bar, then click All file and folders in Search Companion Explorer bar.

    b. Search in the Wired Coffee folder for files that are named or contain the word "customer" as part of the filename.

    c. Close the Search Companion Explorer bar.

6. Copy and move files and folders.

    a. Click the Customer Profile file to select it in the right pane. Click Edit on the menu bar, then click Copy.

    b. Open the Search Companion Explorer bar. Click the Sales folder in the Folders Explorer bar (expand folders if necessary).

    c. Click Edit on the menu bar, then click Paste.

    d. Move the copy of the Customer Profile file into the Marketing folder.

    e. Move the Marketing folder into the Wired Coffee folder.

7. Delete and restore files and folders.

    a. Open the Wired Coffee folder, click the Restore Down button, then resize to display part of the desktop.

    b. Right-click the Marketing folder, drag it to the desktop, then click Move Here on the shortcut menu.

    c. Drag the Marketing folder from the desktop to the Recycle Bin, then click Yes to confirm the deletion, if necessary.

    d. Double-click the Recycle Bin. Right-click a blank area of the taskbar, then click Tile Windows Vertically.

    e. Click File on the Recycle Bin menu bar, click Empty Recycle Bin, then click Yes.

    f. Drag the Marketing folder back to the Wired Coffee folder to restore it, then click the Recycle Bin Close button.

8. Create a shortcut to a file or folder.

    a. Open the Marketing folder.

    b. Create a shortcut to the Customer Profile file, then move the shortcut to the desktop.

    c. Rename the shortcut "Customer Profile," then delete the shortcut on the desktop.

► Independent Challenge 1

As a human resources manager at World Wide Books, you need to organize the folders and files on the company's computer for new employees at store locations around the world. Your job is to create and organize company files and folders.

    a. Open My Computer and create a new folder named **World Wide Books** on the drive and in the folder where your Project Files are located, within which the rest of the organization of files and folders for this independent challenge will appear.

    b. Create a file using WordPad listing at least six international store locations. Save it as **New Store Locations**.

    c. Create a file using WordPad listing employee names. Save it as **Employee App**.

    d. In the World Wide Books folder, create folders named **Store Locations** and **Employees**.

    e. In the Employees folder, create four new folders named with employee names.

    f. Copy the Employee App file into each of the employee folders, then rename each file using the employees' names.

    g. In the folder named Store Locations, create a new folder named **New Stores**.

    h. Move the New Store Locations file to the New Stores folder.

    i. Using paper and pencil, draw the file hierarchy of the World Wide Books folder, then Close My Computer.

► Independent Challenge 2

You are vice president of a carton manufacturing company, Apex Cartons, and you need to organize your Windows files and folders. In addition to folders for typical business related functions, such as correspondence, contracts, inventory, and payroll, you have folders related to company functions, such as manufacturing and material suppliers.

a. Open My Computer and create a new folder named **Apex Cartons** in the drive and in the folder where your Project Files are located, within which the rest of the organization of files and folders for this independent challenge will appear.

b. Create folders named **Manufacturing, Material Suppliers, East Coast** and **West Coast**.

c. Move the East Coast and West Coast folders into the Material Suppliers folder.

d. Create a blank file using WordPad, then save it as **Suppliers Bid** in the Manufacturing folder.

e. Move the Suppliers Bid file into the Material Suppliers folder.

f. Copy the Suppliers Bid file into the Manufacturing folder and rename the copied file **Manufacturing Bids**.

g. Using paper and pencil, draw the file hierarchy of your Apex Cartons folder, then close My Computer.

▶ Independent Challenge 3

You start a mail-order PC business called MO PC, and you use Windows to organize your business files.

a. Open My Computer and create a new folder named **MO PC** on the drive and in the folder where your Project Files are located, within which the files and folders for this independent challenge will appear.

b. Create folders named **Advertising** and **Customers**.

c. Use WordPad to create a letter welcoming new customers. Save it as **Customer Letter** in the Customers folder.

d. Use WordPad to create a list of five tasks to do. Save it as **Business Plan** in the MO PC folder.

e. Use Paint to create a simple logo, then save it as **MO Logo** in the MO PC folder.

f. Move the MO Logo file into the Advertising folder.

g. Create a shortcut to the MO Logo file, then move it into the MO PC folder.

h. Delete the Business Plan file, then restore it.

i. Using paper and pencil, draw the file hierarchy of your MO PC folder, then close My Computer.

Independent Challenge 4

You are a new administrative assistant at Sunrise Bakeries, which recently opened. Your job is to help the owners organize their recipes into different categories and help keep files and folder organized in the future.

a. Open My Computer and create a new folder named **Sunrise Bakeries** on the drive and in the folder where your Project Files are located, within which the files and folders for this independent challenge will appear.

b. Create three files using WordPad and save them as **French Bread, Torte**, and **7-Layer Chocolate** in the Sunrise Bakeries folder on the drive and in the folder where your Project Files are located.

c. In the Sunrise Bakeries folder, create a folder named **Desserts**.

d. Create folders named **Flourless Cakes** and **Flour Cakes** and move them into the Desserts folder.

e. In the Sunrise Bakeries folder, create a folder named **Breads**.

f. Move the Torte file into the Flourless Cakes folder and move 7-Layer Chocolate into the Flour Cakes folder.

g. Move the French Bread file into the Breads folder.

h. Copy the French Bread file into the Breads folder and rename it **Sweet Bread**.

i. Move the Sweet Bread file to your desktop, then drag the file to the Recycle Bin.

j. Double-click to open the Recycle Bin, then restore the Sweet Bread file to the Breads folder.

k. Create a shortcut to the Torte file in the Flourless Cakes folder, then move it into the Sunrise Bakeries folder.

l. Using paper and pencil, draw the file hierarchy of your Sunrise Bakeries folder, then close My Computer.

► Visual Workshop

Re-create the screen shown in Figure C-19, which displays the Search Results window with files from the drive and folder where your Project Files are located. Print the screen. (Press [Print Screen] to make a copy of the screen, open Paint, click Edit on the menu bar, click Paste to paste the screen into Paint, then click Yes to paste the large image if necessary. Click the Text button on the Toolbox, click a blank area in the Paint work area, then type your name. Click File on the Menu bar, click Page Setup, change 100% normal size to 50% in the scaling area, then click OK. Click File on the menu bar, click Print, then click Print.)

FIGURE C-19

Customizing

File and Folder Management

Objectives

- ► **Add a folder to the Favorites list**
- ► **Change folder options**
- ► **Change file details to list**
- ► **Change file and folder list views**
- ► **Display disk and folder information**
- ► **Compress files and folders**
- ► **Use personal folders**
- ► **Customize a personal folder**
- ► **Manage files and folders on a CD**

As you work with files and folders, you'll discover that navigating through a long list of folders can be time consuming. To be more efficient, you can customize the way you work with files and folders to save you time and effort and to suit your personal needs and preferences. In this unit you'll learn how to create links to access files and folders quickly, change folder view options to display the file and folder information you need, store a file in a custom personal folder to quickly view its contents, display disk and folder size information, compress files and folders to save disk space, and use a compact disc to backup and store files for later use in case of problems. John Casey, the owner of Wired Coffee Company, customizes some file management tasks to suit his personal needs.

Windows XP

Adding a Folder to the Favorites List

Rather than navigating through a long list of folders to get to the location you want to display, you can use a Favorites list to locate and organize folders. When you view a folder in My Computer or Windows Explorer that you want to display at a later time, you can add the folder to your Favorites list. Once you add the folder to the Favorites list, you can return to the folder in My Computer or Windows Explorer by opening your Favorites list and selecting the link to the folder you want. In addition to adding folders to the Favorites list, you can also add locations on the Internet. If your list of favorites grows long, you can delete favorites you don't use anymore or move favorites into folders. ◀▬▬▬ John wants to add the Wired Coffee folder to his Favorites list.

Steps

1. **Click the Start button on the taskbar, then click My Computer**
   The My Computer window opens, displaying the contents of your computer, including all disk drives and common folders.

2. **Double-click the drive and folder where your Project Files are located, then double-click the Wired Coffee folder**
   The Wired Coffee window appears, displaying the contents of the Wired Coffee folder.

3. **Click Favorites on the menu bar, then click Add to Favorites**
   The Add Favorite dialog box opens, as shown in Figure D-1.

QuickTip

To specify the location of a favorite on the Favorites list, click Create in in the Add Favorite dialog box, then select a location.

4. **Click to the right of the text to place the insertion point in the Name text box, press [Spacebar], type Company, then click OK**
   You named the favorite "Wired Coffee Company," and added the folder to your Favorites list.

5. **In the left pane under Other Places, click My Computer**
   The My Computer window appears, displaying the contents of your computer.

QuickTip

To display the Favorites list in the Explorer bar, click View on the menu bar, point to Explorer bar, then click Favorites. To close it, click the Close button in the Explorer bar.

6. **Click Favorites on the menu bar, then click Wired Coffee Company**
   The Wired Coffee window appears, displaying the contents of the Wired Coffee folder. To keep the Favorites list organized, you can delete, rename, or move the favorites.

7. **Click Favorites on the menu bar, then click Organize Favorites**
   The Organize Favorites dialog box opens, as shown in Figure D-2.

8. **Click Wired Coffee Company in the Favorites list, click Delete, then click Yes to confirm the deletion to the Recycle Bin**
   The favorite is deleted from the Favorites list and sent to the Recycle Bin.

9. **Click Close**
   The Organize Favorites dialog box closes, and the Wired Coffee window remains open.

FIGURE D-1: Add Favorite dialog box

Name text box

Click button to specify the location of favorite on the Favorites menu

FIGURE D-2: Organize Favorites dialog box

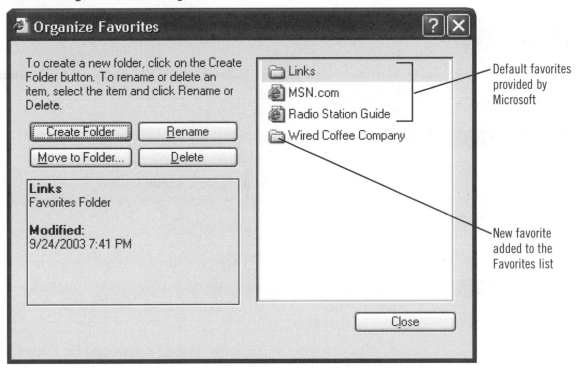

Default favorites provided by Microsoft

New favorite added to the Favorites list

Organizing favorites in folders

If your list of favorites grows long, you can move favorites into folders. To move your favorites, click Favorites on the menu bar, click Organize Favorites, select one or more files or folders from the Favorites list, click Move to Folder to open the Browse for Folder dialog box, select a folder, then click OK. If you want to add a new folder to your Favorites list,

click Create Folder, type the new folder name, then press [Enter]. If you prefer to use another name for a favorite, you can select the favorite you want to rename, click the Rename button, type the new name, then press [Enter]. When you finish making changes, click Close in the Organize Favorites dialog box.

Changing Folder Options

When you work with files and folders, Windows displays folder contents in a standard way, known as the **default**. The default folder view settings are: Tiles view displays files and folders as icons; common task links appear in the left pane; folders open in the same window; and items open when you double-click them, for example. Depending on previous installation or users, your folder view settings might differ. Instead of changing the folder view to your preferred view—Thumbnails, Icons, List, or Details—each time you open a folder, you can change the view permanently to the one you prefer. To change the default view for all the folders or the current folder on your computer, use the View tab in the Folder Options dialog box to apply new folder settings. In addition to the defaults, you can change options such as folder settings to show or hide file extensions for known file types, show or hide hidden files and folders, show the Control Panel in My Computer, and show pop-up descriptions of folders and desktop items. If you don't like the options you set in the Folder Options dialog box, you can restore the dialog box settings to Windows default settings. John wants to experiment with customizing the folder settings to suit his needs.

1. In the Wired Coffee folder, double-click the **Sales folder**, click the **Views button** on the Standard Buttons toolbar, then click **Details**
   The files and folders in the Sales folder appear in Details view.

QuickTip

If you don't like the options you set in the Folder Options dialog box, you can restore the dialog box settings to Windows default settings by clicking Restore Defaults.

2. Click **Tools** on the menu bar, then click **Folder Options**
   The Folder Options dialog box opens, displaying the General tab, as shown in Figure D-3.

3. Click the **Use Windows classic folders option button**
   This option hides the left pane in the folder view that shows common tasks in folders.

4. Click the **View tab**
   The View tab appears, as shown in Figure D-4, displaying folder options relating to the way files and folders appear in My Computer and Windows Explorer.

QuickTip

To restore all folders to original Windows settings, click Reset All Folders.

5. Click **Apply to All Folders**, then click **Yes** to accept the folder views change
   This feature sets all the folders on your computer to match the current folder's view settings, which is currently Details view.

6. In the Advanced settings box, click the **Hide extensions for known file types check box** to select it if necessary
   This option hides the three letter file extension, such as .rtf.

7. In the Advanced settings box, scroll down the list, then click the **Show Control Panel in My Computer check box** to select it
   This option shows a Control Panel icon when you open the My Computer window.

8. Click **OK**
   The Sales window appears without the left pane of common tasks and file extensions at the end of filenames, as shown in Figure D-5.

QuickTip

To display the Control Panel in My Computer, double-click the Control Panel icon.

9. Click the **Back list arrow** ⬅ Back ▾ on the Standard Buttons toolbar, click **My Computer** to display the Control Panel icon in My Computer, click the **Forward list arrow** ➡ ▾ on the Standard Buttons toolbar, then click **Wired Coffee**
   The Wired Coffee window appears, displaying the contents of the folder in Details view. Based on the new folder option settings, all folders appear in Details view.

FIGURE D-3: Folder Options dialog box with the General tab

Default Settings

FIGURE D-4: Folder Options dialog box with the View tab

FIGURE D-5: Sales folder with new folder options

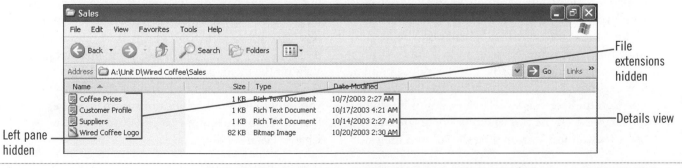

File
extensions
hidden

Details view

Left pane
hidden

Changing File Details to List

You can display files and folders in a variety of different ways, depending on what you want to see and do. When you view files and folders in Details view, a default list of file and folder information appears, which consists of Name, Size, Type, and Date Modified. If the default list of file and folder details doesn't provide you with the information you need, you can add and remove the file and folder information you want to and from the Details view. You use the Choose Details command or right-click a column indicator button to make changes to the details list. John wants to add the owner of a file and image size of picture files to the details list in Details view.

Steps

QuickTip

When you set the default view to Details view, the items you add or remove from the Choose Details dialog box are not included in Details view.

1. **In the Wired Coffee folder, double-click the Sales folder**
   The Sales window appears, displaying the contents of the folder in Details view.

2. **Click View on the menu bar, then click Choose Details**
   The Choose Details dialog box opens, as shown in Figure D-6. The selected check boxes indicate the current columns shown in Details view.

3. **In the Details box, click the Owner check box to select it**
   This options displays the **owner** (the person who can make changes) of files. Yours will be different.

4. **In the Details box, scroll down, then click the Dimensions check box to select it**
   This option displays the size of image files in pixels. A **pixel**, short for picture element, is a single point in a graphic image.

5. **Click OK**
   The additional details are displayed in Details view, as shown in Figure D-7.

6. **Right-click any column indicator button, then click Owner on the shortcut menu to deselect it**
   The Owner column is removed from Details view.

7. **Right-click any column indicator button, then click Date Created on the shortcut menu to select it**
   The Date Created column is added to Details view, as shown in Figure D-8.

CLUES TO USE

Moving columns in Details view

When you display files and folders in Details view, you can change the order of the column details to make it easier to locate the information you need to find. You can change the order of columns by using the Choose Details dialog box or the mouse pointer. The easiest way to move a column detail a short distance on the screen is to drag the column indicator button between the two columns where you want to place the column. As you drag the column indicator button, a blue bar appears, indicating where the column will be placed. If you need to move a column several columns across the screen, the best way to move it is to use the Choose Details dialog box. Click View on the menu bar, click Choose Details to open the Choose Details dialog box, click the column detail you want to move, then click Move Up or Move Down. When you're done, click OK to close the Choose Details dialog box.

FIGURE D-6: Choose Details dialog box

Current column
details in order of
appearance

FIGURE D-7: Columns added in Details view

Column
indicator
buttons

Column details
added

Your name will
differ

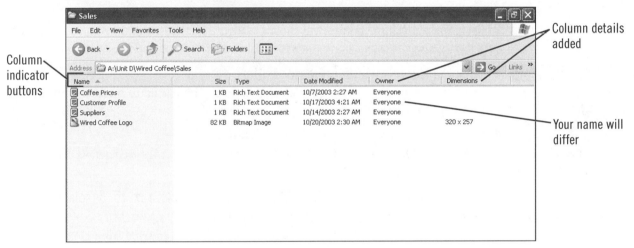

FIGURE D-8: Columns modified in Details view

Owner column
detail removed
and Date
Created column
detail added

Changing File and Folder List Views

Once you choose the details that you want to list in Details view, you can change the order in which the file and folder information is displayed in the columns. If you need to change the way Windows sorts your files and folders, you can use the column indicator buttons in the right pane of Details view. Clicking one of the column indicator buttons, such as Name, Size, Type, or Date Modified in Details view, sorts the files and folders by the type of information listed in the column. John wants to find the date he wrote a letter to the coffee suppliers, so he decides to sort the files in the Business Letters folder by date.

Steps

1. In the Sales folder, click the **Date Modified column indicator button**
   The files and folders are now sorted by their last modification date, as shown in Figure D-9. The gray up arrow in the column indicator button indicates that the list is sorted from earliest (at the top) to latest (at the bottom), and the gray column background indicates that the column is selected. When you point to a column indicator button, a bold orange line appears under the column title.

2. Click the **Date Modified column indicator button**
   The gray arrow changes from up to down, indicating that the list is sorted from latest (at the top) to earliest (at the bottom), as shown in Figure D-10. Each of the column indicator buttons works as a toggle; clicking once sorts the file in one order, and clicking again reverses the order.

3. Click the **Name column indicator button**
   The files and folders are now sorted alphabetically by name from top to bottom. You want to restore folder settings.

4. Click **View** on the menu bar, then click **Choose Details**
   The Choose Details dialog box opens, displaying the currently used details checked at the top of the list.

5. In the Details box, click the **Date Created check box** to deselect it, click the **Dimensions check box** to deselect it, then click **OK**
   The Date Created and Dimensions Column details are removed from Details view.

6. Click **Tools** on the menu bar, then click **Folder Options**
   The folder Options dialog box opens, displaying the file hierarchy.

7. Click **Restore Defaults**, click the **View tab**, click **Restore Defaults**, click **Reset All Folders**, click **Yes** to confirm the reset all folder views, then click **OK**
   The folder options are restored to the Windows default settings. Although Tiles view is the default, the current view doesn't automatically switch back to it when you restore the settings unless you close and re-open the folder.

8. Click the **Views button** ⊞ ▾ on the Standard Buttons toolbar, then click **Tiles**
   The folder view changes to Tiles, as shown in Figure D-11.

9. Click the **Back button** ⊙ Back on the Standard Buttons toolbar
   The Wired Coffee window appears in Tiles view.

FIGURE D-9: Sorting files and folders by date modified (earliest to latest)

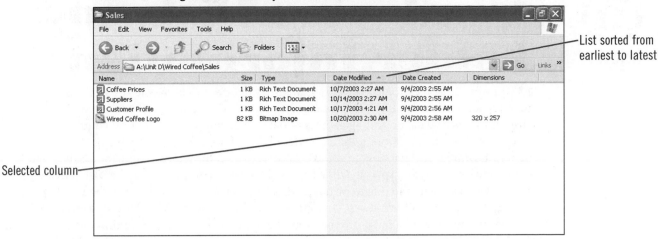

Selected column

List sorted from earliest to latest

FIGURE D-10: Sorting files and folders by date modified (latest to earliest)

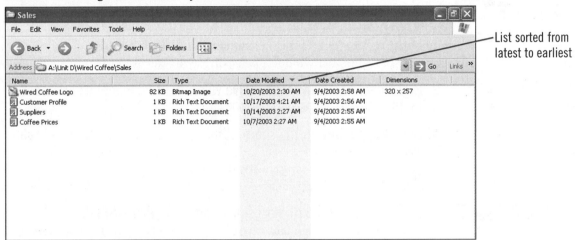

List sorted from latest to earliest

FIGURE D-11: Restoring folder options

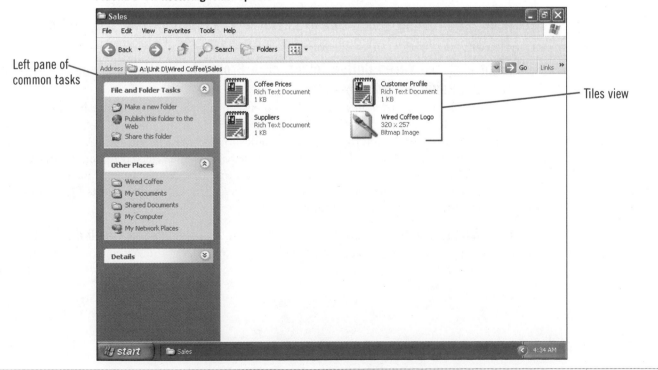

Left pane of common tasks

Tiles view

Displaying Disk and Folder Information

As you work with files, folders, and programs, it's important to know the size of the disk and how much space remains available. A disk can store only a limited amount of data. Hard disks can store large amounts of data, up to 10 gigabytes of data, while floppy disks are limited to 1.4 megabytes of data. A disk that can store 1.44 megabytes of data, for example, is capable of storing approximately 1.4 million characters, or about 3,000 pages of information. You can use the Properties command on a disk to display the disk size, used and free space, and change a **disk label**, which is a name you can assign to a hard or floppy disk. When you label a hard disk, the label appears in the My Computer and Windows Explorer windows. Besides checking hard disk drive or floppy disk information, you can also use the Properties command on a folder to find out the size of its contents. This can be helpful when you want to copy or move a folder to a removable disk or CD. John wants to find out how much space is available on his floppy disk and the size of a folder's contents.

Steps

1. **In the left pane under Other Places, click My Computer**
   The My Computer window opens, displaying the disk drives available on your computer.

2. **Right-click the icon for the drive where your Project Files are located**
   In this example, the drive is the 3½" disk.

3. **Click Properties on the shortcut menu, then click the General tab if necessary**
   The 3½ Floppy (A:) Properties dialog box opens, displaying the General tab, as shown in Figure D-12. There is a pie chart showing the amount of space being used relative to the amount available for the disk. In this example, 872 kilobytes are used and 551 kilobytes are free.

   Trouble?

   If you are working in a lab and your Project Files are located on a hard or network disk, skip Step 4.

4. **Click in the text box if necessary, then type ProjectDisk**
   A disk label cannot contain any spaces, but can be up to 11 characters long.

5. **Click OK**
   The Properties dialog box closes.

6. **Double-click the icon for the drive and folder where your Project Files are located**
   The Wired Coffee folder is displayed.

7. **Right-click the Wired Coffee folder, click Properties on the shortcut menu, then click the General tab if necessary**
   The Wired Coffee Properties dialog box opens, displaying the General tab, as shown in Figure D-13. The Properties dialog box displays the size of the folder (Size) and the actual amount of disk space used by the selected folder (Size on disk). The actual amount of disk space used is either the cluster size or compressed size of the selected folder. A **cluster** is a group of sectors on a disk. A **sector** is the smallest unit that can be accessed on a disk. A sector on a disk cannot always be filled, so the amount is generally higher. If the file or folder is compressed, the Size on disk amount is the compressed size.

8. **Click OK to close the Properties dialog box, then double-click the Wired Coffee folder**
   The Wired Coffee window appears, displaying the contents of the Wired Coffee folder.

FIGURE D-12: General tab in the 3½ Floppy (A:) Properties dialog box

Space on your disk; yours might differ

Pink indicates free disk space

Blue indicates used disk space

FIGURE D-13: General tab in the Wired Coffee Properties dialog box

Folder name

Size of file or folder

Actual amount of disk space used

Your information might differ

Number of files and folders

Understanding file sizes

When you create a file, it takes up space on a disk. Files with text are smaller than files with graphics. The size of a file is measured in bytes. A **byte** is a unit of storage capable of holding a single character or pixel. It's the base measurement for all other incre-

mental units, which are kilobyte, megabyte, and gigabyte. A **kilobyte (KB)** is 1,024 bytes of information while a **megabyte (MB)** is 1,048,576 bytes, which is equal to 1,024 kilobytes. A **gigabyte (GB)** is equal to 1,024 megabytes.

Compressing Files and Folders

You can **compress** files in special folders that use compressing software to decrease the size of the files they contain. Compressed folders are useful for reducing the file size of one or more large files, which frees disk space and reduces the time it takes to transfer files to another computer over the Internet or network. A compressed folder is denoted by a zippered folder icon. You can compress one or more files in a compressed folder by simply dragging them onto the compressed folder icon. When a file is compressed, a copy is used in the compression, and the original remains intact. You can uncompress, or **extract**, a file from the compressed folder and open it as you normally would, or open a file directly from the compressed folder by double-clicking the compressed file icon. When you open a file directly, Windows extracts the file when it opens and compresses it again when it closes.　John wants to compress Wired Coffee graphics in a folder.

Steps

🛑 *If you have a compression program, such as WinZip, installed, you need to uninstall it to perform these steps. See your instructor or technical support person.*

1. In the Wired Coffee folder, double-click the **Graphics folder**, click the **Views button** ▦▾ on the Standard Buttons toolbar, then click **Details**
   The Graphics window appears, displaying the contents of the folder in Details view.

2. Right-click an empty area of the window, point to **New** on the shortcut menu, then click **Compressed (zipped) Folder**
   A new folder, temporarily named New Compressed (zipped) Folder, appears in the right pane.

Trouble?
If a warning dialog box appears, click No to change the name. The filename needs a file extension (.zip). You need to type ".zip" at the end of the folder name.

3. Type **Compressed Graphics**, then click a blank area of the window to deselect the folder
   The Compressed Graphics folder appears, as shown in Figure D-14.

4. Press and hold **[Ctrl]**, click the **Coffee Roast Logo** file, click the **Wired Coffee Color Logo** file, click the **Wired Coffee Logo** file, then release **[Ctrl]**
   The three graphic files are selected.

QuickTip
To compress a folder and its contents, right-click the folder, point to Send To, then click Compressed (zipped) Folder.

5. Drag the selected files to the **Compressed Graphics folder**
   The selected files are copied and compressed into the Compressed Graphics folder. The Size column in Details view shows that the uncompressed graphic files combined are approximately 183 KB, while the compressed folder is only 5 KB.

6. Double-click the **Compressed Graphics folder**
   The Compressed Graphics folder appears, as shown in Figure D-15.

7. In the left pane under Folder Tasks, click **Extract all files** to start the Extraction Wizard, then click **Next** to continue
   The second Extraction Wizard dialog box appears, as shown in Figure D-16.

QuickTip
To extract individual files, click the file, click Move this file in the left pane, select a folder location in the Move Items dialog box, then click Move.

8. In the text box with the directory, select the word **Compressed**, type **Extracted**, click **Next** to extract the files, click the **Show extracted files check box** to deselect it if necessary, then click **Finish**
   The three files are extracted into a folder called Extracted Graphics.

9. Click the **Up button** 🔼 on the Standard Buttons toolbar, press and hold **[Ctrl]**, click the **Extracted Graphics** folder, click the **Compressed Graphics** folder, press **[Delete]**, click **Yes** to confirm the deletion, then click the Graphics window **Close button**
   The graphics are deleted from the Graphics folder, and the Graphics window closes.

FIGURE D-14: **Creating a compressed folder**

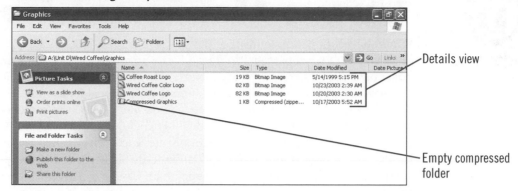

Details view

Empty compressed folder

FIGURE D-15: **Contents of the compressed folder**

Click link to extract all files

Compressed files

FIGURE D-16: **Extraction Wizard dialog box**

Select the word "Compressed" only

Compressing existing files and folders on an NTFS drive

If your hard disk is formatted as NTFS, you need to use a different method to compress existing files and folders. **NTFS** is an advanced file system that provides additional performance, security, and reliability over the standard file system **FAT** (File Allocation Table) or FAT32. To display the file system, select your hard disk icon in My Computer in the left pane under Details. To compress an existing file or folder on an NTFS drive, right-click the file or folder you want to compress, click Properties, click Advanced on the General tab, click the Compress contents to save disk space check box to select it, then click OK twice. In the Confirm Attribute Changes dialog box, select the option you want, then click OK.

Using Personal Folders

Windows makes it easy to manage the personal and business files and folders you work with everyday with a set of **personal folders**. My Documents is a personal folder, which contains additional personal folders, such as My Pictures, My Music, and My Videos. Depending on previous installation, devices installed, or other users, your personal folders might differ. The contents of your personal folders are private, unless you decide to share the contents with others who use your computer. Windows creates personal folders for everyone on your computer to make sure the contents of personal folders remain private. Each personal folder is identified by the user's name. For example, if John Casey and an associate Shawn Brooks use the same computer, there are two sets of personal folders, one named John Casey's Documents and another named Shawn Brooks' Documents. When John logs on to the computer, his personal folders appear as My Documents and Shawn's appear as Shawn Brooks' Documents, but John cannot access them. John wants to open his personal folders and find out more about their functionality.

1. Click the **Start button** on the taskbar, then click **My Documents**
The My Documents window opens, as shown in Figure D-17.

> **QuickTip**
> To open the My Pictures folder from the Start Menu, click the Start button, then click My Pictures.

2. Double-click the **My Pictures folder**
The My Pictures window opens, displaying the contents of the folder as thumbnails. A **thumbnail** is a miniature image of the contents of a file; thumbnails are often used to quickly browse through multiple images. If the folder doesn't contain images, Windows inserts icons instead of thumbnails.

3. Double-click the **Sample Pictures folder**
The Sample Pictures window opens, displaying the contents of the picture folder as a filmstrip, as shown in Figure D-18. Filmstrip is a special view, located on the Views button or View menu, available only for folders with many pictures.

> **QuickTip**
> To rotate pictures in Filmstrip view, click the Rotate Clockwise button ⟳ or the Rotate Counterclockwise button ⟲.

4. Click the **Next Image (Right Arrow) button** ⊙ until the last image in the Sample Pictures folder appears in the filmstrip

5. Click the **Back button** ⊙ Back on the Standard Buttons toolbar twice to display the My Documents folder

6. Double-click the **My Videos folder**
The My Videos folder opens, displaying the contents of the folder as thumbnails. For videos, the first frame appears in the thumbnail.

7. In the left pane under Video tasks, click **Play all**
Windows Media Player opens and plays the sample Windows Movie Maker video.

8. When the video is finished, click the in Windows Media Player **Close button**
Windows Media Player closes.

9. Click the **Back button** ⊙ Back on the Standard Buttons toolbar to display the My Documents folder, then click a blank area to deselect the folder

FIGURE D-17: My Documents folder

General file and folder task links

Personal folders; yours might differ

FIGURE D-18: Sample Pictures folder

Picture specific task links

Buttons to display and modify pictures

Filmstrip view

Pictures in filmstrip

CLUES TO USE

Using the Shared Documents folder

Shared folders are related to your personal folders on a shared computer. They provide a place for you to make files, pictures, and music available to everyone who uses your computer. Your personal folders: My Documents, My Pictures, My Music, and My Videos each have a shared counterpart: Shared Documents, Shared Pictures, etc., in which you can copy files and folders to share with others. To share files and folders on your computer, click the Start button on the taskbar, click My Documents, click the file or folder you want to share, then drag the file or folder to Shared Documents in the left pane under Other Places. To share pictures and music on your computer, open My Documents, double-click the My Pictures or My Music folder, click the file or folder you want to share, click Move this file or Move this folder to open the Move Items dialog box, click the Shared Documents folder, click Shared Pictures or Shared Music, then click Move.

Customizing a Personal Folder

In the My Documents folder you can create your own folders and customize view options based on the contents. In the left pane of the My Pictures, My Music, and My Videos folders, Windows provides links to file management activities specifically related to the contents of the folder and other places on your computer, such as Print pictures in the My Pictures folder, or Play all in the My Music or My Video folders. When you create a new folder, you can customize it for pictures, music, and videos by applying a **folder template**, which is a collection of folder task links and viewing options. When you apply a template to a folder, you apply specific features to the folder, such as specialized task links and viewing options for working with pictures, music, and videos. John wants to customize a folder for pictures in the My Documents folder.

Trouble?

If a folder is selected, this will not be an option. Click a blank area of the window to deselect the folder, then try again.

1. In the My Documents folder, click **Make a new folder** in the left pane under File and Folder tasks, type **Wired Coffee Pictures**, then press **[Enter]**
   The new folder appears.

2. Double-click the **Wired Coffee Pictures folder**
   The empty Wired Coffee Pictures folder appears. General links for file and folder tasks appear in the left pane.

3. Right-click a blank area of the folder, then click **Customize This Folder**
   The Properties dialog box opens, displaying the Customize tab, as shown in Figure D-19.

QuickTip

To choose the picture that displays on a folder icon in Thumbnails view, click Choose Picture in the Customize tab of the Properties dialog box, navigate to the picture, then double-click it.

4. Click the **Use this folder type as a template list arrow**, then click **Pictures (best for many files)**
   When you choose a template, you apply specific features to your folder, such as specialized task links and viewing options for working with pictures, music, and videos.

5. Click the **Also apply this template to all subfolders check box** to select it
   The template is applied to all subfolders within the Wired Coffee Pictures folder.

6. Click **OK**
   The left pane contains common tasks related specifically to pictures, such as Order prints online and Print pictures; the list of available picture tasks changes based on the current selection. See Table D-1 for a list and description of common picture tasks.

7. Click the **Back button** Back to display the My Documents folder

8. Click the **Wired Coffee Pictures folder** to select it if necessary, click **Delete this folder** in the left pane under File and Folder Tasks, then click **Yes** to confirm the deletion to the Recycle Bin
   The Wired Coffee Pictures folder is deleted and sent to the Recycle Bin.

9. Click the **Close button** in the My Documents window
   The My Documents window closes.

FIGURE D-19: Properties dialog box with Customize tab

Folder template

TABLE D-1: Picture tasks in the My Pictures folder

picture task	description
View as a slide show	Displays a full screen version of each picture in the folder for five seconds; click buttons on the Slide Show toolbar to start, pause, and stop the show
Order prints online	Opens the Online Print Ordering Wizard, which helps you order prints of your digital photographs over the Internet
Print this picture or Print the selected pictures	Opens the Photo Printing Wizard, which helps you format and print photographs from a digital camera or scanner
Set as desktop background	Sets the selected picture as the desktop background
Show for pictures online	Opens the Windows XP Pictures Online Web site in your Web browser, where you can find and download pictures over the Internet

Managing Files and Folders on a CD

A **compact disc**, or CD, is a small circular disc that is used to store large amounts of information. The low cost and convenient size of CDs and the popularity of CD recording hardware make using CDs an effective approach to some file management tasks. For example, CDs are an effective way to backup information or transfer large amounts of information to another computer without a network. You can copy, or **write**, files and folders to either a **compact disc-recordable (CD-R)** or a **compact disc rewritable (CD-RW)**. With CD-Rs, you can write files and folders only once, read them many times, but can't erase them. With CD-RWs, you can read, write, and erase files and folders many times, just like a floppy or hard disk. To create a CD, you must have a CD recorder (also known as a writer or burner) and blank CDs. Do not copy more files and folders to the CD than it will hold; anything beyond the limit will not be copied to the CD. Standard CDs hold up to 700 megabytes (MB). High-capacity CDs hold up to 850 MB. When you write to, or **burn**, a CD, Windows needs disk space on your hard disk to store temporary files that are created during the process, so make sure you have 700 MB of free hard disk space when using a standard CD and 1 gigabyte (GB) for a high-capacity CD. John wants to copy the Wired Coffee folder to a CD-RW.

Steps

(STOP) *If you don't have a CD-RW drive, read the steps but do not perform any actions.*

QuickTip

To change CD recording drive properties, right-click the CD recording drive icon in My Computer, click Properties, then click the Recording tab. Select a recording speed or change the Windows space reserve, then click OK.

1. Insert a blank CD-RW into the CD recorder, click the **Start button** on the taskbar, then click **My Computer**

My Computer opens, displaying the drives, including a CD recording drive.

2. Double-click the drive and folder where your Project Files are located, then click the **Wired Coffee folder** to select it

3. In the left pane under File and Folder Tasks, click **Copy this folder**

The Copy Items dialog box opens.

4. In the Folder list, scroll down, click the **CD recording drive**, then click **Copy**

The Wired Coffee folder is copied to the CD recording drive.

QuickTip

If balloon help appears, pointing to an icon in the notification area and indicating you have files waiting to be written to the CD, you can click the balloon to open the CD recording drive.

5. In the left pane under Other Places, click **My Computer**, then double-click the **CD recording drive**

Windows displays a temporary area where files are held before they are copied to the CD, as shown in Figure D-20. Verify that the files and folders that you intend to copy to the CD appear under Files Ready to be Written to the CD

6. In the left pane under CD Writing Tasks, click **Write these files to CD**

The CD Writing Wizard dialog box appears, as shown in Figure D-21.

7. In the CD name text box with the selected text, type **Wired Coffee**, then click the **Next button** to continue

A progress meter appears while the wizard writes the data files to the CD. Then, when finished, the final CD Writing Wizard dialog box appears.

8. Click **Finish**

The CD recording drive opens, displaying the contents of the drive.

9. Click the **Close button** in the CD recording drive window

FIGURE D-20: Files ready to be copied to a CD

Click link to
start writing
to the CD

Folder ready
to be written
to the CD

FIGURE D-21: CD Writing Wizard dialog box

Creating music CDs

With Windows Media Player, you can create your own CDs from music tracks you have stored in Media Library. To create a music CD, you must have a CD recorder and blank CDs (either CD-Rs or CD-RWs). If you use a CD-R to make a one time recording, make sure that the music fits on the CD and that you copy all the music at the same time. A standard CD (700 MB) holds 76 minutes of music, while a high-capacity CD holds 80 minutes. You can copy Windows Media (.wma), mp3, and wav files from the Media Library to a CD. To burn a music CD, insert a blank CD-R or CD-RW in the CD recording drive, start Windows Media Player, add music you want on CD to the Media Library, click Copy to CD or Device on the Taskbar, select the playlist or category of music tracks you want to copy from Media Library, click the recordable CD drive in the Music on Device pane, then click Copy Music. While the burning takes place, do not try to perform any other action on your computer, especially those that access the hard drive, such as opening or saving a file, as that could stop the recording.

Practice

► Concepts Review

Label each element of the screen shown in Figure D-22.

FIGURE D-22

1. Which element points to the sorted column?
2. Which element sorts files and folders by image size?
3. Which element sorts files and folders by file size?
4. Which element contains links?
5. Which element contains personal files and folders?
6. Which element contains compressed files?

Match each term with the statement that describes its function.

7. **Favorite**
8. **Byte**
9. **Personal folder**
10. **Compressed folder**
11. **Extract**

a. A place to store files
b. A way to revisit a folder
c. A place to decrease file sizes
d. A term for uncompressing files
e. A unit of storage

Select the best answers from the following lists of choices.

12. **Which of the following is NOT a default folder view setting?**
    a. Icons view
    b. Show common tasks in folders
    c. Open each folder in the same window
    d. Double-click to open an item

13. Which of the following folder sizes is the largest?
  a. 1 megabyte
  b. 2000 kilobytes
  c. 1 gigabyte
  d. 1,248,896 bytes

14. A cluster is a group of:
  a. Sectors.
  b. Files.
  c. Folders.
  d. Bytes.

15. Extract is another name for:
  a. Uncompress.
  b. Expand.
  c. Compress.
  d. Zipped.

16. Which of the following can read, write, and erase files and folders?
  a. CD-ROM
  b. CD-R
  c. CD-RW
  d. DVD

 # Skills Review

1. Add a folder to the Favorites list.
  a. Open My Computer.
  b. Navigate to the drive and folder where your Project Files are located, then open the Wired Coffee folder.
  c. Create a favorite to the Letters folder named **Wired Coffee Letters**, then click the Back button on the toolbar.
  d. Navigate to the Wired Coffee Letters favorite, then delete the Wired Coffee Letters favorite.

2. Change Folder Options.
  a. Change the view to Details. Change the folder option to use Windows classic folders.
  b. Change the folder option to display the full path in the title bar, then apply the folder options to all folders.
  c. Display the Wired Coffee folder to verify the new folder options.

3. Change file details to list.
  a. Open the Graphics folder in Details view. Add Dimensions and Date Accessed to Details view.
  b. Remove Date Accessed from Details view, then add Date Created to Details view.

4. Change file and folder list views.
  a. In the Graphics folder, sort by smallest to largest, then by date created earliest to latest, then by name in alphabetical order.
  b. Remove Date Created and Dimensions from Details view.
  c. Restore all folder option defaults and reset all folders, change to Tiles view, then display the Wired Coffee folder.

5. Examine disk and folder capacity.
  a. Go to My Computer, then display disk size information for the drive where your Project Files are located.
  b. On paper, write the disk capacity, how much is in use, and how much is available for further use.
  c. Display the Wired Coffee folder, then display folder size information for the Advertising and Letters folders.
  d. On paper, write down the actual size of the folder.
  e. Create a file using WordPad listing the information gathered in Steps b and c. Save it as **Disk Info** in the folder where your Project Files are located, then click the Close button in the WordPad window.

6. Compress files and folders.
  a. Create a compressed folder named **Compressed Logos**. Drag the Graphics folder to the Compressed Logos folder.
  b. Open the Compressed Logos folder, then open the Graphics folder inside.
  c. Extract the Coffee Roast Logo file to the Wired Coffee folder.
  d. In the Wired Coffee folder, delete the Compressed Logos folder and the Coffee Roast Logo file.
  e. Close the Wired Coffee window.

7. Use personal folders.
 a. Open My Documents, then open the My Pictures folder and the Sample Pictures folder.
 b. View all the graphics in the folder, then display My Documents, then open the My Music folder.
 c. Play all the music in the folder, then close Windows Media Player. Display My Documents, then deselect all the folders.

8. Customize a personal folder.
 a. In My Documents, create a folder named **Wired Coffee Music**, then open it.
 b. Customize the folder with a music folder template.
 c. Verify that the common task links changed to Music tasks.
 d. Display My Documents. Delete the Wired Coffee Music folder, then close My Documents.

9. Manage files and folders on a CD.
 a. Insert a CD-RW into the CD recorder. Copy the Advertising and Letters folders to the CD-RW.
 b. Write the file to the CD-RW. Verify that the folders appear on the CD-RW, then close My Computer.

▶ Independent Challenge 1

You own a sewing machine repair business, and you want to use Windows to organize your documents.
 a. Create a WordPad file named **Wilson Letter** thanking Mr. Wilson for his business. Save this file and the other files you create to the drive and folder where your Project Files are located.
 b. Create another WordPad file named **Suppliers**. List the following suppliers in the file:

Apex Sewing Machine Parts	Jones Sewing Repair
PO Box 3645	18th and 3rd Avenues
Tempe, AZ 12345	Brooklyn, NY 09091

 c. Create a third WordPad file named **Bills**. List the following information in the file:

Apex	16453	$34.56
Jones	47354	$88.45
Ott	44412	$98.56

 d. Open My Computer, navigate to the drive and folder where your Project Files are located, then create a folder named **Sewing Works**.
 e. In the Sewing Works folder, create three new folders: **Letters**, **Contacts**, and **Accounts**.
 f. Expand the Sewing Works folder in the Folders Explorer Bar.
 g. Move the file named Wilson Letter to the Letters folder, the file named Suppliers to the Contacts folder, and the file named Bills to the Accounts folder, then add a favorites link to the Letters folder.
 h. Press [Print Screen], open Paint, click Edit on the menu bar, click Paste to paste the screen into Paint, then click Yes to paste the large image if necessary. Click the Text button on the Toolbox, click a blank area in the Paint work area, then type your name. Click File on the menu bar, click Page Setup, change 100 % normal size to 50% in the Scaling area, then click OK. Click File on the menu bar, click Print, then click Print.
 i. Remove the favorites link to the Letters folder.
 j. Close My Computer.

▶ Independent Challenge 2

As manager of the summer program at a day camp, you need to keep your files and folders organized.
 a. Open My Computer, navigate to the drive and folder where your Project Files are located, then create three folders named **Day Camp**, **Campers**, and **Activities**.
 b. Create a WordPad file named **Camper Data**. Save this and other files to the drive and folder where your Project Files are located. Create information on five campers, including names, ages, bunks, and sports.

c. Move the file named Camper Data into the folder named Campers.

d. Create a WordPad file named **Activities Overview**. Add information on five activities, including the activity names, equipment the children need to supply, number of children, and the activity leaders.

e. Move the file named Activities Overview into the folder named Activities.

f. Move the Activities folder and the Campers folder into the Day Camp folder.

g. Apply to all folders: Details view, Windows classic folders, and show extensions for known file types.

h. Open the Campers folder, then copy the Camper Data file to the Activities folder.

i. Open the Activities folder, then print the screen. (See Independent Challenge 1, Step h.)

j. Restore folder options to default settings, then close My Computer.

▶ Independent Challenge 3

The summer fine arts program you manage has different categories of participation for young adults, including two- and four-week programs. To keep track of who participates in each program, you must organize two lists into folders.

a. Open My Computer, navigate to the drive and folder where your Project Files are located, then create a folder named **Summer Program**.

b. In the Summer Program folder, create a folder named **Fine Arts**.

c. In the Fine Arts folder, create two other folders named **2 Weeks** and **4 Weeks**.

d. Create a WordPad file named **2 Weeks Art** on the drive and in the folder where your Project Files are located. Include the following information:

Leni Welitoff	2 weeks	painting
Tom Stacey	2 weeks	ceramics and jewelry

e. Create a WordPad file named **4 Weeks Art** on the drive and in the folder where your Project Files are located. Include the following information:

Kim Dayton	4 weeks	painting and landscape design
Sara Jackson	4 weeks	set construction

f. Move the files you created into their respective folders: 2 Weeks and 4 Weeks.

g. Change folder options to Details view, open each folder in its own window, and do not display the full path in the address bar. Apply to all folders.

h. Open the 4 Weeks folder in the Fine Arts folder, then print the screen (see Independent Challenge 1, Step h.)

i. Restore the folder setting defaults and reset the folders to Tiles view, then close My Computer.

▶ Independent Challenge 4

As head of the graphics department in a small design firm, one of your jobs is to organize the clip-art images used by the company. The two categories in which you want to place images are Lines and Shapes. You can place clip-art images in more than one category as well.

a. In the drive and folder where your Project Files are located, create three different small Paint images and save them using the names: **Ellipses**, **Lines**, and **Curves**.

b. Open My Computer, navigate to the drive and folder where your Project Files are located, then create two folders named **Lines** and **Shapes**.

c. Move the Curves and Lines files into the Lines folder, then move the Ellipses file into the Shapes folder.

d. Copy the Curves file into the Shapes folder, then rename the Ellipses file **Ovals**.

e. Create a compressed folder named **Clip Art**.

f. Place the Lines and Shapes folders in the compressed Clip Art folder.

g. Print the screen (see Independent Challenge 1, Step h), then close My Computer.

► # Visual Workshop

Re-create the screen shown in Figure D-23, which displays the desktop and a compressed folder with pictures from the Sample Pictures folder on the hard disk. Print the screen. (See Independent Challenge 1, Step h for screen printing instructions.)

FIGURE D-23

Customizing
Windows Using the Control Panel

Objectives

- ► Change the desktop background
- ► Customize the desktop
- ► Change the desktop appearance
- ► Change desktop screen settings
- ► Set the date and time
- ► Work with fonts
- ► Add a scheduled task
- ► Customize the taskbar
- ► Customize the Start menu

 If you are concerned about changing the aspects of Windows XP and do not wish to customize, simply read through this unit without completing the steps, or click the Cancel button in any dialog box where you could make a change and don't click the Apply button when instructed.

In this unit you'll learn how to customize Windows XP to suit your personal needs and preferences. You can adjust most Windows features through the Control Panel, a central location for changing Windows settings. The **Control Panel** contains several icons, each of which opens a dialog box or window for changing the **properties**, or characteristics, of a specific element of your computer, such as the desktop, the taskbar, or the Start menu. Each icon represents an aspect of Windows that you can change to fit your own working habits and personal needs. For example, you can use the Display icon to change the background picture or color of the desktop, or the Taskbar and Start Menu icon to customize the taskbar and Start menu. ◆◆◆ John Casey needs to change some of the settings on his computer to make his computing environment more attractive and efficient.

Changing the Desktop Background

The desktop **background**, or wallpaper, is a picture that serves as your desktop's backdrop, the basic surface on which icons and windows appear. You can select a background picture and change how it looks using the Desktop tab in the Display Properties dialog box. Once you select a background picture, you can display it on the screen three different ways: **Tile** displays the picture consecutively across the screen; **Center** displays the picture in the center of the screen; and **Stretch** enlarges the picture and displays it in the center of the screen. Instead of selecting a background picture, which can sometimes make icons on the desktop difficult to see, you can also change the background to a color. John wants to choose a background for his desktop.

Steps

1. **Click the Start button on the taskbar, click Control Panel, then click Switch to Classic View in the left pane under Control Panel if necessary**
   The Control Panel opens, as shown in Figure E-1. Each icon represents an aspect of Windows that you can change to fit your own working habits and personal needs.

2. **Click the Restore Down button in the Control Panel window if necessary, then resize the Control Panel window so you can see desktop changes**

QuickTip

To open the Display Properties dialog box from the desktop, right-click an empty area on the desktop, then click Properties.

3. **Double-click the Display icon** 🖥 **in the Control Panel, then click the Desktop tab**
   The Display Properties dialog box opens, displaying the Desktop tab, as shown in Figure E-2.

4. **Scroll through the Background list, then click Coffee Bean, or make another selection if this one is not available**
   The preview window shows how the background will look on your screen. The Coffee Bean picture is a small picture, so you decide to tile it across the desktop.

5. **Click the Position list arrow, then click Tile, if necessary**
   The background picture appears tiled in the preview window.

6. **Click Apply**
   The background picture appears tiled on the desktop. When you click the Apply button, Windows performs the changes you've made and keeps the dialog box open so that you can select additional options.

7. **In the Background list, click (None)**
   The current color in the Color list appears in the preview window.

8. **Click the Color list arrow, click a color in the list, then click Apply**
   The color in the Color list appears in the preview window and on the desktop.

9. **Select your original background picture or color to restore the desktop, then click Apply**
   The Display Properties dialog box remains open.

FIGURE E-1: Control Panel window

Depending on your computer, your icons might differ

FIGURE E-2: Display Properties dialog box with Desktop tab

Preview selected background; yours may differ

Click an item to select a background

Color list arrow

CLUES TO USE

Setting a picture as the desktop background

Instead of using one of the pictures in the Background list on the Desktop tab in the Display Properties dialog box, you can select a picture on your hard disk or from a Web page as the desktop background. To set a picture as the background, right-click the picture you want to use in My Computer or Windows Explorer, then click Set as Desktop Background, or right-click the picture you want to use on a Web page in your Web browser, then click Set as Background. Acceptable formats for background files are Bitmap (the format of a Paint file), JPEG (the format of an Internet graphic file), or HTM (the format of a Web page). You can use Paint or any graphics program to create new background designs or change existing ones. After you set a picture as the desktop background, the picture is added to the Background list on the Desktop tab in the Display Properties dialog box. When you use a picture from a Web page, it is saved in the Background list as Internet Explorer Background. Each new picture from a Web page you set as a background replaces the previous one. To access the files in the Background list, open the Windows folder, then the Web folder, then the Wallpaper folder, from which you can remove, rename, or modify them.

Customizing the Desktop

Because more and more people are using the Internet, Windows allows you to view Web content on your desktop as you would in a **Web browser**, such as **Internet Explorer**, a program specifically designed to view Web content on the Internet. **Web items** are elements you can place on the desktop to access or display information from the Internet. For example, you can add a Web item to display stock prices or weather information continuously. When you place Web items on the desktop, they are active, which means the Web content is automatically updated as the content changes, while you're connected to the Internet. Using the Display Properties dialog box, you can customize the desktop to display the Web items you want to use. In addition, you can also customize the desktop to show or hide the icons My Documents, My Computer, My Network Places, or Internet Explorer. ◄━━━ John wants to learn how to customize the desktop.

QuickTip
To select your own picture as a background, click Browse, navigate to the drive and folder where your picture is located, select it, then click Open.

1. **On the Desktop tab of the Display Properties dialog box, click Customize Desktop**
   The Desktop Items dialog box opens, displaying the General tab, as shown in Figure E-3. The General tab provides options to display and clean up desktop icons.

2. **Click the My Documents check box to select it, then click the My Computer check box to select it if necessary**
   The My Documents and My Computer icons are set to display on the desktop.

3. **Click the Web tab**
   The Web tab appears, as shown in Figure E-4. The Web tab provides a list of Web items and previews of those items. To enable or disable items on the desktop, you must click the Web item check boxes to select or deselect them.

QuickTip
To add a new desktop item, click New, enter the Web address in the Location text box, then click OK, or click Visit Gallery to access and display Microsoft's Desktop Gallery on the Internet, select the item which you want to add, then click Add to Active Desktop.

4. **Click any Web item check box (such as My Current Home Page) to select it, click OK, then click Apply in the Display Properties dialog box**
   The Web item appears on the desktop. Some Web items require a connection to the Internet. If you don't currently have an Internet connection, you can still add a Web item to your desktop, and an error message will appear in the Web content window.

5. **Click Customize Desktop**
   The Desktop Items dialog box opens, displaying the General tab.

6. **Click the My Documents check box to deselect it, then click the My Computer check box to deselect it if necessary to restore the desktop settings**

7. **Click the Web tab, click the same Web item check box you checked before to deselect it, then click OK**
   You remove the Web item from the desktop.

8. **Click Apply**
   The Display Properties dialog box remains open, and the desktop appears as before.

FIGURE E-3: Desktop Items dialog box with General tab

Click check boxes to show or hide desktop icons

Click button to clean up desktop icons

FIGURE E-4: Desktop Items dialog box with Web tab

Current Web items; yours may differ

Click buttons to add or remove Web items

Cleaning up the desktop

If your desktop gets cluttered with shortcut icons, you can use the Desktop Cleanup Wizard to move shortcuts that you don't use anymore into a folder. The wizard automatically runs every 60 days, or you can start it at any time. To start the wizard, double-click the Display icon ![icon] in the Control Panel in Classic View, click the Desktop tab, click Customize Desktop, then click Clean Desktop Now. Or, right-click an empty area of the desktop, point to Arrange Icons By, then click Run Desktop Cleanup Wizard. In the Desktop Cleanup Wizard dialog box, click Next, click the check boxes for the shortcuts you want to remove in the list to select them, click Next, then click Finish. Windows moves the selected shortcuts into the Unused Desktop Shortcuts folder on the desktop. If you don't want the wizard to run automatically every 60 days, click the Run Desktop Cleanup Wizard every 60 days check box to deselect it in the Desktop Items dialog box.

Changing the Desktop Appearance

You can change the entire appearance of the desktop by using desktop themes. A desktop **theme** changes the desktop background, screen saver, mouse pointers, sounds, icons, and fonts based on a set theme, such as baseball, science, sports, travel, or underwater. You can use one of the predefined desktop themes or create your own. If a theme isn't exactly what you want, you can change the appearance of colors, fonts, and sizes used for major window elements such as title bars, icons, menus, borders, and the desktop itself. You can change each item individually, or use a **scheme**, which is a predefined combination of settings that assures visual coordination of all items. Windows includes many predefined schemes, or you can create your own. When you create a custom scheme or modify an existing scheme, you save your changes with a unique name. Ray Adams, a visually impaired employee of Wired Coffee, needs the Windows classic display that he is more comfortable using and a display configuration with window elements larger than standard size. John decides to create a theme for Ray, who can switch to the theme whenever he uses the computer.

1. Click the **Themes tab** in the Display Properties dialog box

   The Themes tab, shown in Figure E-5, allows you to change the appearance of several desktop elements at once.

2. Click the **Theme list arrow**, then click **Windows Classic**

   The Sample box changes to Windows Classic settings.

3. Click the **Appearance tab**

   The Appearance tab, shown in Figure E-6, allows you to change the appearance of individual desktop elements, such as the menu bar, message box, and selected text, or to select one of several predefined schemes that Windows provides, then modify it as necessary.

4. Click the **Color scheme list arrow**, then click **Windows Classic**

   The color scheme changes to Windows Classic.

5. Click the **Font size list arrow**, then click **Large**

   The font size for text in windows increases in size to make it easier to read.

6. Click **Apply**

   The desktop changes, and the dialog box remains open. Use the Apply button when you want to test your changes, and the OK button when you want to keep your changes and close the dialog box.

7. Click the **Themes tab**, click **Save As**, type **Ray** in the File name text box, then click **Save**

   You save the theme with the name Ray. Now, anytime Ray wants to use the computer, he can easily set up the computer for his needs by clicking the Theme list arrow, then selecting Ray.

8. Click **Delete** to remove the selected theme

9. Click the **Appearance tab**, click the **Windows and buttons list arrow**, click **Windows XP style**, then click **Apply**

   The desktop, windows, and buttons are restored to the Windows XP style and the Display Properties dialog box remains open.

FIGURE E-5: Display Properties dialog box with Themes tab

Theme list arrow

Click button to save a custom designed theme

Preview of selected theme; yours may differ

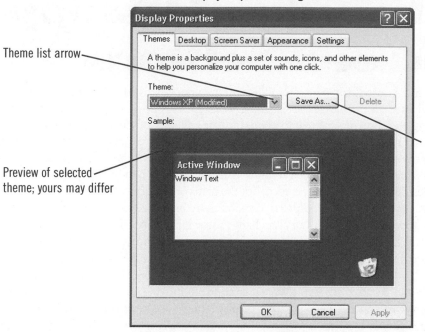

FIGURE E-6: Display Properties dialog box with Appearance tab

Preview of selected scheme

Click list arrow to change the title bar font size

Windows, buttons, and desktop color schemes

Adding sound effects

Besides customizing the desktop appearance of Windows XP, you can also add sound effects to common Windows commands and functions, such as starting and exiting Windows, printing complete, opening and closing folders, or emptying the Recycle Bin. To add sound effects, double-click the Sounds and Audio Devices icon 🔊 in the Control Panel in Classic View, then click the Sounds tab. In the Program events list, click the event to which you want to apply a sound, such as Start Windows. Click the Sounds list arrow, then click the sound you want to link to the event. To hear the sound, click the Play sound button to the right of the Sounds list arrow. To save your settings into a sound scheme, click Save As, type a name, then click OK. When you're done, click OK to apply the sound effect changes to Windows.

Changing Desktop Screen Settings

If you find yourself frequently scrolling within windows as you work or squinting to read small text, you might want to change the size of the desktop on your monitor. A monitor displays pictures by dividing the display screen into thousands or millions of dots, or pixels, arranged in rows and columns. The pixels are so close together that they appear connected. The **screen resolution** refers to the number of pixels on the entire screen, which determines the amount of information your monitor displays. A low screen resolution setting, such as 640 by 480 pixels (width by height), displays less information on the screen, but the items on the screen appear relatively large, while a high setting, such as 1024 by 768 pixels, displays more information on the screen, but the items on the screen appear smaller. You can also change the color quality. The higher the color quality, the more colors can be displayed, which requires greater system memory. The most common color quality settings are: 16-bit, which displays 768 colors, and 24-bit and 32-bit, both of which display 16.7 million colors. If you frequently leave your computer idle, with no movement on your screen for a long time, you should select a **screen saver**, a continually moving display, to protect your monitor from **burn-in**, which occurs when the same display remains on the screen for extended periods of time and becomes part of the screen. ✒ John wants to change the size of the desktop and set a screen saver to start when his computer remains idle for more than five minutes.

Steps

1. Click the **Settings tab** in the Display Properties dialog box
   The Settings tab, shown in Figure E-7, allows you to change the appearance of several desktop elements at once.

2. Drag the **Screen resolution slider** to a different setting
   The new desktop size appears under the slider and in the preview window.

3. Click **Apply**, then click **Yes** in the Monitor Settings dialog box to confirm the change if necessary
   The desktop screen size changes based on your screen resolution setting.

4. Click the **Screen Saver tab**
   The Screen Saver tab, shown in Figure E-8, allows you to select a screen saver.

5. Click the **Screen saver list arrow**, then click **Marquee**
   The Marquee screen saver appears in the preview window. To assign a password to your screen saver, click the On resume, password protect check box or the On resume, display Welcome check box to select it, then click Apply.

6. Click **Settings** to open the Marquee Setup dialog box, type **Wired Coffee Company** in the Text text box if necessary, drag the **Speed scroll box** to the left (slowest speed), then click **OK**
   The options for the Marquee screen saver are set. Not all screen savers have settings.

7. In the Wait box, click the **up arrow** or **down arrow** until it reads **5**
   Your computer will wait five minutes, during which it detects no mouse or keyboard activity, to begin the screen saver.

8. Click **Preview**, move the mouse or press any key to stop the preview, then click **Apply**
   When you preview the screen saver, the entire desktop displays the screen saver pattern.

9. Restore the screen saver to Windows XP, and the screen resolution on the Settings tab to its original settings, then click **OK**
   The Display Properties dialog box closes, and the screen saver and resolution settings are restored.

QuickTip

When (None) is the selected screen saver, no matter how long your computer remains idle, no screen saver appears.

QuickTip

To create your own screen saver slide show, click My Pictures Slideshow from the Screen saver list arrow, then click Settings to add pictures from your hard disk.

FIGURE E-7: Display Properties dialog box with Settings tab

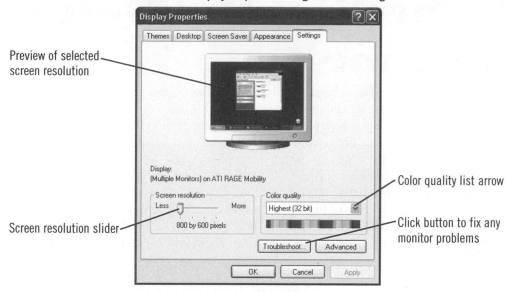

Preview of selected screen resolution

Color quality list arrow

Screen resolution slider

Click button to fix any monitor problems

FIGURE E-8: Display Properties dialog box with Screen Saver tab

Preview window shows how the screen saver will look on your screen

Click button to preview the screen saver on your screen

Click button to customize selected screen saver

Time setting determines when a screen saver begins

The Home Edition command is "On resume, display Welcome screen"

Using more than one monitor

You can increase the size of your workspace on the desktop and your productivity by adding another monitor to your computer. For example, you can work on a document in WordPad on one monitor and search for Web content in your Web browser on the other monitor. One monitor is the primary monitor, which displays the dialog boxes that appear when you start your computer and most programs, and the other monitor is the secondary monitor, which displays windows, icons, and programs you drag to it from the primary monitor. Before you can use more than one monitor, you need to install another **display adapter**, a hardware device that allows a computer to communicate with its monitor, on your computer that supports multiple monitors. After you install the display adapter according to the manufacturer's instructions and restart the computer, Windows detects the new device and installs the related software. In the Control Panel, double-click the Display icon 🖥 in Classic View, click the Settings tab, click the monitor icon that represents the secondary monitor that you want to use, click the Extend my Windows desktop onto this monitor check box to select it, then click Apply to activate the secondary monitor. To arrange multiple monitors, click the monitor icons and drag them in the preview window to the positions you want. You can set different screen resolutions and color settings for each monitor.

Setting the Date and Time

The date and time you set in the Control Panel appear in the lower-right corner of the taskbar. Programs use the date and time to establish when files and folders are created and modified. To change the date and time, you modify the date and time settings on the Date & Time tab in the Date and Time Properties dialog box. When you modify the time, it is important to also verify or update the time zone setting on the Time Zone tab, which is used to accurately display creation and modification dates in a different time zone. In addition to changing the date and time, you can also change their appearance. This is handy if you work on documents from a different country or region of the world. To change the date and time display, you modify the date or settings on the Date/Time tab in the Regional Settings Properties dialog box. ➤➤➤ John is working on an international document and wants to change his date and time settings.

Steps 1234

QuickTip

To open the Date and Time Properties dialog box quickly, double-click the time in the notification area on the taskbar.

1. **Double-click the Date and Time icon 🕒 in the Control Panel**
   The Date and Time Properties dialog box opens, displaying the Date & Time tab, as shown in Figure E-9. To change the date, you choose the month and year you want in the Date section, then click the day you want in the calendar. To change the time, you choose the time increment (hours, minutes, or seconds) you want to modify in the text box in the Time section, then type a new number or click the up or down arrow to select the new time.

2. **Double-click the current minute in the text box in the Time section, click the up arrow three times, then click Apply**
   The new time appears in the running clock in the notification area.

QuickTip

If you have a connection to the Internet, you can click Update Now on the Internet Time tab to update the time on your computer with an accurate time on the Internet.

3. **Click the Time Zone tab, click the list arrow, click (GMT) Greenwich Mean Time : Dublin, Edinburgh, Lisbon, London, then click Apply**
   The adjusted time appears in the running clock in the notification area.

4. **Restore the time zone on the Time Zone tab and the time on the Date & Time tab to their original settings, then click OK**
   The Date and Time Properties dialog box closes.

QuickTip

To change regional format by language and country, click the Standards and formats list arrow, then click a language.

5. **Double-click the Regional and Language Options icon 🌐 in the Control Panel**
   The Regional and Language Options dialog box opens, displaying the Regional Options tab, which shows sample number, currency, time, short date, and long date of the current format settings, as shown in Figure E-10.

6. **Click Customize**
   The Customize Regional Options dialog box opens, displaying tabs that allow you to change the format and symbols used for numbers, currency, time, and date in your files and programs.

7. **Click the Date tab**
   The Date tab appears, as shown in Figure E-11.

8. **Click the Short date format list arrow, click dd-MMM-yy, then click OK**
   The short date format is changed and appears as 07-Sep-03, for example, in the Short date text box on the Regional Options tab.

9. **Click Cancel**
   The Regional and Language Options dialog box closes and the short date format is restored to its original setting.

FIGURE E-9: Date and Time Properties dialog box with Date & Time tab

Month list arrow

Click arrows to change year

Click day to change date

Select time item, then click arrows to change time

FIGURE E-10: Regional and Language Options dialog box

Standards and formats list arrow

Click button to change standards and formats

Current formatting samples

FIGURE E-11: Customize Regional Options dialog box with Date tab

Short date sample of current format

Short date format list arrow

Working with Fonts

Everything you type appears in a **font**, or typeface, a particular design set of letters, numbers, and other characters. The height of characters in a font is measured in points, each point being approximately 1/72 inch, while the width is measured by **pitch**, which refers to how many characters can fit in an inch. You might have heard common font names, such as Times New Roman, Arial, Courier, or Symbol. Windows comes with a variety of fonts for displaying text and printing documents created with programs that are part of Windows, such as WordPad and Paint. Using the Fonts window, you can view these fonts, compare them to each other, see a sample of how a font appears when printed, and even install new fonts. Table E-1 lists the various font-related options on the Fonts toolbar and describes what they do. ➤ John wants to examine different fonts to prepare for a flyer he wants to create.

1. **Double-click the Fonts icon 🗀 in the Control Panel, then click the Maximize button in the Fonts window if necessary**
   The Fonts window opens. The window lists the fonts available on your system and indicates whether each is a TrueType, OpenType, or screen font. **TrueType** and **OpenType** fonts are outline (sometimes called vector or scalable) fonts based on a mathematical equation that creates resizable, or scalable, letters with smooth curves and sharp corners. OpenType is a newer technology and an extension of TrueType, but provides features such as multiplatform support and support for international characters. A **screen font** consists of **bitmapped characters**, which are small dots organized to form a letter. TrueType and OpenType fonts are designed for quality screen display and desktop printer output at any size, while screen fonts are designed for quality screen display and desktop printer output at only the font sizes installed on the computer. Besides the scalability, the main advantage of outline fonts over screen fonts is that they look better, the higher the resolution. Despite the advantages of outline fonts, small outline fonts do not look very good on low-resolution devices, such as display monitors.

2. **Click View on the menu bar, then click Hide Variations (Bold, Italic, etc.)**
   The main font styles appear in the Font window, as shown in Figure E-12.

3. **Double-click the Arial font icon**
   The window displays information about this font and shows samples of it in different sizes, as shown in Figure E-13.

4. **Click Print in the Arial (OpenType) window, then click Print in the Print dialog box**
   A copy of the font information prints.

5. **Click Done**
   The Arial (OpenType) window closes.

6. **Click the Similarity button 🄰🄱 on the Fonts toolbar**
   The Similarity tool helps you find fonts similar to the selected font. All the fonts are listed by how similar they are to Arial, the font listed in the List fonts by similarity to box. You can choose a different font to check which fonts are similar to it by clicking the List fonts by similarity to list arrow, then selecting the font you want to check.

7. **Click the Large Icons button 🔳 on the Fonts toolbar, then click the Back button ◀ Back on the Fonts toolbar**
   You return to the Control Panel.

FIGURE E-12: Fonts window

Font-specific toolbar buttons

Installed fonts; your list might differ

OpenType font

Screen font

FIGURE E-13: Selected font and how it appears in different sizes

Click button to print displayed information

Font information

Sample sizes

TABLE E-1: Font-related buttons on the toolbar

button	description
	Lists fonts by large icon
	Lists fonts alphabetically
AB	Lists fonts by similarity to the selected font
	Lists details of fonts, including filename, font name, size, and date last modified

CLUES TO USE

Installing a font

Although many fonts come with Windows, you can purchase additional fonts and install them easily. To install a new font, click Install New Font on the File menu in the Fonts window, in the Add Fonts dialog box indicate the location of the font you want to install (on the hard drive, a network, or a floppy disk drive), then click OK. This installs the new font so that it's available in the Fonts window of the Control Panel and with all your Windows programs.

Adding a Scheduled Task

Task Scheduler is a tool that enables you to schedule tasks such as Disk Cleanup, a program that removes unnecessary files, to run regularly, at a time convenient for you. Task Scheduler starts each time you start Windows. When Task Scheduler is running on your computer, its icon appears next to the clock on the taskbar. You can double-click the Task Scheduler icon 🖳 on the taskbar in the notification area to open Task Scheduler. With Task Scheduler, you can schedule a task to run daily, weekly, monthly, or at certain times (such as when the computer starts or idles), change the schedule for or turn off an existing task, or customize how a task runs at its scheduled time. Before you schedule a task, be sure that the system date and time on your computer are accurate, as Task Scheduler relies on this information to run. ➤➤➤ John schedules a task to scan his hard disk for corrupted files.

Steps

1. Double-click the **Scheduled Tasks icon** 📝 in the Control Panel
   The Scheduled Tasks window opens, as shown in Figure E-14.

2. Double-click the **Add Scheduled Task icon** 🖳, then click **Next** in the Scheduled Task Wizard dialog box
   The Scheduled Task Wizard displays a list of programs you can schedule to run. If the program or document you want to use is not in the list, click Browse to locate the program on your disk drive or network.

3. In the list of programs, click **Disk Cleanup**, then click **Next**
   The next Scheduled Task Wizard dialog box opens, as shown in Figure E-15, asking you to name and select when you want the task to start.

4. Click the **Weekly option button**, then click **Next**
   The next Scheduled Task Wizard dialog box opens, asking you to select the time and day you want the task to start.

5. In the Start time box, click the **minutes** in the Start time text box, change the time to one minute ahead of the current time, click the current **day of the week check box** to select it, then click **Next**
   Depending on your Windows setting, the next Scheduled Task Wizard dialog box might ask you to enter the name and password of the current user.

6. If asked to enter your password, type your **password** in the Enter the password box, press [Tab], type your **password** in the Confirm password text box, then click **Next**

7. Click **Finish**
   The scheduled task appears in the Scheduled Task window, as shown in Figure E-16.

8. Wait for the clean disk operation to begin, then click **Cancel** in the dialog box
   If you don't know the password, the scheduled task will not run. To be notified when a scheduled task does not run, click Advanced on the menu bar, then click Notify Me of Missed Tasks to select it.

9. Right-click the **Disk Cleanup icon**, click **Delete**, click **Yes** to delete the icon to the Recycle Bin, then click the **Close button** on the Scheduled Tasks window
   You deleted the scheduled task, and the Scheduled Tasks window closes.

FIGURE E-14: Scheduled Tasks window

Double-click icon to add scheduled task

FIGURE E-15: Scheduled Task Wizard

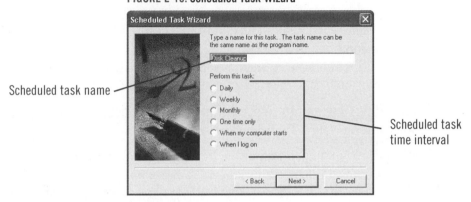

Scheduled task name

Scheduled task time interval

FIGURE E-16: Task added to Scheduled Tasks window

Scheduled task

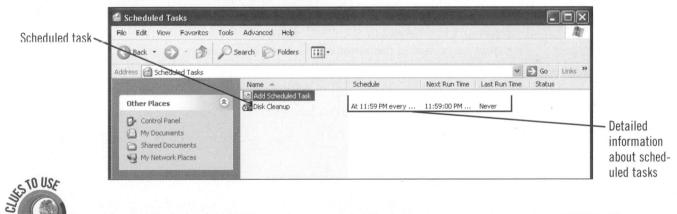

Detailed information about scheduled tasks

Adding new hardware and software to Windows

You can add new hardware, such as a printer, and add or remove programs by using tools in the Control Panel. The Add Hardware Wizard and Add/Remove Programs dialog box walk you through the necessary steps. To start the add new hardware procedure, double-click the Add Hardware icon in the Control Panel, then navigate through the Add Hardware Wizard, making the appropriate selections, and clicking Next to move forward, then clicking Finish when complete. To add or remove a program, double-click the Add or Remove Programs icon, click Add New Programs in the Add or Remove Programs window, click CD or Floppy, then follow the prompts. In both cases, Windows should recognize that new hardware needs to be added or that an installation file needs to be executed. To install a Windows accessory or feature, such as Character Map or Desktop Wallpaper, click Add/Remove Windows Components in the Add or Remove Programs window, double-click a category if necessary, click the check box next to the accessory or feature you want to install, then click OK (you might be asked to insert your Windows installation CD). When you install a new program on your computer, the Start menu highlights the menus you need to click to start the program.

Customizing the Taskbar

The taskbar is initially located at the bottom of the Windows desktop, and is most often used to switch from one program to another. As with other Windows elements, you can customize the taskbar; for example, you can change its size and location, customize its display, or add or remove toolbars to help you perform the tasks you need to do. If you need more room on the screen to display a window, **Auto-hide** can be used to hide the taskbar automatically when it's not in use. If icons in the notification area are hidden when you want to see them, you can customize the notification area to always show the icons you want to use. ⬦⬦⬦⬦ John removes and adds a toolbar to the taskbar, then he learns how to hide the taskbar and show icons in the notification area.

Steps

1. **Place the mouse pointer in an empty area of the taskbar, right-click the taskbar, then point to Toolbars**

   The Toolbars submenu appears, as shown in Figure E-17. You can add or remove a variety of existing toolbars to the taskbar or create a new one.

2. **Click Quick Launch to select it if a check mark doesn't appear next to it**

   You added the Quick Launch toolbar to the taskbar.

3. **Right-click an empty area of the taskbar, then click Properties**

   The Taskbar and Start Menu Properties dialog box opens, displaying the Taskbar tab, as shown in Figure E-18. The Taskbar tab allows you to lock and unlock the taskbar, keep the taskbar visible, group similar taskbar buttons together in one button, and show or hide items, such as the Quick Launch toolbar, clock, and notification icons, on the taskbar.

> **QuickTip**
>
> To open the Taskbar and Start Menu Properties dialog box from the Control Panel in Classic View, double-click the Taskbar and Start Menu icon 🖥️.

4. **Click the Auto-hide the taskbar check box to select it, click the Show Quick Launch check box to deselect it, then click Apply**

   You hid the taskbar at the bottom of the screen and removed the Quick Launch toolbar from the taskbar.

5. **Click Customize**

   The Customize Notifications dialog box opens.

> **QuickTip**
>
> To hide the clock in the notification area, click the Show the clock check box to deselect it in the Taskbar and Start Menu Properties dialog box.

6. **Click an item in the list, click the list arrow as shown in Figure E-19, click Always show, then click OK**

   The Customize Notifications dialog box closes.

7. **Click Apply, then move the mouse pointer to the bottom of the screen**

   The icon you set to always show appears in the notification area. While the mouse pointer is at the bottom of the screen, the taskbar appears. When you move the mouse pointer up, the taskbar is hidden.

8. **In the Taskbar and Start Menu Properties dialog box, click the Auto-hide the taskbar check box to deselect it**

9. **Click Customize, click the same item in the list you modified earlier, click the list arrow, click Hide when inactive, then click OK twice**

   The Auto-hide feature is turned off and the notification icons are hidden when inactive.

FIGURE E-17: **Adding a toolbar to the taskbar**

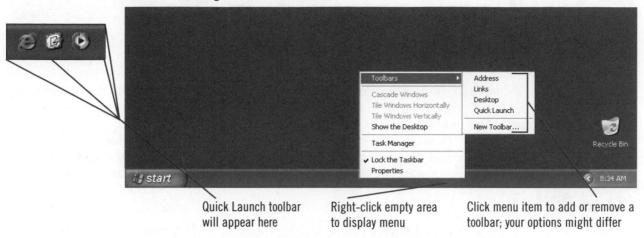

Quick Launch toolbar will appear here

Right-click empty area to display menu

Click menu item to add or remove a toolbar; your options might differ

FIGURE E-18: **The Taskbar and Start Menu Properties dialog box with Taskbar tab**

Click check box to activate Auto-hide

Click button to customize notification area

FIGURE E-19: **Customize Notifications dialog box**

Select item to display list arrow

Click list arrow to change how icons appear

Click button to set default options

Customizing the Start Menu

You can add shortcuts to programs, files, or folders to the Start menu so that you can simply click the Start button, then click the item you want on the Start menu. Adding too many items to the Start menu defeats the purpose, so only add icons for your most frequently used programs and files. To customize the Start menu further, you can display additional menu items on the Start menu. You can also extend a submenu from the Control Panel, Printers, or Network Connections menu items. ▰▰ Because John works with the Calculator program often, he decides to add it to the Start menu.

Steps

1. **Click the Start button on the taskbar, point to All Programs, point to Accessories, then point to the Calculator, but do not click it**
   The Accessories submenu appears with the Calculator program highlighted.

QuickTip

You can also add an item to the Start menu by creating a shortcut to it on the desktop or in Windows Explorer, then dragging the icon anywhere on the All Programs sub-menu on the Start menu.

2. **Right-click the Calculator program as shown in Figure E-20, then click Pin to Start menu**
   The Calculator program appears above the separation line on the Start menu in the permanent menu items section. The menu item stays on the Start menu until you remove it.

3. **Click outside the Start menu to close it, right-click the Start button on the taskbar, then click Properties**
   The Taskbar and Start Menu Properties dialog box opens, displaying the Start Menu tab, which allows you to choose the Start menu style you want: either Start menu (for Windows XP) or Classic Start menu. The Start menu option for Windows XP is selected by default.

4. **Click the Start menu option button if necessary, then next to Start menu, click Customize**
   The Customize Start Menu dialog box opens, displaying the General tab, which allows you to select an icon size for programs, clear the list of recently used programs on the Start menu, indicate the number of programs you want to see on the list, and specify the Internet and E-mail programs to use when you click Internet or E-mail on the Start menu.

QuickTip

To remove all recently used documents from the My Recent Documents sub-menu, click the Advanced tab in the Customize Start Menu dialog box, then click Clear List.

5. **Click the Advanced tab**
   The Advanced tab appears, as shown in Figure E-21. The Advanced tab allows you to modify the way menus appear on the Start menu, add and remove Windows commands to and from the Start menu, and select options to access documents you opened most recently.

6. **In the Start menu items list, click the Display as a menu option button under Control Panel, click OK, then click Apply in the Taskbar and Start Menu Properties dialog box**
   The customized Control Panel option is applied to the Start menu, and the Taskbar and Start Menu Properties dialog box remains open.

7. **Click the Start button on the taskbar, then point to Control Panel to display the submenu of Control Panel options**
   The Control Panel menu options correspond to the icons in the Control Panel window.

8. **Right-click Calculator on the Start menu, then click Remove from This List**
   The Calculator program is removed from the Start menu.

9. **Click Customize in the Taskbar and Start Menu Properties dialog box, click the Advanced tab, click the Display as a link option button under Control Panel in the Start menu items list, then click OK twice**
   The Taskbar and Start Menu Properties dialog box closes, and the Start menu is restored.

FIGURE E-20: Adding a program to the Start menu

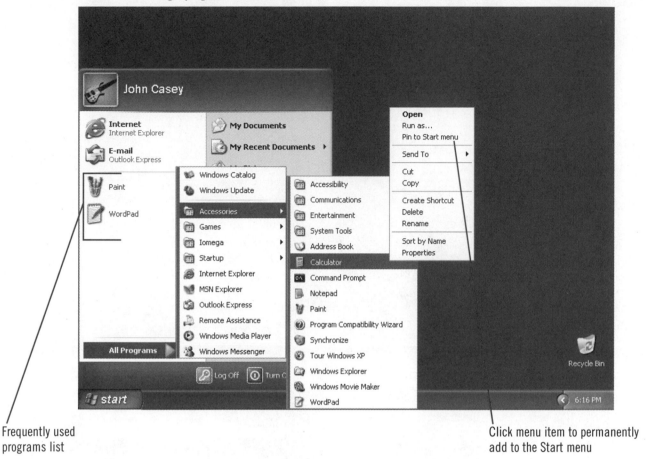

Frequently used
programs list

Click menu item to permanently
add to the Start menu

FIGURE E-21: Customize Start Menu dialog box with Advanced tab

Click options to add
or remove Start
menu items

Click button to remove all
documents listed on My
Recent Documents menu

 CLUES TO USE

Rearranging Start menu items

If you don't like the location of an item on the Start menu, you can move the item to a different location by dragging it. A thick black line appears as you move the mouse pointer, indicating the new location of the item. For example, to move the Windows Explorer menu item from the Accessories submenu to the Start menu, open the Accessories submenu on the All Programs submenu, then drag the Windows Explorer item to the left column of the Start menu in the pinned section above the separator line.

Practice

▶ Concepts Review

Label each element of the screen shown in Figure E-22.

FIGURE E-22

1. Which element points to desktop icons?
2. Which element points to the Quick Launch toolbar?
3. Which element points to an expanded menu?
4. Which element points to recently used programs?
5. Which element points to pinned programs?
6. Which element points to Windows customization utilities?
7. Which element points to the desktop background?

Match each term with the statement that describes its function.

8. **Background**
9. **Screen saver**
10. **Color schemes**
11. **Control Panel**
12. **Start menu**

a. Preset designs for the desktop
b. Used to start programs and open documents
c. Used to change properties of various elements of a computer
d. Preset combinations of desktop colors
e. Used to prevent damage to the monitor

Select the best answers from the following lists of choices.

13. **To customize the desktop, you need to open the:**
    a. Desktop Settings dialog box.
    b. Custom Desktop dialog box.
    c. Folder Options dialog box.
    d. Display Properties dialog box.

14. **An Internet document or Paint file used as a background is called (a):**
    a. Display.
    b. Shortcut.
    c. Web item.
    d. Wallpaper.

15. **Which of the following screen resolutions displays screen elements the largest?**
    a. 640 by 480 pixels
    b. 1024 by 768 pixels
    c. 1280 by 1024 pixels
    d. 1600 by 1200 pixels

16. **Which of the following color quality values displays the smallest number of colors?**
    a. 16-bit
    b. 24-bit
    c. 32-bit
    d. All the same

17. **Which of the following fonts consists of bitmapped characters?**
    a. TrueType
    b. Screen
    c. OpenType
    d. Outline

► Skills Review

1. **Change the desktop background.**
    a. Open the Display Properties dialog box.
    b. Change the background to Santa Fe Stucco, then apply the change.

2. **Customize the desktop.**
    a. Open the Desktop Items dialog box.
    b. Display the My Documents, My Computer, and My Network Places icons on the desktop.
    c. Display the Web tab, select a Web item, then apply the desktop changes.
    d. Restore the desktop icons and the Web item to their original state, then apply the changes.

3. **Change the desktop appearance.**
    a. Display the Themes tab in the Display Properties dialog box. Change the theme to Windows Classic.
    b. Display the Appearance tab. Change the color scheme to Windows Classic, then apply the desktop changes.
    c. Save the theme as **Windows Classic 2**.
    d. Change the theme to Windows XP, then apply the desktop change.
    e. Delete the Windows Classic 2 theme (*Hint:* Select the theme from the Theme list, then click Delete).
    f. Display the Desktop tab, change the background to (None) if necessary, then apply the desktop change.

4. **Change desktop screen settings.**
    a. Display the Settings tab.
    b. Change the Screen resolution to a different setting, then apply the change.
    c. Display the Screen Saver tab. Select the 3D Pipes screen saver, then preview it.
    d. Restore the screen resolution and screen saver to their original settings.
    e. Close the Display Properties dialog box.

5. **Set the date and time.**
    a. Open the Date and Time Properties dialog box.
    b. Change the time to three hours ahead, then apply the change.
    c. Display the Internet Time tab, then update the time (only if you have an Internet connection). Otherwise, change the time back three hours. Close the Date and Time Properties dialog box.

6. Work with fonts.

   a. Open the Fonts window.

   b. Double-click a Times New Roman icon. Print the font information.

   c. Close the Times New Roman and Fonts windows.

7. Add a scheduled task.

   a. Open the Scheduled Tasks window. Start the Scheduled Task Wizard.

   b. Schedule a task for Character Map, or another available program, with the One time only option, then continue.

   c. Change the time to one minute ahead, select the current day, then continue.

   d. If necessary, type your password, press [Tab], type your password again, then continue.

   e. Finish creating the task, wait for the task to take place, then close the program window.

   f. Delete the scheduled task, then close the Scheduled Tasks window.

8. Customize the taskbar.

   a. Display the Quick Launch toolbar on the taskbar.

   b. Open the Taskbar and Start Menu Properties dialog box.

   c. Select the Auto-hide feature and hide the Quick Launch toolbar.

   d. Set any notification icon to display all the time, then apply the changes.

   e. Move the mouse pointer to the bottom of the screen.

   f. Deselect the Auto-hide feature, then restore defaults for the notification icon.

   g. Apply the changes, then close the Taskbar and Start Menu Properties dialog box.

9. Customize the Start Menu.

   a. Point to the Paint program on the Accessories submenu on the Start menu.

   b. Pin the Paint program to the Start menu.

   c. Open the Taskbar and Start Menu Properties dialog box, then display the Advanced tab on the Customize Start Menu dialog box. Show the Favorites menu on the Start menu, then apply the change.

   d. Display the Start menu with the changes.

   e. Remove the Paint program from the Start menu, then hide the Favorites menu.

   f. Close the Taskbar and Start Menu Properties dialog box and the Control Panel.

► Independent Challenge 1

As owner of a small optical laboratory, you are trying to abide by the Americans with Disabilities Act, which states that employers should make every reasonable effort to accommodate workers with disabilities. One worker is visually impaired. Customize the Windows desktop for this employee so that it is easier to work in, desktop items are easier to see and read, and desktop colors strongly contrast with each other. Save this custom configuration.

   a. Open the Display Properties dialog box from the Control Panel.

   b. Change the background to a dark green color.

   c. Set the screen saver for one minute, so you can show employees how it works without waiting too long.

   d. On the Appearance tab, set the Font size to Extra Large Fonts and the Color scheme to Olive Green.

   e. Set the screen resolution to the lowest setting to make it easier for employees to see.

   f. Save the theme as Visible, then apply the changes.

   g. Print the screen. (Press [Print Screen] to make a copy of the screen, open Paint, click Edit on the menu bar, click Paste to paste the screen into Paint, then click Yes to paste the large image, if necessary. Click the Text button on the Toolbox, click a blank area in the Paint work area, then type your name. Click File on the menu bar, click Page Setup, change 100 % normal size to 50% in the Scaling area, then click OK. Click File on the menu bar, click Print, then click Print.)

   h. Delete the scheme Visible, then apply the Windows XP theme.

   i. Set the screen saver for five minutes and restore the screen resolution if necessary.

▶ Independent Challenge 2

You accepted a temporary consulting job in Rome, Italy. After moving into your new home and unpacking your stuff, you decide to set up your computer. Once you set up and turn on the computer, you decide to change the date and time settings and other regional and language options to reflect Rome, Italy.

    a. Open the Control Panel, click Switch to Classic View if necessary, then open the Date and Time Properties dialog box.

    b. Click the Time Zone tab, then click the Time Zone list arrow.

    c. Select Amsterdam, Berlin, Bern, Rome, Stockholm, Vienna from the list (scroll if necessary).

    d. Click the Date & Time tab, change the month and year to June 2003, then click Apply.

    e. Print the screen. (See Independent Challenge 1, Step g, for screen printing instructions.)

    f. Open the Regional and Languages Options dialog box.

    g. On the Regional Options tab, set the language formats to Italian (Italy).

    h. Print the screen. (See Independent Challenge 1, Step g, for screen printing instructions.)

    i. Restore the original date and time zone settings and the regional and language options to English (United States).

    j. Close the Control Panel window.

▶ Independent Challenge 3

As system administrator of a small computer network for a chain of specialty book stores, you want to make sure all the computers don't lose important data. To accomplish this goal, you need to set up a scheduled task to backup the hard disk drives of all computers on a weekly basis.

    a. Open the Scheduled Tasks window.

    b. Schedule the Backup program as a task.

    c. Schedule the task for a monthly time period.

    d. Set the time one minute ahead of the current time.

    e. When the Backup program task appears in the Scheduled Tasks window, print the screen. (See Independent Challenge 1, Step g, for screen printing instructions.)

    f. Delete the Backup scheduled task.

▶ Independent Challenge 4

As owner of Holly's Office Supply, you need to make your business computers easier for your employees to use. One way to do that is to add programs to the Start menu. Your employees use WordPad almost exclusively, and they also use the same documents quite often.

    a. Create a memo to employees about the upcoming company picnic using WordPad, then save the memo as **Company Picnic Memo** in the drive and folder where your Project Files are located.

    b. Close the memo and WordPad.

    c. Add the WordPad program to the Start menu as a pinned item.

    d. Create a shortcut to the Company Picnic Memo file and add it to the Start menu as a pinned item.

    e. Extend the My Computer menu item on the Start menu to display a submenu.

    f. Open the Start menu and point to My Computer.

    g. Print the screen. (See Independent Challenge 1, Step g, for screen printing instructions.)

    h. Open the Company Picnic Memo from the Start menu.

    i. Remove all the shortcuts you created on the Start menu and restore the My Computer menu item to its original state.

▶ Visual Workshop

Re-create the screen shown in Figure E-23, which displays the Windows desktop, then print the screen. Your user name on the Start menu, icons in the Control Panel, and background name (Windows XP Professional) might differ. (See Independent Challenge 1, Step g, for screen printing instructions.)

FIGURE E-23

Unit F

Maintaining
Your Computer

Objectives

► **Format a disk**
► **Copy a disk**
► **Find and repair disk errors**
► **Defragment a disk**
► **Clean up a disk**
► **Restore computer settings**
► **Remove a program**
► **Add a program**
► **Enter DOS commands**

Windows XP offers a number of useful tools for managing such routine tasks as installing and removing programs, and formatting, copying, and repairing disks. Windows XP also provides tools to find and fix disk problems, speed up disk access, clean up disk space, and restore computer settings when problems occur. By periodically finding and repairing disk errors or restoring computer settings, you can keep your files in good working condition and prevent disk problems that might cause you to lose your work. In addition, you can work with the DOS operating system to enter DOS commands or run older DOS-based programs alongside your Windows operating system. John Casey, owner of Wired Coffee Company, formats and copies disks, performs several routine disk management tasks, and uses DOS commands to view his hard disk drive directory.

Formatting a Disk

Formatting a disk prepares it so that you can store information on it. Formatting removes all information from the disk, so you should never format a disk that has files you want to keep. Disks are now usually formatted before you buy them, so you no longer need to format a new disk before you can use it; however, formatting is still a quick way to erase old files from a floppy disk and to scan a disk for errors before you reuse it to store files. See Table F-1 for information about disk capacity, file system, and allocation unit size; default settings are strongly recommended. Do not use the disk that stores your Project Files for this lesson; use a disk that does not contain files you want to keep. ➤ John wants to make a copy of the disk that stores his Project Files for safekeeping, but first he needs to format the disk to which he will copy.

Steps

1. Click the **Start button** on the taskbar, point to **All Programs**, point to **Accessories**, then click **Windows Explorer**

2. Insert a floppy disk in the appropriate drive on your computer
   In this example, the floppy disk drive is the 3½ (A:) drive. Make sure the disk you are using does not contain any files you want to keep.

3. In the left pane of Windows Explorer, click the **drive icon** containing your floppy disk
   Disks and drives appear under the My Computer icon in the left pane of Windows Explorer. The icon representing the 3½ (A:) drive is highlighted, and the files on the disk drive appear in the right pane of Windows Explorer. Review the files on your floppy disk to make sure they are not ones you want to keep.

4. Right-click the **drive icon** containing your floppy disk in the left pane of Window Explorer, then click **Format** on the shortcut menu
   The Format dialog box opens, as shown in Figure F-1. The fastest way to format a floppy disk is with the **Quick Format** option. This option simply formats a previously formatted disk, removing all files from it. The **Full Format** option, which you choose by deselecting the Quick Format check box, removes all files from any floppy disk and scans the disk for bad sectors. You should choose Quick Format only if you are sure that your disk is not damaged. Additional format options include Enable Compression and Create an MS-DOS startup disk. The **Enable Compression** option, supported only on NTFS drives, specifies whether to format the drive so that folders and files on it are compressed. The **Create an MS-DOS startup disk** option formats a disk so that you can start up your computer in MS-DOS, a disk-based operating system, to fix a problem, display information, or run an MS-DOS program using MS-DOS commands; experience with MS-DOS is required.

5. In the Format options area, click the **Quick Format check box** to select it

6. Select any text in the **Volume label text box**, then type **Backup**
   After you format the disk, the volume label appears in Windows Explorer and My Computer to make the floppy disk easier to identify.

7. Click **Start**, then click **OK** in the message box
   A progress meter appears at the bottom of the Format dialog box. After a few moments, the Format Complete message box opens.

8. Click **OK** in the Format Complete message box
   The Format Complete message box closes.

9. Click **Close** in the Format dialog box, then remove the formatted disk from the appropriate drive on your computer
   The disk is now formatted. You will use the formatted disk in the next lesson to make a copy of your Project Files.

FIGURE F-1: Format dialog box

Current format type and file system for selected disk

Click check box to select the Quick Format option

Progress meter

TABLE F-1: Format dialog box options

option	description
Capacity	Specifies how much data the disk or partition can hold, such as the physical size, storage size, and sector size.
File system	Displays the file system for the disk. A file system is the overall structure in which files are named, stored, and organized. NTFS and FAT are types of file systems.
Allocation unit size	Specifies the disk allocation unit size, or cluster size (a group of sectors on a disk). The operating system assigns a unique number to each cluster and then keeps track of files according to which clusters they use. The default allocation size is typically selected.

CLUES TO USE

Protecting against computer viruses

A computer virus is a program that attaches itself to a file, reproduces itself, and spreads to other files. A virus is typically attached to programs and files downloaded from the Internet, electronic mail attachments, or shareware disks containing free or inexpensive software or illegally obtained pirated software. When you open a program or file with the computer virus, the computer becomes infected with the virus and can corrupt or destroy data, or disrupt program or Windows functionality. For example, the Chernobyl virus attempts to erase a computer's hard drive and damage the computer's system settings, making it impossible to access your data. The virus is called the Chernobyl virus because it is timed to go off on April 26, the anniversary of the 1986 Russian nuclear accident, one of technology's worst disasters. The Chernobyl virus didn't propagate quickly because it required a person to open an infected file to contaminate a computer. Many viruses stay dormant on a computer before doing any damage, so catching and destroying these viruses before they cause damage can prevent computer disaster. Antivirus software, or virus detection software, examines the files stored on a disk to determine whether they are infected with a virus, then destroys or disinfects them. Antivirus software typically starts when you start Windows and watches for viruses whenever your computer is on. Popular antivirus software, which needs to be purchased from a software retailer, includes Norton Anitvirus and MacAfee VirusScan. New viruses appear all the time, so it is important that your antivirus software be kept up-to-date to look for the new viruses. You can easily download updates from the Internet. Typically, you should check for updates every three months, or if you hear about a new virus.

Windows XP

Copying a Disk

One way to protect the information on a disk from possible problems is to copy the disk, placing copies of all the files on it to another disk. Then, if information goes bad on a disk, you still have the copied information. You can use Windows to copy information from one disk to another using the same disk drive. When you copy disks, the disk must be the same type, either 3½", or 5¼", and size (1.44 MB or 1.2 MB), and not write-protected. A floppy disk is not write-protected when the tab in the upper-left corner on the back of the floppy disk is pushed down so that you cannot see through the square hole. 5¼" disk drives are common on older computers, but are not standard on new computers. ◄▬▬ John wants to make a copy of the information he has compiled on his floppy disk. He'll copy it to the disk he formatted in the previous lesson.

Trouble?

If you store your Project Files on a network or hard drive, copy the Project Files to a floppy disk before completing this lesson.

1. **Insert the disk that stores your Project Files in the appropriate drive, then right-click the drive icon containing your Project Files in the left pane of Windows Explorer**
   In this example, the icon representing the 3½" disk drive is highlighted, and the shortcut menu for the left pane opens, as shown in Figure F-2.

2. **Click Copy Disk on the shortcut menu**
   The Copy Disk dialog box opens, as shown in Figure F-3. On the left side of the dialog box, you select the **source disk** from which you want to copy. On the right side, you select the **destination disk** to which you want to copy. Both the disk you are copying from (the Project Disk) and the disk you are copying to (the disk you formatted in the previous lesson) are 3½" floppy disks, so the drive shown is the same. The 3½ Floppy (A:) or (B:) icons on both sides of the dialog box are selected by default; no additional drives appear because the computer in this example does not contain additional floppy disk drives, although yours might.

3. **Click Start, then click OK in the Copy Disk message box**
   A progress meter appears in the Copy Disk dialog box with the status message "Reading source disk." After reading the source disk, a Copy Disk message box opens, asking you to insert a destination disk.

4. **Remove your Project Disk, label the blank formatted disk from the previous lesson Copy of Project Disk, insert it into the same drive, then click OK in the Copy Disk message box**
   In the Copy Disk dialog box the progress meter continues with the status message "Writing to destination disk." Upon completion, the status message "Copy completed successfully" appears.

5. **Click Close in the Copy Disk dialog box**
   Now that he has a copy of his disk, John can perform maintenance operations on his disk without worrying about losing any information. Leave the "Copy of Project Disk" disk in the floppy drive for the next lesson.

FIGURE F-2: Windows Explorer with shortcut menu for floppy disk

Disk to copy

Click command
to copy a disk

FIGURE F-3: Copy Disk dialog box

Source disk

Destination disk

Progress meter

Synchronizing files between computers

If you want to work with files that are copied onto two different computers, such as your work computer and your home computer, you can synchronize the files to keep the various copies updated between computers using a Windows feature called Briefcase. Before you can use Briefcase, you need to create one. Open the folder in My Computer where you want the new Briefcase to appear, or display the desktop. Right-click an empty area of the desktop or My Computer, click New, then click Briefcase. To use Briefcase, drag the files you want to copy to your other computer from Windows Explorer to the Briefcase icon. Then, drag the Briefcase icon to the icon for the removable disk drive, and remove the disk. You can now insert the removable disk in a different computer. If you edit the files, you need to synchronize them when you return to your main computer. To synchronize them, reinsert the removable disk, double-click the Briefcase icon, then click Update All on the Briefcase menu to copy the new versions of your files from the removable disk to the hard disk.

Finding and Repairing Disk Errors

Sometimes an unexpected power loss or program error can create inaccessible file segments that take up space on a hard disk or a floppy disk. The **Check Disk** program that comes with Windows helps you find and repair damaged sections of a disk. Check Disk can also be used to find physical disk errors or **bad sectors**. The program doesn't physically repair your media, but it moves data away from any bad sectors it finds. To keep your hard disk drive working properly, you should run Check Disk from time to time. When you run Check Disk, all files must be closed for the process to run. While the Check Disk process is running, your hard disk will not be available to perform any other task. ▟▅▆▂ John wants to make sure his disk has no problems, so he runs Check Disk. For this lesson, use the copy of your Project Disk that you made in the previous lesson.

Steps

1. Close any open files or programs, right-click the **drive icon containing the copy of your Project Disk** in the left pane of Windows Explorer, then click **Properties** on the shortcut menu
   The Properties dialog box opens.

2. Click the **Tools tab**
   The Properties dialog box appears with the Tools tab, as shown in Figure F-4, in which you can start the Check Disk program. The Tools tab also provides you with access to other utilities that can make Windows work more efficiently: defragmentation and backup, which is available only with the Professional version of Windows XP. Defragmentation starts the Disk Defragmenter program and optimizes a disk for better performance, while backup starts the Backup program and copies files and folders to a disk for safe keeping.

QuickTip

For Help, click the Help button [?] in the title bar, then click any item to display a Help screen.

3. In the Error-checking area, click **Check Now**
   The Check Disk dialog box opens, as shown in Figure F-5.

4. Click the **Automatically fix file system errors check box** to select it
   This option repairs most errors automatically using predetermined settings.

5. Click the **Scan for and attempt recovery of bad sectors check box** to select it
   This option makes corrections for any unreadable or bad sectors on the disk.

6. Click **Start**
   A progress meter appears, displaying scanning status. When the process is complete, the Disk Check Complete message box opens.

7. Click **OK** in the Disk Check Complete message box, then click **OK** to close the Properties dialog box

8. Click the Windows Explorer **Close button**

9. Remove the copy of your Project Disk from the appropriate drive on your computer, then insert your original Project Disk

FIGURE F-4: Properties dialog box with Tools tab

Click button to
check the disk

Only available in the
Professional edition

FIGURE F-5: Check Disk dialog box

Click check box to
fix file system errors

Click check box to
recover bad sectors

Progress meter

Backing up files

The more you work with a computer, the more files you create. To protect yourself from losing critical information, it's important to back up, or make copies of your files on a separate disk, frequently. If you are using the Windows XP Professional edition, you can click Backup Now on the Tools tab in the disk drive Properties dialog box to open the Backup program and walk you through the Backup or Restore Wizard to help you back up the files on your hard disk to a floppy or tape drive. You can back up the contents of an entire disk or only certain files. Using the Backup option has several advantages over simply copying files to a floppy, such as compressing files as it copies them so you can fit more onto a floppy disk. It can also split a large file across two or more floppies, something you cannot do with the Copy Disk command.

Defragmenting a Disk

When you delete files from a disk, you create empty spaces that might be fragmented over different areas of the disk. When you create a new file on a fragmented disk, parts of the file are stored in these empty spaces, resulting in a single file that is broken into many parts, which takes longer to retrieve or store when you open or save the file. A file broken up in this way is called a **fragmented file**. To retrieve a fragmented file, the computer must search many areas on the disk, which lengthens retrieval time, but the file is otherwise usable, and it is undetectable to the user that the file is fragmented. You can use the **Disk Defragmenter** program to place all of the parts of a file in one **contiguous**, or adjacent, location. This procedure, which efficiently arranges all of the files and unused space, is called **optimization**. Optimization makes your programs run faster and your files open more quickly. For best results, run Check Disk to check for errors on your disk before you start the disk defragmentation process. While Disk Defragmenter works, you can use your computer to carry out other tasks; however, your computer will operate more slowly. ⟋⟍ John uses Disk Defragmenter to optimize his hard disk; you cannot defragment a floppy disk with Windows XP, although you could with previous Windows versions.

Steps

1. Click the **Start button** on the taskbar, point to **All Programs**, point to **Accessories**, point to **System Tools**, then click **Disk Defragmenter**

   The Disk Defragmenter dialog box opens. You need to choose a hard disk drive, typically, the C: drive.

2. Click the **hard disk drive** if necessary

   Before you perform a complete disk defragmentation, you can analyze the disk to determine the extent of the fragmentation.

QuickTip

To temporarily stop Disk Defragmenter, click Pause, then click Resume when you are ready.

3. Click **Analyze**

   The analyzing process can take a few minutes, depending on the extent of the fragmentation on your disk. You can monitor the process with the progress meter. Upon completion, the Analysis complete message box opens.

4. Click **View Report**

   The Analysis Report dialog box opens, as shown in Figure F-6.

QuickTip

To print the analysis, click Print in the Analysis Report dialog box, then click Print in the Print dialog box.

5. In the Volume information box, click the **down scroll arrow** to display the file fragmentation statistics

   The file fragmentation statistics provide information on the total number of files, average file size, total number of fragmented files and excess file fragments, and average fragments per file.

6. Click **Close** in the Analysis Report dialog box

   The Disk Defragmenter window appears, as shown in Figure F-7. The defragmentation process can take several minutes or more, depending on the extent of the fragmentation on your disk.

Trouble?

If you are working in a lab, check with your instructor or technical support person for authorization to defragment your hard disk drive. If you do not receive authorization, click the Close button in the Defragmentation window and skip Steps 7 and 8.

7. Click **Defragment**

   The Analysis display shows you the defragmentation process. Different colored lines, each representing a disk sector, appear in the Analysis display. The colored lines tell you the defragmentation status of your hard disk drive, and the legend at the bottom of the window explains how to interpret the colors. You can monitor the process with the progress meter. When complete, the Disk Defragmenter window opens, as shown in Figure F-8. The Defragmentation display shows you the result of the defragmentation process.

8. When the defragmentation is complete, click **Close**, then click the **Close button** in the Defragmentation window

   Your disk is now optimized.

FIGURE F-6: Analysis Report dialog box

Scroll down to display fragmentation information; yours will differ

FIGURE F-7: Disk Defragmenter window

Selected volume for disk defragmentation

Defragmented files in red

Analysis of disk defragmentation

Legend for disk defragmentation

FIGURE F-8: Disk defragmentation process completed

Defragmented disk; no red areas

Cleaning Up a Disk

Cleaning up a disk involves removing unneeded files to make room for other files on your computer, which can be difficult if you don't know the significance of each file. You can use a Windows XP program called **Disk Cleanup** to clean up your hard disk drive safely and effectively. You can also empty the Recycle Bin to clear space on the hard disk. Disk Cleanup searches your drive, then lists temporary files, Internet cache files, and unnecessary program files that you can safely delete. You can select the types of files you want Disk Cleanup to delete. Before you select and delete files, make sure you will not need them in the future. Disk Cleanup also gives you the option to remove Windows components and installed programs that you no longer use. ✏ John decides to clean up his hard disk.

Trouble?

If you have more than one hard disk, the Select Drive dialog box opens. Click the drive list arrow, click the hard drive for the computer, then click OK to open the Disk Cleanup dialog box.

QuickTip

To clean up Windows components, installed programs, and restore points, click the More Options tab, then click the appropriate button.

Trouble?

If you are working in a lab, check with your instructor or technical support person for authorization to delete the Recycle Bin or any other files. If you do not receive authorization, click Cancel to close the dialog box, then skip Step 6.

1. Click the **Start button** on the taskbar, point to **All Programs**, point to **Accessories**, point to **System Tools**, then click **Disk Cleanup**

   Disk Cleanup selects your hard drive and calculates how much disk space you can free on the drive, then the Disk Cleanup for (C:) dialog box opens (the hard drive is C: in this example), displaying the Disk Cleanup tab with types of files to remove and the amount of disk space taken up by each type of file, as shown in Figure F-9. Your list of files to delete might differ.

2. In the Files to delete list, click **Recycle Bin** (but not the check box), then click **View Files**

   The Recycle Bin window opens, listing the files currently stored in the Recycle Bin.

3. Click the **Close button** in the Recycle Bin window

4. In the Files to delete box, click the **check boxes** next to any item with a check mark to deselect them (be sure to scroll through the entire list)

5. In the Files to delete box, click the **Recycle Bin check box** to select it

   The check mark indicates that you want to delete all the files in the Recycle Bin, as shown in Figure F-10.

6. Click **OK** in the Disk Cleanup dialog box, then click **Yes** in the message box to confirm the deletion

   The Disk Cleanup for (C:) message box opens, and a progress meter appears, displaying deletion status. After a few moments, the message box closes. If you open the Disk Cleanup dialog box after deleting the Recycle Bin files, the amount of disk space taken up by the Recycle Bin will be 0 KB.

FIGURE F-9: Disk Cleanup for (C:) dialog box

Types of files and space taken up; your list might differ

Click button to open the folder for the selected item

FIGURE F-10: Disk Cleanup for (C:) dialog box with Recycle Bin selected

Selected item to be deleted

Terminating an inactive program

If a program stops responding to mouse or keyboard commands, you can use the Windows Task Manager to terminate and exit the program, after which you can restart it. To terminate an inactive program, right-click an empty area on the taskbar, then click Task Manager to open the Windows Task Manager window. Click the Applications tab if necessary. Click the program you want to terminate in the task list, then click End Task. Sometimes it takes a few moments to terminate the program. If the program still doesn't terminate, click End Task again. When the program termination process completes, click the Close button in the Windows Task Manager window.

Windows XP

Restoring Computer Settings

Windows XP is a reliable operating system, but anytime you make changes to your computer, such as adding or removing software and hardware, you run the risk of causing problems with your operating system. To alleviate potential problems, you can use **System Restore**, a program installed with Windows XP Professional, to undo harmful changes to your computer and restore its settings. System Restore returns your computer system, but not your personal files, to an earlier time, before the changes were made to your computer, called a **restore point**. As you work with your computer, System Restore monitors your changes and automatically creates restore points on a daily basis or at important system events, but you can also create your own restore point at any time. If you have recently performed a system restoration, you can use System Restore to undo your most recent restoration. System Restore is turned on by default when you install the Windows XP operating system, but you can turn it off or make other System Restore changes on the System Restore tab in the System Properties dialog box. ◄━━━ John wants to make some changes to his computer, so he creates a restore point in case problems arise.

Steps 1 2 3 4

QuickTip

To restore your computer, start the System Restore program, click the Restore my computer to an earlier time option button if necessary, click Next, select a date and a restore point, click Next to restore and reboot the computer, then click OK in the Restoration Complete dialog box.

1. **Click the Start button on the taskbar, point to All Programs, point to Accessories, point to System Tools, then click System Restore**
   The Welcome to System Restore window opens, as shown in Figure F-11. The window displays an introduction to the process and two or three (or more) options: Restore my computer to an earlier time, Create a restore point, and Undo my last restoration, which will appear only if you have previously performed a restoration.

2. **Click System Restore Settings**
   The System Properties dialog box opens, displaying the System Restore tab, as shown in Figure F-12. The System Restore tab allows you to turn off System Restore, which stops the automatic creation of restore points and changes the amount of disk space available for System Restore. Windows needs space on your hard disk to save restore points. When you decrease the available disk space, you reduce the number of restore points. System Restore requires a minimum of 200 MB of available space on your hard disk. If System Restore runs out of disk space, it becomes inactive until sufficient disk space is made available.

Trouble?

Check with your instructor or technical support person for authorization to change the disk space usage; if you do not receive it, skip Step 3, then click Cancel.

3. **If your disk space usage is greater than 20%, drag the Disk space to use slider to 20%, then click OK**
   The Welcome to System Restore window appears.

4. **Click the Create a restore point option button, then click Next**
   The Create a Restore Point window appears, asking you to type a description for your restore point.

QuickTip

To delete all but the most recent restore point, start the Disk Cleanup program, click the More Options tab, click Clean up under System Restore, then click Yes to confirm the deletion.

5. **In the Restore point description text box, type Default Windows XP installation, then type your initials**
   The restore point cannot be changed after you create it, so make sure you have the name you want.

6. **Click Create**
   Windows creates a restore point, which includes the current date and time. The Restore Point Created window opens, displaying the day, date, time, and name of the new restore point.

7. **Click Close**
   The Restore Point Created window closes.

FIGURE F-11: Welcome to System Restore window

Click link to open the System Properties dialog box with System Restore tab

System restore options; yours might differ

FIGURE F-12: System Properties dialog box with System Restore tab

Select check box to turn off System Restore

Disk space usage slider

Recover from a system failure

If your computer doesn't start properly for any reason, known as system failure, System Restore will not help you unless you can start the program. You need an Automated System Recovery (ASR) disk to start and recover your computer. To create an ASR with Windows XP Professional, click the Start button on the taskbar, point to All Programs, point to Accessories, point to System Tools, click Backup to start the program, then click Advanced Mode in the Backup Utility Wizard. Click Tools on the menu bar, click ASR Wizard, and then follow the instructions in the Automated System Recovery Preparation Wizard.

During the process, you'll need a blank 3½" floppy disk to save your system settings. You will also need backup media, such as a floppy disk or tape, to contain the backup files. Only those system files necessary for starting up your system will be backed up; personal files will need to be backed up separately, so you only need to do this once. To recover from a system failure using ASR, insert the original Windows XP installation CD in your CD drive, restart your computer from the CD, press [F2] when prompted during the text-only mode section of Setup, insert the ASR floppy disk when prompted, then follow the recovery instructions.

Unit F — Windows XP

Removing a Program

Adding and removing programs gives you the flexibility to use the programs you need when you need them and to maximize the free space on your hard drive. If you do not use a program very often and want to free some space, you can remove the program. You can always reinstall it. Windows XP comes with many programs called Windows components. If you want to free space on your hard drive, use Add or Remove Programs to remove a component. If you have installed a program that is not included on the Windows XP installation CD, such as Microsoft Office XP, you should avoid using Windows Explorer to delete the program because program files and other information might be located in other places, and you might not find everything. Also, some programs share files with other programs, so deleting them can cause damage to other programs. The Change or Remove Programs feature in Add or Remove Programs will make sure all of the program files are removed, except those which are shared with other programs. ➤ John needs more space on his hard drive, so he decides to remove some game programs.

Steps

STOP **If you do not have the Windows XP installation CD-ROM to reinstall the program in the next lesson, don't remove the program in this lesson and simply read through this lesson and the next without completing the steps.**

Trouble?

Click **Switch to Classic view** if necessary.

▶ **1.** Click the **Start button** on the taskbar, then click **Control Panel**
The Control Panel opens in Classic view.

2. Double-click the **Add or Remove Programs icon** 🗔 in the Control Panel
The Add or Remove Programs window opens, as shown in Figure F-13, and Setup searches for currently installed non-operating system programs on your computer.

3. Click **Add/Remove Windows Components**
The Windows Components Wizard dialog box opens, and the wizard searches for components installed on your computer. The Components list shows all the components of Windows XP, as shown in Figure F-14. Each component contains one or more parts that you can install or remove. A blank box means that none of the parts of that component are installed; a shaded box means that only some of the parts of the component are installed; and a checked box means that all of the parts of that component are installed. To display what is included in a component, click the component name (but not the check box), then click Details. The Accessories and Utilities component at the top of the list is selected.

4. Click **Details** to display Accessories and Utilities subcomponents, click **Games** in the Subcomponents list, then click **Details**
The Games dialog box appears, listing the Windows game components. Windows XP comes with five games that you can play over the Internet. The games take up 8.5 MB of hard disk space, so you want to remove them for now and will reinstall them later.

Trouble?

If you are working in a lab, check with your instructor or technical support person for authorization to remove the program or instructions to remove another one. If you do not receive authorization, skip Steps 5, 6, and 7, then click Cancel three times.

▶ **5.** Click the **Internet Games check box** to deselect it
The Internet Games check box clears. When you clear a check box, Windows removes the component. Make sure that you do not change any other settings.

6. Click **OK** in the Games dialog box, click **OK** in the Accessories and Utilities dialog box, then click **Next** in the Windows Components Wizard dialog box

7. Click **Finish** in the Windows Components Wizard, then click **Close** in the Add or Remove Programs window
The Windows Components Wizard removes the software and reconfigures Windows.

FIGURE F-13: **Add or Remove Programs window**

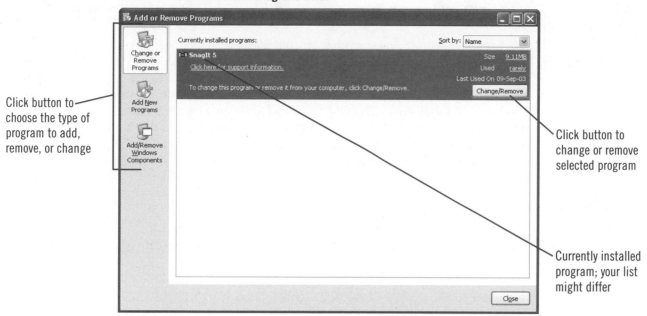

Click button to choose the type of program to add, remove, or change

Click button to change or remove selected program

Currently installed program; your list might differ

FIGURE F-14: **Windows Components Wizard dialog box**

Size of component's contents

Description of high-lighted component

Windows components list; yours might differ

Click button to display details for highlighted components

Updating Windows using the Web

You can use the Windows Update feature to add the latest Windows updates and new features from the Internet to your Windows XP installation. Windows Update is a Microsoft Web site that helps you keep your computer up-to-date. Windows Update provides a central location where you can find and add new Windows features, system updates, and device drivers. To add features from Microsoft Windows Update, connect to the Internet, click the Start button on the taskbar, point to All Programs, click Windows Update, then follow the instructions on the Web site. Windows Update can review device drivers and system software on your computer, compare those findings with a master database on the Web, and then recommend and install updates specifically for your computer. Windows Update indicates the approximate download time and whether an update is already installed on your computer. You can also restore to a previous device driver or system file using the uninstall option. Updates are continually added to the Web site, so it is important to check for important new content on a regular basis. If you want to be notified when updates occur, you can set up Windows XP to let you know when they happen. Double-click the System icon in the Control Panel in Classic view, click the Automatic Updates tab, click the notification setting you want, which includes turning it off, then click OK.

Windows XP

Adding a Program

Windows XP comes with many programs; a typical installation installs only the most common programs, but you can install any additional components as needed. You can use Add or Remove Programs to add Windows components you chose not to include in the original installation or that you removed to free space on a disk. When you install a Windows component, you need the Windows XP installation CD-ROM to complete the process. You can also use the Add New Programs feature in Add or Remove Programs to install programs that are not included on the Windows XP installation CD, such as Microsoft Office XP, or to add the latest Windows updates and new features from the Internet. ◀━━ John deleted some files to free space on his hard disk, so he can reinstall the Internet games he previously removed.

Steps

 If you did not remove the program in the previous lesson, simply read through this lesson without completing the steps.

1. Double-click the **Add or Remove Programs icon** 📷 in the Control Panel
   The Add/Remove Programs window opens. At the same time, the Setup program searches for currently installed programs on your computer, which may take a few moments.

> **QuickTip**
>
> For a currently installed program, click Change/Remove to modify or delete a program installation.

2. Click **Add/Remove Windows Components**
   The Windows Components Wizard dialog box opens, and the wizard searches for components installed on your computer. The Components list shows all the components of Windows XP. The Accessories and Utilities component at the top of the list is selected.

3. Click **Details** to display the Accessories and Utilities subcomponents, click **Games** in the Subcomponents list, then click **Details**
   The Games dialog box appears, listing the Windows game components. The check boxes indicate which parts are currently installed on your computer.

4. Click the **Internet Games check box** to select it
   The Internet Games check box is selected, as shown in Figure F-15. When you select a check box, Windows installs the component. Make sure that you do not change any other settings.

> **Trouble?**
>
> If you do not have the Windows XP installation CD-ROM, see your instructor or technical support person.

5. Insert the Windows XP installation CD-ROM in the appropriate drive, if the Welcome to Windows screen appears click **Exit** if necessary, click **OK** in the Games dialog box, click **OK** in the Accessories and Utilities window, then click **Next** in the Windows Components dialog box
   A status bar appears, indicating progress as the wizard copies files from the installation CD-ROM to your hard drive.

6. Click **Finish** in the Windows Components Wizard dialog box, click **Close** in the Add or Remove Programs window, then click the **Close button** in the Control Panel

7. Click the **Start button** on the taskbar, point to **All Programs**, then point to **Games**
   The Start menu highlights the menus and submenus to indicate where the new programs are located, as shown in Figure F-16.

8. Click an empty area of the desktop to close the Start menu, then remove the Windows XP installation CD-ROM from the appropriate drive

FIGURE F-15: Windows Components Wizard dialog box for Games

Selected item to install

Your computer might have different components installed

FIGURE F-16: Start menu with a highlighted path

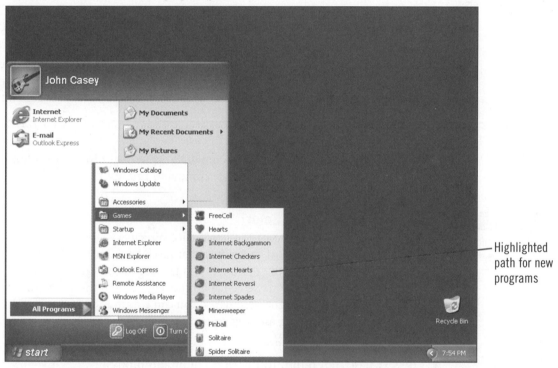

Highlighted path for new programs

Getting older programs to run on Windows XP

If you have an older program, such as a game, that was written for an earlier version of Windows and doesn't run on Windows XP, you can run the Program Compatibility Wizard to help you fix the problem. The wizard steps you through the process of testing your program in different Windows environments, such as Windows 95, and with various settings, such as screen resolution and color quality. To start the Program Compatibility Wizard, click the Start button on the taskbar, point to All Programs, point to Accessories, click

Program Compatibility Wizard, read the introduction, click Next, then follow the step-by-step instructions. If you have problems installing a program on Windows XP, you can run the Program Compatibility Wizard on the setup file, such as Setup.exe, for the program. If you are comfortable working with the compatibility settings, you can manually set the properties. Right-click the program you want to change, click Properties, click the Compatibility tab, change the compatibility settings you want, then click OK.

Entering DOS Commands

Besides running Windows XP programs, you can also enter commands and run programs written in Windows 3.1 and MS-DOS. **MS-DOS** stands for Microsoft Disk Operating System. MS-DOS, or DOS, employs a **command-line interface** through which you must type commands at a **command prompt** to run different tasks. A character such as a > or $ appears at the beginning of a command prompt. Each DOS command has a strict set of rules called a **command syntax** that you must follow when expressing a command. Table F-2 lists common DOS commands and their syntax. You can also start Windows XP programs from within DOS; for example, you can type "explorer" after the command prompt to start Windows Explorer. ➤➤➤➤ For some tasks, John prefers to enter commands at the DOS prompt. He decides to display the Command Prompt window on his computer and run a few simple commands.

Steps 1 2 3 4

1. **Click the Start button on the taskbar, point to All Programs, point to Accessories, then click Command Prompt**
   The Command Prompt window opens, displaying the DOS command prompt, as shown in Figure F-17. The command prompt indicates the current directory, in this case the Documents and Settings directory for John Casey. You can view the contents of the current directory using the dir command.

2. **Type cd c:\, then press [Enter]**
   DOS changes from accessing the Documents and Settings directory for John Casey to accessing the hard drive (C:) directory. The command prompt changes from C:\Documents and Settings\John Casey> to C:\>.

Trouble?
If the contents of the directory don't fill the page, type cd c:\ program files, then press [Enter] to change the directory.

3. **Type dir /p, then press [Enter]**
   DOS displays the contents of the hard drive directory. The "/p" part of what you type is called an **argument**, part of the syntax that gives DOS more information about what you want it to do. By adding the optional /p argument to the dir command, DOS displays the contents of the directory one screen at a time. Figure F-18 shows the first screen, also called the **output**, or results, of the command. You can continue viewing the directory listing one page at a time by pressing any key, or you can return to the DOS command prompt at any time by pressing [Ctrl][C].

QuickTip
To view information about a particular DOS command, type the command name, type /?, then press [Enter] at the DOS command prompt.

4. **Press [Ctrl][C] to return to the DOS command prompt**

5. **Type exit, then press [Enter]**
   The Command Prompt window closes, and you return to Windows.

CLUES TO USE

Controlling the appearance of the Command Prompt window

Windows XP gives you several options for controlling the appearance of the Command Prompt window, including a Control Panel program called Console. To open the Console, right-click the Command Prompt window title bar, then click Properties. In the "Command Prompt" Properties dialog box, you can click the Options tab to change the cursor size and display options, click the Font tab to change font sizes and styles, click the Layout tab to change the window size and position and screen buffer size, then click the Colors tab to change screen text, screen background, popup text, and popup background colors.

FIGURE F-17: Command Prompt window

DOS command prompt

FIGURE F-18: Results of dir /p command

File size

Filename or directory name

Output of dir /p command in C: directory

Filename extension

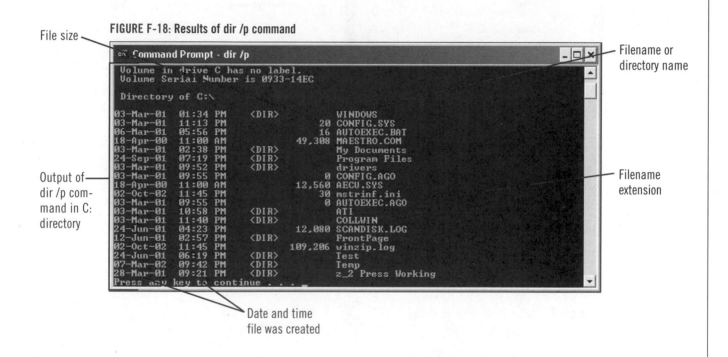

Date and time file was created

TABLE F-2: Common DOS commands (arguments are in italics)

command	purpose
cd *foldername*	Opens the folder named *foldername*
dir /p	Lists the contents of the current folder, one screen at a time if you use the /p argument
dir at*.doc	The asterisk is a wildcard and represents any number of characters in a filename. The command matches at back.doc, ati.doc, and atlm.doc
exit	Closes the Command Prompt window
more *filename*	Displays the contents of a file, one screen of output at a time
type *filename*	Displays the contents of the text file named filename

Practice

► Concepts Review

Label each element of the screen shown in Figure F-19.

FIGURE F-19

1. Which element optimizes a disk?
2. Which element deletes files from a disk?
3. Which element copies files from disk to disk?
4. Which element fixes and repairs a disk?
5. Which element accepts MS-DOS commands?
6. Which element copies files from disk to tape?

Match each term with the statement that describes its function.

7. **Reinstalls computer files**   a. Disk Cleanup
8. **Optimizes disk access**   b. Check Disk
9. **Deletes files**   c. Disk Defragmenter
10. **Stores files**   d. System Restore
11. **Finds and repairs disk errors**   e. Formatted disk

Select the best answers from the following lists of choices.

12. **Which option performs a disk format that removes all files from a disk and scans the disk for bad sectors?**
    a. Quick Format selected   c. Full Format selected
    b. Quick Format deselected   d. Full Format deselected

13. **When copying a floppy disk, the disks that you use do NOT need to be:**
   a. Formatted.
   b. The same size.
   c. The same type.
   d. Non write-protected.

14. **Which of the following locations is NOT a tool on the drive properties dialog box?**
   a. Error checking
   b. Defragmentation
   c. Maintenance
   d. Backup

15. **Which of the following is NOT a Check Disk function?**
   a. Finds damaged sections of a disk
   b. Moves data away from damaged sections of a disk
   c. Repairs damaged sections of a disk
   d. Physically repairs a damaged disk

16. **Disk defragmentation arranges:**
   a. Data files.
   b. Unused space.
   c. System files.
   d. All of the above.

17. **Which of the following is NOT a Disk Cleanup file type?**
   a. Program Files
   b. Recycle Bin
   c. Temporary files
   d. Temporary Internet files

18. **When you type the DOS command _more text.txt_, DOS:**
   a. Displays the contents of the file text.txt.
   b. Finds the file text.txt.
   c. Displays the contents of the file text.txt one screen at a time.
   d. Displays more information about the file text.txt.

▶ Skills Review

 If you are working in a lab, check with your instructor or technical support person for authorization to perform Steps 4-8; if you do not receive authorization, skip Steps 4-8.

1. **Format a disk.**
   a. Start Windows Explorer.
   b. Insert a disk in the floppy drive. (You can reuse the disk "Copy of Project Files Disk" that you created in this unit.)
   c. Right-click the drive icon containing your floppy disk, then click Format.
   d. Click the Quick Format check box to deselect it if necessary, click Start, then click OK in the warning box.
   e. Click OK in the message box, then click Close in the Format dialog box.
   f. Remove the formatted disk from the floppy drive.

2. **Copy a disk.**
   a. Insert the disk with your Project Files in the floppy drive.
   b. In Windows Explorer, right-click the floppy disk drive, then click Copy Disk.
   c. In the Copy Disk dialog box, click the drive containing the disk with your Project Files, click Start, then click OK in the message box.
   d. When prompted, remove the floppy disk with your Project Files, insert the blank disk you just formatted (not the disk with your Project Files) in the floppy drive, then click OK.
   e. Click Close in the Copy Disk dialog box when done and leave the disk in the floppy drive.

3. **Find and repair disk errors.**
   a. In Windows Explorer, right-click the drive icon containing your Project Files, then click Properties.
   b. Click the Tools tab, then click Check Now.
   c. Click the Automatically fix file system errors check box to select it.
   d. Click the Scan for and attempt recovery of bad sectors check box to select it, then click Start.

    e. Click OK in the message box, click OK in the Properties dialog box, then click the Close button.

    f. Remove the floppy disk, then insert your original disk containing your Project Files.

4. Defragment a disk.

    a. Start Disk Defragmenter.

    b. Click the hard disk drive (typically, the C: drive), then click Analyze.

    c. Click View Report, click Print, then click Print in the Print dialog box.

    d. Click Close in the Analysis Report dialog box, then click the Close button.

5. Cleanup a disk.

    a. Start Disk Cleanup.

    b. If necessary, click the drive list arrow, click the hard disk drive, then click OK.

    c. In the Files to delete list, click Temporary Internet Files (but not the check box), then click View Files.

    d. Click the Content window Close button.

    e. Click the check boxes next to any items with check marks to deselect the items. (Be sure to scroll through the entire list.) Click the Temporary Internet Files check box to select it.

    f. Click OK in the Disk Cleanup dialog box, then click Yes in the message box.

6. Restore computer settings.

    a. Start System Restore. Create a restore point with your name, then close System Restore.

7. Remove a program.

    a. Open the Add or Remove Programs window from the Control Panel.

    b. Open the Windows Components Wizard dialog box.

    c. Open the details for Accessories and Utilities, then open the details for Accessories.

    d. Deselect the Character Map check box if necessary, then complete the wizard to remove the program.

8. Add a program.

    a. Open the Add or Remove Programs window from the Control Panel.

    b. Open the Windows Components Wizard dialog box.

    c. Open the details for Accessories and Utilities, then open the details for Accessories.

    d. Select the Character Map check box.

    e. Insert a Windows XP installation disk or CD-ROM, then complete the wizard to add the program.

    f. Remove the installation CD-ROM, then close the Control Panel.

9. Enter DOS commands.

    a. Start Command Prompt.

    b. Type **cd c:\program files**, then press [Enter]. Type **dir /w**, then press [Enter].

    c. Type **exit**, then press [Enter].

▶ Independent Challenge 1

You own Wilkenson & Associates, an international public relations firm that specializes in overseas travel. You want to protect important company data from software viruses.

    a. Format a blank floppy disk using the Full Format type and the label Backup. You can use the copied disk you made in this unit if you want, but not the disk with your Project Files.

    b. Copy the files **2003 Income Projections** and **2003 Expense Budget** from the disk with your Project Files to a blank formatted disk.

    c. Scan the floppy disk for errors. Label the disk for easy identification.

► Independent Challenge 2

You are the network administrator at Robotz, Inc., a toy company that specializes in the production and distribution of robots. You want employees to update their computer systems with the latest Windows XP components. You check out the Windows Update Web site and determine which components you want the employees to install.

a. Start the Add/Remove Programs utility in the Control Panel. Connect to the Internet as necessary.

b. Click Add New Programs, then click Windows Update to access the Windows Update Web site in your browser.

c. Click the About Windows Update link. If you are starting Windows Update for the first time, you might be prompted to install additional software.

d. Click the Support Information link. Click the Pick updates to install link.

e. Display and print the Critical Updates page and the Windows XP page with the software updates for your Windows system.

f. Close the Add/Remove Programs window and the Control Panel.

g. Close your Web browser and disconnect from the Internet.

► Independent Challenge 3

You are a course developer at EZSoft Inc., a computer training company that specializes in training beginner- to expert-level software users. You are developing a new course on maintaining a computer. You are currently working on a lesson to teach students how to speed up disks by using the Windows system tools Check Disk and Disk Defragmenter.

a. Open WordPad, then create a document called **Win Tools Training** on the drive and folder where your Project Files are located that instructs students on how to use the Check Disk and Disk Defragmenter system tools.

b. Follow the steps in the WordPad document to check and defragment the hard disk drive (see your instructor or technical support person for authorization to defragment your hard disk), and take at least one print screen of the Check Disk and Disk Defragmenter window as you go through the material, and insert the picture in the WordPad document. To take a print screen of the current window and then insert it into the WordPad document, press [Alt][Print Screen] to copy the picture to the Clipboard, switch to the WordPad document, place the insertion point where you want the picture, then click the Paste button on the WordPad toolbar.

c. Save the document, print it, then close WordPad.

► Independent Challenge 4

You are an employee at an insurance firm. Since installing Windows XP, one of your DOS programs has been behaving erratically. To help figure out the problem, you need to display the autoexec.bat or config.sys file in DOS.

a. Click the Start button on the taskbar, point to All Programs, point to Accessories, then click Command Prompt.

b. Type **cd c:\Windows** at the DOS prompt, then press [Enter].

c. Type **More win.ini** at the DOS prompt, then press [Enter].

d. Press [Enter] to step through the file. (*Hint:* press [Ctrl] [C] to cancel at any time.)

e. Print the screen. (Press [Alt][Print Scrn] to make a copy of the window, open Paint, click Edit on the menu bar, click Paste to paste the screen into Paint, then click Yes to paste the large image, if necessary. Click the Text button on the Toolbox, click a blank area in the Paint work area, then type your name. Click File on the menu bar, click Page Setup, change 100 % normal size to 50% in the Scaling area, then click OK. Click File on the menu bar, click Print, then click Print.)

f. Press [Spacebar] to advance to the next screen if necessary, then type **exit** to return to Windows.

▶ Visual Workshop

Re-create the screen shown in Figure F-20, which shows the results of using the Disk Cleanup for (C:) dialog box. Print the screen. (See Independent Challenge 4, Step e for screen printing instructions.) If you are working in a lab, check with your instructor or technical support person for authorization to delete all the files in the Disk Cleanup for (C:) dialog box.

FIGURE F-20

Windows XP

Unit G

Exploring
the Internet with Microsoft Internet Explorer

Microsoft Internet Explorer 6, a component included with Windows XP, is a software program that helps you access the World Wide Web. In this unit, you learn about the benefits of the World Wide Web, examine the basic features of Internet Explorer 6, connect to the Internet, and access Web pages. Before you begin the lesson, check with your instructor or technical support person to see if it's possible for you to connect to the Internet. If not, simply read the lessons to learn about using Internet Explorer. Wired Coffee Company is a growing business that wants to take advantage of Internet technology. John uses Internet Explorer to open the company Web page and find information related to the coffee business.

Understanding the Internet and Web Browsers

The **Internet** is a global collection of more than 75 million computers (and growing) linked together to share information. The Internet's physical structure includes telephone lines, cables, satellites, and other telecommunications media, as depicted in Figure G-1. Using the Internet, computer users can share many types of information, including text, graphics, sounds, videos, and computer programs. The **World Wide Web** (also known as the Web or WWW) is a part of the Internet that consists of Web sites located on different computers around the world. A **Web site** contains Web pages linked together to make searching for information on the Internet easier. **Web pages** are documents that contain highlighted words, phrases, and graphics, called **hyperlinks** (or simply **links**) that open other Web pages when you click them. Some Web pages contain frames. A frame is a separate window within a Web page. Frames let you see more than one Web page at a time. Figure G-2 shows a sample Web page. **Web browsers** are software programs that you use to "browse the Web," or access and display Web pages. Browsers make the Web easy to navigate by providing a graphical, point-and-click environment. This unit features Internet Explorer 6, a popular browser from Microsoft that comes with Windows XP. Netscape (formally Netscape Navigator and Netscape Communicator) is another popular browser. John realizes that there are many uses for Internet Explorer in his company.

Internet Explorer will allow John to do the following:

▶ **Display Web pages from all over the world**
John can look at Web pages for business purposes, such as checking the pages of other coffee companies to see how they market their products.

▶ **Display Web content on his desktop**
John can make his desktop look and work like a Web page. John can display Web content, such as the Microsoft Investor Ticker, ESPN SportsZone, Expedia Maps Address Finder, or MSNBC Weather Map, directly on his desktop and have the content updated automatically.

▶ **Use links to move from one Web page to another**
John can click text or graphical links (which appear either as underlined text or as graphics) to move from one Web page to another, investigating different sources for information. Because a Web page can contain links to any location on the Internet, he can jump to Web pages all over the world.

▶ **Play audio and video clips**
John can click links that play audio and video clips, such as the sound of coffee grinding or a video of workers picking coffee beans. He can also play continuous audio and video broadcasts through radio and television stations over the Internet.

▶ **Search the Web for information**
John can use search programs that allow him to look for information about any topic throughout the world.

▶ **Make favorite Web pages available offline**
John can create a list of his favorite Web pages to make it easy for him to return to them at a later time. He can also make a Web page available offline. When he makes a Web page available offline, he can read its content when his computer is not connected to the Internet.

▶ **Print the text and graphics on Web pages**
If John finds some information or images that he wants to print, he can easily print all or part of the Web page, including the graphics.

FIGURE G-1: Structure of the Internet

Satellite connection

Phone line connection

Fiber-optic cable connection

FIGURE G-2: Sample World Wide Web page

Web page title
and browser
name

Graphic hyperlink   Text hyperlink

CLUES TO USE

The history of the Internet and World Wide Web

The Internet has its roots in the Advanced Research Projects Agency Network (ARPANET), which the United States Department of Defense started in 1969. In 1986, the National Science Foundation formed NSFNET, which replaced ARPANET. NSFNET expanded the foundation of the U.S. portion of the Internet with high-speed, long-distance data lines. In 1991, the U.S. Congress expanded the capacity and speed of the Internet further and opened it to commercial use.

The Internet is now accessible in over 300 countries. The World Wide Web was developed in Switzerland in 1991 to make finding documents on the Internet easier. Software programs designed to access the Web, known as Web browsers, use point-and-click interfaces. The first such Web browser, Mosaic, was introduced at the University of Illinois in 1993. Since the release of Mosaic, Microsoft Internet Explorer and Netscape have become the two most popular Web browsers.

Windows XP

Connecting to the Internet

Universities and large companies are most likely connected to the Internet via expensive, high-speed wiring that transmits data very quickly. Home computer owners, however, usually must rely on a modem and the phone lines already in place, as shown in Figure G-3. In some areas, **ISDN** (Integrated Services Digital Network) or **DSL** (Digital Subscriber Lines) **lines**, wires that provide a completely digital connection, or **cable modems**, which use cable television lines, are becoming available and affordable. DSL and cable modems, also known as **broadband** connections, are continually turned on and connected and use a network setup, so you don't need to establish a connection using a dial-up modem. Data travels slower over phone wires than over digital lines and cable modems. Whether you use a phone line or an ISDN or DSL line or cable modem, Windows can help you establish a connection between your computer and the Internet using the New Connection Wizard. First, you need to select an **ISP** (Internet Service Provider), which is a company that sets up an **Internet account** for you and provides Internet access. ISPs maintain servers connected directly to the Internet 24 hours a day. You pay a fee, sometimes by the hour, but more often a flat monthly rate. To connect to the Internet, you need to obtain an Internet account and connection information from your ISP or your system administrator. ➤ John has signed up with an ISP. He uses the New Connection Wizard to set up the service.

Trouble?

If the vocation information dislog box opens, enter the necessary user information, then click OK.

1. Click the **Start button**, point to **All Programs**, point to **Accessories**, point to **Communications**, then click **New Connection Wizard**
   The New Connection Wizard dialog box opens, displaying a welcome message. If your ISP provides you with an installation program that sets up the connection for you, install and run that program and skip this lesson.

2. Read the introduction, then click **Next**
   The next wizard dialog box asks you to choose a network connection type. You can choose to connect to the Internet (which is the default), the network at my workplace, an existing home or small office network, or another computer directly.

3. Click the **Connect to the Internet Option button** if necessary, then click **Next**
   The next wizard dialog box asks you to choose how you want to connect to the Internet. You can select from a list of ISPs, set up the connection manually, or use the CD from your ISP.

Trouble?

If you connect to the Internet through a network, follow your instructor's or technical support person's directions to establish your connection.

4. Click the **Set up my connection manually option button**, then click **Next**
   The next wizard dialog box asks you to choose how to connect to the Internet, as shown in Figure G-4. The first option helps you connect to the Internet using a dial-up modem, while the next two options help you connect using a broadband connection.

5. Click the **Connect using a dial-up modem option button**, then click **Next**

6. In the next wizard dialog box, type the name of your ISP in the text box, click **Next**, type the area code and telephone number of your ISP in the text box, then click **Next**
   Your ISP documentation provides the numbers you should use.

7. Type your **user name** in the User name text box, press **[Tab]**, type your **password**, press **[Tab]**, then type your **password** again
   Your ISP documentation provides you with the user name and password you should use. As you type the password, bullets appear instead of characters.

8. Click **Next**, then click **Finish** to complete the Internet connection

FIGURE G-3: Modem and phone line connection to the Internet

Modem inside your computer

Phone jack on the wall

Phone lines connect your computer to your ISP's server

Computers and networks on the Internet

Your ISP maintains a server directly connected to the Internet

FIGURE G-4: Selecting an Internet connection option

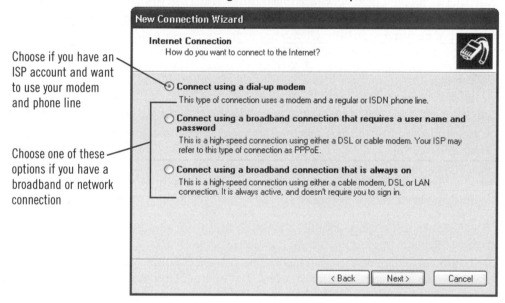

Choose if you have an ISP account and want to use your modem and phone line

Choose one of these options if you have a broadband or network connection

Sharing an Internet connection

If you have a home or small office network using Windows XP Professional, you can use Internet Connection Sharing (ICS) to connect all the computers on the network to the Internet using one connection, which saves you money on multiple connections. To enable ICS, click the Start button on the taskbar, point to All Programs, point to Accessories, point to Communications, click Network Setup Wizard to start the Network Setup Wizard, then follow the step-by-step wizard instructions.

Starting Internet Explorer

Internet Explorer is a Web browser that you use to search the World Wide Web. You can start Internet Explorer using the Start menu, the Internet Explorer icon on the desktop, or the button on the Quick Launch toolbar on the taskbar. After you start Internet Explorer, you might need to connect to the Internet by selecting a dial-up or broadband service and entering a user name and password. The elements of the Internet Explorer window allow you to view, print, and search for information on the Internet. Table G-1 describes the various elements of the Internet Explorer window. You can have more than one Internet service connection. One connection might provide your business Internet service, another might be for home or family use, and another might access a university or institutional account. Once you establish a connection to the Internet, you are ready to explorer Web pages on the Internet. ➤ Before John can take advantage of the many features of the World Wide Web, he must start Internet Explorer.

Steps

Trouble?
If Internet Explorer doesn't appear on the left column of the Start menu, it's available on the All Programs submenu.

1. Click the **Start button** on the taskbar, then click **Internet** (with Internet Explorer in gray below it) in the left column of the Start menu

Internet Explorer opens. If you connect to the Internet through a network, follow your instructor's or technical support person's directions to log on. If you connect to the Internet by telephone using a dial-up networking connection, you need to select a connection and enter your user name and password in the Dial-up Connection dialog box, as shown in Figure G-5. See your instructor or technical support person for this information.

Trouble?
If your computer is not connected to the Internet, check with your instructor or technical person to see if it's possible for you to connect.

2. If necessary, click the **Connect to list arrow**, select the name of your ISP from the previous lesson, type your **user name**, press **[Tab]**, type your **password**, then click **Connect**

Upon completion of the dial-up connection, you are connected to the Internet (unless an error message appears; if so, search for the Modem Troubleshooter in the Help and Support Center). A Connection icon 🖳 appears in the notification area on the taskbar to indicate you are connected. You can now view Web pages, check your e-mail, or use any other Windows communications features.

3. If necessary, click the **Maximize button** to maximize the Internet Explorer window

Internet Explorer displays a Web page, as shown in Figure G-6. The Web page on your screen will differ from the one shown in Figure G-6. Later in this unit, you will learn how to change the Web page that appears when you first start Internet Explorer.

Getting help with Internet Explorer

If you want information on a general topic or a specific task, you can find the information you are looking for in Microsoft Internet Explorer Help. To access Help, click Help on the menu bar, then click Contents and Index. The Microsoft Internet Explorer Help window appears and works in the same way Windows Help does. You can find help information you need by using a table of contents, index, or keyword search. If you need more help with Internet Explorer on the Web, you can click Help on the menu bar, then click Online Support. You can also get tips on how to use Internet Explorer more effectively. To display a tip, click Help on the menu bar, then click Tip of the Day. A Tip pane appears at the bottom of the Internet Explorer window. Read the tip, then click the Next tip link to display another tip. Click the Close button in the Tip pane to close the pane.

FIGURE G-5: Dial-up Connection dialog box

Dial-up connection name

Your user name and password will differ

Click button to change dial-up settings

FIGURE G-6: Elements of Internet Explorer window

Title bar

Menu bar

Address bar

Web page window; yours will differ

Status bar

Toolbar

Status indicator

Links bar

Go button

TABLE G-1: Elements of the Internet Explorer window

option	description
Title bar	Displays the name of the Web page and the name of the browser you are using at the top of the window
Menu bar	Provides access to a variety of commands, much like other Windows programs
Toolbar	Provides buttons for easy access to the most commonly used commands in Internet Explorer
Address bar	Displays the address of the current Web page or the contents of a local or network computer drive; you can also type the address of a site you want to visit in the Address bar, then press [Enter]
Go button	Displays the current Web address or Web search information about a particular topic in the Address bar
Links bar	Displays link buttons to Web pages on the Internet or to documents on a local or network drive
Status indicator	Located below the Close button; waves the Windows logo to indicate a new Web page is loading
Web page window	Displays the current Web page or the contents of a local or network computer drive; you may need to scroll down the page to view its entire contents
Status bar	Displays information about your connection progress with new Web pages that you open, including notification that you have connected to another site, the percentage of information transferred from that site, and locations of the links in the document window as you move your mouse pointer over them

Opening a Web Page and Following Links

You can open a Web page quickly and easily by entering a Web address in the Address bar. A **Web address** is a unique place on the Internet where you can locate a Web page. A Web address is also called a **URL**, which stands for **Uniform Resource Locator**. If you change your mind, or the Web page takes too long to **download**, or open on the screen, you can click the Stop button on the toolbar. If you stop a Web page while it is downloading, and the page doesn't completely open, you can click the Refresh button on the toolbar to update the screen. Often, Web pages connect to each other through links that you can follow to obtain more information about a topic, as shown in Figure G-7. A link can move you to another location on the same Web page, or it can open a different Web page altogether. To follow a link, simply click the highlighted word, phrase, or graphic. The mouse pointer changes to 🖑 when it is over a link. If you open a Web page written in different languages, Internet Explorer asks you to update your computer with character sets you need to view the page correctly. ➤ John contracts with a Web development company to create a Web site for Wired Coffee. He wants to access the Web site and follow some of its links in order to give feedback to the developer. John knows that the URL for the Web page is www.course.com/illustrated/wired/.

Steps

1. Click anywhere in the **Address bar**
   The current address is highlighted, and any text you type replaces the current address. If the current address isn't highlighted, select the entire address.

Trouble?

If you receive an error message, type one of the URLs listed in Table G-2 instead to open a Web page, then follow a link found on the Web page.

2. Type **www.course.com/downloads/illustrated/wired/**, then press **[Enter]**
   Be sure to type the address exactly as it appears. When you enter a Web address, Internet Explorer automatically inserts "http://" in the Address bar before the URL. The status bar displays the connection process. After downloading for a few seconds, the Web page appears in the document window.

3. Locate the **menu link** on the main page, then move the mouse pointer over the link, as shown in Figure G-8
   When you move the mouse pointer over a link, the mouse pointer changes to 🖑. This indicates that the text or graphic is a link. The address of the link appears in the Status bar.

QuickTip

To listen to media files and Internet radio stations using the Media bar while you browse the Web, click the Media button 🌐 Media on the toolbar.

4. Click the **menu link**
   The status indicator waves as you access and open the new Web page. The menu Web page appears in the document window.

5. Move the mouse pointer over the **Wired Coffee logo** in the upper-left corner, then click the **logo**
   The Wired Coffee Company page appears in the document window.

6. Click the **Back button** ⬅ Back on the toolbar
   The previous Web page, menu, appears in the document window.

QuickTip

To expand the document window to fill the screen, click View on the menu bar, then click Full Screen. Press [F11] to return to the normal view.

7. Click the **Forward button** ➡ on the toolbar
   The Wired Coffee Company page appears in the document window again. You also could have clicked the Wired Coffee logo link to return to the Wired Coffee Company page.

8. Click the **Back button list arrow** ⬅ Back ▾ on the toolbar, then click **Home Page**
   The Wired Coffee Home Page appears in the document window. Notice that when you have already visited a link, the color of the link changes.

FIGURE G-7: Web pages connected through links

Graphic link; click to jump
to InfoZone Web page

FIGURE G-8: Wired Coffee Company Web page

Graphic links appear
without any distin-
guishing marks

Mouse pointer changes to
a hand when positioned
over a link

Web page address

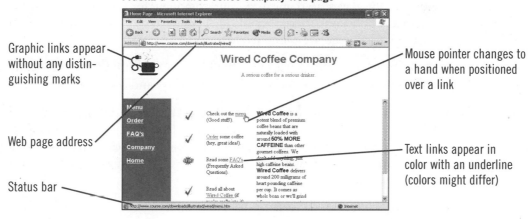

Text links appear in
color with an underline
(colors might differ)

Status bar

TABLE G-2: URLs of coffee companies' Web sites

company name	URL
Peet's Coffee & Tea	www.peets.com
Seattle's Best Coffee	www.seabest.com
Starbucks Coffee	www.starbucks.com

CLUES TO USE

Understanding a Web address

The address for a Web page is called a URL. Each Web page has a unique URL that is typically composed of four parts: the protocol (a set of rules that allows computers to exchange information), the location of the Web site, the name that maintains the Web site, and a suffix that identifies the type of site. A URL begins with a protocol, followed by a colon, two slashes, location of the Web site, a dot, name of the Web site, a dot, and a suffix. The Web site is the computer where the Web pages are located. At the end of the Web site name, another slash may appear, followed by one or more folder names and a filename. For example, in the address, http://www.course.com/downloads/illustrated/wired/main.htm, the protocol is *http* (HyperText Transfer Protocol), the location of the Web site is *www* (World Wide Web), the name of the Web site is *course*, and the suffix is *com* (a commercial organization); folders at that site are called */downloads/illustrated/wired*; and within the wired folder is a file called *main.htm*.

Windows XP

Adding a Web Page to the Favorites List

Rather than memorizing URLs or keeping a handwritten list of Web pages you want to visit, you can use a Favorites list to store and organize the addresses. When you display a Web page in your document window that you want to display again at a later time, you can add the Web page to your Favorites list. You add Web pages in the Internet Explorer window to your Favorites list in the same way you add folders in the My Computer or Windows Explorer window to the list. Once you add the Web page to the Favorites list, you can return to the page by opening your Favorites list and selecting the link to the page you want. ➤ John wants to add the Wired Coffee Web page to his Favorites list.

Steps

1. Click Favorites on the menu bar, then click Add to Favorites

The Add Favorite dialog box opens, as shown in Figure G-9. You have the option to make the Web page available for offline viewing. When you make a Web page available for **offline viewing**, the pages are copied to your computer for viewing after you disconnect your Internet connection. This is helpful when you want to read a Web page without worrying about how long you are connected to the Internet.

2. In the Name text box, select the current text, type Wired Coffee Company, then click OK

You name the Web page "Wired Coffee Company" and add it to your Favorites list.

QuickTip

You can browse folders on your hard disk drive and run programs from the Address bar. Click anywhere in the Address bar, then type the location of the folder or program. For example, typing "C:\Windows\" opens the Windows folder.

3. Click anywhere in the Address bar, type www.course.com, then press [Enter]

When you type a Web address in the Address bar, a feature called **AutoComplete** suggests possible matches from previous entries you made for Web addresses. If a suggestion in the list matches the Web address you want to enter, click the suggestion from the Address bar list, then press [Enter].

4. Click the Favorites button ☆ on the toolbar

The Explorer bar opens on the left side of the document window and displays the Favorites list. The Favorites list contains several folders, including a Links folder and individual favorite Web pages that come with Internet Explorer.

QuickTip

You can import favorites, known as bookmarks, from Netscape or another browser by clicking File on the menu bar, clicking Import and Export, then following the steps in the Import/Export wizard.

5. Click Wired Coffee Company in the Favorites list

The Wired Coffee Company Web page appears in the document window, as shown in Figure G-10. The Favorites list also includes folders to help you organize your Favorites list. You can click a folder icon in the Favorites list to display its contents.

6. Click the Links folder in the Favorites list

The Favorites list in the Links folder expands and appears in the Explorer bar, as shown in Figure G-11. To open a favorite in the Links folder, position the 🖑 pointer over the favorite you want to open, then click the mouse button.

7. Click the Links folder in the Favorites list again

The Favorites list in the Links folder collapses to display the Links folder icon only. If you no longer use a favorite, you can delete it from the Favorites list, as described in the Clues to Use "Organizing favorites."

FIGURE G-9: Add Favorite dialog box

Click check box to make Web page available offline

Displays the name of the Web page as it will appear in your Favorites list

Click button to save the current page in another folder

FIGURE G-10: Internet Explorer window with Favorites list

Explorer bar displays Favorites list

Folder to help organize your favorites

Individual favorites; your list might differ

Click button to close Explorer bar

FIGURE G-11: Links folder in Favorites list

Click folder to display or hide the Favorites list in the Links folder

Organizing favorites

If your list of favorites grows long, you can delete favorites you don't visit anymore or move favorites into folders. To delete and move your favorites, click Favorites on the menu bar, then click Organize Favorites. In the Organize Favorites dialog box, select one or more files from the Favorites list, then click the Delete button or the Move to Folder button. If you want to add a new folder to your Favorites list, click the Create Folder button, type the new folder name, then press [Enter]. If you prefer to use another name for a favorite, you can select the favorite you want to rename, click the Rename button, type the new name, then press [Enter]. When you finish making changes, click Close to exit.

Windows XP

Making a Web Page Available Offline

When you make a Web page available offline, you can read its content when your computer is not connected to the Internet or network. For example, you can view Web pages on your laptop computer when you have no Internet or network connection. Or, you might want to read Web pages at home but not want to tie up a phone line. When you make a Web page available offline, you save, or **synchronize**, the latest online version of your Web page on your hard disk drive for offline viewing. You can specify how much content you want available, such as an individual Web page or a Web page and all of its linked Web pages, and choose how you want to update that content on your computer. When you choose to view a Web page and all its linked pages offline, be aware that the additional linked pages take up a lot of hard drive space. ➤ John wants to make the Wired Coffee Company Web site on the Favorites list available for offline viewing. After viewing the offline version of the Web site, John updates the offline version to make sure he has the latest data.

QuickTip
To make the current Web page available offline, click Favorites on the menu bar, click Add to Favorites, click the Make available offline check box to select it, click Customize, follow the Offline Favorite Wizard instructions, click Finish, then click OK.

1. Click **Favorites** on the menu bar, then click **Organize Favorites**
   The Organize Favorites dialog box opens.

2. In the Favorites list, click **Wired Coffee Company**
   Status information about the Wired Coffee Company favorite appears in the Organize Favorites dialog box, as shown in Figure G-12.

3. Click the **Make available offline check box** to select it, then click **Close**
   The Synchronizing dialog box opens and synchronizes the Wired Coffee Company Web page, then the dialog box closes. The latest version of your Web page is now saved on your hard disk drive for offline viewing.

QuickTip
When you choose to work offline, Internet Explorer starts in offline mode until you click File on the menu bar, then click Work Offline again to clear the check mark.

4. Click the **Home button** 🏠 on the toolbar, click **File** on the menu bar, then click **Work Offline**
   You disconnect Internet Explorer from the Internet or network.

5. In the Favorites list, click **Wired Coffee Company**
   When you access the Wired Coffee Company Web site in offline mode, Internet Explorer displays the offline version of the Web page that is on your hard disk drive. You can view any offline Web page, but if you click a link to a Web page not available offline, Internet Explorer asks you to reconnect to the Internet or network.

6. Click **File** on the menu bar, then click **Work Offline** to deselect it
   When you re-establish the connection to the Internet or network, you can synchronize with the latest online version of the Wired Coffee Web page to update the offline version on your hard disk drive.

QuickTip
To specify a schedule for updating that page and how much content to download, select the link, then click Properties, then click the Schedule tab. You can also click Setup to schedule updating when you log on or log off your computer and when your computer becomes idle.

7. Click **Tools** on the menu bar, then click **Synchronize**
   The Items to Synchronize dialog box opens, as shown in Figure G-13. You can select which Web pages or files you want to synchronize and specify when and how you want them updated.

8. Click the **Wired Coffee Company check box** to select it if necessary, deselect all other check boxes if necessary, then click **Synchronize**
   The Synchronizing dialog box opens, then closes when the download is complete. The Wired Coffee Company Web page is resynchronized, with the latest online version of the Web page on your hard disk drive and ready for offline viewing.

9. Right-click **Wired Coffee Company** in the Favorites list, click **Delete**, click **Yes** to confirm the deletion to the recycle bin, then click the **Close button** in the Explorer bar

FIGURE G-12: Organize Favorites dialog box

Selected favorite

Favorites list

Status information about the selected favorite

Click check box to make the favorite available offline

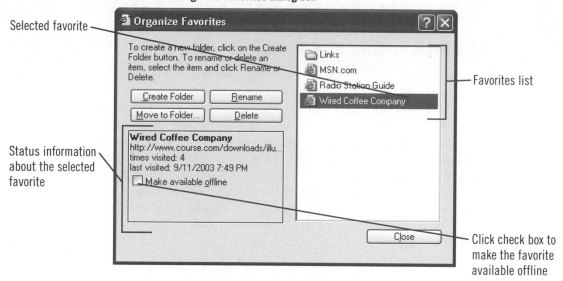

FIGURE G-13: Items to Synchronize dialog box

Select the items you want to synchronize

Click button to change offline synchronize settings

Click button to synchronize selected Web pages

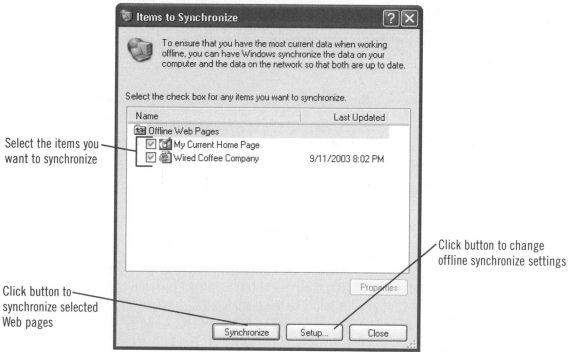

Saving a Web page and a Web graphic

If you want to view a Web page offline, but you don't ever need to update its content, such as a published article whose content will not change, you can save the page on your computer. There are several ways you can save the Web page, from just saving the text to saving all of the graphics and text needed to display that page as it appears on the Web. To save a Web page, click File on the menu bar, then click Save As. In the Save Web Page dialog box, specify the drive and folder in which you want to save the file, type the name you want for the file, click the Save as type list

arrow, select the file format type you want, then click Save. When you save a complete Web page, Internet Explorer saves all the graphic and text elements in a folder. If you want to save an individual graphic on a Web page, point to the graphic you want to save to display a toolbar on the graphic 🖫🖫🖿🖳, then click the Save this image button 🖫. If the toolbar doesn't appear, right-click the graphic, then click Save Picture As. You can also use the toolbar on a graphic to print 🖨 or e-mail 🖂 the graphic and open the My Pictures folder 🖳.

Changing Your Home Page and Adding a Link Button

Your **home page** in Internet Explorer is the page that opens when you start the program. When you first install Internet Explorer, the default home page is the Microsoft Network (MSN) Web site. If you want a different page to appear when you start Internet Explorer and whenever you click the Home button, you can change your home page. You can choose one of the millions of Web pages available through the Internet, or you can select a particular file on your hard drive. The Links bar, located to the right of the Address bar, provides easy access buttons to display Web pages. The Links bar comes with predefined buttons to Microsoft-related Web pages, but you can add or remove buttons, or change the Web pages associated with the buttons on the Links bar to customize it to meet your needs. John decides to change his home page to the Wired Coffee Company Web page and add a link button to the Links bar.

Steps 123 4

QuickTip

You change your home page back to www.msn.com in the Skills Review exercise at the end of this unit. If you want to change it back at any other time, type "www.msn.com" in the Address bar, press [Enter], then complete Steps 1 through 3 of this lesson.

1. Click **Tools** on the menu bar, click **Internet Options**, the Internet Options dialog box opens, then click the **General tab** if necessary
   The Internet Options dialog box, as shown in Figure G-14, allows you to change a variety of Internet Explorer settings and preferences. See Table G-3 for a description of each tab.

2. In the Home page section, click **Use Current**
   The address of the Wired Coffee Company Web page appears in the Address text box.

3. Click **OK**
   You associate the Home button on the toolbar with the current Web page, Wired Coffee Company.

4. Click the **FAQ's link**, then click the **Home button** 🏠 on the toolbar
   The home page appears in the document window.

Trouble?

If the Links bar doesn't move, you need to unlock it. Click View on the menu bar, point to Toolbars, then click Lock the Toolbars to deselect it.

5. Double-click the word **Links** on the Links bar
   The Links bar opens and may hide the Address bar. The Links bar contains buttons with links to Web pages. You can drag a link on a page or a Web site address in the Address bar to a blank area on the Links bar to create a new Links button.

6. Place 🖑 over the **Order link**, click the **left mouse button**, then drag the **Order link** on the main page to the left of the first button on the Links bar, the mouse pointer changes to a black bar to indicate the placement of the button, then release the mouse button
   A new link button appears on the Links bar with the name associated with the Web site, as shown in Figure G-15. You can delete or change the properties of a links button. Simply right-click the link button you want to change, then click the Delete or Properties command on the shortcut menu.

7. Click the **Order button** on the Links bar, then click the **Back button** ⬅ Back on the toolbar

8. Right-click the **Order button** on the Links bar, click **Delete**, then click **Yes** to confirm the deletion to the Recycle Bin
   The home page appears in the document window.

QuickTip

To display buttons on a hidden toolbar, click ⮟ on the right side of the toolbar.

9. Position the ⬉ pointer over the word **Links**, click the **Links bar**, the mouse pointer changes to ✛, drag the **Links bar** to the right to hide it, then relock the toolbars if previously locked

FIGURE G-14: Internet Options dialog box

Click button to use
current Web page
as home page

Click button to insert MSN
Web address in Address box

Click button to clear
current History list

Click arrows to change number of days
to keep a Web page in History list

FIGURE G-15: New button on Links bar

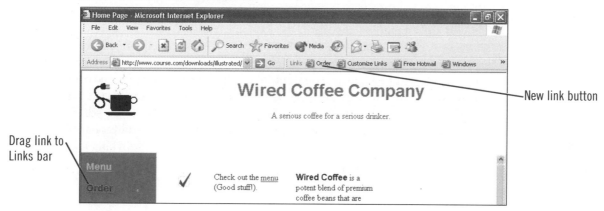

New link button

Drag link to
Links bar

TABLE G-3: Internet Options dialog box tabs

tab	allows you to
General	Change your home page, temporary file settings, and history settings
Security	Select security levels for different parts of the Internet
Privacy	Select privacy levels for cookie usage on your computer; a **cookie** is a file created by a Web site that stores information on your computer, such as your preferences, when visiting that site
Content	Set up a rating system for Internet content and personal information for typing Web addresses and buying items over the Internet
Connections	Change connection settings (phone and network)
Programs	Choose which programs (Mail, News, and Internet call) you want to use with Internet Explorer
Advanced	Change individual settings for browsing, multimedia, security, printing, and searching

CLUES TO USE

Viewing and maintaining a History list

Sometimes you run across a great Web site and simply forget to add it to your Favorites list. With Internet Explorer there's no need to try to remember all the sites you visit. The History feature keeps track of where you've been by date, site, most visited, or order visited today. To view the History list, click the History button 🕙 on the toolbar, then click a day or week in the Explorer Bar to expand the list of Web sites visited. Because the History list can grow to occupy a large amount of space on your hard drive, it's important that you control the length of time you retain Web sites in the list. Internet Explorer deletes the History list periodically, based on the settings you specify in the General tab of the Internet Options dialog box, as shown in Figure G-14.

Searching the Web

You can find all kinds of information on the Web. The best way to find information is to use a search engine. A **search engine** is a program you access through a Web site and use to search through a collection of Internet information to find what you want. Many search engines are available on the Web, such as MSN, AltaVista, Google, AOL Search, and Excite. When performing a search, the search engine compares the words or phrases, known as **keywords**, you submit that best describe what you want to retrieve, with words the search engine finds on various Web sites on the Internet. If it finds your keywords in the stored database, it lists the matched sites on a Web page. These matched sites are sometimes called **hits**. The company that manages the search engine determines what information its database stores, so search results of different search engines vary. ✎ John wants to search for other coffee-related Web sites to check out the competition.

Steps

QuickTip

To customize search options, click Change preferences in the Search Companion, click the options you want, then click OK if necessary.

1. Click the **Search button** 🔍 on the toolbar

The Search Companion appears in the Explorer bar, as shown in Figure G-16. You can select search options to find a personal or business address, display a list of links to previous searches, and find a map for a specific address. Each search option requires different search criteria, which is information related to what you want to find. To search for a Web page containing the information you want, you need to enter a keyword or words in the search text box. The more specific your search criteria, the better list of matches you receive from the search engine. You can also search directly from the Address bar. Type keywords in the Address bar, press [Enter], and Internet Explorer displays a list of sites that match what you are searching for.

QuickTip

To search for other items using a search engine, such as a file, computer, or person, click Search this computer for files in the Search Companion, then click the type of items in which you want to search.

2. In the text box, type **find coffee imports**

Now you're ready to start the search.

3. Click **Search** in the Search Companion

The search engine, in this case MSN, retrieves and displays a list of Web sites that match your criteria, as shown in Figure G-17. The total number of Web sites found is listed at the top. The search results appear in order of decreasing relevance. If the search results return too many hits, you should narrow the search by adding more keywords. As you add more keywords, the search engine finds fewer Web pages that contain all of those words. See Table G-4 for other techniques to narrow a search.

QuickTip

To perform a new search, click Start a new search at the bottom of the Search Companion.

4. Click any **link** to a Web site in the list of matches

The Web site that you open appears in the right pane of the document window. You can follow links to other pages on this Web site or jump to other Web sites. When you finish, close the Search Companion.

5. Click **Close button** in the Search Companion

The Search Companion closes.

6. Click the **Home button** 🏠 on the toolbar

You return to the Wired Coffee Company home page.

CLUES TO USE

Searching for people on the Web

Internet Explorer includes several directory services to help you find people you know who may have access to the Internet. To find a person on the Internet, click the Start button, click Search, click Computers or people, then click People in your address book to open the Find People dialog box, which shows a directory service, WhoWhere? in the Find People dialog box. Select the directory service you want to use, type the person's name, then click Find Now. Each directory service accesses different databases on the Internet, so if you don't find the person using the first service, try a different directory service.

FIGURE G-16: Explorer Bar with Search Companion

Type search criteria here

Click to search for other items

Click to change search options

Search animation character

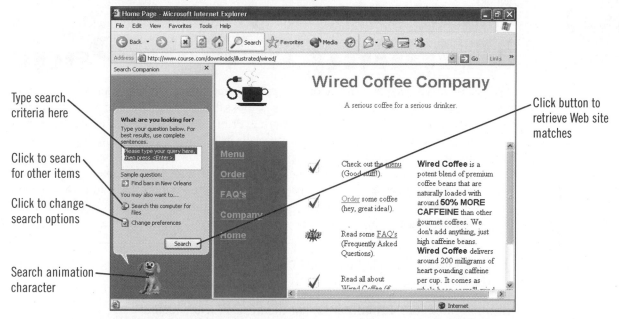

Click button to retrieve Web site matches

FIGURE G-17: Search results

Additional search options; yours might differ

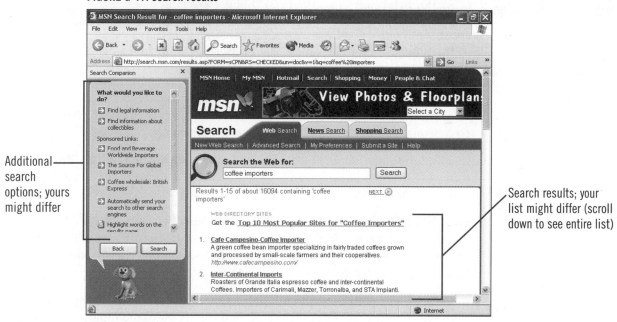

Search results; your list might differ (scroll down to see entire list)

TABLE G-4: Techniques to narrow a search

technique	example
Use descriptive, specific words	Beaches surfing Pacific
Use plain English phrases	Surfing beaches on the Pacific Ocean
Place exact phrases and proper names in quotes	"Sunset Beach"
Use a + sign between words your results must contain	Surf + beach
Use a - sign between words your results should not contain	Surf + beach - Atlantic
Use AND to find results containing all words	Surf AND sea AND sand
Use OR to find results containing at least one word	Surf OR beach

Windows XP

Previewing and Printing a Web Page

Web pages are designed for viewing on a computer screen, but you can also print all or part of one. Before you print, you should verify that the page looks the way you want. You save time, money, and paper by avoiding duplicate or wasteful printing. Print Preview shows you exactly how your Web page will look on the printed page. This is especially helpful when you have multiple pages to print. When you are ready to print, Internet Explorer provides many options for printing Web pages. For Web pages with frames, you can print the page just as you see it, or you can elect to print a particular frame or all frames. You can even use special Page Setup options to include the date, time, or window title on the printed page. You can also choose to print the Web addresses from the links contained on a Web page. ➤ John previews and prints a Web page, then exits Internet Explorer.

Steps

1. **Click File on the menu bar, then click Print Preview**
   The Print Preview window opens, as shown in Figure G-18.

2. **Click the Zoom Out button 🔍 on the Print Preview toolbar**
   The entire page appears in the Print Preview window.

QuickTip

You can also click the Print button 🖨 on the Internet Explorer toolbar to print the current page directly or click File on the menu bar, then click Print to open the Print dialog box.

3. **Click the Print button on the Print Preview toolbar**
   The Print dialog box opens, displaying the General tab, as shown in Figure G-19.

4. **In the Select Printer box, select the printer you want to use**

5. **Click the Pages option button**
   This option prints the pages specified, in this case, pages 1 to 1. The Print dialog box also gives you several options to print the frames. You can print the Web page as laid out on the screen, only the selected frame, or all frames individually.

6. **Click the Options tab, then click the As laid out on screen option button if necessary**
   Instead of handwriting links to a Web page, you can automatically print a list of the Web site addresses for each link.

7. **Click the Print table of links check box to select it, then click Print**
   The Print Preview window closes, and the Web page prints on the selected printer. You do not need to save the page before you exit because you only view documents with Internet Explorer; you do not create or change documents.

Trouble?

If you connect by telephone, you can right-click the Connect icon 🖥 in the notification area of the taskbar, then click Disconnect.

8. **Click the Close button in the Internet Explorer window**
   The Internet Explorer window closes. If you connected to the Internet by telephone, a disconnect dialog box opens. If you connected to the Internet through a network, follow your instructor's or technical support person's directions to close your connection.

9. **If the disconnect dialog box opens, click Disconnect**

FIGURE G-18: Preview a Web page

Click button to
print Web page

Click buttons to zoom
in or zoom out

Click button to close
Print Preview

Preview of Web page

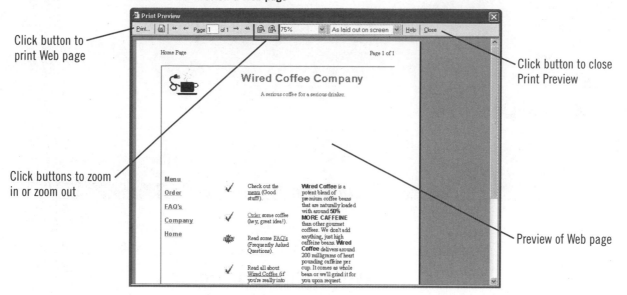

FIGURE G-19: Print dialog box

Click options to
select the pages
you want to print

Click icon to select a
printer; your printer
icons might differ

CLUES TO USE

Setting up the page format

When you print a Web page, you can use the Page Setup
dialog box to control the printing of text and graphics on
a page. The Page Setup dialog box, shown in Figure G-20,
specifies the printer properties for page size, orientation,
and paper source; in most cases, you won't want to
change them. From the Page Setup dialog box, you can
also change header and footer information. In the
Headers and Footers text boxes, you can type text to
appear as a header and footer of a Web page you print. In
these text boxes, you can also use variables to substitute
information about the current page, and you can combine text and codes. For example, if you type "Page &p of
&P" in the Header text box, the current page number
and the total number of pages print at the top of each
printed page. Check Internet Explorer Help for a complete list of header and footer codes.

FIGURE G-20: Page Setup dialog box

Practice

► Concepts Review

Label each element of the screen shown in Figure G-21.

FIGURE G-21

1. Which element displays status information?
2. Which element indicates a Web page is loading?
3. Which element represents a graphic link?
4. Which element represents a text link?
5. Which element displays the address of the current Web page?
6. Which element indicates the position of a link?

Match each term with the statement that describes its function.

7. Address bar	a. Spins as Internet Explorer loads a page
8. Toolbar	b. Displays the URL for the current page
9. Favorites button	c. Provides shortcuts for options on the menu bar
10. Status indicator	d. Displays a list of selected Web pages and folders to organize them
11. Back button	e. Displays the previously viewed page

Select the best answers from the following lists of choices.

12. **Software programs used to access and display Web pages are called:**
    a. Web sites.
    b. Search engines.
    c. Web utilities.
    d. Web browsers.

13. **If you want to save the name and URL of a Web page in Internet Explorer and return to it later, you can add it to a list called:**
    a. Favorites.
    b. Bookmarks.
    c. Home pages.
    d. Preferences.

14. **The international telecommunications network that consists of linked documents is called the:**
    a. NSFNET.
    b. Netscape Communicator.
    c. Internet Explorer.
    d. World Wide Web.

15. **In Internet Explorer, where are the buttons that perform common functions, such as moving to a previous Web page?**
    a. Address bar
    b. Toolbar
    c. Status bar
    d. Menu bar

16. **Which of the following is a valid URL?**
    a. http:/www.usf.edu/
    b. htp://www.usf.edu/
    c. htp:/ww.usf.edu/
    d. http//www.usf.edu/

17. **Underlined words that you click to jump to another Web page are called:**
    a. Explorers.
    b. Favorites.
    c. Web browsers.
    d. Hyperlinks.

18. **The URL of the current Web page appears in the:**
    a. Title bar.
    b. Document window.
    c. Address bar.
    d. Status bar.

▶ Skills Review

1. **Connect to the Internet.**
   a. Create a dial-up Internet connection using the New Connection Wizard.

2. **Start Internet Explorer.**
   a. Start Internet Explorer.
   b. Identify the toolbar, menu bar, Address bar, Links bar, status bar, status indicator, URL, document window, and scroll bars.
   c. In the toolbar, identify icons for searching, viewing favorites, viewing history, and moving to the previous page.

3. **Open a Web page and follow links.**
   a. Click in the Address bar, type **www.cnet.com**, then press [Enter].
   b. Explore the Web site by using the scroll bars, toolbar, and hyperlinks.
   c. Click in the Address bar, type **www.sportsline.com**, then press [Enter].
   d. Follow the links to investigate the content.

4. **Add a Web page to the Favorites list.**
   a. Click in the Address bar, type **www.loc.gov**, then press [Enter].
   b. Click Favorites on the menu bar, then click Add to Favorites.
   c. Click OK.
   d. Click the Favorites button.
   e. Click the Home button.
   f. Click the Library of Congress Home Page link in the Favorites list.

5. Make a Web page available offline.

   a. Click Favorites on the menu bar, then click Organize Favorites.

   b. In the Favorites list, click Library of Congress.

   c. Click the Make available offline check box to select it, then click Close.

   d. Click the Home button.

   e. Click File on the menu bar, then click Work Offline to select it. Click Stay Offline in the Message box if necessary.

   f. Click Library of Congress Home Page in the Favorites list.

   g. Click File on the menu bar, then click Work Offline to deselect it.

   h. Click Tools on the menu bar, then click Synchronize.

   i. Click the Library of Congress Home Page check to select it if necessary, then deselect all other check boxes if necessary.

   j. Click Synchronize.

   k. Right-click Library of Congress Home Page in the Favorites list, click Delete, then click Yes.

   l. Click the Close button in the Favorites list.

6. Change your home page and add a link button.

   a. Click in the Address bar, type www.msn.com (or your home page), then press [Enter].

   b. Click Tools on the menu bar, then click Internet Options.

   c. Click the General tab if necessary.

   d. Click Use Current.

   e. Click OK.

   f. Click the Back button.

   g. Click the Home button.

7. Search the Web.

   a. Click the Search button.

   b. Type job computer training in the text box.

   c. Click the Search button.

   d. Click a link to a Web site from the matches list.

   e. Click the Close button in the Search Companion.

   f. Click the Home button.

8. Preview and print a Web page.

   a. Click File on the menu bar, then click Print Preview.

   b. Click the Zoom Out button on the Print Preview toolbar.

   c. Click the Print button on the Print Preview toolbar.

   d. In the Select Printer box, click a printer.

   e. Click the Pages option button. Use the range 1-1.

   f. Click Print.

   g. Click the Close button to exit Internet Explorer.

   h. Click Yes to disconnect if necessary.

▶ Independent Challenge 1

You will soon graduate from college with a degree in business management. Before entering the workforce, you want to make sure that you are up-to-date on all advances in the field. You decide that checking the Web would provide the most current information. In addition, you can look for companies with employment opportunities.

a. Use Internet Explorer to investigate one or two of the business related sites from Table G-5, or search for other business sites if these are not available.

b. Click the necessary links on the page to locate information about employment opportunities that sound interesting to you.

c. When you find a promising page, print the page.

TABLE G-5: Business related sites

Career Builder	www.careerbuilder.com
College Grad	www.collegegrad.com
Small Business Solutions	www.bcentral.com

▶ Independent Challenge 2

You leave tomorrow for a business trip to France. You want to make sure that you take the right clothes for the weather and decide that the best place to check France's weather might be the Web.

a. Use Internet Explorer to access one or two of the weather sites from Table G-6, or search for other weather sites if these are not available.

b. Click the necessary links on the page to locate information about the weather in Paris.

c. Print at least two reports on the Paris weather.

TABLE G-6: Weather sites

The Weather Channel	www.weather.com
National Weather Service	www.nws.noaa.gov
CNN Weather	www.cnn.com/WEATHER

▶ Independent Challenge 3

Your boss wants to buy a new desktop computer (as opposed to a laptop). He assigns you the task of investigating the options. You decide that looking on the Web would be more expedient than visiting computer stores in the area.

a. Use Internet Explorer to visit two of the Web sites from Table G-7, or search for other computer company sites if these are not available.

b. Click the necessary links to find a page from each of the two that you think offer the best deal.

c. Add the pages to your favorites.

d. Make the pages available offline and synchronize them.

e. Print a page from each of the two that you think offer the best deal.

f. Delete the two favorites.

TABLE G-7: Computer companies' Web sites

IBM	www.ibm.com
Apple	www.apple.com
Dell	www.dell.com
Gateway	www.gateway.com

▶ Independent Challenge 4

During the summer, you want to travel to national parks in the United States. Use one of the Search Companions through your Web browser to find Web sites with maps of the national parks. Visit four or five sites from the match list, and print a page from the one that you think offers the best maps and related information for park visitors.

► Visual Workshop

Re-create the screen shown in Figure G-24, which displays the Internet Explorer window with the Favorites list and a Web site. Print the Web page, then print the screen. (Press [Print Screen] to make a copy of the screen, open Paint, click Edit on the menu bar, click Paste to paste the screen into Paint, then click Yes to paste the large image, if prompted. Click the Text button on the Toolbox, click a blank area in the Paint work area, then type your name. Click File on the menu bar, click Page Setup, change 100% normal size to 50% in the Scaling area, then click OK. Click File on the menu bar, click Print, then click Print.)

FIGURE G-22

Exchanging

Mail and News

Objectives

► Start Outlook Express

► Explore the Outlook Express window

► Add a contact to the Address Book

► Compose and send e-mail

► Retrieve, read, and respond to e-mail

► Manage e-mail messages

► Select a news server

► View and subscribe to a newsgroup

► Read and post a news message

 If you are not connected to the Internet and do not have an e-mail account, you cannot work through the steps in this unit; however, you can read the lessons without completing the steps to learn what you can accomplish using Outlook Express.

Windows XP includes Microsoft Outlook Express 6, a powerful program for managing **electronic mail**, known as e-mail. With an Internet connection and Microsoft Outlook Express, you can exchange e-mail messages with anyone on the Internet and join any number of **newsgroups**, collections of e-mail messages on related topics posted by individuals to specified Internet locations. ◄───── John Casey, owner of the Wired Coffee Company, uses Outlook Express to send and receive e-mail messages and join a newsgroup about the coffee industry.

Starting Outlook Express

Whether you want to exchange e-mail with colleagues and friends or join newsgroups to trade ideas and information, Outlook Express provides you with the tools you need. When you install Windows XP, a menu item for Outlook Express appears on the left column of the Start menu and the All Programs submenu. If your computer is not connected to the Internet or you do not have an e-mail account, check with your instructor or technical support person to see if it's possible for you to connect or set up an e-mail account. Otherwise, read through the lessons in this unit without completing the steps. John wants to use Outlook Express to exchange e-mail with his employees.

1. **If necessary, establish a connection to the Internet via the network or telephone**
   If you connect to the Internet through a network, follow your instructor's or technical support person's directions to establish your connection. If you connect by telephone, create a new connection using the New Connection Wizard to establish your connection or use an existing dial-up networking connection. To start the New Connection Wizard, click the Start button on the taskbar, point to All Programs, point to Accessories, point to Communications, then click New Connection Wizard.

2. **Click the Start button on the taskbar, then click E-mail (with Outlook Express in gray below it) in the left column of the Start menu**
   The Outlook Express window opens and displays the Outlook Express Start Page, as shown in Figure H-1. Depending on past use, your folders and contacts may differ. If you connect to the Internet through a network, follow your instructor's or technical support person's directions to log on. If you connect to the Internet by telephone using a dial-up networking connection, you might need to enter your user name and password. See your instructor or technical support person for this information.

3. **If necessary, click the Connect to list arrow, select the name of your ISP, type your user name, press [Tab], type your password, then click Connect**
   Upon completion of the dial-up connection, you are connected to the Internet (unless an error message appears; if so, search for the Modem Troubleshooter in the Help and Support Center). When you start Outlook Express for the first time, you need to use the Set up a Mail account link on the Start Page to start the Internet Connection Wizard and enter your e-mail account set-up information. See your instructor or technical support person for this information.

4. **If available, click the Set up a Mail account link on the Start Page, in the Internet Connection Wizard dialog box type your name, click Next, type your e-mail address, click Next, select an incoming mail server type, type the name of the incoming mail server, type the name of the outgoing server, click Next, type your e-mail account name, type your password, click Next, then click Finish**
   Your mail account is set up. The Set up a Mail account link is replaced on the Start Page in the E-mail area with the Read Mail and new Mail message links.

5. **If necessary, click the Maximize button to maximize the Outlook Express window**

Trouble?
If Outlook Express doesn't appear on the left column of the Start menu, it's available on the All Programs submenu.

Trouble?
If the Internet Connection Wizard opens, follow the step-by-step instructions to setup your e-mail account.

QuickTip
To modify or add an account, click Tools on the menu bar, click Accounts, click an account, then click Properties, or click Add, click an account type, then follow the wizard instructions.

FIGURE H-1: Outlook Express window with Start Page

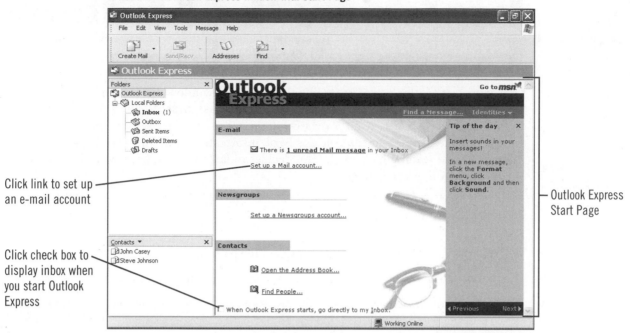

Click link to set up an e-mail account

Click check box to display inbox when you start Outlook Express

Outlook Express Start Page

Understanding e-mail account information

Before you can set up an e-mail account, you need your account name, password, e-mail server type, and the names of your incoming and outgoing e-mail servers from your ISP or network administrator. The Internet Connection Wizard helps you connect to one or more e-mail servers. Outlook Express allows you to send and retrieve e-mail messages from different types of **e-mail servers,** which are the locations where your e-mail is stored before you access it. Outlook Express supports three types of incoming e-mail servers: **POP3** (Post Office Protocol), **IMAP** (Internet Message Access Protocol), and **HTTP** (Hypertext Transfer Protocol). A **Protocol** is a set of

rules and standards that control the transmission of content, format, sequencing, and error management for information over the Internet or network like rules of the road govern the way you drive. POP3 servers allow you to access e-mail messages from a single Inbox folder, while IMAP servers allow you to access multiple folders. HTTP servers are used on Web sites, such as Hotmail, and allow you to send and receive e-mail messages in Outlook Express or on a Web site. When you use POP3 or IMAP e-mail servers, you also need to provide an outgoing e-mail server. **SMTP** (Simple Mail Transfer Protocol) is generally used to send messages between e-mail servers.

Starting Outlook Express from your Web browser

You can set Outlook Express as your default e-mail program, so that whenever you click an e-mail link on a Web page or choose the mail command in your Web browser, Outlook Express opens. You can also set Outlook Express as your default news reader, so that when you click a newsgroup link on a Web page or choose the news reader command in your Web browser, Outlook Express opens. To set Outlook Express as your default e-mail or newsgroup

program, start Internet Explorer, click Tools on the menu bar, click Internet Options, click the Programs tab, click either the E-mail or Newsgroups list arrow, click Outlook Express, then click OK. In Internet Explorer, you can click the Mail button on the toolbar, then click Read Mail to check your e-mail or click Read News to check your newsgroup messages in Outlook Express.

Windows XP

Exploring the Outlook Express Window

After you start Outlook Express, the Outlook Express window displays the Outlook Express Start Page, as shown in Figure H-2. The **Outlook Express Start Page** displays tools that you can use to read e-mail, set up a newsgroup account, read newsgroup messages, compose e-mail messages, enter and edit Address Book information, and find people on the Internet. Before reading his e-mail, John decides to familiarize himself with the components of the Outlook Express window.

He notes the following features:

► The **title bar** at the top of the window displays the name of the program.

► The **menu bar** provides access to a variety of commands, much like other Windows programs.

► The **Toolbar** provides icons, or buttons, for easy access to the most commonly used commands. See Table H-1 for a description of each toolbar button. These commands are also available on menus.

► The **Go to MSN link** opens your default Web browser program and displays the MSN Web page.

► The **Folders list** displays folders where Outlook Express stores e-mail messages. You can also use folders to organize your e-mail messages.

► The **Contacts list** displays the contact names in the Address Book.

► The **new Mail message link** opens the New Message dialog box, where you can compose and send e-mail messages.

► The **Read Mail link** jumps to the Inbox, where you can read and reply to incoming e-mail messages.

► The **Set up a Newsgroups account link** creates a newsgroup account and appears instead of the Read News link if you have not set up a newsgroup account using the Internet Connection Wizard.

► The **Read News link** connects to newsgroups that you can view and subscribe to, and appears instead of the Set up a Newsgroup account link if you have already set up a newsgroup account.

► The **Open the Address Book link** opens the Address Book, where you can enter and edit your contacts list.

► The **Find People link** opens the Find People dialog box, where you can search for people on the Internet or in your Address Book.

► The **Tip of the day** pane appears on the right side of the window and displays an Outlook Express tip; click Next and Previous at the bottom of the pane to move between the tips.

► The **status bar** displays information about your Internet connection with a mail or news group server.

FIGURE H-2: Outlook Express window with Start Page

Title bar

Menu bar

Toolbar

Folders list; your list might differ

Contacts list; your list might differ

Go to MSN link

Outlook Express Start Page links

Click links to display an Outlook Express tip

Status bar

TABLE H-1: Outlook Express Start Page toolbar buttons

button	name	description
	Create Mail	Opens the e-mail message composition window
	Send/Recv	Sends e-mail messages and checks for new messages
	Addresses	Opens the Address Book
	Find	Finds e-mail messages, text in an e-mail message, or people on the Internet

CLUES TO USE

Getting help in Outlook Express

If you need help connecting to the Internet to get mail or learning how to use Outlook Express features, you can get help from several different sources. To get Outlook Express Help, you can use the Help system that comes with the program or view Outlook Express Web sites on the Internet. To open Outlook Express Help, click Help on the menu bar, then click Contents and Index. To learn more about Outlook Express from Web sites on the Internet, click Help on the menu bar, point to Microsoft on the Web, then click Product News. Your browser starts and displays the Outlook Express Web site.

Windows XP

Adding a Contact to the Address Book

A **contact** is a person or company that you communicate with. You can store a contact's information, such as the contact's title, street address, phone number, and personal Web page address, in the **Address Book**. You can organize your contacts into **contact groups**, which are groups of related people with whom you communicate regularly, or into folders. ➤ John wants to add a new employee to his Address Book.

Steps

QuickTip

You can also click the Addresses button 📖 on the toolbar to open the Address Book.

1. **Click the Open the Address Book link on the Outlook Express Start Page**
   The Address Book window opens, as shown in Figure H-3, displaying the current contacts in the Address Book. The Address Book toolbar is above the list of contacts. See Table H-2 for a description of each toolbar button. These commands are also available on the menu bar.

2. **Click the New button 🖼️▾ on the Address Book toolbar, then click New Contact**
   The Properties dialog box opens, displaying the Name tab. On the Name tab, you enter name and e-mail information. You can use other tabs to enter additional information.

3. **Type Shawn in the First text box, press [Tab] twice, then type Brooks in the Last name text box**
   The name of the new contact appears in the Display text box as it will appear in the contacts list, unless you click the Display list arrow and choose a different name.

QuickTip

Once you add an e-mail address to the Address Book, click Edit to modify it. If an e-mail address is no longer in use, click Remove to delete it.

4. **Click in the E-Mail Addresses text box, type shawnbrooks@course.com, then click Add**
   The e-mail address appears in the box below the E-Mail Addresses text box, as shown in Figure H-4. E-mail addresses are not case-sensitive, so capitalization doesn't matter, and they cannot contain spaces. The e-mail address includes the text "(Default E-Mail)," which indicates this e-mail address is the one used if a contact has multiple e-mail addresses.

5. **Click OK**
   The Properties dialog box closes, and you return to the Address Book.

QuickTip

To create a contact group, click the New button on the Address Book toolbar, click New Group, type a group name, click Select Members, double-click names from the Address Book, click OK, then click OK again.

6. **Click any contact in the right pane, then position the mouse pointer over Shawn Brooks in the Address Book to display a ScreenTip**
   To remove the ScreenTip, move the mouse pointer, or wait a moment and it will close on its own. To edit a contact, double-click anywhere on the contact's entry in the Address Book.

7. **Double-click Shawn Brooks in the Address Book**
   The Shawn Brooks Properties dialog box opens and displays the selected contact's information.

8. **Click the Business tab, click in the Phone text box, type 925-555-3084, then click OK**
   Shawn's business phone number appears in the Address Book. Scroll, if necessary, to view it.

9. **Click the Close button in the Address Book window**

FIGURE H-3: Address Book window

Address Book toolbar

Folders and groups of contacts for use on a shared computer

Type name here to find contact

Current contacts; your list might differ or be blank

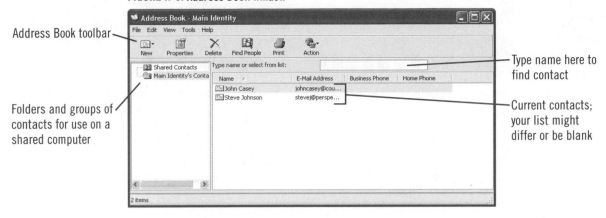

FIGURE H-4: Properties dialog box with new contact

Enter e-mail address here

Enter name information here

Click button to add e-mail address after typing it in text box

Click buttons to edit or delete e-mail address

E-mail address added here

TABLE H-2: Address Book toolbar buttons

button	name	description
	New	Creates a new contact, group, or folder
	Properties	Opens property information for the selected contact
	Delete	Deletes the selected contact
	Find People	Finds people in the Address Book or on the Internet
	Print	Opens the Print dialog box
	Action	Sends mail, dials a connection, or places an Internet call

CLUES TO USE

Printing contacts from the Address Book

You can print your contact information in a variety of formats, such as Memo, Business Card, and Phone List. The Memo style prints all the information you have for a contact with descriptive titles. The Business Card style prints the contact information without descriptive titles. The Phone List style prints all the phone numbers for a contact or for all your contacts. To print contact information, open the Address Book, select a specific contact (if desired), click the Print button 🖨 on the toolbar, select a print range, print style, and the number of copies you want to print, then click Print in the Print dialog box.

Composing and Sending E-mail

E-mail is becoming the primary form of written communication for many people. E-mail messages follow a standard memo format, with fields for the sender, recipient, date, and subject of the message. To send an e-mail message, you need to enter the recipient's e-mail address, type a subject, then type the message itself. You can send the same message to more than one individual, to a contact group, or to a combination of individuals and groups. You can personalize your e-mail messages and newsgroup messages with stationery templates, or you can design your own stationery. ◄■■■ John wants to send an e-mail message to the new employee whose contact information he added to the Address Book in the previous lesson.

Steps 1 2 3 4

1. Click the **Create Mail list arrow** ⬚ ▾ on the toolbar, click **Clear Day** or another available stationery, then click the **Maximize button** in the message window if necessary
The New Message window opens and is maximized, as shown in Figure H-5, displaying the Clear Day stationery in the message box.

2. Click the **To button** 📖 next to the To text box
The Select Recipients dialog box opens, as shown in Figure H-6, displaying the contacts from the Address Book.

3. Scroll in the list of contacts if necessary, click **Shawn Brooks**, then click **To**
The contact's name, Shawn Brooks, appears in the Message recipients To box. You can also add additional recipients to this list, select another recipient and click the **Cc (carbon copy)** button to send a copy of your e-mail message to that person, or click the **Bcc (blind carbon copy)** button to send a copy of your e-mail message to another person whose name will not appear in the e-mail message. Bcc is useful when sending e-mails to a large group of unrelated people, and allows for privacy for the recipients.

4. Click **OK**
Shawn's name appears in the To text box. Shawn's e-mail address is associated with the name selected even though it does not appear. You include a subject title.

5. Click in the **Subject text box**, then type **Welcome aboard!**
The message title bar changes from New Message to the subject text "Welcome aboard!" Since the subject text is the first information the recipient sees about the e-mail, it should provide a short, concise summary of the message contents.

6. Click the first line in the **text box** at the bottom of the message window
The Formatting toolbar is now activated and appears just below the Subject text box.

7. Type **Dear Shawn:**, press **[Enter]** twice, type **I would like to welcome you to the Wired Coffee Company. We are excited that you have joined our team. Wired Coffee is a growing company, and I believe your contributions will make a big difference. Please come to a luncheon for new employees this Thursday at 12:30 in the company cafe.**, press **[Enter]** twice, then type **John**

8. Click the **Send button** 📧 on the toolbar, then click **OK** in the information box if necessary
The New Message window closes. The e-mail message is placed temporarily in the Outbox, a folder for storing outgoing messages, then it is sent automatically to the recipient. A copy of the outgoing message remains in the Sent Items folder so that you can reference the message later. To send a message later, click File on the menu bar, then click Send Later. To send, open the Outbox, then click 📧.

QuickTip
To create a new message without stationery, you can click the New Mail button on the toolbar, click the new Mail message link in the Outlook Express window, or double-click a name in the Contacts list.

QuickTip
To remove a name from the Message recipients list, click the person's name in the Message recipients list box, then press [Delete].

QuickTip
To save an incomplete message, click File on the Menu bar, then click Save. The e-mail message is saved with the name of the subject and placed in the Drafts folder.

FIGURE H-5: New Message window with Clear Day stationery

Click button to select recipient from Address Book

Click text box to enter subject text

Click here to begin typing message

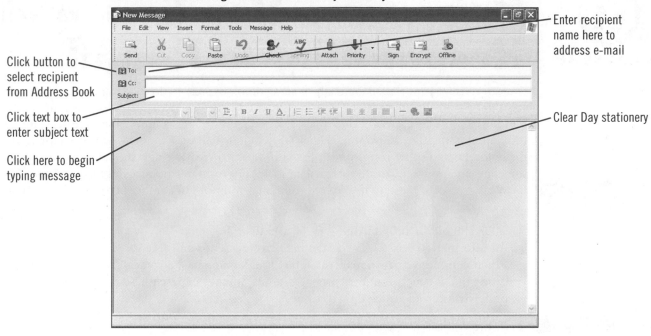

Enter recipient name here to address e-mail

Clear Day stationery

FIGURE H-6: Selecting recipients for e-mail message

Enter name here to find recipient, or click the Find button

Folder location of addresses

Select a contact from this list; your list might differ

Click button to move contact to recipient list

Recipient(s) for this message appear here

CLUES TO USE

Attaching a file to an e-mail message

You can easily share a file, such as a picture or a document, using e-mail by attaching it to an e-mail message. Upon receiving the e-mail, the recipient can open the file in the program that created it or save it on disk. For example, suppose that you are working on a report that you created using WordPad and that a colleague working in another part of the country needs to present the report today. After you finish the report, you can attach the report file to an e-mail message and send the message to your colleague, who can then open, edit, and print the report. To attach a file to an e-mail message, create the message, click the Attach button 🔖 on the toolbar in the Insert Attachment dialog box, navigate to the drive and folder location of the file you want to attach, select the file, then click Attach.

Retrieving, Reading, and Responding to E-mail

You can retrieve your e-mail manually or set Outlook Express to do so automatically. New messages appear in the Inbox along with any messages you haven't stored elsewhere or deleted. **Message flags** may appear next to a message. See Table H-3 for common message flags. You can respond to a message in two ways: either reply to it, which creates a new message addressed to the sender(s) and other recipients, or forward it, which creates a new message you can send to someone else. In either case, the original message appears in the message response. ✎ John forwards an e-mail message he received from Shawn Brooks to another person at the company.

Steps 1 2 3 4

1. Click the **Send/Recv button** 📧 on the toolbar
   An information box displays as Outlook Express sends and receives your e-mail messages. When you receive new e-mail, the Inbox folder name in the Folders list is boldfaced, indicating that it contains unread messages, and a number in parentheses indicates the number of newly received e-mail messages.

> **QuickTip**
>
> To display the Inbox when you start Outlook Express, click the When Outlook Express starts, go directly to my Inbox check box on the Outlook Express Start Page.

2. In the Folders list, click **Inbox**
   The Inbox folder opens. The **preview pane** displays the messages in your Inbox. The **display pane** displays the e-mail message selected in the preview pane. E-mail messages that appear with boldfaced subject or heading text are ones you have not opened.

3. Click the **message** you received from Shawn Brooks, as shown in Figure H-7
   The display pane displays the e-mail message from Shawn Brooks selected in the preview pane.

> **Trouble?**
>
> If you didn't receive a message from Shawn Brooks, click the Send/Recv button on the toolbar again. It may take a few minutes for the message to arrive.

4. Double-click the **message** you received from Shawn Brooks in the preview pane, then click the **Maximize button** in the message window if necessary
   When you receive a short message, you can quickly read it by clicking the message and then reading the text in the display pane. Longer messages are easier to read in a full window instead of in the display pane. You can reply to the author, reply to all recipients, forward the message, or simply close or delete the message.

> **QuickTip**
>
> To print an e-mail message, open the message, then click the Print button 🖨 on the message window toolbar.

5. Click the **Forward button** 📧 on the message toolbar, then click the **Maximize button** in the message window if necessary
   The Forward Message window opens, as shown in Figure H-8, displaying the original e-mail subject title in the Subject text box with the prefix "Fw:" (short for Forward) and the original message you sent in the message box. You can add additional text to the message.

6. Click in the upper-left corner of the message box, then type **Please add Shawn Brooks to Thursday's luncheon guest list.**

> **Trouble?**
>
> If you don't know an e-mail address to send the forwarded message to, click the Close button in the message window, then continue to the next lesson.

7. Click the **To text box**, type the e-mail address of your instructor, technical support person, or someone else you know, then click the **Send button** 📧 on the toolbar
   You send the e-mail message. To verify that your message was sent, view the Sent Items folder. If the recipient of the e-mail message is a contact in the Contacts list, you can type the name of the recipient instead of the e-mail address in the To text box. As you type a recipient name, **AutoComplete** suggests possible matches from the Contacts list. Click the suggestion from the list that matches the contact you want.

8. In the Folders list, click **Sent Items** to display e-mail messages you have sent

9. In the Contacts list, right-click **Shawn Brooks**, click **Delete**, then click **Yes**

FIGURE H-7: Outlook Express window with Inbox

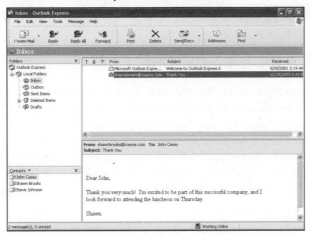

FIGURE H-8: Forward Message window

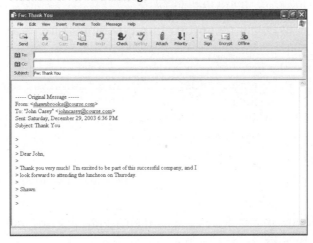

TABLE H-3: Mail message flag icons

icon	description	icon	description
	Unread message; message heading text appears bold		One or more files attached to message
	Read message		Sender marked message as high priority
	Replied to message		Sender marked message as low priority
	Forwarded message		

Checking the spelling and content in e-mail messages

Before you send an e-mail message, you should spell check the text and read through the content to make sure your spelling is accurate and your content conveys the message you want to the recipient(s). If you have Microsoft Word, Microsoft Excel, or Microsoft PowerPoint installed on your computer, Outlook Express uses the spelling checker from the program to spell check your e-mail messages. If you do not have one of these programs installed, the Spelling command is not available, and you need to check spelling manually. To start the spell checker, type your e-mail message, click Tools on the menu bar, then click Spelling. To have Outlook Express automatically check all of your e-mail messages before sending them, display the Outlook window, click Tools on the menu bar, click Options, click the Spelling tab in the Options dialog box, click the Always check spelling before sending check box to select it, then click OK.

Managing E-mail Messages

A common problem with using e-mail is an overcrowded Inbox. To keep your Inbox organized, you should move messages you want to save to other folders and subfolders, delete messages you no longer want, and create new folders as you need them. Storing incoming messages in other folders and deleting unwanted messages makes it easier to see the new messages you receive and to keep track of messages to which you have already responded. ➤ John wants to create a new folder for his important messages in the Local Folders location, move a message from the Inbox to the new folder, then delete the messages he no longer needs.

Steps 1 2 3 4

1. **Click File on the menu bar, point to New, then click Folder**
   The Create Folder dialog box opens, displaying the list of folders contained in the Outlook Express folder, as shown in Figure H-9.

2. **Click in the Folder name text box, type Important, then click Local Folders in the Folders list**
   You name the new folder Important, and it will appear in the Folders list under Local Folders. To create a **subfolder** (a folder in a folder), you select one of the folders in the Folders list under Local Folders. The Folders list works like the left pane of Windows Explorer. When you create a subfolder, the Expand Indicator ⊞ appears next to the name of the folder that contains the subfolder.

3. **Click OK**
   The new folder, Important, appears in the Folders list under Local Folders at the bottom of the list.

> **QuickTip**
> To delete a message, select the message in the preview pane, then click the Delete button ✕ on the toolbar.

4. **Click Inbox in the Folders list, then right-click the message you received from Shawn Brooks in the preview pane of the Inbox**
   A shortcut menu appears, displaying commands, such as Move to Folder, Copy to Folder, Delete, Print, and Add Sender to Address Book, to help you manage your e-mail messages.

5. **Click Move to Folder on the shortcut menu**
   The Move dialog box opens, allowing you to specify the folder where you want to move the selected message.

> **QuickTip**
> To move a message to a folder, drag the message from the preview pane to the folder in the Folders list.

6. **Click the Important folder, then click OK**

7. **In the Folders list, click the Important folder**
   The e-mail message you just moved appears in the preview and display panes, as shown in Figure H-10.

> **QuickTip**
> To sort messages by sender, subject, date, priority or flag, click a header in the preview pane.

8. **In the Folders list, right-click the Important folder, click Delete, then click Yes to confirm the deletion**
   You place the Important folder in the Deleted Items folder. The Deleted Items folder works just like the Recycle Bin. The folder temporarily stores deleted messages until you automatically or manually delete them.

9. **In the Folders list, right-click the Deleted Items folder, click Empty 'Deleted Items' Folder, then click Yes to confirm the deletion**
   You permanently delete the Important folder and all of its contents.

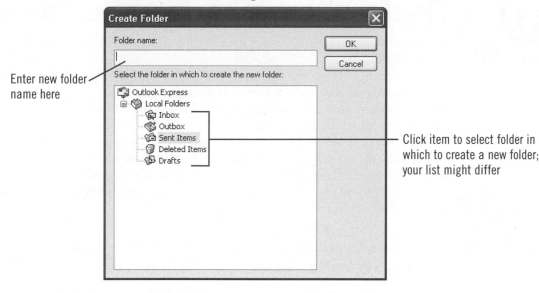

FIGURE H-9: Create Folder dialog box

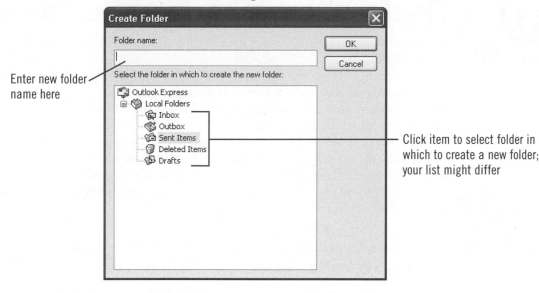

Enter new folder name here

Click item to select folder in which to create a new folder; your list might differ

FIGURE H-10: Important folder

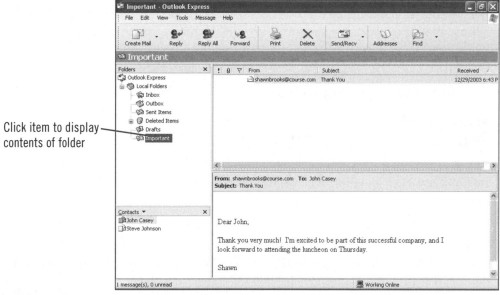

Click item to display contents of folder

Diverting incoming e-mail to folders

Outlook Express can direct incoming messages that meet criteria to other folders in the Folders list rather than to your Inbox. For example, your friend loves sending you funny e-mail, but you often don't have time to read it right away. You can set message rules to store any messages you receive from your friend in a different folder so they won't clutter your Inbox. When you are ready to read the messages, you simply open the folder and access the messages just as you would messages in the Inbox. To set criteria for incoming messages, click Tools on the menu bar, point to Message Rules, then click Mail. If the New Mail Rule dialog box opens, no previous message rules exist. Otherwise, the Message Rules dialog box opens, and you click New to create a new message rule. In the New Mail Rule dialog box, select the conditions for your rule, select the actions for your rule, click any undefined value (such as the e-mail address you want to divert and the folder where you want to store the diverted messages) and provide information. Type a name to identify the rule, then click OK. If you receive unwanted e-mail from a specific address, you can block all messages from that sender. To block all messages from a sender, click the message from the sender, click Message on the menu bar, then click Block Sender.

Selecting a News Server

A newsgroup is an electronic forum where people from around the world with a common interest can share ideas, ask and answer questions, and comment on and discuss any subject. You can find newsgroups on almost any topic. Before you can participate in a newsgroup, you must select a news server. A **news server** is a computer located on the Internet, which stores newsgroup messages, also called **articles**, on different topics. Each news server contains several newsgroups from which to choose. The Internet Connection Wizard walks you through the process of selecting a news server. This wizard also appears the first time you use Outlook Express News. To complete the wizard process and the steps in this lesson, you need to get the name of the news server you want to use from your instructor, technical support person, or Internet service provider (ISP), and possibly an account name and password. ➤ John wants to add a news server account so he can access coffee-related newsgroups.

Steps

Trouble?

If you have not already selected a news server, the Internet Connection Wizard opens. Skip to Step 4 to complete the wizard. If you already have a news server, continue to Step 2.

1. In the Folders list, click **Outlook Express**, then click the **Read News link** or click the **Set up a Newsgroups account link** in the Outlook Express Start Page

2. Click **Tools** on the menu bar, click **Accounts**, then click the **News tab** in the Internet Accounts dialog box
   The Internet Accounts dialog box opens, as shown in Figure H-11, displaying the News tab with your list of available news servers. Using the Internet Accounts dialog box, you can add, remove, and view properties for news servers, mail servers, and directory services.

QuickTip

To add a new e-mail account, click Add, click Mail, then follow the Internet Connection Wizard instructions.

3. Click **Add**, then click **News** on the shortcut menu
   The Internet Connection Wizard dialog box opens.

4. Type your **name** if necessary, then click **Next**
   The name you enter appears in messages you post to a newsgroup.

5. Type your **e-mail address** if necessary, then click **Next**
   Individuals participating in the newsgroup need to know your e-mail address so they can reply to your news messages, either by posting another news message or by sending you an e-mail message.

6. Type the **name of the news server** provided by your instructor, technical support person, or ISP, as shown in Figure H-12, click the **My news server requires me to log on** check box to select it if required by your ISP, then click **Next**

7. If you selected the My news server requires me to log on check box in the previous step, type **your user name** and **your password** in the appropriate text boxes, then click **Next**

QuickTip

To change a news server name, right-click the news server in the Folders list, click Properties, type a name in the News Accounts text box, then click OK.

8. Click **Finish**, click **Close** if the Internet Accounts dialog box is still open, then click **No** when prompted to download a list of available newsgroups
   The news server name appears in the Folders list, as shown in Figure H-13. You view a list of available newsgroups in the next lesson.

FIGURE H-11: Internet Accounts dialog box

Click tab to select
server type

Available
news server

Click button to
add server

FIGURE H-12: Internet Connection Wizard dialog box

Enter new server
here; your news
server might differ

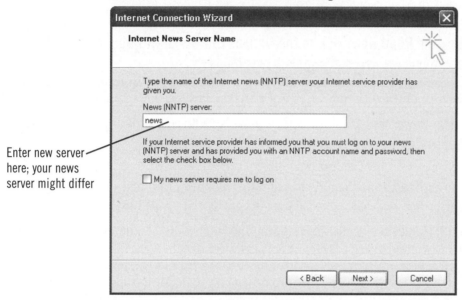

FIGURE H-13: Outlook Express window with news server

News server; your
news server name
might differ

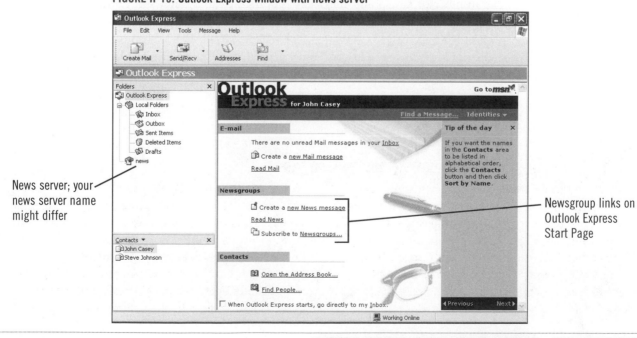

Newsgroup links on
Outlook Express
Start Page

Windows XP

Viewing and Subscribing to a Newsgroup

When you add a news server account to Outlook Express, it retrieves a list of newsgroups available on that server. Often this list is quite lengthy. Rather than scroll through the entire list looking for a particular topic, you can have Outlook Express search the list for that topic. Similarly, you can search all the messages you retrieve from a newsgroup for a particular message. Once you select a newsgroup, you can merely view its contents, or, if you expect to return to the newsgroup often, you can subscribe to it. Subscribing to a newsgroup places a link to the group in the news server folder in your Outlook Express Folders list, providing easy access to the newsgroup. ◄━━ John wants to find and subscribe to a newsgroup for coffee drinkers, so he can keep track of what people want from a coffee company.

Steps

Trouble?

If a log in message appears, click OK.

1. Click the **Read News link** in the Outlook Express Start Page, then click **Yes** if necessary, to view a list of available newsgroups
   The Newsgroup Subscriptions dialog box opens, as shown in Figure H-14, displaying news servers on the left (if more than one exists) and related newsgroups on the right.

2. In the News server list, click the **news server** you added in the previous lesson if necessary
   A list of the newsgroups you subscribe to appears in the preview pane. Your list might be empty.

QuickTip

To download new newsgroup messages, click the news server in the Folders list, click the newsgroup in the right pane, click Settings, click New Messages Only on the shortcut menu, then click Synchronize Account.

3. Type **coffee** in the Display newsgroups which contain text box
   Newsgroups related to coffee appear in the Newsgroup list box, as shown in Figure H-15.

4. Scroll if necessary, click any newsgroup from your list, then click **Go to**
   The newsgroup name you choose appears selected in the Folders list, and the newsgroup messages appear in the preview pane of the Outlook Express window, as shown in Figure H-16. You think this newsgroup looks promising, so you decide to subscribe to it.

5. Right-click the **newsgroup name** in the Folders list, then click **Subscribe**
   The number of newsgroup messages appears next to the newsgroup name in the Folders list. The icon next to the newsgroup changes from gray to color to indicate the subscription is complete.

Filtering unwanted newsgroup messages

After you become familiar with a newsgroup, you might decide that you don't want to retrieve messages from a particular person, about a specific subject, of a certain length, or older than a certain number of days. This is called filtering newsgroup messages. To filter unwanted messages, click Tools on the menu bar, point to Message Rules, then click News. If the New News Rule dialog box opens, no previous message

rules exist. Otherwise, the Message Rules dialog box opens, and you click New to create a new message rule. In the New Mail Rule dialog box, select the conditions for your rule, select the actions for your rule, click any undefined value (such as the e-mail address you want to divert and the folder where you want to store the unwanted messages) and provide information, type a name to identify the rule, then click OK.

FIGURE H-14: Newsgroup dialog box

Click icon to select
a new server; your
list of news servers
might differ

Click button to subscribe
to selected newsgroup

Click button to view
selected newsgroup

List of newsgroups
available on selected
news server

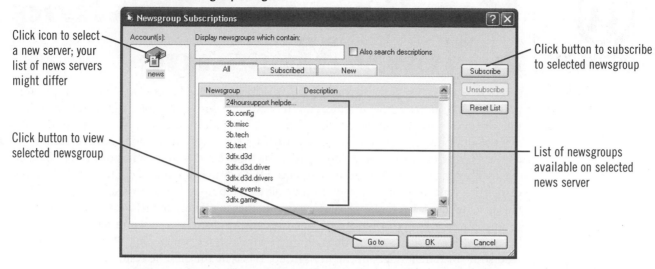

FIGURE H-15: List of newsgroups relating to coffee

List of newsgroups
that contain the
word "coffee"

FIGURE H-16: Outlook Express window with newsgroup

Messages in
selected newsgroup

Newsgroup

Reading and Posting a News Message

After retrieving new newsgroup messages, you can read them. Newsgroup messages appear in the preview pane, just as e-mail messages do. To view a newsgroup message in the display pane, click the title of the message in the preview pane. If the Expand Indicator ⊞ appears to the left of a newsgroup message, then the message contains a conversation thread. A **conversation thread** consists of the original message on a particular topic along with any responses that include the original message. To read the responses, click ⊞ to display the message titles, then click the title of the message you want to read. To hide all the responses to a conversation thread, click the Collapse Indicator ⊟ to the left of a newsgroup message. Icons appear next to the news messages to indicate whether a conversation thread is expanded or collapsed, and whether or not it has been read. See Table H-4 for a description of common message icons. ⟵ John decides to read some of the messages in the newsgroup. When he finishes, he restores his news server settings by unsubscribing from this newsgroup and removing the news server from the Folders list.

Steps

Trouble?

If a newsgroup message has no ⊞, click a message without a ⊞, then skip to Step 3.

1. Click a **newsgroup message** in the preview pane with ⊞ to the left of the title, then read the message in the display pane
   The newsgroup message appears in the display pane.
2. Click ⊞ next to the newsgroup message
   The titles of the responses to the original message appear under the original newsgroup message, as shown in Figure H-17.

QuickTip

To view only unread messages, click View on the menu bar, point to Current View, then click Hide Read Messages.

3. Click each **reply message** under the original message, then read the reply
   As you read each message, you can choose to compose a new message, send a reply message to everyone viewing the newsgroup (known as **posting**), send a reply message to the author's private e-mail address (rather than posting it on the newsgroup), or forward the message to another person.
4. After reading the last reply message, click the **Reply Group button** 🗊 on the toolbar, then click the **Maximize button** if necessary
5. Type a response to the newsgroup message, as shown in Figure H-18
   To see the exchange of messages and replies, click a message in the thread, click Message on the menu bar, then click Watch Conversation.
6. Click the **Send button** 🗊 on the toolbar, then click **OK**
   Your reply message appears in the preview pane along with the other replies to the original message. Everyone viewing the newsgroup can download and read your response.

Trouble?

If another warning message appears, click No to subscribe to the Newsgroup, then click No to view a list of newsgroups.

7. Right-click the **newsgroup** in the Folders list, click **Unsubscribe**, then click **OK**
8. Right-click the **news server** in the Folders list, click **Remove Account**, then click **Yes**
9. Click **File** on the menu bar, click **Exit**, then click **Yes** if necessary to disconnect from the Internet

TABLE H-4: Newsgroup message icons

icon	description	icon	description
🗋	Unopened message; message heading text appears in bold	🗋	Message unavailable on server
🗋	Read message	🗋	Replied to message
🗋	Read message and stored on your computer	🗋	Forwarded message
🗋	Unopened message and stored on your computer	✳	Newsgroup new on server

FIGURE H-17: Reading a newsgroup message

Click button to create a new message

Click Collapse Indicator to hide replies to messages

Click Expand Indicator to display replies to messages

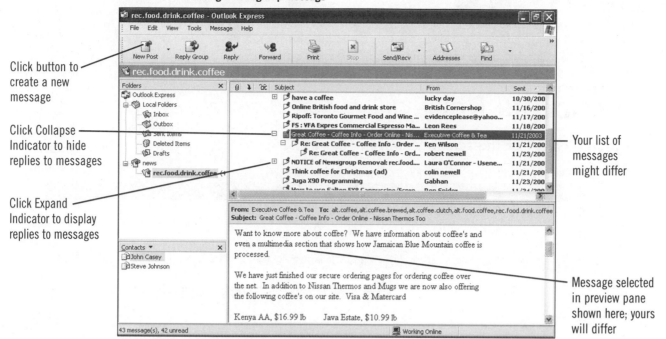

Your list of messages might differ

Message selected in preview pane shown here; yours will differ

FIGURE H-18: Posting a newsgroup message

Click button to post message to newsgroup

The original message will differ

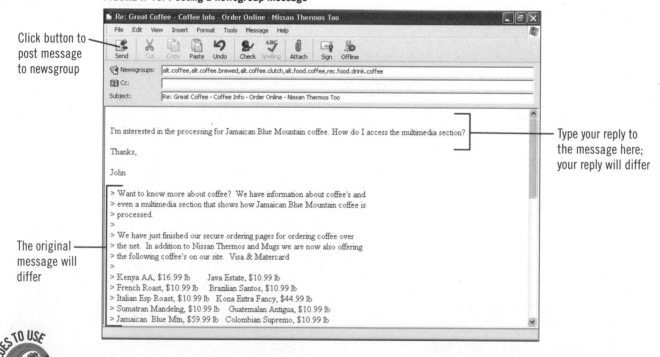

Type your reply to the message here; your reply will differ

CLUES TO USE

Deleting old news messages

Newsgroup messages are stored on your hard drive, so you should delete unneeded messages to free disk space. Outlook Express gives several clean-up options to help you optimize your hard drive space. You can delete entire messages (titles and bodies), compress messages, remove just the message bodies (leaving the title headers), or reset the information stored for selected messages, which allows you to refresh messages (download again). To clean up files on your local hard drive, select a news server in the Folders list, click Tools on the menu bar, click Options, then click the Maintenance tab. You can select any of the clean-up options to delete or compress news messages at a specified time, or click Clean Up Now, then click the button for the clean-up option you want to perform.

Practice

► Concepts Review

Label each element of the screen shown in Figure H-19.

FIGURE H-19

1. Which element displays new e-mail messages?
2. Which element points to an e-mail message?
3. Which element points to a newsgroup?
4. Which element points to the display pane?
5. Which element displays the contents of a folder?
6. Which element points to the preview pane?
7. Which element displays e-mail commands?

Match each term with the statement that describes its function.

8. **Message flag**   a. A computer on the Internet that stores articles
9. **Outlook Express**   b. Displays e-mail, contacts, and newsgroups
10. **Message Rules**   c. An icon that indicates e-mail priority
11. **Outlook Express window** d. Diverts selected incoming e-mail folders
12. **News server**   e. A program that exchanges e-mail on the Internet
13. **Newsgroup**   f. A collection of articles on related topics

Select the best answers from the following lists of choices.

14. The location that allows you to jump to folders and open tools is called the:
- **a.** Outlook Express window.
- **b.** Outlook Express Start Page.
- **c.** Folders list.
- **d.** Outlook Express Link Page.

15. To compose a message, you can:
- **a.** Click the new Mail message link.
- **b.** Click Create Mail button on the toolbar.
- **c.** Click Message on the menu bar, then click New Message.
- **d.** All of the above

16. A contact is a:
- **a.** Person with whom you communicate.
- **b.** Mailing address.
- **c.** Newsgroup.
- **d.** Program.

17. When you click the Send button on the toolbar in the New Message window, you first send an e-mail message to the:
- **a.** E-mail address.
- **b.** Outbox.
- **c.** Internet.
- **d.** Cc and Bcc addresses.

18. ✉ indicates that the message has:
- **a.** Not been read.
- **b.** Been read.
- **c.** One or more files attached to it.
- **d.** Been marked as low priority by the sender.

► Skills Review

1. Start Outlook Express and explore the Outlook Express window.
- **a.** Connect to the Internet.
- **b.** Start Outlook Express.
- **c.** Identify the title bar, menu bar, toolbar, Internet Explorer link, Folders list, Read Mail link, Read News link, new Mail message link, Open the Address Book link, Find People link, and status bar.
- **d.** On the toolbar, identify icons for opening the Address Book, sending and receiving e-mail messages, composing a message, and finding a message.
- **e.** If necessary, enter your user name and password, then click Connect.

2. Add a contact to the Address Book.
- **a.** Click the Address Book button.
- **b.** Click the New button, then click New Contact.
- **c.** Type John in the First name text box, press [Tab] twice, then type Asher.
- **d.** Click in the E-Mail Addresses text box, then type johna@course.com.
- **e.** Click Add, then click OK. Click the Address Book Close button.

3. Compose and send e-mail.
- **a.** Click the New Mail button, then click the Maximize button if necessary.
- **b.** Click the To button.
- **c.** Click the name John Asher.
- **d.** Click To, then click OK.
- **e.** Click the Subject text box, then type Financial Update Request.
- **f.** Press [Tab] to move to the message window, then type John: Please send year-end financial report ASAP. Thanks.
- **g.** Click the Send button.

4. Retrieve, read, and respond to e-mail.
- **a.** Click the Send/Recv button. It may take a few minutes before you receive a message from John Asher.
- **b.** In the Folders list, click Inbox. Click the message you just received from John Asher.
- **c.** Click the Forward Message button, then click the Maximize button if necessary.

    d. Click the To text box, then enter your e-mail address. Enter a response in the message window.

    e. Click the Send button.

5. Manage e-mail messages.

    a. Click File on the menu bar, point to New, then click Folder.

    b. Type **Archive**. Click Local Folders in the Folders list, then click OK.

    c. Right-click the message received from John Asher, then click Move To Folder on the shortcut menu.

    d. Click Archive, then click OK.

    e. In the Folders list, click the Archive folder.

    f. Right-click the message received from John Asher, then click Delete on the shortcut menu.

    g. Right-click the Archive folder, click Delete, then click Yes.

    h. Click the Address Book button.

    i. Click John Asher, click the Delete button, then click Yes. Click the Close button.

6. Select a news server.

    a. In the Folders list, click Outlook Express.

    b. Click the Read News link or the Set up a Newsgroup account link.

    c. If the Internet Connection Wizard appears, skip to Step e. Otherwise, click Tools on the menu bar, click Accounts, then click the News tab.

    d. Click Add, then click News.

    e. Type your name, then click Next. Type your e-mail address, then click Next.

    f. Type the name of a news server (see your instructor, technical support person, or ISP for a name), then click Next.

    g. Click Finish, click Close if necessary, then click No.

7. View and subscribe to a newsgroup.

    a. Click the Read News link, then click Yes if necessary.

    b. In the News server list, click the news server you just added (if available).

    c. Type **caffeine**. (If no items appear, type **tea** or **chocolate**.)

    d. Click a newsgroup. Click Go To.

    e. Right-click the newsgroup in the Folders list, then click Subscribe.

8. Read and post a news message.

    a. Click a newsgroup message with a ⊞.

    b. Click ⊞ next to the newsgroup message.

    c. Click and read each reply.

    d. Click the Reply Group button, then type a response.

    e. Click the Send button, then click OK.

    f. Right-click the newsgroup in the Folders list, click Unsubscribe, then click OK.

    g. Right-click the news server in the Folders list, click Remove Account, then click Yes.

    h. Click File on the menu bar, click Exit, then click Yes if necessary to disconnect.

► Independent Challenge 1

You are a new lawyer at Bellig & Associates. You have a home computer with Windows XP and Outlook Express that you often use to do work on while you are at home. Because e-mail is an important method of communication at the law firm, you want to use the Outlook Express Address Book to enter e-mail addresses of colleagues with whom you need to communicate while working out of the office.

    a. Start Outlook Express, then open the Address Book.

    b. Enter the following names and e-mail addresses:

        Greg Bellig   gregb@bellig_law.com

Jacob Bellig   jacobb@bellig_law.com
Derek Quan   derekq@bellig_law.com

c. Print the Address Book in both the Business Card and Memo styles.

d. Delete the names and e-mail addresses you just entered in the Address Book.

▶ Independent Challenge 2

As president of Auto Metals, you just negotiated a deal to export metal auto parts to an assembly plant in China. Your lawyer, Josh Higgins, drew up a preliminary contract. You want to send Josh an e-mail indicating the terms of the deal so he can finish the contract. When Josh responds, move the e-mail into the Legal folder. If you do not have a connection to the Internet, ask your instructor or technical support person for help completing this challenge.

a. Open a New Message window using the stationery called Technical, or another option.

b. Type **jhiggins@course.com** in the To text box in the message window, then type **China Deal Contract** in the Subject text box.

c. Enter the following message:

Dear Josh,

I have completed the negotiations with the assembly plant. Please modify the following terms in the contract:

1. All parts shall be inspected before shipping.

2. Ship 20,000 units a month for 3 years with an option for 2 more years.

Sincerely yours,

[your name]

d. Send the e-mail.

e. Print the e-mail you receive from Josh Higgins.

f. Create a new folder called Legal, then move the e-mail message you received from Josh Higgins to the new folder.

g. Delete the Legal folder.

▶ Independent Challenge 3

You are a legal assistant at a law firm specializing in international law. Your boss asks you to research international contracts with China. You decide to start your research with newsgroups on the Internet.

a. Select a news server. (See your instructor, technical support person, or ISP to obtain a news server.)

b. Subscribe to a newsgroup about China, then read several newsgroup messages and replies.

c. Reply to a message, then post a new message.

d. Print the newsgroup messages, including the original message and replies.

e. Unsubscribe to the newsgroup, then remove the newsgroup server.

▶ Independent Challenge 4

You like to play sports, watch sports, read about sports, and talk about sports all the time, so you decide to join a sports newsgroup.

a. Select a news server. (See your instructor, technical support person, or ISP to obtain a news server.)

b. Subscribe to a newsgroup about sports, then read several newsgroup messages and replies.

c. Reply to a message, then post a new message.

d. Print the newsgroup messages, including the original message and replies.

e. Unsubscribe to the newsgroup, then remove the newsgroup server.

► Visual Workshop

Re-create the screen shown in Figure H-20, which displays the Outlook Express window with a message that has been sent. Print the Outlook Express window. (Press [Print Screen] to make a copy of the screen, open Paint, click Edit on the menu bar, click Paste to paste the screen into Paint, then click Yes to paste the large image if necessary. Click the Text button on the Toolbox, click a blank area in the Paint work area, then type your name. Click File on the menu bar, click Page Setup, change 100% normal size to 50% in the Scaling area, then click OK. Click File on the menu bar, click Print, then click Print.)

FIGURE H-20

Windows XP

Unit I

Communicating
over the Internet

Objectives

- ► **Set up Internet security**
- ► **Protect your Internet privacy**
- ► **Protect your Internet identity**
- ► **Create a .NET Passport**
- ► **Browse the Web with MSN Explorer**
- ► **Send and receive instant messages**
- ► **Communicate with others**
- ► **Share graphical content**
- ► **Get remote assistance**

Windows XP makes communicating with other computers over the Internet more secure and easier than ever. It includes Control Panel utilities that allow you to set security and privacy settings, and accessories that allow you to connect to other computers and to the Internet, communicate with users on other computers, collaborate with others during online conferences, and ask for or get remote online assistance from a contact. This unit shows you how to set up Internet security and privacy settings and how to use Windows communication features such as MSN Explorer and Windows Messenger, which are useful for home and business. ◢ John Casey, the owner of Wired Coffee Company, recently purchased a computer so he can work from home. He wants to take advantage of Windows communications features for his business.

Windows XP

Setting up Internet Security

Windows provides Internet security options to prevent users on the Internet from gaining access to personal information without your permission, such as credit card information while you shop online, and to protect your computer from unsafe software downloaded or run from the Internet. Internet security is divided into zones, to which you can assign different levels of security. There are four security zones: Internet, Local intranet, Trusted sites, and Restricted sites. See Table I-1 for a description of each security zone. When you access a Web page or download content from the site, Internet Explorer checks its security settings and determines the Web site's zone, which you can see on the right side of the Internet Explorer status bar. All Internet Web sites are assigned to the Internet zone until you assign individual Web sites to other zones. In addition to security zones, you can also control the Web content that appears on your computer with the Content Advisor. The **Content Advisor** allows you to prevent access to Web sites that contain material you deem inappropriate, such as language or violence, and to create a supervisor password to prevent other users from making changes to the settings, which is a helpful content security system for children. ⬛➤ John wants to check the security settings on his computer.

1. Click the **Start button** on the taskbar, click **Control Panel**, click **Switch to Classic View** if necessary, then double-click the **Internet Options icon** 🌐 in the Control Panel window
   The Internet Properties dialog box opens, displaying the General tab.

2. Click the **Security tab**
   The Security tab appears, displaying the Internet zone and its current security level, as shown in Figure I-1. You move the slider up for a higher level of security or down for a lower level of security. The security levels are: High, Medium, Medium-low, and Low. If a security level doesn't meet all your needs, you can customize it for a selected zone. Simply click Custom Level on the Security tab, select the settings you want to disable, enable, or prompt for a response, then click OK.

   Trouble?

   If the slider is not available, click Default Level to change the security level to Medium and display the slider.

3. Drag the slider up or down to adjust the security level, then click **Yes** if a Warning message dialog box opens
   A detailed description appears next to the security level, which changes when you change the security level.

4. In the Web content zone box, click the **Trusted sites icon** ✅
   The security level for Trusted sites appears, in which you can add and remove your own trusted sites or change custom security level settings.

5. Click the **Content tab**
   The Content tab appears, displaying settings to control Internet content, protect your Internet identity, and create a personal profile.

   QuickTip

   To create a password to change Content Advisor settings, click the General tab in the Content Advisor dialog box, click Create Password, type and confirm a password and related hint as indicated, then click OK.

6. In the Content Advisor section, click **Enable**
   The Content Advisor dialog box opens, displaying the Ratings tab with current rating levels for the RSACi (Recreational Software Advisory Council on the Internet) Language category, as shown in Figure I-2. You can select any of the categories to change their rating levels independently of the others. The higher the rating level (0 through 5), the more restrictive access to Web sites becomes.

7. Drag the slider to adjust the content rating level
   When you change the rating level, the detailed description below the rating level changes.

8. Click **Cancel** in the Content Advisor dialog box, then click **Cancel** in the Internet Properties dialog box

FIGURE I-1: **Internet Properties dialog box with Security tab**

Internet zones

Security level slider

Currently security setting for the Interent zone; yours might differ

FIGURE I-2: **Content Advisor dialog box**

Rating service

Rating categories

Rating level slider

Current rating level for selected category

Click button for Web information on rating service

TABLE I-1: **Security zones**

zone	description	default setting
Internet	Contains all Web sites that are not assigned to any other zone	Medium
Local intranet	Contains all Web sites that are on your organization's intranet and don't require a proxy server	Medium
Trusted sites	Contains Web sites that you trust not to threaten the security of your computer	Low (allows all cookies)
Restricted sites	Contains Web sites that you believe threaten the security of your computer	High (blocks all cookies)

Windows XP

COMMUNICATING OVER THE INTERNET   WINDOWS XP I-3 ◄

Protecting Your Internet Privacy

When you browse the Internet, you can access and gather information from Web sites, but Web sites can also gather information about you without your knowledge unless you set up Internet security on your computer. You can set Internet privacy options to protect your personal identity from unauthorized access. When you visit a Web site, the site creates a **cookie** file, known as a **first-party cookie**, which stores information on your computer, such as your Web site preferences or personal identifiable information including your name and e-mail address. Not all cookies are harmful; many first-party-cookies save you time re-entering information on a return visit to a Web site. However, there are also **third-party cookies** such as advertising banners, which are created by Web sites you are not currently viewing. Once a cookie is saved on your computer, only the Web site that created it can read it. The privacy options allow you to block or permit cookies for Web sites in the Internet zone; however, when you block cookies, you might not be able to access all the features of a Web site. When a Web site violates your cookie policy, a red icon appears on the status bar. To find out if the Web site you are viewing in Internet Explorer contains third-party cookies or if any cookies have been restricted, you can get a privacy report. The privacy report lists all the Web sites with content on the current Web page and shows how all the Web sites handle cookies. John wants to check the privacy settings on his computer and get a privacy report for a Web page.

QuickTip
To delete all the cookies currently on your computer, click the General tab, click Delete Cookies, then click OK.

1. **In the Control Panel window, double-click the Internet Options icon** 🪐
   The Internet Properties dialog box opens, displaying the General tab.

2. **Click the Privacy tab**
   The Privacy tab appears, displaying a slider in which you can select a privacy setting for the Internet zone, as shown in Figure I-3. You move the slider up for a higher level of privacy or down for a lower level of privacy.

3. **Drag the slider to adjust the privacy setting**
   When you change your privacy settings, a detailed description appears next to the level. When you apply the privacy changes, they might not affect cookies that are already on your computer, but they will affect any new ones. If you set the privacy level to a high setting, which blocks all or most cookies, or a low setting, which blocks only a few or no cookies, you can click Edit in the section below to override cookie handling for individual Web sites.

4. **Click Cancel to close the Internet Properties dialog box without making changes**
   You return to the Control Panel window.

5. **Click the Start button on the taskbar, then click Internet (with Internet Explorer in gray below it) in the left column of the Start menu**
   Internet Explorer opens, displaying your home page.

QuickTip
To view a Web site's privacy policy summary, select a Web site in the Privacy Report dialog box, then click Summary.

6. **Click View on the menu bar, then click Privacy Report**
   The Privacy Report dialog box opens, displaying all the Web sites associated with the current Web page and their handling of cookies, as shown in Figure I-4.

7. **Click Close to close the Privacy Report dialog box, then click the Close button on the Internet Explorer window**
   Internet Explorer closes.

FIGURE I-3: Internet Properties dialog box with Privacy tab

Privacy level slider

Current privacy setting information

FIGURE I-4: Privacy Report dialog box

Cookie information
for each Web site

Web sites with content
on the Web page

Protecting your computer from the Internet

When you connect to the Internet, you can access Web sites and information on the Internet, but others on the Internet can also access information on your computer. You can prevent this by activating Internet Connection Firewall (ICF), another security layer of protection. A firewall is a security system that creates a protective barrier between your computer or network and others on the Internet. ICF is software that monitors all communication between your computer and the Internet and prevents unsolicited inbound traffic from the Internet from entering your private computer. ICF discards all unsolicited communications from reaching your computer unless you specifically allow it to come through. If your computer is directly connected to the Internet, you should activate ICF. If you are using Internet Connection Sharing (ICS) on your network to provide Internet access on multiple computers, you should activate ICF on the ICS computer only, otherwise it might create network communication problems. To set up an ICS, double-click the Network Connections icon 🌐 in the Control Panel window, right-click your Internet connection icon, click Properties on the shortcut menu, click the Advanced tab in the Properties dialog box if necessary, click the Protect my computer and network by limiting or preventing access to this computer from the Internet check box to select it if necessary, then click OK.

Protecting Your Internet Identity

To further protect your privacy, you can use certificates to verify your identity and protect important information, such as your credit card number, on the Internet. A **certificate** is a statement verifying the identity of a person or the security of a Web site. You can obtain your personal security certification from an independent Certification Authority (CA). A personal certificate verifies your identity to a secure Web site that requires a certificate, while a Web site certificate verifies its security to you before you send them information. When you visit a secure Web site (one whose address may start with "https" instead of "http"), it automatically sends you its certificate, and Internet Explorer displays a lock icon on the status bar. A certificate is also known as a **Digital ID** in other programs, such as Microsoft Outlook or the Address Book. ➤ John wants to check the privacy settings on his computer and import a certificate he issued to himself.

Steps

1. **In the Control Panel window, double-click the Internet Options icon** 🌐
   The Internet Properties dialog box opens, displaying the General tab.

2. **Click the Content tab, then click Certificates**
   The Certificates dialog box opens, displaying the Personal tab. The Personal tab stores your individual certificates, while the other tabs store certificates based on the purpose on the tab. You want to insert a certificate issued by John Casey. The certificate in this example is for example purposes only and not issued by a certification authority. Since the certificate is not yours and not issued by a CA, you want to import and store it under the Other People tab.

3. **Click the Other People tab, click Import to start the Certificate Import Wizard, then click Next**
   The next Certificate Import Wizard dialog box appears, asking you to specify the certificate file you want to import.

4. **Click Browse, navigate to the drive and folder where your Project Files are located, double-click the file JohnCasey.cer, then click Next**
   The next Certificate Import Wizard dialog box appears, asking you to specify the location in which you want to place the certificate, as shown in Figure I-5. The Other People option is selected.

5. **Click Next to display a summary screen, click Finish, then click OK in the successful import message box**
   The John Casey certificate appears in the Certificates dialog box, as shown in Figure I-6. To obtain a personal certificate, find a certification authority on the Trusted Root Certification Authorities tab in the Certificates dialog box or search for one on the Internet. The certification authority works with you to create the certificate file and import it to your computer.

6. **Double-click the John Casey certificate**
   The Certificate dialog box opens, as shown in Figure I-7, displaying information about the specific certificate, including its trustworthiness and the date until which it's valid.

7. **Click OK to close the Certificate dialog box, click the John Casey certificate to select it if necessary, click Remove, then click Yes in the message box to confirm the deletion**

8. **Click Close to close the Certificates dialog box, then click Cancel to close the Internet Properties dialog box without making changes**
   You return to the Control Panel window.

FIGURE I-5: Certificate Import Wizard dialog box

Stores imported certificate in the Other People lab

FIGURE I-6: Certificates dialog box

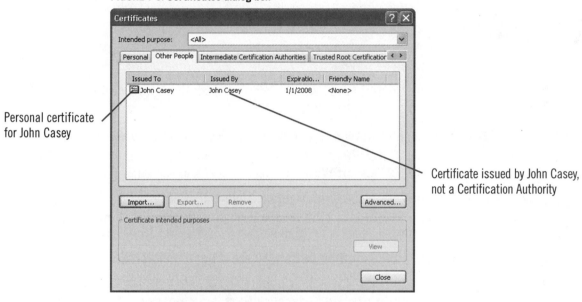

Personal certificate for John Casey

Certificate issued by John Casey, not a Certification Authority

FIGURE I-7: Certificate dialog box

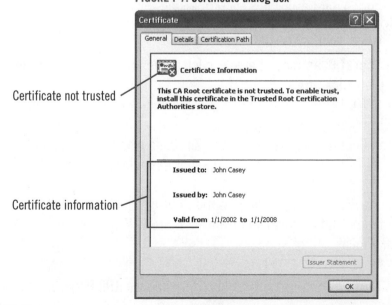

Certificate not trusted

Certificate information

Windows XP

Creating a .NET Passport

Microsoft .NET Passport is an online service that makes it possible for you to use your e-mail address and a single password to securely sign in to any participating .NET Passport Web site or service around the world. It also enables you to make faster and more secure online purchases with .NET Passport **wallet**, which is a single place to securely store personal financial information, such as your credit card number. The .NET Passport wallet uses certificates issued by a trusted certification authority to keep transactions secure. Each user on a computer must have a .NET Password to access all MSN Internet Access Web sites and use MSN related software, such as MSN Explorer and Windows Messenger. You use the .NET Passport Wizard to help you quickly associate a .NET Password to any existing e-mail address or create one while you sign up for a free MSN or Hotmail e-mail account. Once you create a .NET Passport, you can quickly sign in at any participating Web site by clicking the .NET Passport button **Sign In** or sign in when you start MSN related software, such MSN Explorer and Windows Messenger. When you finish working with a participating Web site, you can click **Sign Out** to sign out. John creates a .NET Password so that he can use MSN Explorer and Windows Messenger.

 Steps

(STOP) *If you already have a .NET Passport, you can skip this lesson.*

1. In the Control Panel window, double-click the **User Accounts icon**
   The User Accounts window opens.

   Trouble?

   If you have an existing Passport and want to change it, click Change my .NET Passport, then continue with Step 3.

2. Depending on your network setup, click your user account, then click **Set up my account to use a .NET Password**, or click the **Advanced tab**, then click **.NET Password Wizard**
   The .NET Passport Wizard dialog box opens, as shown in Figure I-8.

3. Read the welcome information, then click **Next**
   The next .NET Passport Wizard dialog box appears, as shown in Figure I-9, asking if you have an e-mail account. In most cases, you'll already have an e-mail account.

   Trouble?

   If you don't have an e-mail address, click the No, I would like to open a free MSN.com e-mail account now option button, click Next, follow the instructions to create one, then skip to Step 9.

4. Click the **Yes option button** if necessary, then click **Next**
   The next .NET Passport Wizard dialog box appears, asking you to enter an e-mail account.

5. Type your e-mail address, click **Next**, type a password as indicated, then click **Next**
   If you used an existing Hotmail or MSN address, click Finish, then skip to Step 9. The next .NET Passport Wizard dialog box appears, asking you to choose and answer a secret question, which is a security measure put in place for identification purposes when you want to make changes to your password.

6. Click the **Secret Question list arrow**, click a question, type the answer in the Answer text box, then click **Next**
   The next .NET Passport Wizard dialog box appears, asking you to indicate the region where you live.

7. Specify the Country/Region, State, and ZIP Code where you live, then click **Next**
   The next .NET Passport Wizard dialog box appears, asking you to accept or decline the MSN Terms of Use agreement to use the service.

8. Click the **I accept the agreement option button**, click **Next**, select the check boxes with the type of information you want to share with participating sites, click **Next**, then click **Finish**
   The User Accounts window appears with the .NET Passport added to the account.

9. Click the **Close button** in the User Accounts and Control Panel windows

FIGURE I-8: **.NET Passport Wizard dialog box welcome screen**

Click link to view the
Microsoft privacy policy

FIGURE I-9: **.NET Passport Wizard dialog box**

Click the option that
applies to you

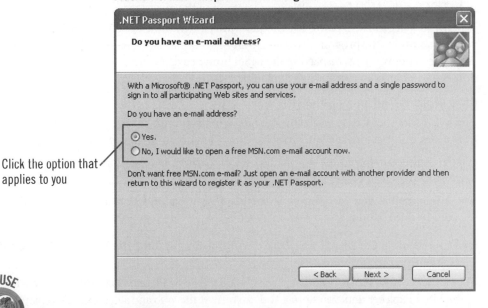

Making changes to a .NET Passport

You can find out more about .NET Passport and a directory of participating Web sites by visiting the Microsoft .NET Passport Web site at www.passport.com. At the Web site, you can click the Member Services link to change your .NET Passport information, reset your password, and find out answers to frequently asked questions. You can also access the Web site from your account in the User Accounts window. In User Accounts, you can also delete a .NET Passport association with a user account. To delete the association, open your user account in the User Accounts window, click Manage my network passwords in the task pane, select your e-mail address or Passport.Net, click Remove, click OK, then click Close. This doesn't delete the .NET Passport, just

the association with the user account. To delete a .NET Passport, you need to close your MSN Hotmail or MSN e-mail account or contact .NET Passport member services. For those who make online purchases, you can also find out how to store financial information in .NET Passport wallet, which helps you make faster, safer online purchases at any .NET Passport express purchase Web site. To create a .NET Passport wallet, click the Member Services link, click the Create or edit my .NET Passport wallet link, sign in if necessary, click Yes to create a certificate by a trusted certification authority, then follow the Web site instructions. When you want to make an online express purchase with .NET Passport, click Passport express purchase.

Browsing the Web with MSN Explorer

MSN Explorer is Internet software you can use to browse the Web, send e-mail and instant messages to friends, listen to music, watch videos, and manage finances online. MSN Explorer combines Microsoft's Internet software technologies, such as Microsoft Internet Explorer, Microsoft Windows Media Player, and MSN Messenger Service, with its leading Web services, such as Hotmail and CNBC Money. You don't have to be an MSN member to use MSN Explorer, but you do need to have a Microsoft .NET Passport, which you can obtain when you associate an existing e-mail address with a User Account using the .NET Passport wizard, or sign up for a free Hotmail or MSN e-mail account during the setup process. With MSN Explorer you can search the Web and access Web sites as in Internet Explorer. John Casey wants to learn about the capabilities of MSN Explorer.

Steps

(STOP) *If MSN Explorer is not installed on your computer, install it from the Internet at www.explorer.msn.com. Your steps may vary.*

Trouble?

If a message dialog box appears asking you to use MSN Explorer on the Start menu, click the Don't show me this message again check box to select it, then click No.

1. Click the **Start button** on the taskbar, point to **All Programs**, click **MSN Explorer**, then sign in to MSN at the MSN Explorer Welcome screen with your name and password if necessary
   When you start MSN Explorer for the first time, a light blue Welcome screen appears, asking you to customize the program, and create an MSN account and sign in if necessary. The MSN Explorer window opens, displaying the MSN home page. At the top of the MSN Explorer window is a toolbar with buttons listed in Table I-2.

2. Click **Help & Settings** on the title bar
   The MSN Member Center Web site appears, where you can change account information, add new users, and personalize your MSN settings, as shown in Figure I-10.

QuickTip

To display or hide the status bar on the bottom of the window, press [Ctrl][Shift][S].

3. Click the **Address bar** under the toolbar, type **www.windowsmedia.com**, then press **[Enter]**
   The MSN WindowsMedia.com Web site appears where you can play music, movies, radio, and other media. You can also click the Music button on the toolbar to play other music selected by MSN and create a music favorites list.

4. Click links as necessary to start a streaming media clip, then click the **Close button** in any window that opens
   The music video or movie plays in a small Windows Media Player window in the lower-left corner of the MSN Explorer until you stop it. You can browse the Web and still continue to play the media.

Trouble?

If a survey appears the first time you display MSN Hotmail, scroll down to the bottom, then click Continue as necessary to complete it.

5. Click the **E-mail button** 📧 on the toolbar, then click **No** if necessary to avoid copying your address book from Outlook Express to MSN
   The MSN Hotmail Web site appears, from which you can send, receive, and manage your e-mail messages, as shown in Figure I-11.

6. Click the **Stop button** on the Windows Media Player, then click the **Money button** 💰 on the toolbar
   The MSN Money CNBC Web site appears where you can manage your finances online, including investments, banking and bills, taxes, insurance, savings, and loans.

7. Click **My Calendar** 🕐 in the left pane, then click **Yes** in the message box if necessary
   The MSN Calendar Web site appears. You can create your own online calendar in which you can add new appointments and tasks and set reminders.

8. Click **Sign Out** on the title bar to sign out of MSN and close the MSN Explorer window, then click the **Close button** in the Welcome MSN Explorer window

FIGURE I-10: MSN Explorer window with Help & Settings

Click buttons to move back or forward

Address bar

Click buttons to customize MSN

Click button to view other options

Click button to view more buttons

MSN Explorer toolbar

MSN settings; your screen might differ

FIGURE I-11: MSN Explorer window with MSN Hotmail

Click button to display and organize e-mail folders

Windows Media Player with streaming media; your content will differ

E-mail messages; yours will differ

Click button to stop media

TABLE I-2: MSN Explorer toolbar buttons

button	used to	button	used to
Home	Display your home page	Money	Manage your finances
E-mail	Send and receive e-mail	Shopping	Purchase goods and services online
Favorites	Access frequently used Web sites	Music	Play MSN selected music
Online Contacts	Send and receive instant messages	Games	Play Internet games
People & Chat	Participate in chats and online communities		

Sending and Receiving Instant Messages

You can use Windows Messenger to exchange instant messages with a designated list of contacts over the Internet. An **instant message** is an online typewritten conversation in real-time between two or more contacts. E-mail messages collect in an e-mail program and can be viewed at a later time, whereas instant messages require both parties to be online, and the communication is instantaneous. As you type an instant message, you can also insert graphical symbols called **emoticons**, such as a happy face, which help convey your emotions. The list of emoticons is available in the Conversation window. You and your contacts don't have to be MSN members to use Windows Messenger, but you both need a .NET Passport. You can have as many as 150 different contacts and include up to five people in a conversation. John Casey wants to communicate with Holly Todd, a Wired Coffee stockholder, about the next stockholders' meeting, so he sends and receives instant messages.

Steps

 For the next four lessons, ask someone with Windows XP, an Internet connection, and the same version of Windows Messenger to start Windows Messenger and be signed in when you start this lesson.

QuickTip

To sign in with a different account, click File on the menu bar, click Sign Out, click the To sign in with a different account, click here link, enter your e-mail address and password, then click OK.

1. Click the **Start button** on the taskbar, point to **All Programs**, click **Windows Messenger**, then sign in to MSN if necessary

The Windows Messenger window opens. You can also double-click the Windows Messenger icon on the taskbar in the notification area to start the program, which appears as either 🧍 (if you're already signed in) or 🧍 (if you need to sign in).

2. Click **I want to** in the Actions pane if necessary to display more comments if necessary

With the available commands, you have quick access to commonly performed tasks, such as add a contact. If your contact is already online and appears in Windows Messenger, skip Steps 3 and 4.

QuickTip

To add someone from your Contacts list in Outlook Express 6 or later to the Windows Messenger, right-click the contact name, then click Set as Online Contact.

3. In the Actions pane, click **Add a Contact**, click the **By e-mail address or sign-in name option button** if necessary, then click **Next**

The Add a Contact Wizard dialog box appears, asking you for a contact's e-mail address, as shown in Figure I-12. If the wizard can't add the contact to your list, it provides an option to help you send an e-mail to your contact with information to help your contact get connected.

4. Type your contact's complete e-mail address, click **Next**, then click **Finish**

The Windows Messenger window appears, as shown in Figure I-13.

5. Double-click your contact in the list of contacts currently online

The Conversation window opens; in the status bar, Windows Messenger shows when the other person is typing, as well as the date and time of the last message you received.

QuickTip

If you don't want to receive messages, you can change your status to one of many choices, such as Busy. In the Windows Messenger window, click File on the menu bar, point to My Status, then click a status option.

6. Click the **message box**, type a **message**, then click **Send**

The message appears in the Conversation window. To insert an emoticon in your message, click the Emoticon button 😊 in the Conversation window, then click an icon.

7. Wait for a response, then continue to converse in this manner

The conversation appears in the Conversation window, as shown in Figure I-14.

8. Click the **Close button** on the Conversation window

FIGURE I-12: Add a Contact Wizard dialog box

Enter e-mail address here

FIGURE I-13: Windows Messenger window

MSN member signed in

Click link to open the MSN Hotmail Web site

Contacts currently online

Contacts not currently online

Click here to display or hide a list of commands

Your list of contacts will differ

Actions pane

FIGURE I-14: Conversation window

Instant message conversation; yours will differ

Type instant message here

Click button to send each message

Other Windows Messenger tasks

Sorting contacts by groups

As your Contacts List grows, you may want to organize them into groups. Windows Messenger makes it easy to organize your contacts into predefined groups and groups that you create. To display your contacts by groups, click Tools on the menu bar in the Windows Messenger window, point to Sort Contacts By, then click Groups. Four predefined groups appear by default: Coworkers, Family, Friends, and Other Contacts. To add a group, click Tools on the menu bar, then point to

Manage Groups. Click Add a Group, type a name, then press [Enter]. To delete or rename a group, click Tools on the menu bar, point to Manage Groups, point to Delete a Group or Rename a Group, then click a group. Once you have organized your groups, you can simply drag contacts from one group to another. To hide and display contacts in a group, click the Up button and Down button next to the group name.

Communicating with Others

When used with Windows XP, Windows Messenger provides state-of-the-art computer communications features. With Windows Messenger, you can talk to others over the Internet as you do on a regular phone, use video to see others and let others see you as you converse, share programs and files with others, and collaborate on documents and even share a whiteboard (a drawing canvas). Once you set up your computer hardware and software, you're ready to communicate over the Internet. You have two communication choices: audio only, and audio and video. With audio only, you speak into a microphone and hear the other person's response over your computer's speakers. With audio and video, you send video to others so they receive live images as well as sound. If the person you are calling doesn't have a video camera, they will see you, but you won't see them. If your computer is located on a network behind a firewall, you can communicate with people who are behind the same firewall, but you might not be able to communicate with those outside the firewall; check with your network administrator for details. John wants to confer with Bruce Clemons, a Wired Coffee Company stockholder who lives in California, about a stockholders' meeting.

Steps

STOP *In order to use the audio and video features of Windows Messenger, you need to have speakers, a microphone, and a video camera attached and installed on your computer. If you have only speakers and a microphone, you can complete part of the lesson. If you don't have any of the hardware, read the lesson without completing the steps to learn what is possible in Windows Messenger.*

> **Trouble?**
>
> If the Audio and Video Tuning Wizard dialog box opens, follow the step-by-step instructions to select and test your media hardware.

1. In the Windows Messenger window, right-click the name of your online contact, then click **Start a Voice Conversation**

The Conversation window opens and sends an invitation to your online contact to have a voice conversation, as shown in Figure I-15.

2. Wait for an acceptance response from your online contact

3. When you receive an acceptance, start talking back and forth

As you converse, you can adjust the speaker balance and the volume left or right.

> **Trouble?**
>
> If you and your contact don't have video cameras, skip to Step 7.

4. In the right pane of the Conversation window, click **Start Camera** and have your contact do the same if available

A video screen graphic appears in the right pane of the Conversation window without the live video until you accept the invitation to the video conversation.

5. Click the **Accept** link to have a video conversation, then start talking back and forth

Live video appears in the right pane of the Conversation window, as shown in Figure I-16.

6. Instruct your contact to click **Stop Camera** in the right pane of the Conversation window, then you click **Stop Camera**

A message appears in the message window indicating the video conversation has ended, and the video screen closes, but the audio connection remains until you stop it.

> **QuickTip**
>
> To block a contact from seeing or contacting you, click the Block button 🚫 in the Conversation window.

7. Instruct your contact to click **Stop Talking** in the right pane of the Conversation window, then you click **Stop Talking**

When you end the voice conversation, all audio and any video stops.

8. Click the **Close button** on the Conversation window

The Conversation window closes and the Windows Messenger window appears.

FIGURE I-15: Conversation window with audio

Invitation sent for a voice conversation

Speaker balance and volume controls

Click links to perform other tasks

FIGURE I-16: Conversation window with video

Live video; yours will differ

Invitation and acceptance for a video conversation

CLUES TO USE

Sending a file or e-mail from Windows Messenger

While you are conversing in Windows Messenger, you can send a contact a file or an e-mail message. You can send many different types of files, including documents, pictures, and music. To send a file, right-click the contact you want to send the file to, click Send a File or Photo, navigate to and select the file you want to send, then click Open. A request to transfer the file is sent to your contact. You are notified when it is accepted or declined. If your computer is located on a network behind a firewall, you might not be able to send files to those outside the firewall. If you want to send files to those behind the firewall, you need to manually open the connection;

check with your network administrator for details. Before you receive files over the Internet, make sure you have virus protection software on your computer. When you receive a file, a message dialog box related to viruses might open. You can click the link in the Conversation window to open the file or click File on the menu bar, then click Open Received Files. If you want to send a contact an e-mail message to follow up on a conversation in Windows Messenger, right-click the contact, then click Send E-mail (*e-mail address*). In the message window, type your message, then click Send.

Sharing Graphical Content

Windows Messenger includes **Whiteboard**, a program that you can use to display and share graphical content. All participants in the Windows Messenger can access a shared whiteboard and make changes interactively to the graphics it displays. A whiteboard can have multiple pages, which users can easily add and delete. You can copy and paste items between the whiteboard and other programs. You can emphasize key points using a highlighter tool or a pointer. Changes to one whiteboard are automatically synchronized with all other whiteboards, unless the user chooses to remove synchronization. John wants to show Bruce a graphic he has found that he thinks may work well with the company logo. He uses Windows Messenger to share it with him and get his ideas.

Steps

1. In the Windows Messenger window, right-click the name of your online contact, then click **Start Whiteboard**

   The Conversation window opens and sends an invitation to your online contact to have a voice conversation.

2. Wait for an acceptance response from your online contact

   When you receive an acceptance, the Sharing Session window opens and then the Whiteboard window opens in front of it on both computers. Whiteboard works in a similar way as the Paint program, and many of the buttons in the Toolbox are the same.

3. Draw a picture on the canvas or paste one that you copied from another program

   Because the Whiteboards on both computers are synchronized, your contact sees the same thing that you see. You can use the Select Area button ⬚ or Select Window button ⬚ in the Toolbox to help you quickly paste a selection or window contents into Whiteboard.

4. Click the **Remote Pointer On button** ☞ on the Toolbox

   The remote pointer 👉 appears on the Whiteboard, as shown in Figure I-17. This pointer also appears on your contact's Whiteboard. As you drag the pointer around the Whiteboard, the pointer moves in the same way on your contact's Whiteboard.

5. Click ☞ again

   The pointer no longer appears on the Whiteboard.

6. Click the **Text button** 𝗔 on the Toolbox, then type some sample text on the Whiteboard

7. Click the **Pen button** ✐ on the Toolbox, then draw some sample lines and curves on the Whiteboard

   As shown in Figure I-18, John writes the text, "This color needs to be changed" and draws a line pointing to the coffee cup. The same changes and comments appear on your contact's Whiteboard. You also sees any edits that your contact makes on his Whiteboard.

   QuickTip

   To save the contents of the Whiteboard, click File on the menu bar, click Save As, specify a location, then click Save.

8. Click **File** on the Whiteboard menu bar, then click **Exit** to close the Whiteboard window, but do not save any changes

9. Click the **Close Connection button** 🖳 on the Sharing Session window, then click the **Close button** on the Conversation window

   The sharing session ends and both windows close.

FIGURE I-17: Opening a Whiteboard

Toolbox

Remote pointer

Your contents will differ

Click buttons to insert and view other Whiteboard pages

FIGURE I-18: Editing a Whiteboard

Click button to synchronize or unsynchronize changes on both computers

Click button to lock or unlock screen contents

Your contents will differ

This color needs to be changed

CLUES TO USE

Sharing documents and programs in Windows Messenger

If you need to share information in a specific document or program with others in the conference, you can use Windows Messenger to share your documents and programs. To start application sharing in Windows Messenger, open the document or program you want to share, right-click the contact with whom you want to share, then click Start Application Sharing. Upon acceptance of the invitation, click the App Sharing button in the Sharing Session window, click the name of the program in the list of open programs that appears in the Sharing dialog box, then click Share. Others can see your document and the program on their computer screens. They cannot work with the document until you give them access to it, which you do by clicking Allow Control in the Sharing dialog box. You can click Close in the Sharing dialog box to work in the shared program. The user who clicks the program window "takes control" of the program and can then run any menu commands or make changes to the document. To discontinue sharing, click the program you want to stop sharing in the Sharing dialog box, then click Unshare. When you're finished, click the Close Connection button to close the sharing session. If you have a multi-player game, such as Age of Empires II, installed on both computers, you can play the game using Windows Messenger. To invite a contact to play, right-click the contact in the Window Messenger window, then click Start *program name*. Any game installed on your computer that uses the DirectPlayLobby interface appears as an option on the menu.

Getting Remote Assistance

Sometimes the best way to fix a computer problem is to get help from a friend or colleague who knows how to solve it. If your friend or colleague lives too far away to help you in person, you can use Remote Assistance and an Internet connection to help you get the support and answers you need. With Remote Assistance in Windows Messenger, you can ask a trusted contact in another location to connect to your computer over the Internet and provide support in real-time. After connecting to your computer, you can invite a contact to view your desktop, chat online using instant messages, talk online using a microphone and speakers, and send files. Instead of simply talking about a solution, sometimes you need someone to show you how to perform the steps before you fully understand the procedure. With Remote Assistance, you can give a contact control of your computer whereby he can demonstrate how to perform the procedure using his mouse and keyboard while you watch in real-time. If your computer is located on a network behind a firewall, you might not be able to use remote assistance; check with your network administrator for details. ◢ Bruce Clemons asks John to show him how to make changes in the Control Panel, so he gives John control of his computer using Remote Assistance.

1. **In the Windows Messenger, have your contact right-click your contact name, then click Ask for Remote Assistance**
   The Conversation window opens, and you receive an invitation from your online contact for remote assistance.

2. **Click the Accept link**
   When you receive an acceptance, the Remote Assistance window opens. Your contact receives a Remote Assistance message dialog box.

3. **Have your contact click Yes to let you view his screen and chat, then click Scale Window if necessary to display the entire desktop**
   Your contact's entire desktop appears in the Remote Assistance window, as shown in Figure I-19.

4. **Click the Take Control button 🖥 on the toolbar**
   Your contact receives a Remote Assistance message dialog box.

5. **Have your contact click Yes to let you take control of their screen**
   The Remote Assistance—Web Page Dialog box appears on your computer, indicating you are now sharing control of your contact's computer.

6. **Click OK to take control of your contact's computer**

7. **Click the Minimize button in the open windows, click the Start button, then click Control Panel**
   The open windows minimize on the taskbar, and the Control Panel window opens in your Remote Assistance window and on your contact's computer, as shown in Figure I-20. As you demonstrate how to make changes in the Control Panel, each step of the procedure appears in your Remote Assistance window and on his desktop.

8. **Click the Release Control button 🖥 on the toolbar, then click the Close button on the Remote Assistance window and Conversation window**
   The Windows Messenger window appears.

9. **Click File on the menu bar, click Sign Out, then click the Close button on the Windows Messenger window to close it**
   If you close the Windows Messenger window without signing out, Windows Messenger stays active in the notification area on the taskbar with the icon 👤.

FIGURE I-19: Connecting to a remote computer using Remote Assistance

Status information

Instant messages

Contact's Conversation window

Type instant messages here

Click button to display contact's entire desktop

Contact's Remote Assistance window

Contact's desktop

FIGURE I-20: Controlling a remote computer using Remote Assistance

Results appear here and on contact's computer

Perform actions here

CLUES TO USE

Making a phone call in Windows Messenger

Windows Messenger allows you to dial regular phones through a voice service provider using a modem on your computer. Once the modem connects to the number you are dialing, called the remote party, you can pick up your phone and talk. This feature is useful for people who spend long periods of time near their computers because it allows them to place calls without first dialing numbers on a phone. When you use Windows Messenger, having your modem's speakers on is helpful so you can hear what is actually happening with the connection. To make a phone call from Windows Messenger, click Actions on the menu bar, then click Make a Phone Call. If you need a voice service provider, click Get Started Here and follow the instructions to sign up. In the Phone window, type a phone number, including area code (even for local calls), then click Dial. If your computer is located on a LAN behind a firewall, you might not be able to make phone calls; check with your network administrator for details. When you're done, click Hang Up to end the call.

Practice

► Concepts Review

Label each element of the screen shown in Figure I-21.

FIGURE I-21

1. Which element indicates you are online in Windows Messenger?
2. Which element indicates a contact is online in Windows Messenger?
3. Which element displays Remote Assistance information?
4. Which element displays online chat messages from your computer?
5. Which element displays online chat messages from your contact's computer?
6. Which element displays invitations to communicate?

Match each term with the statement that describes its function.

7. **Instant message**   a. A window in Windows Messenger that allows you to have a typewritten conversation
8. **Certificate**   b. A security system that creates a protective barrier between your computer and
9. **Firewall**   others on the Internet
10. **Whiteboard**   c. A window in Windows Messenger that allows you to share graphical content
11. **Remote Assistance**   d. A window in Windows Messenger that allows you to take control of a computer
                              e. A statement that verifies the identity of a person or the security of a Web site

Select the best answer from the list of choices.

12. **Which of the following is NOT a security zone?**
    a. Internet
    b. Intranet
    c. Trusted sites
    d. Restricted sites

13. **Which of the following are types of certificates?**
    a. Personal and Web site
    b. Trusted and approved
    c. Trusted and personal
    d. Personal and approved

14. **You need a .NET Passport to sign in to:**
    a. MSN Explorer.
    b. Windows Messenger.
    c. MSN Internet Web sites.
    d. All of the above.

15. **Which of the following is NOT allowed in an instant message?**
    a. Text
    b. Emoticons
    c. Formatted text
    d. Attachments

16. **With Windows Messenger, you can:**
    a. Talk with others over the Internet.
    b. Share a document.
    c. Provide online help.
    d. All of the above.

17. **Which of the following might cause communication problems with Windows Messenger?**
    a. Cookies
    b. Certificates
    c. Firewalls
    d. Emoticons

▶ Skills Review

1. **Set up Internet security.**
   a. Open the Control Panel, then open the Internet Properties dialog box and display security settings.
   b. Change the security level if possible.
   c. Display content settings, open the Content Advisor dialog box, then change the content rating for Violence.
   d. Close the Content Advisor and Internet Properties dialog box without accepting any changes.

2. **Protect your Internet privacy.**
   a. In the Control Panel, open the Internet Properties dialog box and display privacy settings.
   b. Change the privacy level to Low.
   c. Close the Internet Properties dialog box without accepting any changes.

3. **Protect your Internet identity.**
   a. In the Control Panel, open the Internet Properties dialog box and display content settings.
   b. Open the Certificates dialog box.
   c. Import the file JoeJackson.cer from the drive and folder where your Project Files are located into the Other People tab.
   d. Remove the Joe Jackson certificate, then close the Certificates dialog box.
   e. Close the Internet Properties dialog box without accepting any changes.

4. **Create a .NET Passport.**

    If you already have a .NET Passport, you can skip this section.

   a. In the Control Panel, open the User Accounts window.
   b. Depending on your network setup, click your computer administrator account and click Set up my account to use a .NET Password, or click the Advanced tab and click .NET Password Wizard.
   c. Follow the step-by-step wizard instructions to attach a password to an existing e-mail address or a new one, which you can create using the wizard.
   d. Close the User Accounts window and the Control Panel window.

5. **Browse the Web with MSN Explorer.**
   a. Start MSN Explorer and sign in if necessary. Switch to Help & Settings and change the picture that represents your account.
   b. Open the www.windowsmedia.com Web site, then play streaming media with the built-in Windows Media Player.
   c. Stop the streaming media, sign out, then close MSN Explorer.

6. **Send and receive instant messages.**
   a. Start Windows Messenger and sign in if necessary.
   b. Double-click a contact currently online, type and send a message, wait for a response, then continue to converse in this manner.
   c. Print the screen. (Press [Print Screen] to make a copy of the screen, open Paint, click Edit on the menu bar, click Paste to paste the screen into Paint, then click Yes to paste the large image if necessary. Click the Text button on the Toolbox, click a blank area in the Paint work area, then type your name. Click File on the menu bar, click Page Setup, change 100 % normal size to 50% in the Scaling area, then click OK. Click File on the menu bar, click Print, then click Print.)
   d. Close the Conversation window.

7. **Communicate with others.**
   a. In Windows Messenger, start and have a voice conversation with an online contact.
   b. If available, start a video conversation, then stop the camera when you're done.
   c. Stop talking, then close the Conversation window.

8. **Share graphical content.**
   a. In Windows Messenger, start Whiteboard.
   b. Use the Whiteboard tools to draw an image that includes text. Synchronize the content and use the remote pointer.
   c. Exit the Whiteboard window without saving changes, close the connection, then close the Conversation window.

9. **Get remote assistance.**
   a. In Windows Messenger, ask for remote assistance from an online contact.
   b. Instruct your contact to accept the invitation, then click Yes to let the contact view your screen and chat.
   c. Instruct your contact to scale the window to display the entire desktop if necessary.
   d. Instruct your contact to take control of your desktop and perform a task for you to see.
   e. Instruct your contact to release control back to you, then close the Remote Assistance window.
   f. If you are working on a lab computer, delete any contacts that you added to Windows Messenger.
   g. Sign out in Windows Messenger, then close the program window.

▶ Independent Challenge 1

You work at a small pet shop supply company called PetStop. Because you have some experience with computers and the Internet, your manager asks you to set Internet security and privacy settings for company computers.
   a. Open the Internet Properties dialog box from the Control Panel.
   b. Display security settings, then change the security level for the Internet to High if possible.
   c. Print the screen. (Refer to Step 6c in the Skills Review for screen printing instructions.)
   d. Display privacy settings, then change the privacy level to High.
   e. Print the screen. (Refer to Step 6c in the Skills Review for screen printing instructions.)
   f. Override cookie handling for a Web site you choose, then close the Per Site Privacy Actions dialog box.
   g. Close the Internet Properties dialog box and the Control Panel without accepting any changes.

▶ Independent Challenge 2

You manage an international computer security company called Secure-One International. You want to test out your security system with noncertified certificates. Joe Jackson, an employee, created his own certificate and tries to pass it off as an authorized certificate from a trusted Certification Authority.

a. Open the Internet Properties dialog box from the Control Panel. Display content settings, then open the Certificates dialog box.

b. Import the file **JoeJackson.cer** from the drive and folder where your Project Files are located into the Other People tab.

c. Print the screen. (Refer to Step 6c in the Skills Review for screen printing instructions.) Draw a circle around the name or organization who issued the certificate.

d. Remove the Joe Jackson certificate, then close the Certificates dialog box.

e. Close the Internet Properties dialog box and the Control Panel without accepting any changes.

▶ Independent Challenge 3

You are working in a regional office as a financial service advisor for Point Financial Services. As the financial markets move up and down during the day, you want to send instant messages to clients and other advisors at the main office.

a. Select a partner who has access to a Windows XP computer with an Internet connection and Windows Messenger, and add your partner to your Contacts list if necessary.

b. Choose a time for instant messaging, then start Windows Messenger. Select your contact and send an instant message.

c. Wait for a response (this may take a few moments), then continue to converse in this manner.

d. Save the online chat text as **PointFS** on the drive and folder where your Project Files are located.

e. If you are working on a lab computer, delete any contacts that you added to Windows Messenger.

f. Sign out and close the Windows Messenger window.

▶ Independent Challenge 4

You are a student at Midwest University, and you will collaborate with another student on a project this semester. Because you commute to the university from a distance, you want to be able to work on the project on your home computer while communicating efficiently with your partner.

a. Select a partner who has access to a Windows XP computer with an Internet connection and Windows Messenger, and add your partner to your Contacts list if necessary.

b. Choose a time for an audio and video conference, then start Windows Messenger.

c. Select your contact, then use audio and video (if available) to communicate about your project.

d. Print the screen. (Refer to Step 6c in the Skills Review for screen printing instructions.)

e. Open one of your software programs (such as Microsoft Word), create a document for your project (such as a short project proposal), then share the document with your partner.

f. Print the screen. (Refer to Step 6c in the Skills Review for screen printing instructions.)

g. Stop the audio and video conversation and the application sharing.

h. If you are working on a lab computer, delete any contacts that you added to Windows Messenger.

i. Sign out and close the Windows Messenger window, then close any other open windows.

▶ Visual Workshop

Re-create the screen shown in Figure I-22, which displays the Remote Assistance window in Windows Messenger. Some of the information on the screen, such as contact names, will differ. Print the screen. (Refer to Step 6c in the Skills Review for screen printing instructions.)

FIGURE I-22

Managing
Shared Files Using a Network

Objectives

- ► **Understand network services**
- ► **Examine network computer properties**
- ► **Open and view a network**
- ► **Create a shared folder**
- ► **Map a network drive**
- ► **Copy and move shared files**
- ► **Open and edit a shared file**
- ► **Disconnect a network drive**

STOP *If you are not connected to a network, you can not work through the steps in this unit; however, you can read the lessons without completing the steps to learn what is possible in a network environment.*

Windows XP comes with a powerful tool for managing files and folders across a network called **My Network Places**. A **network** is a system of two or more computers connected together to share resources. My Network Places is integrated with Windows Explorer and My Computer, allowing you to view the entire network and to share files and folders with people from other parts of the network. John Casey, owner of Wired Coffee Company, uses network tools to manage files and folders for use by multiple users on the company network.

Understanding Network Services

Windows is a secure, reliable network operating system that allows people using many different computers to share resources, such as programs, files, folders, printers, and an Internet connection. A single computer on the network, called a **server**, can be designated to store these resources. Other computers on the network, called **clients** or **workstations**, can access the resources on the server instead of having to store them. You can share resources using two or more client computers, or you can designate one computer to serve specifically as the server. If the workstation computers are close together in a single building or group of buildings, the network is called a **local area network (LAN)**. If the workstation computers are spread out in multiple buildings or throughout the entire country using dial-up or wireless connections, the network is called a **wide area network (WAN)**. To set up a network with multiple computers, you need to install a network adapter for each computer on your network and connect each computer to a network hub using network cable or wireless technology. Network adapters are usually hardware cards, called **network interface cards**, or **NICs**, inserted in a slot, or **USB (Universal Serial Bus)**, port in the back of your computer that connects it to the network. A **network hub** is a hardware device that connects multiple computers at a central location. When data arrives at one port of the network hub, it is copied to the other ports so that all connected network devices see the data. If you have two LANs or two sections of the same LAN on different floors of the same building with different network adapter types, you can connect them together with a hardware device called a **bridge**. If you have any number of LANs, you can connect them together with a hardware device called a **router**. If you want to share a printer or Internet connection with the computers on a network, you simply connect the printer or modem to the server, a computer on the network, or directly to a network hub, router, or bridge. ◄— John knows that there are many benefits to using the Wired Coffee network to manage files and folders and wants to learn about networking.

John realizes that using a network enables his employees to do the following:

► **Share central resources through client/server networking**

Windows offers a network configuration called **client/server networking**. Under this arrangement, a single computer is designated as a server, allowing access to resources for any qualified user. Client/server networking provides all users on a network a central location for accessing shared files. Figure J-1 shows an example of a typical client/server network configuration.

► **Share resources through peer-to-peer networking**

Windows also offers a network configuration called peer-to-peer networking. **Peer-to-peer networking** enables two or more computers to link together without designating a central server. In this configuration, any computer user can access resources stored on any other computer, as long as those resources are available for sharing. Peer-to-peer networking allows individual computer users to share files and other resources, such as a printer, with other users on the network without having to access a server.

► **Share resources through network connections**

Windows provides connectivity between your computer and a network, another computer, or the Internet using **Network Connections**. Whether you are physically connected using a direct cable or connected remotely using a dial-up or cable modem, you can connect securely to a network over the Internet using a **Virtual Private Network (VPN)** connection or set up your computer to let other computers connect to yours using an **incoming network connection**. VPN and incoming network connection are examples of WANs.

► **Share designated files and folders on your computer with other network users**

Windows provides support for security, so even though your computer is connected to a network, you can designate which resources on your computer you want to share with others. Before network users can use any resources on your computer, they must be granted the required permission.

FIGURE J-1: Typical client/server network

Wireless signal

Workstation

WAN or Internet

Phone line and modem network connection

Network printer

LAN

Network router

Network server

Network hub

Workstation

Understanding a Home Phoneline Network

If you have several computers located in different rooms of your home, you can create a Home Phoneline Network (HPN) using the existing phone lines and telephone cable to connect the computers together without a network hub and special cables stretched from room to room. An HPN is an example of peer-to-peer networking. With an HPN, you can share files, printers, and an Internet connection among your computers like you can with any peer-to-peer network. Before you can set up an HPN, you need to install a Home Phoneline Network Adapter (HPNA) for each computer on your network and use telephone cable to physically connect each HPNA to a phone jack. Each phone jack functions like a port on a network hub, eliminating the need for a separate hardware device. An HPN uses existing phone lines, yet operates on a different band of frequencies, so it doesn't interfere with normal telephone calls.

Windows XP

Examining Network Computer Properties

Names and locations are used to identify computers on a network. The computer's name refers to the individual machine, and the computer's location refers to how the machine is grouped together with other computers. In a peer-to-peer network, individual computers are often organized into workgroups. A **workgroup** is a group of computers that perform common tasks or belong to users who share common duties and interests. In a client/server network, individual computers are often grouped into domains. A **domain** is a collection of computers that the person managing the network creates to group together computers used for the same tasks and to simplify the set up and maintenance of the network. The difference between a domain and a workgroup is that the network administrator defines the domains that exist on the network and controls access to computers within those domains. In a workgroup, each user determines who has access to his or her computer. Computers anywhere on the network can be located easily through the naming hierarchy and can be addressed individually by name. You can find the name and workgroup or domain of a computer on the network by examining the system properties. Workgroups are available on all Windows XP computers, but domains are available only with the Professional edition. John decides to check the properties of his network computer.

1. Click the **Start button** on the taskbar, click **Control Panel**, then click **Switch to Classic View** if necessary
   The Control Panel opens in Classic view.

Trouble?

References to domains and Network ID button appear only in the Professional Edition.

2. Double-click the **System icon** 💻, then click the **Computer Name tab** in the System Properties dialog box
   The Computer Name tab of the System Properties dialog box appears, as shown in Figure J-2. If you are not connected to a network domain, you can click Network ID to start the Network Identification Wizard to join a domain and create a local user account.

3. Click **Change**
   The Computer Name Changes dialog box opens, displaying the computer name and current membership, either domain or workgroup name, of this computer, as shown in Figure J-3. In this case, the network computer name is LAPTOP and the domain name is NETONE.

4. Click **Cancel**
   The System Properties dialog box appears.

5. Click **OK**, then click the **Close button** in the Control Panel window
   The Control Panel window closes.

Joining a network domain

If you are not connected to a network domain, you can use the Network Identification Wizard to join a domain and create a local user account. Before you start the Network Identification Wizard, you need to connect your computer to a client/server network using a network adapter and network cable. After you connect a network adapter to your computer and start Windows XP Professional, your computer automatically detects the network adapter and creates a local area connection. A local area connection is the only type of network connection that Windows automatically creates. To start the Network Identification Wizard, double-click the System icon in the Control Panel, click the Computer Name tab in the System Properties dialog box, then click Network ID. When the Network Identification Wizard dialog box opens, read the welcome, click Next, select the business network option, click Next, select the network with a domain option, then follow the step-by-step instructions to enter your user name, password, user account domain, computer name, and computer domain. Upon completion, Windows asks you to restart your computer.

FIGURE J-2: System Properties dialog box with Computer Name tab

Computer name; yours might differ

Domain name in Professional edition, or workgroup name; yours might differ

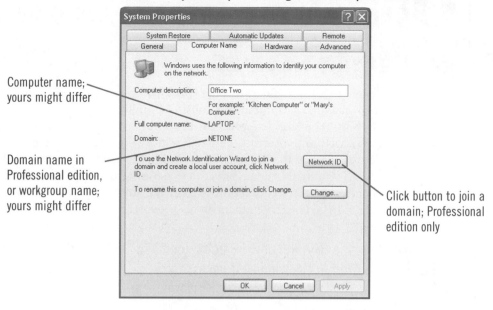

Click button to join a domain; Professional edition only

FIGURE J-3: Computer Name Changes dialog box

Domain available in Professional edition only

Domain or workgroup name appears here; yours might differ

Viewing network properties

A computer that uses a Windows network must be configured so that other machines on the network recognize it. On a small network, you might be responsible for configuring your computer, or that responsibility might fall to the network administrator. You can view and modify some of the network settings for your computer using the Network Connections window. In the Control Panel, double-click the Network Connections icon 🖧 to display current network connections. Right-click a network connection icon, then click Properties to display network settings. The network dialog box opens displaying the General tab with the name of your network interface card and a list of available network components. The network connection consists of three types of components: client, service, and protocol. The client type allows you to access computers and files on the network. The service type allows you to share your computer resources, such as files and printers, with other networked computers. Protocol is the language that the computer uses to communicate with other computers on the network. Understanding which components are installed on your computer helps you understand the capabilities and limitations of your computer on the network.

Opening and Viewing a Network

The key to managing files and folders in a network environment is understanding the structure of your particular network. Most networks consist of multiple types of computers and operating systems. My Network Places lets you view the entire network or just your part of the network to give you access to the servers, domains, and workgroups on the network. The Entire Network window allows you to view a list of servers not in your workgroup and to view other network domains. If you want to add a server to your workgroup, you can use the Add Network Place Wizard to help you through the process. John uses Windows networking to see where his computer fits with all the others on his network.

Trouble?

If the My Network Places icon is not on the desktop, right-click the desktop, click Properties, click the Desktop tab, click Customize Desktop, click the My Network Places check box to select it, then click OK twice.

1. Double-click the **My Network Places icon** 🖳 on the desktop, then click the **Maximize button** in the window if necessary
   The My Network Places window opens, displaying shared folders available on your immediate network.

2. In the Other Places section of the task pane, click **Entire Network**, or click **My Network Places** in the Address bar, type **Entire Network**, then press **[Enter]**
   The Entire Network window appears, displaying various segments and computers connected to your network, such as Microsoft Windows Network. If you are on a large network, you might have other choices that display more segments of the network.

3. Double-click the **Microsoft Windows Network icon** 🌐 in the network window
   The Microsoft Windows Network window appears, displaying current domains in your network, as shown in Figure J-4.

4. Double-click a **domain icon** 🖧 in the network window
   The network computers connected to the domain appear, as shown in Figure J-5. You decide to view the contents of a computer connected to your network.

5. Double-click a **network computer icon** 🖳 in the network window
   The computer connected to your network opens and displays the contents of the drive or folder, as shown in Figure J-6. In this case, the computer contains a shared printer and folder, access to other printers and faxes, and scheduled tasks.

6. Click the **Close button** in the network window
   The network window closes.

Creating a shortcut to a network location

Instead of clicking numerous icons in My Network Places to access a network location, by using the Add Network Place Wizard you can create a shortcut to the network location in the My Network Places window for easy access. The wizard provides step-by-step instructions to select the network location and create a shortcut. The wizard also allows you to create a shortcut to a Web or FTP (File Transfer Protocol) site. If you need storage space on the Internet to manage, organize, and share documents, you can also use the Add Network Place Wizard to help you sign up for a service that offers online storage space. To start the Add Network

Place Wizard, double-click the My Network Places icon on the desktop, then click Add a network place in the Network Tasks section of the task pane. When the Add Network Place Wizard dialog box opens, click Next, click Choose another network location, click Next, click Browse, select the network location to which you want to connect, click OK, click Next, enter a shortcut name for the network location, click Next, then click Finish. Upon completion, the network location window appears, and the shortcut with the 🖳 icon appears in the My Network Places folder.

FIGURE J-4: Microsoft Windows Network window

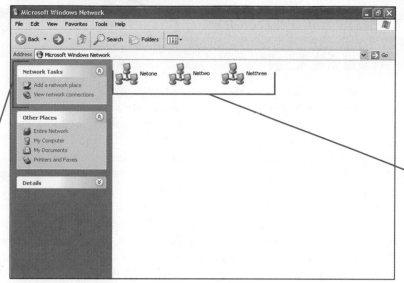

Network Task options are different depending on your network type, either domain or workgroup

Current domains; your list might differ

FIGURE J-5: Contents of a domain

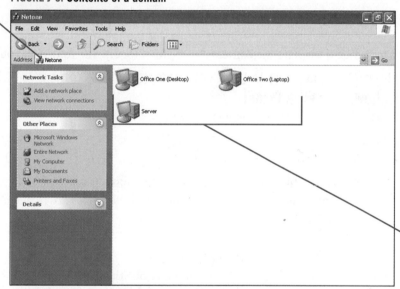

Current domain; yours might differ

Current servers or shared computers; your list might differ

FIGURE J-6: Contents of a server or shared computer

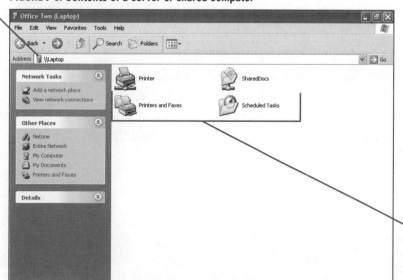

Current server or shared computer; yours might differ

Your contents might differ

Creating a Shared Folder

Windows XP

To create a shared folder on a network, you use many of the file management skills you learned with My Computer and Windows Explorer. You can create a new folder to share or use an existing one anywhere on your computer. For example, you can create a shared folder in a subfolder within your My Documents folder. After you select the folder you want to share, you use the Sharing and Security command in My Computer or Windows Explorer to share the folder and its contents on a network and to specify whether you want to give network users permission to change the contents of the shared folder. When you create a shared folder, you have the option to use the name of the folder or another name as the **share name**, which is the name network users see on the network in My Network Places. If you use a different share name, the original folder's name remains the same. Unless you have a very good reason for naming it differently, it's best to make the shared name the same as the folder name. Keeping the names consistent helps to avoid confusion. If you are not working in a network environment, you may not be able to complete these steps. In this case, simply read the steps without completing them. John has decided to create a shared folder on his computer called Sales that will allow employees from anywhere on the network to add information to Sales files.

1. Click the **Start button** on the taskbar, then click **My Documents**
   The window displays the contents of the My Documents folder on your hard drive.

2. Right-click anywhere in the My Documents window (except on a file or folder), point to **New**, then click **Folder**
   A new folder, named New Folder, appears in the window.

3. Type **Sales**, then press **[Enter]**
   The folder is now named Sales.

4. Right-click the **Sales folder icon**, then click **Sharing and Security** on the shortcut menu
   The Sales Properties dialog box opens. You can use the Sales Properties dialog box to adjust the settings to allow other users access to the files in your shared folder. The Sharing tab allows you to designate the kind of access you want other users to have for the folder you just created.

Trouble?

If you are connected to a workgroup instead of a domain, the Sharing tab commands are different. Click the Share this folder on the network check box to select it, click the Allow network users to change my files check box to select it, then skip to Step 8.

5. Click the **Share this folder option button**
   Figure J-7 shows the sharing information about the Sales folder. The sharing tab includes a text box for entering the shared name of the folder. By default, Windows automatically enters the name of the folder as the shared name and sets the file permission to full control.

6. Click **Permissions**
   The Permissions for Sales dialog box opens, displaying permission settings. The default permission settings provide full control to any user.

7. Click **OK** to close the Permissions for Sales dialog box

Trouble?

If a Server service error message box appears, you need to install file sharing. Double-click the Network Connections icon 🖧 in the Control Panel, right-click the network connection icon, click Properties, click Install, click Service, click Add, click File and Print Sharing for Microsoft Networks, then click OK twice.

8. Click **OK** to close the Sales Properties dialog box
   Anyone can now access the Sales folder, shown in Figure J-8, from anywhere on the network. The 🗁 icon indicates that the folder is a shared folder.

FIGURE J-7: Sales Properties dialog box with Sharing tab

Shared folder name

Click option to specify maximum number of users at a time

Click button to specify permission settings

FIGURE J-8: Shared folder within the My Documents folder

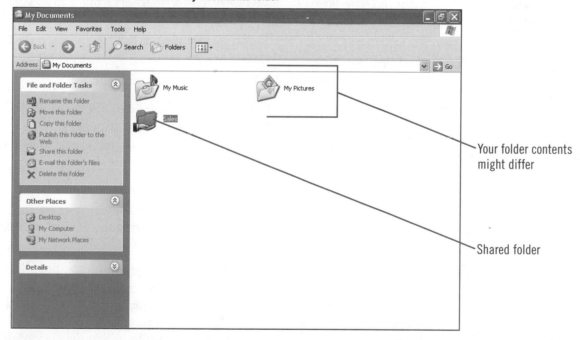

Your folder contents might differ

Shared folder

CLUES TO USE

File permission properties

Every file in the Windows file system includes permissions for each user, or settings that designate what each user can and cannot do to each file. Two basic types of file permissions are available for users: read and full. Read permission allows the user to open and view the file but not to make changes that can be saved in the file. When you open a read-only file, the words "Read Only" appear in the title bar. You can makes changes, but an error message appears when you try to save the file. You can save the file with a new name in a different location and have full access to it. Full permission allows the user to edit and save changes to the file (or "write") and execute programs on server or client computers. Qualified users or system administrators use file permissions and passwords to control who can access any specific area of the network. In this way, the network remains secure against unauthorized use.

Windows XP

Mapping a Network Drive

Windows networking enables you to connect your computer to other computers on the network quite easily. If you connect to a network location frequently, you might want to designate a drive letter on your computer as a direct connection to a shared drive or folder on another computer. Instead of spending unnecessary time opening My Network Places and the shared drive or folder each time you want to access it, you can create a direct connection, called **mapping** a drive, to the network location for quick and easy access. ✎━━━ At John's request, the network administrator creates a shared folder called Wired Coffee on the computer named Server. Now John uses My Network Places to map a drive letter from his computer to that folder so that he can easily move files to this central location for others to share. To complete these steps, you need to map to a network computer and a folder specified by your instructor or technical support person.

Steps

Trouble?

Before beginning, ask your instructor which networked computer you can map onto your computer. If you do not have a networked computer available, read the steps without completing them.

1. Click the **Address list arrow**, scroll if necessary, then click **My Network Places**
Windows networking shows all the active computers in your immediate network.

2. Click **Tools** on the menu bar, then click **Map Network Drive**
The Map Network Drive dialog box opens, as shown in Figure J-9. By default, the Map Network Drive dialog box assigns network drive letters from Z to A. Local drives, such as your hard drive or removable store drives, are assigned letters from A to Z. You decide that the default network drive letter choice is okay. Now you want to select the shared folder.

QuickTip

To use a different drive letter, click the Drive list arrow, then click the drive letter you want to use. To reassign a drive letter after it has been assigned, disconnect from the drive, then remap the drive.

3. Click **Browse**
The Browse For Folder dialog box opens, as shown in Figure J-10.

4. Click the **Expand indicator** ⊞ as necessary to navigate to the **networked computer icon** supplied by your instructor or technical support person
In this case, the networked computer called Server opens. The window for the networked computer opens and displays the folders available for file sharing.

5. Click the shared **Wired Coffee folder** (or the folder specified by your instructor or technical support person) to select it, then click **OK**
The Map Network Drive dialog box appears, displaying the network path to the server. You want to reconnect to the drive every time you log on.

Trouble?

If your mapped drives do not automatically reconnect when you log on, make sure your user name and password are the same for all the networks to which you connect.

6. If not already checked, click the **Reconnect at logon check box**, then click **Finish**
The Map Network Drive dialog box closes, and Windows networking maps a drive connecting your computer to the shared Wired Coffee folder (or to the shared folder specified by your instructor or technical support person). When the connection is complete, a window appears for the newly mapped drive, allowing you to view the files within the mapped drive, as shown in Figure J-11. You can now easily copy folders and files from your floppy disk into the shared folder.

7. Click the **Close button** in the mapped drive window
The My Network Places window appears.

FIGURE J-9: **Map Network Drive dialog box**

Drive letter

Select check box to
reconnect drive
automatically each
time you log on

Click button to select
folder on the network

Sample network path

FIGURE J-10: **Browse For Folder dialog box**

Wired Coffee folder
located on Server

FIGURE J-11: **Wired Coffee folder window on Server**

Your contents
might differ

Creating a network connection

Network Connections provides connectivity between your computer and a network, another computer, or the Internet. With the New Connections Wizard, you can set up a home or small office network, connect to the Internet, connect to a remote network using a dial-up or Virtual Private Network (VPN) connection, connect directly to another computer using a cable, or accept incoming connection access to your computer, which means your computer running Windows XP can operate as a remote access server, or as a dial-up network server. To establish any one of these connection types, click the Start button on the taskbar, point to All Programs, point to Accessories, point to Communications, click New Connection Wizard, click Next, click the connection option you want, and then follow the instructions in the Network Connection Wizard. To connect to the network, double-click the connection icon in the Network Connections window.

Copying and Moving Shared Files

Once you create shared folders and map your network drives, copying and moving shared files and folders in Windows is as easy as managing files on your own computer. The only difference is that data transfer can take longer over a network than it does on your local computer. You can copy and move files using any of the Windows file management tools: My Network Places, My Computer, or Windows Explorer. My Network Places works just like My Computer. ➤ John wants to copy files from his floppy disk into the shared Sales folder on his hard drive to make them accessible to the other users on his network. He also needs to move a file from the shared Sales folder to the Wired Coffee folder on the network drive (Z:) to make it accessible to another department. Since he's copying files to several locations, John uses Windows Explorer to drag and drop the files.

Steps

Trouble?

If you are using a floppy disk for your Project Files, make a copy of the disk before you use it and insert the copy into your disk drive. See your instructor or technical support person for assistance.

1. Make sure a copy of the disk or drive where your Project Files are located is available

2. In the Windows networking window, click the **Address list arrow**, click the drive where your Project Files are located, then double-click the folder where your Project Files are located
   The Windows networking window displays the contents of your Project Files.

3. Right-click the **Wired Coffee folder**, click **Explore**, then click the **Sales folder** in the Folders Explorer Bar
   Windows Explorer opens, displaying the available folders and drives in the left pane, as shown in Figure J-12. You can now copy or move files easily from your computer to anywhere on the network. Next you copy the files named Coffee Prices, Customer Profile, and Suppliers to the shared Sales folder you created on Drive C.

Trouble?

If you click the shared Sales folder by mistake, click the Sales folder from your Project Disk, then go to Step 5.

4. In the Folders Explorer Bar, click the **Expand indicator** ⊞ next to the My Documents folder to display the shared Sales folder (the one with a hand), but do not click the folder

5. Click **Edit** on the menu bar, click **Select All**, then drag the files from the right pane to the shared **Sales folder** in the Folders Explorer Bar
   This copies files to the shared Sales folder on the hard drive. Anyone who has access to your computer can now share the files.

6. In the Folders Explorer Bar, click the shared **Sales folder**, then click the **down scroll arrow** in the Folders Explorer Bar until you can see the icon representing the mapped network folder
   Windows Explorer lists the contents of the Sales folder, as shown in Figure J-13.

7. Right-click the **Suppliers file**, drag the file to the mapped networked folder in the Folders Explorer Bar, then click **Move Here** on the shortcut menu
   The Suppliers file is now in the networked folder.

8. Click the **mapped network folder** in the Folders Explorer Bar to view the Suppliers file, then click the **Close button** in both windows

FIGURE J-12: Sales folder on Project Disk

Contents
of Sales
folder on
Project Disk

Mapped drive; your list might differ

FIGURE J-13: Shared Sales folder

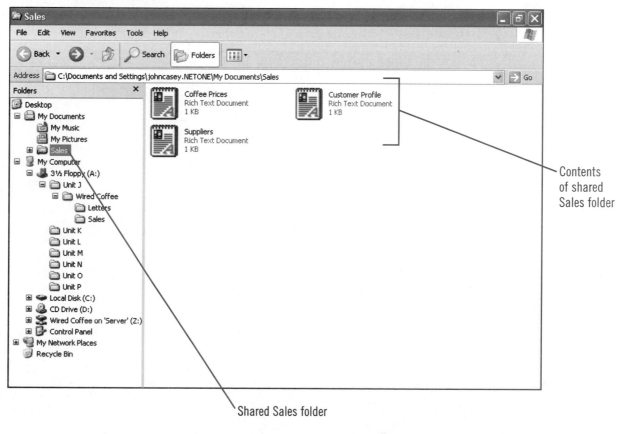

Contents
of shared
Sales folder

Shared Sales folder

Windows XP

Opening and Editing a Shared File

Working with shared files on a network is simple with Windows. Once you map all the necessary drives to your network folders, you can use network files in any program from your computer. For example, you can use WordPad to edit text files or Paint to create a graphic. You might also be able to use programs installed on the server specifically for the use of individual clients. Ask your system administrator about available options. ⟶ John uses WordPad to make corrections in the Suppliers file that he placed in the Wired Coffee folder on the server.

Steps

1. Click the **Start button** on the taskbar, point to **All Programs**, point to **Accessories**, then click **WordPad**
   The WordPad window opens.

2. Click **File** on the menu bar, click **Open**, then click the **Look in list arrow**
   The Open dialog box opens, as shown in Figure J-14, displaying the Look in list with local and networked drives. From here you can open files located on all drives and folders, including the drives mapped to the network.

3. Click the **icon** for the mapped network drive to the Wired Coffee shared folder
   A list of files stored in the networked folder appears in the Open dialog box, as shown in Figure J-15.

4. Click **Suppliers**, then click **Open**
   The file named Suppliers opens. You want to add another supplier to the list.

5. Click the bottom of the list, then type **Homegrown USA Coffee**

6. Click the **Save button** 💾 on the toolbar
   WordPad saves the changes to the file Suppliers.

7. Click the **Close button** in the WordPad window

FIGURE J-14: Open dialog box with Look in list

Look in list arrow

Mapped drive; your list might differ

FIGURE J-15: Open dialog box with files on mapped drive

Wired Coffee folder on Server

Files on mapped drive Z; your list might differ

CLUES TO USE

Network traffic

Large networks can serve hundreds of users simultaneously. Like water flowing through pipes, only a certain amount of data can pass through the wires connecting the individual computers at any given time. If the amount of network traffic is sufficiently heavy, then the flow of data might slow considerably, causing file operations, such as opening, saving, and copying, to take longer to complete.

Disconnecting a Network Drive

Windows XP

Usually, you map a network drive to reconnect automatically every time you log on. However, sometimes you might find it necessary to disconnect a mapped drive manually. Your system administrator might add a new hard drive to the server, or she might reorganize the directory structure of the network, making the network path for the mapped drive incorrect. When this occurs, Windows makes the process of disconnecting a mapped drive very easy. ⟍ The system administrator informs John that a network reorganization will take place over the weekend. To prepare for the reorganization, John cleans up his hard drive and the mapped drive. Then he disconnects the drive mapped to (Z:) until he finds out what changes have been made.

1. Click the **Start button** on the taskbar, click the **My Computer icon**, then double-click the **mapped drive**
   The contents of the mapped drive appear. You want to delete the Suppliers file.

2. Right-click the **Suppliers file**, click **Delete**, then click **Yes** to confirm the deletion

3. In the Other Places section of the task pane, click **My Documents**
   You want to delete the shared folder.

4. Right-click the shared **Sales folder**, then click **Delete**
   The Confirm Folder Delete dialog box opens. You confirm the deletion.

5. Click **Yes** to confirm the folder deletion, click **Yes** in the sharing message box if necessary, then click the **Close button** in the My Documents window
   After cleaning up your hard drive and the mapped drive, you disconnect the mapped drive.

QuickTip

To disconnect a network drive in Windows Explorer, right-click the mapped network drive in the left pane, then click Disconnect.

6. Right-click the **My Network Places icon** 🖥 on the desktop
   A shortcut menu appears, as shown in Figure J-16. This menu provides several options for working in a network environment. See Table J-1 for a description of the options available on this menu.

7. Click **Disconnect Network Drive** on the shortcut menu
   The Disconnect Network Drives dialog box appears, as shown in Figure J-17. The dialog box lists all the network drives that you have mapped from your computer. You should check with your system administrator or instructor before actually disconnecting a drive. To quit without actually disconnecting a drive, click Cancel.

8. To disconnect the drive you mapped, click the **mapped drive** with the Wired Coffee folder, click **OK**, then click **Yes** in the warning message if necessary
   Windows disconnects the drive you selected and closes the Disconnect Network Drives dialog box.

Network paths

The path to a shared network directory is like the path to a file on a hard or floppy disk. For example, the path to the Suppliers file on your Project Files Disk is A:\Wired Coffee\Sales\Suppliers. Network paths replace the drive designation with the host computer name, as in \\Server\Wired Coffee. In either case, the path tells the computer where to look for the files you need.

FIGURE J-16: Shortcut menu for My Network Places

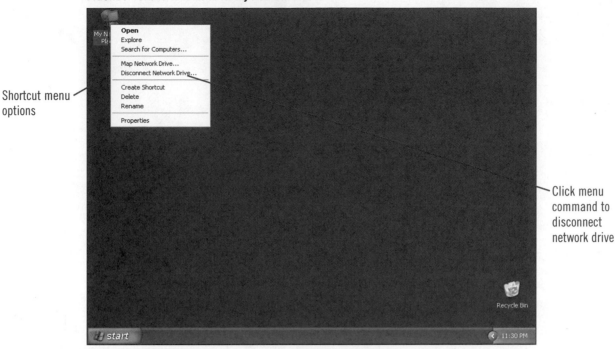

Shortcut menu options

Click menu command to disconnect network drive

FIGURE J-17: Disconnect Network Drives dialog box

Your list of drives might differ

TABLE J-1: Shortcut menu commands for My Network Places

option	function
Open	Starts My Network Places
Explore	Opens Windows Explorer in order to copy and move files or folders from one folder to another, whether on your local computer or the network
Search for Computers	Finds a computer whose name you know but not its location
Map Network Drive	Maps a drive from your computer to a shared directory on another computer
Disconnect Network Drive	Disconnects a drive on your computer from a shared directory on another computer
Create Shortcut	Creates a shortcut to My Network Places
Rename	Renames the My Network Places icon
Properties	Views the properties of your network

Practice

► Concepts Review

Label each element of the screen shown in Figure J-18.

FIGURE J-18

1. Which element points to a domain?
2. Which element points to a folder on a network server?
3. Which element points to a network file?
4. Which element points to a network server?
5. Which element creates a shortcut to a network location?
6. Which element displays network locations?

Match each of the terms with the statement that describes its function.

7. Shared folder
8. File permissions
9. Client
10. Network path
11. Server

a. Determines who can read, write, or execute files
b. A location where multiple users can access the same files
c. The address for an individual computer on a network
d. A computer on a network that uses shared resources
e. A computer on a network designated to share resources

Select the best answers from the following lists of choices.

12. **A network in which the computers are connected close together is called a:**
    a. LAN.
    b. WAN.
    c. VPN.
    d. HPN.

13. **A Virtual Private Network is an example of a:**
    a. LAN.
    b. WAN.
    c. HPN.
    d. USB.

14. **What hardware device connects multiple LANs together?**
    a. Network interface card
    b. Router
    c. Hub
    d. Client

15. **In a client/server network, computers are organized into:**
    a. Workgroups.
    b. Domains.
    c. Clients.
    d. Servers.

16. **What network component allows you to share your computer resources?**
    a. Client
    b. Service
    c. Protocol
    d. NIC

17. **The Windows XP network management tool that allows you to inspect the configuration of your network is called:**
    a. Windows Explorer.
    b. My Computer.
    c. Network Neighborhood.
    d. My Network Places.

18. **To disconnect a network drive:**
    a. Double-click the drive letter in My Network Places.
    b. Highlight the drive letter, click File on the menu bar, then click Delete.
    c. Click the drive letter, then drag it to the Recycle Bin.
    d. Right-click the My Network Places icon, then click Disconnect Network Drive.

19. **When you highlight a drive letter in My Network Places, click File on the menu bar, then click Explore:**
    a. My Computer starts, allowing you to manage files and folders.
    b. My Network Places displays the entire network.
    c. Windows Explorer starts, allowing you to manage files and folders.
    d. File Manager starts, allowing you to manage files and folders.

20. **When you map a networked drive:**
    a. Windows networking displays a graphic showing the entire structure of the network.
    b. You can use the shared files and folders of another computer on the network.
    c. The computer you are using is attached to the network.
    d. Windows networking adds your computer to the network path.

21. **If the file permissions for a shared folder are set to read only:**
    a. No one can read the files in the folder.
    b. You can edit the file and save your changes.
    c. Everyone can read the files but not write to the files.
    d. Everyone can execute files but not write to the files.

▶ Skills Review

1. **Examine network computer properties.**
   a. Open the Control Panel, then open System Properties.
   b. Display the network computer name and domain.
   c. Click OK, then close the Control Panel.

2. **Open and view a network.**
   a. Open My Network Places, display the Entire Network, then display the Microsoft Windows Network.
   b. Display the domain supplied by your instructor or technical support person.
   c. Double-click the network computer supplied by your instructor or technical support person.
   d. Close the network window.

3. **Create a shared folder.**
   a. Display My Documents, right-click in the My Documents window, point to New, then click Folder.
   b. Name the new folder **Memos**, then press [Enter].
   c. Click File on the menu bar, then click Sharing and Security.
   d. Click the Share this folder option button. (If you are working in a Workgroup, close the Share this folder on the network check box to select it, click the Allow network users to change My files check box to select it, then skip to Step 3f.)
   e. Click Permission, select the Read-Only setting, then click OK.
   f. Click OK.

4. **Map a network drive.**
   a. Display My Network Places.
   b. Navigate to the network computer to which you want to map.
   c. Click the shared folder to which you want to map.
   d. Click Tools on the menu bar, then click Map Network Drive.
   e. Click the Reconnect at logon check box to select it, click OK, then click the Close button.

5. **Copy and move shared files.**
   a. Make sure a copy of the disk or drive where your Project Files are located is available.
   b. Click the Address list arrow, click the drive where your Project Files are located, then double-click the folder where your Project Files are located.
   c. Click the Wired Coffee folder, then display the Folder Explorer Bar.
   d. Click the Letters folder in the Explorer Bar.
   e. Click the Expand icon next to the My Documents folder.
   f. Select all the files, then drag them to the shared Memos folder you created in the My Documents folder.
   g. Click the shared Memos folder in the Explorer Bar.
   h. Move the IRS Letter file to the mapped networked folder in the Explorer Bar.
   i. Click the mapped networked folder in the Explorer Bar to view the file, then close both windows.

6. **Open and edit a shared file.**
   a. Open the IRS Letter file from the shared Memos folder on your hard drive in WordPad.
   b. Change the date in the body of the letter from April 25 to May 10.
   c. Save the file, print it, then close the file and WordPad.

7. **Disconnect a network drive.**
   a. Open My Computer, double-click the mapped drive, then delete the IRS Letter file.
   b. Display My Documents, delete the shared Memos folder, then close My Documents.
   c. Right-click the My Network Places icon, then click Disconnect Network Drive.
   d. Select the drive you mapped in Step 4, click OK, then click Yes if necessary.

► Independent Challenge 1

As the new clerk at a craft store called Holly's, you are asked to create a list of suppliers' names. Your task is to enter the supplier information in a new file and place that file in two places for others to use. You must create a shared folder on your computer to store the file, then map a drive to a network folder that will also contain the file.

 If you are not connected to a network, ask your instructor or technical support person for help in completing this independent challenge. If you are working in a lab environment, you may not be able to create a shared folder. If so, do not create a shared folder; use the folder supplied by your instructor instead.

a. Open the My Documents folder and display the Folders Explorer bar.
b. Create a shared folder called Suppliers with read-only permissions.
c. Open WordPad and enter the following information in a new document:

Name	Address	City & State or Country
Baskets & Things	101 Hopyard Road	Chicago, IL
Frames R Us	1934 Hummingbird Lane	Los Angeles, CA
Season's	125 34th Street	New York, NY
Royal Touch	34 Birkshire Street	London, England
Ming's Crafts	2685 Queen Street	Hong Kong, China

d. Save the file as Supplier List in the newly created Suppliers folder, then print the file.
e. Map a drive to a shared folder on another computer to which you have permission.
f. Create a World Wide Suppliers folder on that drive.
g. Copy the Supplier List file from the Suppliers folder on the local computer to the World Wide Suppliers folder on the mapped drive.

h. Print the screen. (Press [Print Screen] to make a copy of the screen, open Paint, click Edit on the menu bar, click Paste to paste the screen into Paint, then click Yes to paste the large image if necessary. Click the Text button on the Toolbox, click a blank area in the Paint work area, then type your name. Click File on the menu bar, click Page Setup, change 100% normal size to 50% in the Scaling area, then click OK. Click File on the menu bar, click Print, then click Print.)

i. Delete the Suppliers folder on your hard drive and the World Wide Suppliers folder on the mapped drive.

j. Disconnect the network drive you mapped, and delete the shared folder you created.

Independent Challenge 2

As president of your company, you decide to increase the pay rates of two of your employees, Jessica Thielen and Debbie Cabral. You use WordPad to write a memo that you can edit and use for both employees. After completing the memos, you print the documents for the employees. You also want to copy the documents to the company server so they can be stored in the employees' folders.

a. Create a **Memos** folder on the drive and in the folder where your Project Files are located.

b. Open WordPad and type the following memo in a new document:
   Dear Jessica,
   Your service to this company is greatly appreciated. To show my appreciation to such an outstanding employee as yourself, I have decided to give you a 10% raise in salary. The raise will go into effect with the next pay period.
   Sincerely yours,
   Your Name

c. Save the document **Thielen Raise** to the Memos folder, then print the document.

d. Change **Dear Jessica** to **Dear Debbie** in the Thielen Raise memo.

e. Save the file as **Cabral Raise** in the Memos folder, print the document, close the file, then close WordPad.

f. Map a drive to a shared folder on another computer to which you have permission.

g. Create a folder called **Thielen** on the mapped drive, and copy the Thielen Raise file from your Project Disk into the Thielen folder.

h. Create a shared folder called **Cabral** on the mapped drive, and copy the Cabral Raise file into the Cabral folder.

i. Print the screen. (See Independent Challenge 1, Step h for screen printing instructions.)

j. Delete the Thielen and Cabral shared folders on the mapped drive, then disconnect the network drive you mapped.

► Independent Challenge 3

You are the system administrator for your company's computer network. During peak usage of the network, you want to monitor who is on the network. You use the Properties command in the My Network Places to learn who is connected to the network.

a. Open My Network Places.

b. Display the network identification for two connected computers to learn their names and domain.

c. Print the screen for the network identification for the connected computers. (See Independent Challenge 1, Step h for screen printing instructions.)

d. Map two drives to a shared folder on another computer to which you have permission.

e. Display the network identification for the mapped drives.

f. Print the screen for the network identification for the mapped drives (See Independent Challenge 1, Step h for screen printing instructions.)

g. Disconnect the network drives you mapped.

▶ Independent Challenge 4

The system administrator for your network calls and informs you that he needs to make some changes to the directory structure. He advises you to move any files you put on the server recently and to disconnect any mapped drives.

a. Map a drive to a shared folder on another computer to which you have permission, and copy two files from your Project Files to this mapped drive.

b. Using My Network Places, create a shared folder on your local hard disk called **Network Files**.

c. Move the files from the folder on the network drive to the shared Network Files folder on the local hard disk.

d. Print the screen. (See Independent Challenge 1, Step h for screen printing instructions.)

e. Disconnect the mapped drive from the network, then delete the shared folder on your local hard drive.

▶ Visual Workshop

Re-create the screen shown in Figure J-19, which displays the files on a local hard drive and files on a network drive. Print the screen. (See Independent Challenge 1, Step h for screen printing instructions.)

FIGURE J-19

Sharing
Information among Programs

Objectives

- ► **Understand object linking and embedding**
- ► **Embed a new object**
- ► **Embed an existing object**
- ► **Edit an embedded object**
- ► **Embed a video clip**
- ► **Modify a video clip**
- ► **Link an object**
- ► **Update a link**

You can supplement text in a document with pictures and other visuals to make your document more interesting. Charts, tables, and pictures, when combined with text, can convey your message much more effectively than text alone. Windows XP makes it easy to insert a file or part of a file that was created in one program into a file that was created in a different program. The ability to share files and information among different programs is called **object linking and embedding** (**OLE**, pronounced "oh-lay"). With OLE, you can work with a document in WordPad and take advantage of the specialized tools in a program, such as Paint or Microsoft Excel, at the same time. John Casey, owner of Wired Coffee Company, will use OLE to place a picture of his signature and a picture of his company logo in a sales promotion document. He will also use OLE to insert a video clip in a promotional document and to link a picture to a flier.

Understanding Object Linking and Embedding

OLE involves sharing information between two programs. The information, often referred to as an **object**, can be a picture from a graphics program, a chart from a spreadsheet program, a video clip, text, or almost anything else you can create on a computer. The program that creates the object is called the **source program**; the program that creates the file into which you want to insert the object is called the **destination program**. Likewise, the file that originally contained the object is called the **source file**, and the file where you want to insert the object is called the **destination file**. Both embedding and linking involve inserting an object into a destination file; they differ in where their respective objects are stored. With **embedding**, a copy of the object becomes part of the destination file. If you want to edit the object, you make changes in the destination file, and the original file remains intact. With **linking**, a representation of the object appears in the destination file, but the object is stored in the source file. If you want to edit the linked object, you make changes in the source file or its representation in the destination file, and the changes will be reflected in the other file the next time you open it. Figure K-1 illustrates the process of embedding an object into a document, and Figure K-2 illustrates the process of linking an object to a document. Table K-1 can help you decide whether to embed or link an object. John wants to explore the benefits of sharing information between programs.

By using OLE, John will be able to do the following:

► **Access features from other programs**
With OLE, John can put information from one program into another. For example, he can insert a picture into WordPad (a word processing program) by using Paint (a drawing program).

► **Edit data easily**
When you embed or link an object, you can edit the object directly in the embedded program. For example, if John embeds or links a Paint drawing into a WordPad document, he can edit the drawing from WordPad while using Paint tools. The Paint tools are made available in the destination program through the object.

► **Update to the latest information**
Some of your documents may contain objects from source files that other users access, such as financial information or artwork. If you insert the object with a link, Windows will update the object automatically if a user changes the source file. For example, John can link a Paint drawing to his WordPad document. If someone changes the Paint drawing, John's WordPad document is updated with the changes the next time he opens the document in WordPad.

► **Save space**
When you link an object to a document, a representation of the object, which takes up less disk space than the object itself, appears in the document. The actual object is stored in the source file, and the destination file stays small. Embedding, on the other hand, can require more disk space because the object is actually copied to the destination file. John can use linking to keep the file size of his documents small, thereby saving disk space on his computer.

FIGURE K-1: **Embedding an object**

Destination program (WordPad)

Embedded object

Destination program (WordPad) with embedded object (in Paint)

FIGURE K-2: **Linking an object**

Destination program (WordPad)

Representation of the object

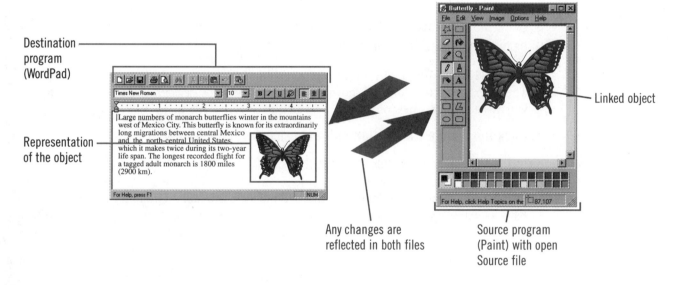

Linked object

Any changes are reflected in both files

Source program (Paint) with open Source file

TABLE K-1: **Embedding versus linking**

situation	action
You are the only user of an object, and you want it to be part of your document	Embed
You want to access the object in its source program, even if the original file is not available	Embed
You want to update the object manually while working in the destination program	Embed
You always want an updated object	Link
The object's source file is on a network where others can change or access it	Link
You want to keep your document file size small	Link

Windows XP

Embedding a New Object

Sometimes an application isn't capable of creating the data you need to display. For example, if you wanted to include a picture in a WordPad document, which does not have drawing features, you could start Paint, create a picture in Paint, copy it, switch to WordPad, and paste the picture into your document. Instead of switching back and forth between programs to create and insert a picture, you can embed a Paint object from WordPad. When you embed a Paint object into your WordPad document, Paint automatically starts in the WordPad program window, so you can create and edit the drawing without leaving WordPad. Embedding can be done with the Insert Object command, and the Copy and Paste Special commands. John wants to create a picture of his signature and place the picture at the bottom of a sales document.

Steps

1. Click the **Start button** on the taskbar, point to **All Programs**, point to **Accessories**, then click **WordPad**
   WordPad opens with a blank document.

2. Open the file **WIN K-1** from the drive and folder where your Project Files are located, then save it as **Sales Promotion**
   The Sales Promotion file opens in the WordPad window.

3. Click the **Maximize button** in the WordPad window if necessary, then click one line below the phrase **"Sincerely yours,"** to place the insertion point

4. Click **Insert** on the menu bar, then click **Object**
   The Insert Object dialog box, shown in Figure K-3, lets you select an object type and specify whether to create a new object or insert an object from a file that already exists.

5. Click the **Create New option button** to select it if necessary

6. In the Object Type list box, scroll to and click **Paintbrush Picture**, then click **OK**
   An empty Paint canvas appears inside a selection box (indicated by gray slanted lines) in the WordPad document, and Paint's menus and tools are available. Though it appears that you have switched to Paint (the source program), the title bar confirms that you are still in WordPad. As long as the Paint object is selected, however, you can use the Paint tools as if you were in the stand-alone Paint program.

7. Click the **Pencil tool** 🖉 on the Toolbox if necessary, then drag in the Paint object to draw the name **John**, as shown in Figure K-4
   If you don't like how a line appears, use the Undo command on the Edit menu.

QuickTip

To delete an object in the destination program, click the object, then press [Delete].

8. Click outside of the drawing area to exit Paint
   The source program closes, and the embedded Paint object becomes part of your document; it is a graphic object that can be moved or resized just like any other object. Sizing handles appear around the embedded object, indicating that it is currently selected.

9. Click outside of the object to deselect it, then click the **Save button** 🖫 on the toolbar to save the document
   Compare your screen to Figure K-5.

FIGURE K-3: **Insert Object dialog box**

Insert Object options

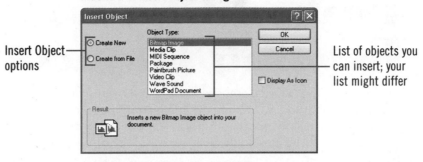

List of objects you can insert; your list might differ

FIGURE K-4: **Embedded Paint object**

Title bar shows you are still in WordPad

Pencil tool

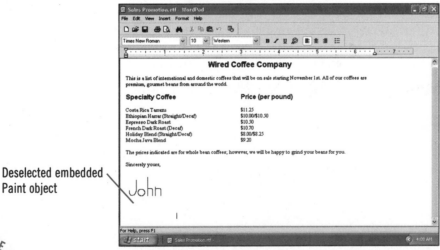

Paint Toolbox

Embedded Paint project

FIGURE K-5: **WordPad document with Paint object**

Deselected embedded Paint object

Viewing object properties

If you need to find out the type, size, or location of an object in a document, you can select the object, then click Object Properties on the Edit menu to display this information. The General tab appears with the object information, including the object's type and original location. You can also change the appearance of an object with the View tab in the Object Properties dialog box. An embedded object can appear as editable information, such as a picture or chart, or as an icon. By default, an object appears as editable information, but you can change an object to appear as an icon in order to save disk space. Depending on the type of object, such as a graphic file, you can also change the size of the object.

Windows XP

Embedding an Existing Object

In addition to creating and embedding an object from scratch, you can also embed an existing file. When you embed an existing file into a document, a copy of the file is stored in the destination document as an object. The original file remains unchanged, and the object becomes part of the document. ⟍ John wants to embed the company logo into his sales document.

Steps 1 2 3 4

1. In the WordPad document, scroll if necessary, then click in the blank line above the title "Wired Coffee Company"
This places the insertion point where you want the company logo to appear.

> **QuickTip**
> To place the insertion point at the beginning of a document, press [Ctrl][Home].

2. Click **Insert** on the menu bar, then click **Object**
The Insert Object dialog box opens.

3. Click the **Create from File option button**
The Object Type list box changes to the File text box.

> **QuickTip**
> To insert an icon in a document in place of an object, click the Display As Icon check box to select it in the Insert Object dialog box. To view the object, double-click the icon in the document.

4. Click **Browse**
The Browse dialog box opens, from which you can select the file to insert.

5. Navigate to the drive and folder where your Project Files are located, click **Wired Coffee Logo**, then click **Open**
As shown in Figure K-6, the full path name appears in the File text box. The object type for Wired Coffee Logo is a bitmap image. A bitmap image (BMP) is a common file format for pictures that are used by drawing programs.

> **QuickTip**
> When you insert an existing file into a document, the source program for the embedded object does not start. You can start the source program and make changes by double-clicking the object.

6. Click **OK**
The embedded object is inserted into the WordPad document. Compare your screen to Figure K-7. Sizing handles appear around the embedded object, indicating that it is selected. Sizing handles are the small black boxes around the edge of a selected object. In WordPad, as in other Windows programs, sizing handles are used to change the shape and size of an object.

7. Click the **Save button** 🖫 on the toolbar to save the document

CLUES TO USE

Embedding objects by copying and pasting

Instead of using the Insert Object command to embed files, you can also embed files by copying and pasting. For example, if you want to embed a slide from Microsoft PowerPoint to a Word document, you can open the PowerPoint file, select the slide, click the Copy button on the Standard toolbar, open the Word document, place the insertion point where you want to embed the object, click Edit on the menu bar, click Paste Special, click the Paste option button, click the embedded object type (in this case Microsoft PowerPoint Slide Object), then click OK. When embedding is not supported by a program, such as Notepad, the object you copied is simply pasted into the document instead of embedded.

FIGURE K-6: Insert Object dialog box

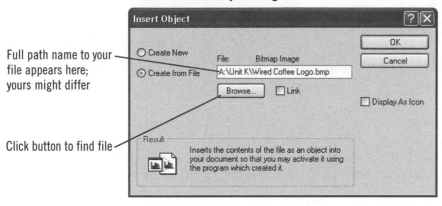

Full path name to your file appears here; yours might differ

Click button to find file

FIGURE K-7: WordPad document with embedded object

Embedded object

Sizing handle

Placing part of a file on the desktop

If you have part of a document, either text or graphic, that you want to use in multiple documents, you can create a scrap on the desktop, which you can drag to other documents or programs. A scrap is a file that is created when you drag part of a document to the desktop. If the programs you are using support OLE drag-and-drop functionality, such as WordPad, you can create a scrap on the desktop. If you can drag-and-drop text or graphics in a file window, the program supports OLE, and you can create a scrap. To place part of a file on the desktop, resize the file window so you can see the desktop, select the text or graphic you want to become a scrap, then drag the selected text or graphic to the desktop. An icon appears on the desktop with the name "Scrap" or the name of the program from which you copied the information followed by "Scrap" and part of the text copied. For example, if you drag the text "Sincerely yours," to the desktop from WordPad, the scrap document name is "WordPad Document Scrap 'Sincerely yours,...'."

Editing an Embedded Object

After you insert an embedded object, you can edit or change the contents of the embedded object any time you want. To edit the information in an embedded object, you can double-click the object in the destination file. Windows locates the object's source program and starts it within the destination program. You can then use tools and features of the source program to edit the object. When you're done, you click outside the object and the source program closes. John wants to enlarge and add color to the Wired Coffee Logo in the sales document.

1. Double-click the **Wired Coffee logo**
   The source program (Paint) opens within the WordPad document. If you can't see the entire object in WordPad, scroll bars will appear around it, so you might need to resize the viewing area of the object in WordPad.

Trouble?

If large resize handles appear around the object, double-click it to edit it.

2. If necessary, position the sizing pointer ↖ over the lower-right sizing handle of the embedded object, then drag the **sizing handle** to match Figure K-8
   As you drag the sizing handles of an embedded object, the border size of the object changes.

3. Click the **Fill With Color button** 🖋 on the Paint Toolbox

4. Click the **red color cell** (third from the left in the second row) on the Paint Color box
   The Foreground color in the Paint Color box changes to red, as shown in Figure K-9.

5. Position the mouse pointer over the Paint object
   Notice that the pointer changes to 🖋 when you move it in the Paint object.

Trouble?

If scroll bars appear around the Paint object, then resize the object as in Step 2.

6. Click the tip of 🖋 inside the coffee cup
   The Fill With Color tool fills only the area inside the lines. If you fill the wrong area, use the Undo command to reverse the action and try again.

7. Click the **blue color cell** (seventh from the left in the second row) on the Paint Color box, then click the tip of 🖋 inside the saucer below the cup
   The saucer is filled with blue.

8. Click outside the object to exit Paint, then click to the right of the embedded object
   Paint closes and the object is deselected. Compare your screen to Figure K-10. The changes you made to the embedded object appear only in this document. If you opened the Wired Coffee Logo in Paint, you would see that it is still black and white.

9. Click the **Save button** 💾 on the toolbar to save the document

Saving an embedded object

If you have changed an embedded object, and you decide to save the object not only in the destination program but also in a separate file, you can save a copy of the embedded object. For example, to save a copy of the color Wired Coffee logo in a separate file, you would select the image, click Edit on the WordPad menu bar, point to Bitmap Image Object, then click Open. The Paint program opens with the company logo in a separate Paint window that is in front of the WordPad window. Click File on the menu bar, click Save Copy As, then save the file. To exit Paint and return to WordPad, click File on the menu bar, then click Exit & Return to Sales Promotion.

FIGURE K-8: Editing an embedded object in Paint

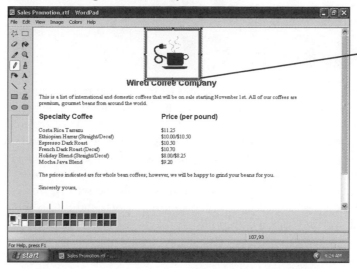

Drag this sizing handle to resize object and remove scroll bars

FIGURE K-9: Paint Color box

Fill With Color pointer

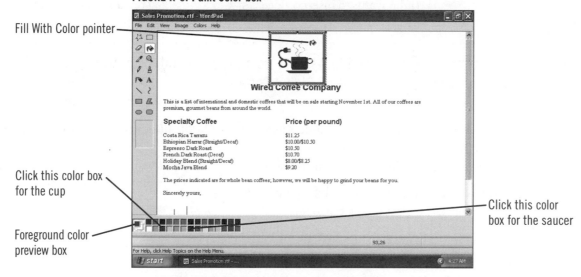

Click this color box for the cup

Click this color box for the saucer

Foreground color preview box

FIGURE K-10: WordPad document with edited object

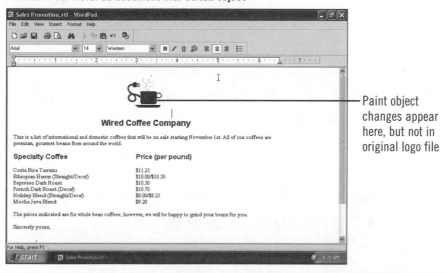

Paint object changes appear here, but not in original logo file

Embedding a Video Clip

You can enhance a simple document with multimedia by adding a video or sound clip. Showing a video or playing a sound clip can help convey your message better than text. When you embed a video or sound clip into a document, it becomes part of the document, so you don't have to keep track of the clip as an external file. As a single document, you can send it in an e-mail attachment, but be aware, video and sound clips can greatly increase the size of a document. You can play back the clip with Media Player, an accessory that comes with Windows XP that plays audio, video, or animation files, and controls the settings for multimedia hardware devices. Media Player is designed to play common video and audio formats, such as .avi (Video for Windows) and .wav, a common sound type. See Table K-2 for a description of the Media Player media types. If you insert a file with the .wmv (Windows Media Video) or .wma (Windows Media Audio) format, the Windows Media Player opens to play the file. To hear the sound on a video clip that has audio, you need to have a sound card and speakers. You can still play a video without a sound card or speakers, but you won't get any sound. When you print a document with an embedded video or sound clip, the printed page appears just like the image on the screen. John wants to insert a video clip into a WordPad document in order to promote international coffee.

Steps 1 2 3 4

1. In WordPad, open the file **WIN K-2** from the drive and folder where your Project Files are located, then save it as **Global Coffee**
   WordPad closes the Sales Promotion document and opens the new document.

2. In the Global Coffee document, click in the **second blank line** below the title "Wired Coffee Company"
   This places the insertion point where you want the video to appear.

3. Click **Insert** on the menu bar, then click **Object**
   The Insert Object dialog box opens.

4. Click the **Create from File option button**
   The Object Type list box changes to the File text box.

5. Click **Browse**, in the Browse dialog box, navigate to the drive and folder where your Project Files are located, click **Globe**, then click **Open**
   The full path name of the video clip object appears in the File text box. The file's object type, Video Clip, appears above the File text box.

6. Click **OK**
   The video clip is embedded in the WordPad document. Sizing handles appear around the embedded object, as shown in Figure K-11.

7. Double-click the **video clip object** to play it, then quickly click the **Pause button** [‖] on the Control bar
   The video clip plays until you pause it, as shown in Figure K-12, or until it reaches the end of the video clip. When you play a video clip, a Control Bar appears with playback buttons, such as Play, Stop, and Pause, which are similar to those on a VCR.

8. Drag the **slider** all the way to the left to rewind the video

9. Click the **Play button** [▶] on the Control bar
   The video plays from the beginning until the end. The Control bar closes when the video stops.

FIGURE K-11: WordPad document with video clip

Double-click the globe to play the video clip

Sizing handles

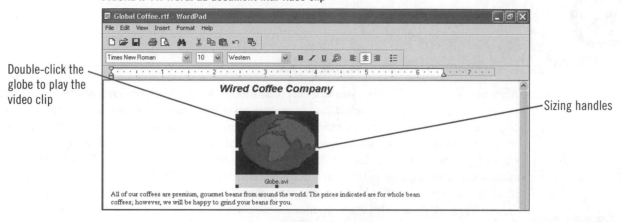

Wired Coffee Company

Globe.avi

All of our coffees are premium, gourmet beans from around the world. The prices indicated are for whole bean coffees; however, we will be happy to grind your beans for you.

FIGURE K-12: Embedded video clip with Control bar

Click button to stop video

Drag slider to rewind or forward video

Click button to play video

Control bar

TABLE K-2: Media Player media types

media type	media format	hardware	description
Video	Video for Windows (.avi) Moving Pictures Experts Group (.mpeg, .mpg)	None	Continuous digital video
Animation	Video for Windows (.avi)	None	A series of graphic images
Audio	CD Audio (.cda) Sound (.wav)	Sound card and speakers	A series of sound waves
Musical Instrument Device Interface (MIDI)	MIDI Sequencer (.mid, .rmi, .midi)	Sound card and speakers	Electronic instructions to play sheet music

Inserting a sound

You can insert a new or existing sound into a document in the same way that you insert a video clip. To insert a sound, click Insert on the menu bar, then click Object to open the Insert Object dialog box. To embed an existing sound file, click the Create from File option button, click Browse, double-click a sound, then click OK. To create a new sound, click the Wave Sound object type, then click OK. When you create a new sound to embed, the Sound Recorder embedded program opens, and you need a microphone to create a sound effect. Sound Recorder allows you to adjust volume and speed, add echo, play in reverse, and mix sound elements to create the effect you want. When you close Sound Recorder, a small speaker icon appears in your document. When you insert an existing sound file, the Media Player or a small speaker icon appears in your document depending on the sound format. Before you can play a sound, you need to install a sound card and speakers.

Modifying a Video Clip

After you insert a video clip, you can edit it or modify its playback options. Media Player offers basic editing capabilities to select, cut, copy, and paste segments of a video clip. If you need more advanced editing, recording, or compressing of video clips, you can use Windows Movie Maker, which comes with Windows XP. Media Player also allows you to set the video clip to automatically repeat or rewind, to display the Control bar, and to set display and playback options. For example, if you want to print your document with an embedded video clip, but don't want to include the caption at the bottom, you can change the Media Player option setting to hide the Control bar. ◄══════ John wants to modify the playback options of the Globe video clip so that it repeats and so that the Control bar does not appear.

1. **Right-click the Globe video clip object, point to Video Clip Object, then click Edit**
   The Media Player menus and toolbar open in WordPad, as shown in Figure K-13. You change the playback options of the Globe video clip, so they look better in the document.

2. **Click Edit on the menu bar, then click Options**
   The Options dialog box opens, as shown in Figure K-14.

3. **Click the Control Bar On Playback check box to deselect it if necessary**
   The Control Bar On Playback option is deselected, and the Control bar will not appear when you play the video clip.

4. **Click the Auto Repeat check box to select it if necessary**
   The Auto Repeat option is checked, and the video will repeat when it is done playing.

5. **Click OK**
   The video clip appears without the Control bar.

6. **Click the Play button ▶ on the Media Player toolbar**
   The video clip plays without the Control bar, as shown in Figure K-15, and automatically repeats until you click the Stop button.

7. **Click the Stop button ■ on the Media Player toolbar**

8. **Click Edit on the menu bar, click Options, click the Auto Repeat check box to deselect it, click the Control Bar On Playback check box to select it, type Globe in the Caption text box, then click OK.**

9. **Click a blank area of the WordPad window to exit Media Player, click the Save button 🖫 on the WordPad toolbar, then click the Close button in the WordPad window**

FIGURE K-13: Embedded Media Player program in WordPad

Media
Player
menu bar

Length of
video clip

Control bar
with video
length

Media
Player
toolbar

Embedded
video clip

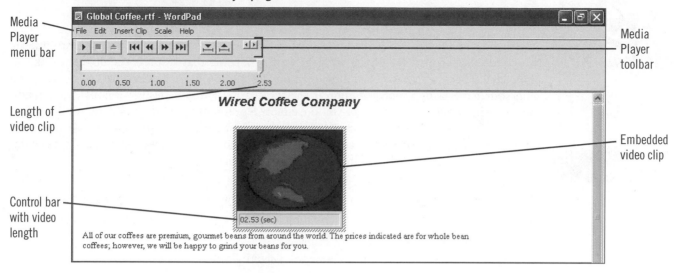

FIGURE K-14: Options dialog box

Click check box to
select the Auto
Repeat option

Click check box
to deselect the
Control bar
option

FIGURE K-15: Video clip without Control bar

Linking an Object

When you want to keep source and destination files in sync with each other, you can link the source file that created the object with the destination file that displays the object. Unlike an embedded object, which is stored directly in the destination file, a linked object remains stored in its source file. Only a representation of the object appears in the destination file. You can edit the object itself in the source file, or you can edit its representation in the destination file—either way, changes you make will be updated in the other file the next time you open it. John wants to link a picture of a coffee cup to an informational flier he is creating so that if he decides to change the picture, it will be changed in the flier as well.

Steps

1. Click the **Start button**, point to **All Programs**, point to **Accessories**, click **Paint**, open the file **Coffee Cup** from the drive and folder where your Project Files are located, save it as **Coffee Cup Image**, then exit Paint
   Saving the Paint file with a new name will keep the original file intact.

2. Click the **Start button**, point to **All Programs**, point to **Accessories**, click **WordPad**, open the file **WIN K-3** from the drive and folder where your Project Files are located, then save it as **Roasting Flier**

3. In the WordPad document, click in the **blank line** two lines below the title "Wired Coffee Company"
   The insertion point appears in the center of the blank line. You will insert a link to the Coffee Cup Image file you just created in Paint into the WordPad document.

4. Click **Insert** on the menu bar, click **Object**, then click the **Create from File option button** in the Insert Object dialog box
   The current folder, typically My Documents, appears in the File text box. The Insert Object dialog box has a Browse button to select a file to insert, and a Links check box to link instead of embed the selected file.

5. Click **Browse**, in the Browse dialog box, navigate to the drive and folder where your Project Files are located, click **Coffee Cup Image**, then click **Open**
   So far you have done the same steps that you would do for embedding; however, you want to link the two files, so when you change the coffee cup image in Paint or in the destination file, the revisions are seen in all of the documents linked to the source file.

6. Click the **Link check box** to select it, as shown in Figure K-16, then click **OK**
   The linked object appears on the WordPad page, as shown in Figure K-17. The linked object looks just like an embedded object; the difference is that any changes you make will affect both files.

7. Click **Edit** on the menu bar, then click **Links**
   The Links dialog box opens, as shown in Figure K-18. In this dialog box, you can open the source file, change the source file, or break the link. You can also check or change the way linked objects are updated; the default setting is automatic.

8. In the Update section, click the **Manual option button**
   This changes the update status of the object so that it will be updated with changes made to the source object only when you choose. For supported programs, you can set a linked object to be updated automatically when the source file is revised and saved, or manually when you click Update Now in the Links dialog box. If a source object is located on a removable disk, it's a good idea to change the update status to manual.

9. Click **Close** in the Links dialog box, then click the **Save button** 🖫 on the WordPad toolbar to save the document
   The Links dialog box closes, and your changes are saved to disk.

FIGURE K-16: Insert Object dialog box

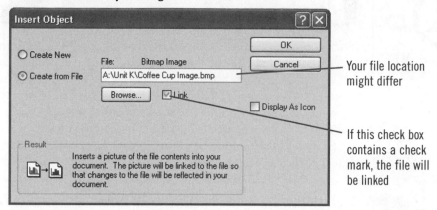

Your file location might differ

If this check box contains a check mark, the file will be linked

FIGURE K-17: WordPad document with linked object

Linked Paint object

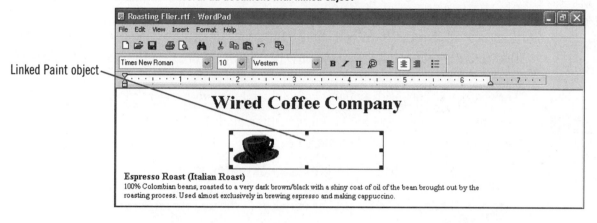

FIGURE K-18: Links dialog box

Link status; your file location might differ

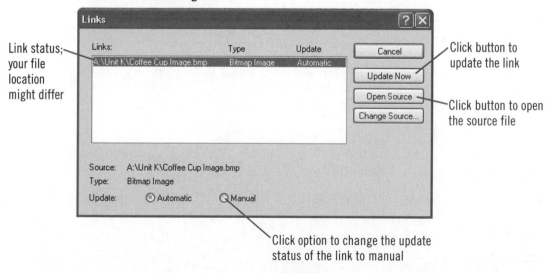

Click button to update the link

Click button to open the source file

Click option to change the update status of the link to manual

Linking objects by copying and pasting

Instead of using the Insert Object command to link files, you can also link files by copying and pasting. For example, if you want to link a chart from Microsoft Excel to a Word document, you can open the Excel file, select the chart, click the Copy button on the Standard toolbar, open the Word document, place the insertion point where you want to link the object, click Edit on the menu bar, click Paste Special, click the Paste Link option button, then click OK.

Updating a Link

Windows XP

When you want to edit a linked object, you can double-click it in the destination file just as you do with embedded objects, or you can start the source program, open the source file, then make and save your changes. When you double-click a linked object in the destination file, the source program and source file open in a separate window from the destination file. Remember that the object in the destination file is only a representation; any changes made to the object are done in the source file, whether you access it by double-clicking the object in the destination file or by opening it in the source program. ➤ John wants to add some text to the coffee cup image. He'll open the linked Paint object, add some information, then update the linked object in WordPad.

Steps 1 2 3 4

QuickTip

To open a linked object, the object's source program and source file must be available on your computer or network.

1. Click the **Start button**, point to **All Programs**, point to **Accessories**, click **Paint**, then open the file **Coffee Cup Image** from the drive and folder where your Project Files are located
   Paint starts, displaying the linked file.

2. Click the **Maximize button** in the Paint program window if necessary, click the **Text button A** on the Paint Toolbox, then drag to create a text box, as shown in Figure K-19
   The text box appears with an insertion point, and the Fonts toolbar appears.

Trouble?

If you can't see the Fonts toolbar, click View on the menu bar, then click Text Toolbar.

3. Click the **Font list arrow** on the Fonts toolbar, click **Arial Black** or a similar font, click the **Font Size list arrow**, then click **12**

4. Click the **text box**, then type **A great cup of coffee is all in the roasting!**
   The text automatically wraps inside the text box. When the text box appears, you can edit the text. Press [Backspace] to correct any mistakes. Compare your screen to Figure K-20.

5. Click outside of the text box within the object
   When you deselect the text box, the text becomes part of the image.

6. Click the **Close button** in the Paint window, then click **Yes** to save the changes
   Paint closes, and the WordPad window appears.

7. Click the **linked object** to select it if necessary, click **Edit** on the menu bar, then click **Links**
   The Links dialog box opens.

8. Click **Update Now**, then click **Close**
   The linked object in the Roasting Flier is updated with the changes you made to the source file in Paint, as shown in Figure K-21.

9. Click the **Close button** in the WordPad window, then click **Yes** to save the changes

FIGURE K-19: Paint object with text box

Fonts toolbar

Drag to create text box

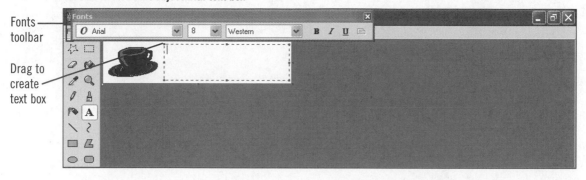

FIGURE K-20: Paint object with new text

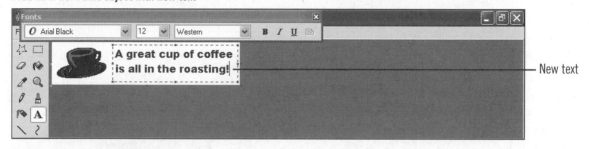

New text

FIGURE K-21: WordPad document with updated object

Updated Paint object in WordPad

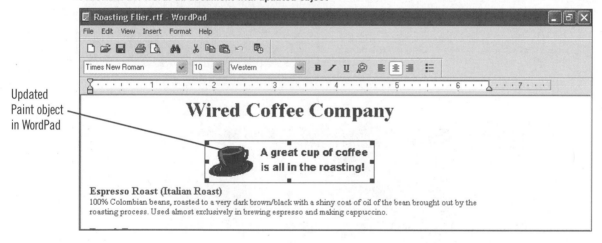

Finding, changing, and breaking a linked object

Instead of opening a linked object from the source file to make changes, you can open a linked object from the destination file using the Open Source button in the Links dialog box. The Open Source button finds the source file containing the linked object and opens that file. After making changes, you exit and return to the destination file. The Links dialog box keeps track of the source file location. You can change the linked source to a different file by using the Change Source button. If you want to disregard a link and change it to an embedded object, select the linked object in the destination file, click Edit on the menu bar, click Object Properties, click the Link tab, click Break Link, click Yes in the message box, then click OK. On the Link tab in the Object Properties dialog box, you can also open or change the source file, change update options, and update the source for the selected object.

Practice

► Concepts Review

Label each element of the screen shown in Figure K-22.

FIGURE K-22

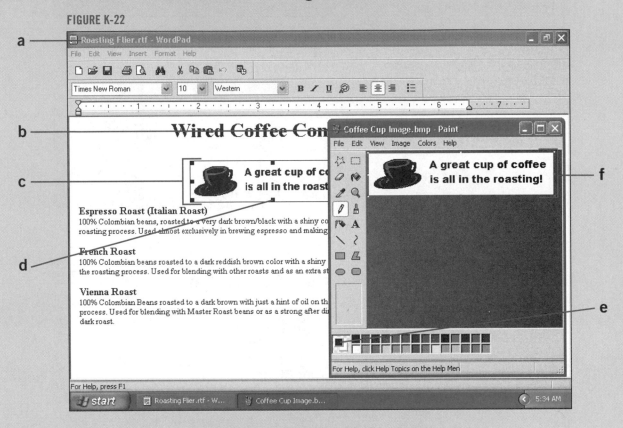

1. Which element points to the destination program?
2. Which element points to the embedded object?
3. Which element points to the source program?
4. Which element points to the source contents?
5. Which element points to a sizing handle?
6. Which element points to the foreground color?

Match each term with the statement that describes its function.

7. **Object**
8. **Embedded object**
9. **Links**
10. **Link**
11. **Destination file**
12. **Source file**

a. An object created in one program and stored in another
b. The place where an embedded object is stored
c. The WordPad menu command you use to embed a file
d. The place where a linked object is stored
e. WordPad menu command you use to check the status of a document's links
f. The connection between an object from a source file and the respective destination file

Select the best answers from the following lists of choices.

13. Which of the following objects can be embedded into WordPad?
a. Video clip
b. Picture
c. Microsoft Excel chart
d. All of the above

14. Which type of object is stored only in its source file?
a. A linked object
b. An embedded object
c. A text placeholder
d. None of the above

15. Which program would you most likely use to create an embedded object that resembles a drawing?
a. Media Player
b. Microsoft Word
c. Microsoft Paint
d. Microsoft Excel

16. Which of the following is NOT true about embedded objects?
a. Embedded objects can be edited from the destination file.
b. Embedded objects are stored in the destination file.
c. Embedded objects are displayed in the destination file.
d. Embedded objects are stored in the source file.

17. Which of the following is NOT false about linked objects?
a. To edit a linked object, you must open its source file.
b. A linked object is an independent object embedded directly into a document.
c. You can access a linked object even when the source file is not available.
d. A linked object substantially increases your destination file size.

18. Which of the following is NOT true about updating a link?
a. You can manually update a link.
b. You can update a linked object even when the link is broken.
c. When you link an object, the default setting for updating is "automatic."
d. An automatic link updates when the source file is saved.

19. Which command on the Edit menu can you use to update a link?
a. Links
b. Paste Special
c. Object
d. Object Properties

► Skills Review

1. **Embed a new object.**
   a. Start WordPad.
   b. Open the file WIN K-4 from the drive and folder where your Project Files are located.
   c. Save the document as Company Memo.
   d. Click the first blank line below the phrase "Sincerely yours."
   e. Click Insert on the menu bar, then click Object.
   f. Click the Paintbrush Picture object type, then click OK.
   g. Use the Pencil tool to draw the signature John in the embedded object.
   h. Click outside the object to exit Paint.
   i. Save the WordPad document.

2. **Embed an existing file.**
   a. Click the blank line above the title at the top of the WordPad document.
   b. Click Insert on the menu bar, then click Object.
   c. Click the Create from File option button, click Browse, then navigate to the drive and folder where your Project Files are located.
   d. Click the file Wired Coffee Logo.
   e. Click Open, then click OK.
   f. Click outside of the object to deselect it.
   g. Save the WordPad document.

3. **Edit an embedded object.**
   a. Double-click the Wired Coffee Company Logo at the top of the WordPad document.
   b. Use the Rounded Rectangle tool to draw a rectangle around the Wired Coffee Company Logo in the embedded object.
   c. Click the Fill With Color tool, choose a color, then click a blank area inside the rectangle to change the background to a different color.
   d. Click outside the object to exit Paint.
   e. Save the WordPad document.

4. **Embed a video clip.**
   a. Click the second blank line below the title in the WordPad document.
   b. Click Insert on the menu bar, click Object, click the Create from File option button, then click Browse.
   c. Navigate to the drive and folder where your Project Files are located, then click the Globe file.
   d. Click Open, then click OK.
   e. Play the video clip.
   f. Save the WordPad document.

5. **Modify a video clip.**
   a. Right-click the video clip, point to Video Clip Object, then click Edit.
   b. Click Edit on the menu bar, then click Options.
   c. Click the Control Bar On Playback check box to deselect it.
   d. Click the Auto Repeat check box to select it, then click OK.

e. Play the video clip, then stop it.

f. Change the options to turn off Auto Repeat, display the Control Bar on playback, and add Globe as the caption.

g. Click outside the object to exit Media Player.

h. Save the WordPad document, then close WordPad.

6. Link an object.

a. Start Paint.

b. Open the file Burst Sign from the drive and folder where your Project Files are located.

c. Save the file as **Burst Sign Image**, then close Paint.

d. Start WordPad.

e. Open the file WIN K-5 from the drive and folder where your Project Files are located.

f. Save the document as **Holiday Sale**.

g. Click the second blank line below the title of the WordPad document.

h. Click Insert on the menu bar, click Object, click the Create from File option button, then click Browse.

i. Navigate to the drive and folder where your Project Files are located, click the file Burst Sign Image, then click Open.

j. Click the Link check box to select it, then click OK.

k. Click Edit on the menu bar, click Links, click the Manual option button, then click Close.

l. Save the document.

7. Update a link.

a. Start Paint.

b. Open the file Burst Sign Image from the drive and folder where your Project Files are located.

c. Click the Text tool, then drag to create a text box inside the burst sign.

d. Type **Sale** (do not click outside the text box yet).

e. Click the Font Size list arrow on the Fonts toolbar, then click 18, or a similar font size that matches the text above the burst.

f. Click outside the text box. Add your name to the document.

g. Save your changes to the file, then close Paint.

h. Make sure the Burst image is selected in the WordPad document, click Edit on the menu bar, then click Links.

i. Click Update Now, then click Close.

j. Save and print the document.

k. Close WordPad.

▶ Independent Challenge 1

You opened a small arts and craft store called Stamp By Me. You want to create a flier that contains sales and promotional information for the next three months.

a. Start Paint, open the file WIN K-6 from the drive and folder where your Project Files are located, then create a sales logo for the store. You can create your own or use the Text tool and the Rectangle tool to place the name of the store inside a rectangle.

b. Save the image as **Sales Logo**, then close Paint.

c. Start WordPad. In a blank document enter store information, including the name, address, city, state, zip, phone number, and store hours of the arts and craft store.

d. Save the flier as **Stamp By Me** to the drive and folder where your Project Files are located.

e. Enter store specials. They can include Buy one, get one of equal or lesser value at 50% discount, 25% off, or anything else.

f. Create a list of important dates such as the following: January 5, Introduction to Stamping, March 2, Introduction to Stamping, and March 19, Masking, Reverse Images, and Other Tricks.

g. Format the information in the document.

h. Above the name of the arts and craft store, embed the Sales Logo image from the drive and folder where your Project Files are located.

i. Embed a new bitmap image of your signature at the bottom of the document.

j. Close Paint and return to WordPad.

k. Proofread your flier and correct any errors, print the flier, then close WordPad.

Independent Challenge 2

You are the owner of Hiezer Bakery. In an attempt to increase sales to businesses, you want to create a new catering menu with pastries and desserts. Using WordPad, enter and format text, then embed and edit a drawing to make the menu appealing.

a. Start Paint, open the file WIN K-7 from the drive and folder where your Project Files are located, then create a menu sign for the bakery. Add appropriate text using the Text tool.

b. Save the image as **Menu Sign**, then close Paint.

c. Start WordPad, then create a menu with descriptions of at least five items.

d. Save the document as **Hiezer Menu** to the drive and folder where your Project Files are located.

e. Format the menu information to make it readable and attractive.

f. At the top of your menu, embed the Menu Sign file from the drive and folder where your Project Files are located.

g. Edit the embedded object from WordPad so that it contains the text **Now offering catering!** inside a circle.

h. Proofread your document and correct any errors.

i. Print the document, then close WordPad.

j. Start Paint, open and print the Menu Sign file, then close Paint.

▶ Independent Challenge 3

You are the director of sales at Classified Collectibles, a large international distributor of stamps, pins, coins, and other rare items. You are seeking rights to distribute Olympic memorabilia to retail stores across the country. Write a letter to persuade the United States Olympic Committee to grant you the exclusive rights. Assume the following facts:

- The company currently distributes United States collectible stamps and coins.
- The company currently distributes 45,000 items through 50 distribution centers in the United States, Europe, Asia, and South America.
- There are four direct-sales centers with toll-free numbers.

a. Start Paint, then open the file WIN K-8 from the drive and folder where your Project Files are located.

b. Create a logo for Classified Collectibles using the Ellipse tool. (To make perfect circles, press [Shift] while you drag the Ellipse tool.) The logo can be similar to the Olympic rings logo, or you can use other tools to make it quite different.

c. Save the image as **Classified Collectibles Logo**, then close Paint.

d. Start WordPad, then write a letter to convince the Olympic Committee to award you the contract, and format the letter as needed.

e. Save the WordPad file as **Olympic Letter** to the drive and folder where your Project Files are located.
f. Link the Classified Collectibles Logo file on the drive and folder where your Project Files are located to your document.
g. Start Paint and open the Classified Collectibles Logo file.
h. Add the text **Classified Collectibles** to the logo, save the logo, then close Paint.
i. Update the linked file in your WordPad document.
j. Print the document.
k. Save the file, then close WordPad.

► Independent Challenge 4

You are the president of Garfield Graffiti Removal, Inc., a company that specializes in the removal of graffiti. The company's patented RemoveX system removes paint from all types of surfaces. After removing the paint, GGRI restores surfaces with PreventX, a special clear coating that makes graffiti easier to clean up in the future. Write a letter to persuade the Los Angeles City Council to award GGRI the contract to remove graffiti from city property.

a. Start Paint, then open the file WIN K-9 from the drive and folder where your Project Files are located.
b. Create a logo for GGRI.
c. Save the logo as **GGRI Logo** to the drive and folder where your Project Files are located, then close Paint.
d. Start WordPad, then write a letter to convince the city council to award GGRI the contract, and format the letter as needed.
e. Save the document as **LA Graffiti** to the drive and folder where your Project Files are located.
f. In your letter, link the file GGRI Logo from the drive and folder where your Project Files are located.
g. Start Paint and open the GGRI Logo.
h. Add graffiti to the GGRI Logo using the Airbrush tool (the fifth tool in the left column), then close Paint.
i. Update the linked file in your document.
j. Print the document.
k. Save the file, then close WordPad.

▶ Visual Workshop

Create a document that looks like the example in Figure K-23. Use WordPad as the destination program and Paint as the source program; use linking to save disk space. Save the document as Accident Report to the drive and folder where your Project Files are located. Print the document.

FIGURE K-23

Unit L

Working

with Windows Media

Objectives

► **Take pictures with a digital camera**
► **Get pictures from a scanner**
► **View pictures**
► **Make a photo album**
► **Format and print photos**
► **Send a photo in an e-mail**
► **Publish files to the Web**
► **Copy and play music from a CD**
► **Create a playlist**

Windows XP comes with several visual tools and wizards to help you find and work with pictures and photographs, and to choose a graphic or determine the right settings to scan a picture without using a graphics program. In this unit, you'll learn how to get pictures from a digital camera or scanner using a wizard, view pictures in a photo album and several other ways to make them easier to find, format and print photographs using a wizard, send a picture in an e-mail message, and publish files on the Web using a wizard. You'll also learn how to use Windows Media Player to help you copy music from a CD and create a playlist, which is a list of media files that play in a customized order. John Casey, the owner of Wired Coffee Company, uses Windows visual tools and wizards to transfer pictures and photographs to his computer and then distribute them to others. He also copies music from a personal CD to his computer so he can play the music in a custom sequence while he works.

Taking Pictures with a Digital Camera

The Scanner and Camera Wizard guides you through the process of taking pictures with a digital still camera or video camera. A **digital still camera** stores pictures digitally rather than on film. The major advantage of digital still cameras is that making photos is fast and inexpensive. To print a photo from your computer, you need a color printer and special photo paper. A digital video camera displays live or recorded digital video, which is higher in quality than nondigital. You can also edit and e-mail digital video and still photographs with your computer. With the Scanner and Camera Wizard, you can capture digital snap shots or view ones you took already with the camera and save them in a folder on your computer, view device properties, delete pictures from your camera, or print photos. In order to use the digital camera features of Windows XP, you need to have a digital still or video camera attached and installed on your computer. ✒ John wants to take some pictures to test out a new digital camera.

Steps 1 2 3 4

 If you don't have a digital video or still camera attached and installed on your computer, read this lesson without completing the steps if necessary.

▶ 1. Click the **Start button** on the taskbar, click **Control Panel**, click **Switch to Classic View** if necessary, then double-click the **Scanners and Cameras icon** 🖳
The Scanners and Cameras window opens, displaying installed scanners and digital cameras.

> **Trouble?**
> If the Scanner and Camera Wizard opens when you attach your camera, click Next in the first wizard dialog box, and skip Steps 1 and 2.

2. Double-click the **digital video camera icon** 📹, then click **Next**
The next wizard dialog box asks you to take and select the picture that you want to copy to a folder. A real time image from the digital camera appears in the Preview box.

> **QuickTip**
> To rotate the selected picture, click the Rotate Clockwise button 🔄 or the Rotate Counterclockwise button 🔄.

▶ 3. Click the **Take Picture button** 📷 if available to take several pictures
The pictures appear in the Pictures box with check boxes selected in the upper-right corner, as shown in Figure L-1. The selected check boxes indicate which picture will be saved, or click Clear All to deselect them all.

4. Clear the check boxes next to the pictures you don't want to save, then click **Next**
The next wizard dialog box asks you to select a folder name and destination, as shown in Figure L-2.

> **QuickTip**
> To view the contents of the Picture box, click the Back button ⬅ Back.

▶ 5. In the name text box (number 1), type **Family Pictures** if necessary
The new folder name appears in the name text box and the place box (number 2). The default folder destination is My Pictures. The pictures you take with the Scanner and Camera Wizard remain in the Pictures box even if you exit and start the wizard, unless you delete them using the check box at the bottom of the dialog box.

6. Click the **Delete pictures from my device after copying them check box** to select it, then click **Next**
The next wizard dialog box saves only the selected pictures in the specified folder in consecutive order as Family Pictures 001, Family Pictures 002 and so on. After completing the process, the next wizard dialog box asks if you want to perform additional tasks.

7. Click the **Nothing. I'm finished working with these pictures option button** if necessary, click **Next**, then click **Finish** to open the Family Pictures folder

8. Click **My Pictures** in the task pane, click the **Family Pictures folder** to select it if necessary, click **Delete this folder** in the task pane, click **Yes** to confirm the folder deletion, then close all open windows

FIGURE L-1: Taking digital pictures with a video camera

Clear check box to not save picture

Click button to take live picture

Digital pictures

Click buttons to rotate pictures or get property information

FIGURE L-2: Selecting a folder name and destination

Folder name

Folder destination

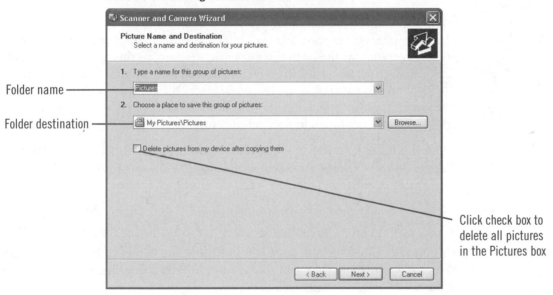

Click check box to delete all pictures in the Pictures box

CLUES TO USE

Taking pictures from the camera window

Instead of using the Scanner and Camera Wizard to take pictures from a digital camera that is attached to your computer, you can also open the camera window from My Computer and take snap shots in the window. As you take pictures, you can delete individual pictures or all of the pictures and save them to your My Pictures folder. To view pictures from the camera window, click the Start button on the taskbar, click My Computer, then double-click the digital video camera icon 📷 to open the camera window.

Windows initializes the camera and displays a real time image. To take a picture, click Take a new picture in the task pane. The picture appears as a thumbnail at the bottom of the window. You can continue to take pictures, save them to the My Pictures folder, or delete them. To delete or save an individual picture, right-click it, then click Delete or Save in My Pictures. To delete all the pictures, click Delete all pictures on camera in the task pane.

Getting Pictures from a Scanner

Windows XP makes it easy to get pictures from a scanner with the Scanner and Camera Wizard. A **scanner** is like a photocopy machine on which you can lay photographs, books, and other documents that you want to save in digital form on your computer. In addition to scanning photographs, many high resolution scanners also allow you to scan a negative from a film strip and enlarge it. With the Scanner and Camera Wizard, you can choose scanning preferences, such as picture type, preview the scanned picture, adjust the scan area, and select a graphic format. In order to use the scanner features of Windows XP, you need to have a scanner attached and installed on your computer. ◀━━━ John wants to scan a picture to test out a new scanner.

Steps

🛑 *If you don't have a scanner attached and installed on your computer, read this lesson without completing the steps to learn what is possible with scanners.*

▶ 1. Click the **Start button** on the taskbar, click **Control Panel**, click **Switch to Classic View** if necessary, then double-click the **Scanners and Cameras icon** 📇
The Scanners and Cameras window opens, displaying installed scanners and digital cameras.

Trouble?

If your scanner is not installed, plug in the hardware as directed, click Add an imaging device in the task pane if necessary, then follow the Scanner and Camera Installation Wizard instructions to help you install the device.

2. Double-click the **scanner icon** 📇, then click **Next**
The next wizard dialog box asks you to preview the scanned picture and choose scanning preferences, such as the picture type. There are four picture type options: Color picture, Grayscale picture, Black and white picture or text, and Custom. Grayscale is the use of many shades of gray to represent a graphic, while black and white uses only black and white to represent a graphic, such as a line drawing. The Custom option allows you to adjust contrast, brightness, and resolution in dots per inch (dpi).

3. Place the picture on the scanner, click a picture type option, then click **Preview**
The wizard scans the picture based on the picture type option and displays it in the Preview pane with a selection rectangle and red resize handles at the corners, as shown in Figure L-3.

Trouble?

If you accidentally click the Preview pane instead of a red resize handle, the selection rectangle changes to a dot. Use ╋ to reselect the picture with green resize handles at the corners.

▶ 4. Position ╋ over the red resize handles in the Preview pane, the pointer changes to ↖ or ↗, drag to crop the picture to the size you want if necessary, click 🔳 to enlarge and preview the selection, click ▦ to restore the enlarged picture, then click **Next**
The next wizard dialog box asks you to select a folder name, destination, and format for the pictures.

5. In the name text box (number 1), type **Family Pictures** if necessary
The new folder name appears in the name text box and the place box (number 3). Now you select a graphic format: BMP (bitmap image), JPG (JPEG Image, the default), TIF (TIF Image), and PNG (PNG Image).

QuickTip

The pictures are saved in consecutive order as Family Pictures, Family Pictures 001, Family Pictures 002, and so on.

▶ 6. Click the **Select a file format list arrow**, click the format you want, then click **Next**
The next wizard dialog box scans the picture, as shown in Figure L-4, and saves it in the specified folder, then asks if you want to perform additional tasks.

7. Click the **Nothing. I'm finished working with these pictures option button** if necessary, click **Next**, then click **Finish** to open the Family Pictures folder

8. Click **My Pictures** in the task pane, click the **Family Pictures folder** to select it if necessary, click **Delete this folder** in the task pane, click **Yes** to confirm the folder deletion, then **close** all open windows

---

FIGURE L-3: Previewing a scanned picture

Choose scanning options

Preview of scanned picture

Click button to preview the scanned picture

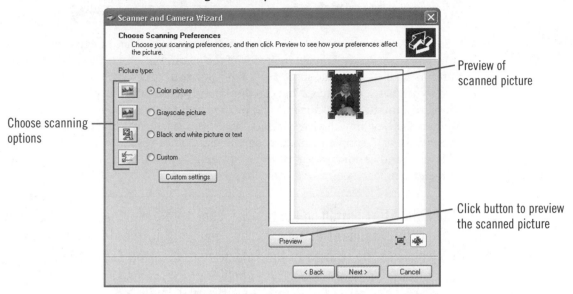

FIGURE L-4: Scanning a picture

Scanned picture's filename and location

Scanned picture

Scanning progress meter

Selecting the appropriate file format

Each file type has a different format and recommended use. JPG (Joint Photographic Experts Group; also known as JPEG) and PNG (Portable Network Graphics) are graphic file formats commonly used on Web pages, while BMP (Bit-mapped) and TIF (Tagged Image File Format, also known as Tiff) are file formats used in documents. The format specifies how the information in the file is organized internally. JPG and PNG formats are compressible, which means that the file size is smaller and transfers over the Internet faster. Each file format uses a different compression method, which produces different results when you display the graphic files. JPG is designed for photographs and supports millions of colors, but loses some image quality by discarding image data to reduce the file size. PNG is designed for Web graphics and supports millions of color without losing image quality, but not all Web browsers fully support its capabilities without using a plug-in, which is a software add-on installed on your computer. TIF is designed for all graphics and colors and one of the most widely used graphic formats, but the file size is large. BMP is the standard Windows graphic format and similar to TIF.

Viewing Pictures

Windows XP gives you several ways to view pictures in a folder. In My Computer, you can use **Thumbnails** view to see a miniature image of the pictures in a folder, or to see a larger view of the pictures in a full screen slide show, switch to **Filmstrip** view, which includes buttons to make it easy to switch between pictures. You can display the pictures in a folder as a full screen slide show. If you have a mixture of documents and pictures in a folder or receive faxes sent directly to your computer, the best way to view the pictures is to open them in the Windows Picture and Fax Viewer, which is a simple graphics program that comes with Windows XP that allows you to quickly view and annotate select pictures. ✏ John wants to view pictures several different ways to determine the best way to view his pictures.

Steps

1. Click the **Start button** on the taskbar, click **My Documents**, click the **Folders button** on the Standard Buttons toolbar, navigate to the drive and folder where your Project Files are located in the Folders list using the **Expand indicator** ⊞ (do not click the folder icon), drag the **Family Pictures folder** in the Folders list to the My Documents folder in the right pane, then click again
   The Family Pictures folder is copied to the My Documents folder.

QuickTip

To display pictures in a larger view such as filmstrip, click the Views button ▦ ▾ on the Standard Buttons toolbar, then click Filmstrip.

2. In the right pane, double-click the **Family Pictures folder**, click the **Views button** ▦ ▾ on the Standard Buttons toolbar, then click **Thumbnails** if necessary
   The Family Pictures folder opens, displaying the contents of the folder as thumbnails.

3. In the task pane, click **View as a slide show**, then move the mouse to display the Slide Show toolbar in the upper-right corner
   The pictures in the folder appear in full screen in display order for five seconds. With the Slide Show toolbar you can play, pause, and stop the slide show and display the previous or next slide. The Slide Show toolbar hides after five seconds of inactivity.

4. Click the **Close the window button** ⊗ on the Slide Show toolbar to return to the Family Pictures folder, then double-click the first picture in the Family Pictures folder
   The Windows Picture and Fax Viewer window opens, displaying the first picture in the folder, as shown in Figure L-5. At the bottom of the window are buttons you can use to: display other pictures in the folder; change the picture size and orientation; open the picture in another program for editing; and delete, print, and save the picture.

5. Click the **Next Image (Right Arrow) button** ▷ until the last image (Family Pictures 003) in the Family Pictures folder appears in the window
   A picture in the TIF format appears in the window. When you open a fax or TIF file in the Windows Picture and Fax Viewer window, **annotation tools**, which appear at the bottom of the window, allow you to draw lines and shapes, highlight areas, add text or an attached note, change annotation properties, and switch between pages in a fax.

QuickTip

To change the font style, size, and color of the annotation, click the Edit Info button 📝 to open the Font dialog box.

6. Click the **New Text Annotation button** 𝐀, drag ▯ to draw a rectangle on the picture, click in the rectangle to open the text box, type **Brett 2 Years Old**, resize the text box as necessary, press **[Esc]**, drag the box to the top right corner of the picture, then click outside the text box
   The text annotation appears on the picture, as shown in Figure L-6.

7. Click the **Copy To button** 💾 to open the Copy To dialog box in the Family Pictures folder, click **Save**, then click **Yes** to replace the current Family Pictures 003 file

8. Click the **Close button** on the Windows Picture and Fax Viewer window, click **No** (if asked) to save the annotation, then click the **Close button** on the My Documents window

FIGURE L-5: Windows Picture and Fax Viewer window

Your filename
might include
an extension

Click button
to get help

Click buttons to move
between pictures

FIGURE L-6: Adding a text annotation to a picture

Picture in TIF
format

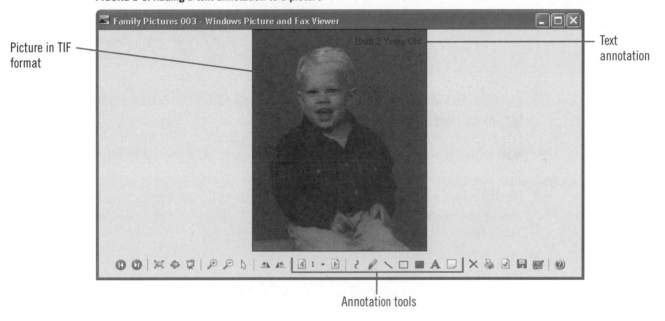

Text
annotation

Annotation tools

CLUES TO USE

Using pictures as a screen saver

Instead of using screen savers provided by Windows XP, you can use your own pictures to create a slide show screen saver. To use pictures as a screen saver, create a folder on your computer, place the pictures you want to use in the slide show in the folder, then double-click the Display icon 🖼 in the Control Panel. In the Display Properties dialog box, click the Screen Saver tab, click the Screen saver list arrow, click My Pictures Slideshow, then click Settings. In the My Pictures Screen Saver Options dialog box, click Browse to open the Browse for Folder dialog box, choose the folder with your pictures, click OK, specify the size and for how long you want the pictures to appear in the slide show and other options, then click OK. You can click Preview to view the screen saver slide show.

Making a Photo Album

When you create a new folder in the My Documents folder, you can customize it for pictures, music and videos by applying a folder template, which is a collection of folder task links and viewing options. When you apply a template to a folder, you apply specific features to the folder, such as specialized commands in the task pane and viewing options for working explicitly with pictures, music, and videos. For example, when you apply a music or video template to a folder, the Play all command appears in the task pane. If you have a folder with pictures, you can use the Photo Album folder template to display the pictures in the folder as a filmstrip by default when you open the folder. Filmstrip is a special view available only for folders with pictures. Since Filmstrip view displays a large image of the selected picture in the folder, the Photo Album template works best for picture storage folders with only a few pictures. Otherwise, you would need to continually scroll to locate and display pictures in the folder. ◄──── John wants to make a photo album for pictures in the Family Pictures folder.

Steps

1. **Click the Start button** on the taskbar, click **My Documents**, right-click the **Family Pictures folder**, then click **Properties**
   The Properties dialog box opens.

2. **Click the Customize tab**
   The Customize tab, shown in Figure L-7, allows you to change the folder template, choose the picture that appears on a folder in Thumbnails view, and change the folder icon for all views except Thumbnails.

3. **Click the Use this folder type as a template list arrow**, then click **Photo Album (best for fewer files)** if necessary
   When you choose a template, you apply specific features to your folder, such as specialized task links and viewing options for working with pictures, music, and videos. See Table L-1 for a list and description of the folder templates.

4. **Click the Also apply this template to all subfolders check box** to select it if necessary
   This option applies the Photo Album template folder to all existing subfolders, as well as any subfolders you create, in the Family Pictures folder.

5. **Click OK**
   When you open a folder with photos, the left pane contains common tasks related specifically to pictures, such as Order prints online and Print pictures; the list of available picture tasks changes based on the current selection.

6. **Double-click the Family Pictures folder**
   The Family Pictures window opens, displaying the contents of the picture folder as a filmstrip, as shown in Figure L-8.

7. **Click the Next Image (Right Arrow) button** ⊙ until the last image in the Family Pictures folder appears in the window

8. **Click the Back button** ◐ Back on the Standard Buttons toolbar to display the My Documents folder

FIGURE L-7: Folder Properties dialog box with Customize tab

Click list arrow to display folder templates

Click button to change folder picture

FIGURE L-8: Family Pictures folder in Filmstrip view

First picture in Filmstrip view

Pictures in folder

TABLE L-1: Folder templates

folder template name	description
Documents (for any file type)	Displays the contents of a folder in Tiles view and specialized picture commands in the task pane
Pictures (best for many files)	Displays the contents of a folder in Thumbnails view and specialized picture commands in the task pane
Photo Album (best for fewer files)	Displays the contents of a folder in Filmstrip view and specialized picture commands in the task pane
Music (best for audio files and playlists)	Identifies the contents of the folder as general sound and playlist files and displays specialized music commands in the task pane
Music Artist (best for works by one artist)	Identifies the contents of the folder as music by one artist and displays specialized music commands in the task pane
Music Album (best for tracks from one album)	Identifies the contents of the folder as tracks from an album by the same artist and displays specialized music commands in the task pane
Videos	Identifies the contents of the folder as videos and displays specialized video commands in the task pane

Formatting and Printing Photos

Windows XP

Windows XP makes it easy to format and print photographs with the Photo Printing Wizard, which allows you to print photographs from a digital camera, scanner, or your computer. With the wizard, you can select the photo(s) to print, the paper type, and a page layout, such as full page prints, contact sheet prints, 8 × 10-inch prints, 5 × 7-inch prints, 4 × 6-inch prints, 3.5 × 5-inch prints, and wallet size prints. In order to get the best results when you print photographs, set your printer resolution to the highest setting for the best quality output, and use high-quality glossy paper designed specifically for printing photographs. Check your printer documentation for best resolution setting suited to print your photographs. When you print photographs with a high resolution setting, the printing process might take longer. Many printer manufacturers also make paper designed to work best with their printers; check your printer manufacturer's Web site for more information. 🖊 John purchased photo paper for his color printer and wants to print a family photo. If you don't have a color printer or special glossy photo paper, you can still complete this lesson, but your printout will not be high quality.

1. **In the My Documents folder, double-click the Family Pictures folder**
   The Family Pictures window opens, displaying the contents of the picture folder as a filmstrip.

2. **In the task pane, click Print pictures**
   The Photo Printing Wizard dialog box opens.

QuickTip

When you select a picture, the command in the task pane changes to Print this picture.

3. **Click Next to continue**
   The next Photo Printing Wizard dialog box appears, asking you to select the pictures that you want to print. The pictures in the Family Pictures folder appear in the Pictures box with check boxes selected in the upper-right corner. The selected check boxes indicate which pictures will be printed by the wizard. You can deselect individual check boxes for the pictures you don't want to print or click Clear All to deselect them all.

4. **Click the check boxes to deselect all but one of the photos, then click Next**
   The next Photo Printing Wizard dialog box appears, asking you to select a printer and print preferences, such as the paper type, print quality settings, and print color, as shown in Figure L-9.

5. **If necessary, click the Printer list arrow, then click an available printer**

6. **Click Printing Preferences**
   The printer Properties dialog box opens. Your dialog box tabs and settings will differ depending on your printer manufacturer and model.

7. **Check to make sure your paper type (plain, matte, photo, etc.) matches the paper in the printer and printer resolution setting is set at the highest possible setting, then click OK**
   The Photo Printing Wizard dialog box appears with printing options.

8. **Click Next, then click a page layout for the selected photos (in the Available layouts list (scroll down if necessary)**
   The next Photo Printing Wizard dialog box appears, asking you to select a page layout for the selected photos, such as Full page photo print, 4 × 6 inch cutout prints (three per page, cropped and rotated to fit), and Wallet prints, as shown in Figure L-10.

9. **Click Next, then click Finish**
   The Photo Printing Wizard sends the photographs to the printer and completes the process. The Family Pictures folder appears.

FIGURE L-9: Printing options in Photo Printing Wizard

Current printer; yours might differ

Click button to change printing preferences

Current paper selection; yours might differ

FIGURE L-10: Photo layouts in Photo Printing Wizard

Photo layouts

Preview of selected photo layout; your photo orientation might differ

CLUES TO USE

Ordering photo prints from the Web

If you have digital photographs taken from a digital camera or scanned into your computer, you can send your digital photographs to an online printing company where they create photo prints and send them to your mailing address. Windows XP makes the process easy with the Online Print Ordering Wizard, which steps you through the ordering process. To place a print order, you need an Internet connection. To order prints of your digital photographs, open My Documents, move your pictures into the My Pictures folder and open the folder, click Order prints online in the task pane to open the Online Print Ordering Wizard, read the welcome message, click Next, select the pictures you want to create prints of, click Next, select a company to print your photos, click Next, then follow the remaining steps to place an order with the specific printing company. You'll need to provide print sizes, quantities, and billing and shipping information to complete the order. The printing company sends the prints to your shipping address.

Sending a Photo in an E-mail

If you have one or more photos, pictures, or documents that you want to share with others, you can send them in an e-mail as attachments. Before you send photos or pictures in an e-mail as an attachment, you typically need to resize them in a separate graphics program so your recipient can view them with minimal scrolling, open your e-mail program, and then attach the files. With Windows XP you can send a photo or picture in an e-mail message without having to resize it in a separate graphics program, or even open your e-mail program. Using the E-mail command in the task pane of any folder window, Windows XP simply asks how you want to size the photos and pictures, then opens an e-mail message window with the attached files from your default e-mail program. All you need to do is address the message, add any message text, and send it. John wants to send a family photo to family and friends.

Steps

1. **In the Family Pictures folder, click the photo you want to send in an e-mail**
   The selected file appears in the Family Pictures folder.

2. **In the task pane, click E-mail this file**
   The Send Pictures via E-Mail dialog box opens, as shown in Figure L-11. When you select multiple pictures, the command in the task pane changes to E-mail the selected items.

3. **Click the Make all my pictures smaller option button if necessary**
   This option makes pictures the best size for viewing in an e-mail message window. If you choose to keep pictures at their original sizes, it will typically require e-mail recipients to scroll horizontally and vertically to view the pictures.

4. **Click OK, then click the Maximize button on the e-mail message window if necessary**
   The Send Pictures via E-Mail dialog box closes and an e-mail message window opens with the selected picture attached from your default e-mail program, such as Outlook Express, as shown in Figure L-12.

5. **In the To box, type the e-mail address of your instructor, technical support person, or someone else you know, then type a message if necessary**

6. **Click the Send button on the toolbar**
   The e-mail message is sent. The Family Pictures folder appears.

7. **Click the Start button on the taskbar, click E-mail (with your default e-mail program in gray below it) in the left column of the Start menu, then click the Maximize button on the e-mail program window if necessary**
   The Outlook Express window opens, displaying the Inbox; your default e-mail program might differ.

8. **In the Folders list, click Sent Items, then click the e-mail message you sent with the attached picture**
   The e-mail message appears with the picture below the message text in the preview pane.

9. **Click the Close button on your e-mail program window**
   The Family Pictures folder appears.

QuickTip

If you know the specific size you want for your picture, click Show more options to expand the dialog box; options include: 640 by 480 window, 800 by 600 window, or 1024 by 768 window, which are typical screen resolutions.

Trouble?

Your e-mail program might require different steps to display the e-mail message you sent with the attached picture.

FIGURE L-11: **Send Pictures via E-Mail dialog box**

Click to display more
sizing options

FIGURE L-12: **E-mail message window with picture attached**

Attached
resized
picture

Publishing Files to the Web

Windows XP

With the Web Publishing Wizard, you can copy an individual file or a folder of files from your computer to your own Web site or a network location, such as a shared folder. When you publish your files to a Web site, you can let others view your pictures and documents using their Web browser. If you don't have a Web site to publish your files, you can create a personal Web site in MSN Communities. MSN Communities is a service that allows you to create a personal Web site to display pictures and documents, and create an online community to share messages, create a photo album, hold chat sessions, manage a calendar, and add Web pages to your site. You don't have to be an MSN member to use MSN Communities, but you do need to have a Microsoft .NET Passport. You can obtain a .NET Passport when you associate an existing e-mail address with a User Account using the .NET Passport wizard or sign up for a free Hotmail or MSN e-mail account during the setup process. After you publish a file or folder to the Web, a shortcut link to that Web site is placed in My Network Places on your computer. When you are connected to the Internet, you can access your published files from My Network Places and add or delete the files in the same way you would on any network. John wants to publish some family photos on a personal Web site in MSN Communities for family and friends to view over the Internet.

Steps 1234

(STOP) *In order to use the Web Publishing Wizard, you need to have a Microsoft .NET Passport. If you don't have a Passport, one will be created for you during the publishing process.*

1. In the Family Pictures folder, click the photo you want to publish on the Web
The selected file appears in the Family Pictures folder.

2. In the task pane, click **Publish this file to the Web**
The Web Publishing Wizard dialog box opens.

> **QuickTip**
> When you don't select any pictures, the command in the task pane changes to Publish this folder to the Web.

3. Click **Next**, click the check boxes to deselect all but one of the photos if necessary, then click **Next**
The next Web Publishing Wizard dialog box appears, asking you to select a service provider to host your Web site, as shown in Figure L-13.

4. Click **MSN Communities** if necessary, then click **Next**
The next Web Publishing Wizard dialog box appears, asking you where you want your files stored.

> **Trouble?**
> If a connection dialog box opens, type your .Net Passport user name and password, then click OK or click Get a .NET password to create an account.

5. Click **My Web Documents (Personal)** if necessary (if not available, click Cancel, then skip to Step 8), click **Next**, then click **Next** to publish the photo to your personal community on the Web
The next Web Publishing Wizard dialog box appears, asking you to resize your photo.

> **Trouble?**
> If the .NET Passport connection dialog box opens, type your user name and password, then click OK.

6. Click a picture sizing option if necessary, click **Next** to copy the files, click **Next** upon completion, then click **Finish**
Your files are published to a personal Web site associated with your .NET Passport. Your Web browser opens, displaying your Web community, as shown in Figure L-14; your Web page, navigation controls, and links might differ.

7. Click the link(s) necessary to view a list of photo filenames, click the photo link to display the image, follow the Web site instructions to delete the photo, then click the **Close button** on your Web browser window and all other open windows

8. Click the **Start button** on the taskbar, click **My Documents**, click the **Family Pictures folder** to select it if necessary, click **Delete this folder** in the task pane, click **Yes** to confirm the folder deletion, then click the **Close button** on the My Documents window

FIGURE L-13: Selecting a service provider for Web publishing

Your list
might differ

FIGURE L-14: MSN Communities Web site with published photo

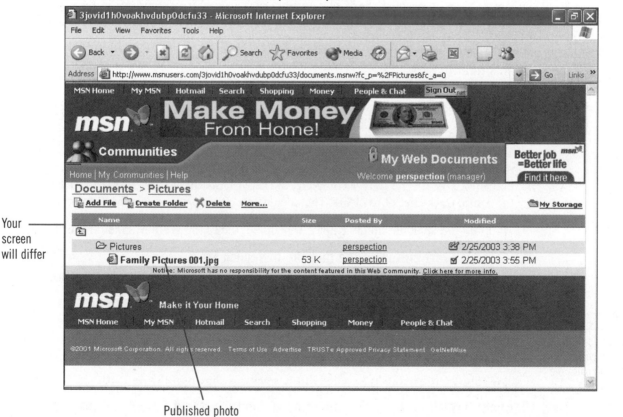

Your
screen
will differ

Published photo

Copying and Playing Music from a CD

Windows XP

Windows Media Player can also copy one music track or an entire album from a music CD to your computer. When you copy music from a CD or download music from the Web to your computer, Windows automatically copies music by the same artist into one folder in the My Music folder, and creates subfolders for each album. Windows gives you several ways to play the music on your computer. In the My Music folder, you can click Play all or Play selection in the task pane or double-click an individual music file to open and play the music in Windows Media Player. If you click Play all in the My Music folder, Windows Media Player opens and plays all the music in your My Music folder and subfolder in random order. If you click Play all in a sub-folder within your My Music folder, Windows Media Player opens and plays all the music in the folder in consecutive order. John wants to copy a few music files from a personal music CD to his computer.

Steps

(STOP) *You need a personal music CD to complete the steps in this lesson. If you don't have access to a personal music CD, read through the steps but do not perform any actions.*

1. Insert a music CD into the CD-ROM drive, then start Windows Media Player and click the play button if necessary
   The Windows Media Player window opens and starts to play the first track on the CD.

QuickTip

Before you copy music to your computer, you should make sure you have enough free space; music tracks typically use between 1.5 MB and 4 MB of disk space.

2. Click **Copy from CD** on the taskbar
   The Windows Media Player window displays a list of music tracks on the CD, as shown in Figure L-15. A selected check box appears next to each track and indicates which music tracks will be copied from the CD. You can deselect check boxes you don't want to copy.

3. Click the check boxes to deselect all but three music tracks, then click the **Copy Music button** ●
   The Windows Media Player copy music protection dialog box opens.

4. Read the dialog box message, click the **Do not protect content check box** to select it, then click **OK**
   The copying process starts with the first selected music track. The Copy Status column for the first selected music track, changes from "Pending" to "Copying," followed by a progress percentage. When the copy is complete, the copy status changes to "Copied to Library," and the music track check box clears. The default copy location is in your My Music folder.

5. When all the selected music tracks are copied, **close** the Windows Media Player window

6. Click the **Start button** on the taskbar, then click **My Music**
   The My Music folder opens, displaying the folder to which you copied the music tracks, which is named the artist's name.

Trouble?

When Windows Media Player doesn't recognize the artist name on a CD, it names the folder Unknown Artist.

7. Double-click the artist folder
   The subfolder contains a music album folder, which contains the music tracks on the album.

8. Double-click the music album folder
   The subfolder contains the copied music tracks, as shown in Figure L-16.

9. Click **Play all** in the task pane to open Windows Media Player and play the music, click the **Stop button** when you're done, then remove the CD from the CD-ROM drive
   Leave the Windows Media Player open for the next lesson.

FIGURE L-15: Copying music from a CD using Windows Media Player

Album name

Artist name

Taskbar

Status information

Controls to play, pause,
and stop the player

Current CD in CD-ROM
drive; yours will differ

Click button to copy
selected items to the
My Music folder

Music tracks on CD

FIGURE L-16: Music tracks copied to the My Music folder

Album folder

Music tracks copied
from a CD; your
music will differ

Copying music to your portable device

A portable device is a small handheld piece of hardware equipment that combines computing, telephone/fax, Internet/e-mail, and networking. Portable handheld devices, such as Pocket PCs and Personal Digital Assistants (PDAs), provide a convenient way to stay connected to others and get some work done while you are on the road. Many of these portable devices also allow you to download or copy music files to it, so you can listen to music. Windows Media Player makes it easy to copy the music you want to a portable device. To copy files to your portable device, connect your portable device to your computer, click the Start button on the taskbar, point to All Programs, click Windows Media Player to start the program, click Copy to CD or Device on the taskbar, click the playlist, category, or files you want to copy in the Music to Copy pane, clear the check boxes for any files you do not want to copy, click the device you want to copy files to in the Music on Device pane, then click Copy Music. Windows Media Player verifies that there is enough space for the selected files on the portable device, then starts the copying process. As the music copies, the amount of used and free space on the portable device is displayed at the bottom of the Music on Device pane.

Creating a Playlist

Instead of playing **digital media** files, such as music tracks, video clips, and DVD segments, one at a time or in sequential order from a CD or DVD, you can use Windows Media Player to create a playlist. A **playlist** is a customized list or sequence of digital media that you want to listen to or watch. A playlist allows you to group together media files and specify the order in which you want to play back the media. You can mix and match the media files on your computer, your network, your writable CD, or the Internet to create your own personal juke box that you can access quickly from Windows Media Player and play in the background as you work with other programs. John wants to create a playlist for the music he copied from a CD onto his computer.

1. In the Windows Media Player, click **Media Library** on the taskbar
   The Media Library appears.

2. Click the **New playlist button** 🖿 to open the New Playlist dialog box, type **Favorite Playlist** in the Enter the new playlist name text box, then click **OK**
   The new playlist appears in the My Playlists folder in the Media Library list.

3. In the Album folder under the Audio folder and Media Library list, click the album name in which you copied files from a CD if necessary
   The music tracks from the album appear in the right pane, as shown in Figure L-17.

4. Click the first music track in the right pane, press and hold **[Shift]**, then click the last music track in the list to select all the music tracks

5. Click the **Add to playlist button** 🖿, then click **Favorite Playlist**
   The files are added to the playlist.

6. In the Media Library list, under the My Playlists folder, click **Favorite Playlist**
   The music tracks in the Favorite Playlist appear in the right pane, as shown in Figure L-18. If the playlist is not in the order that you like, you can drag an item in the playlist to another position in the list.

7. Click the **Play button** to play the files in the Favorite Playlist, then click the **Stop button** when you're done listening
   Windows Media Player opens and plays all the music tracks in the folder until you stop it. The music stops when you close the Windows Media Player. The album folder window in the My Music folder appears.

8. In the Media Library list, right-click **Favorite Playlist**, click **Delete** to delete the playlist, then click the **Close button** on the Windows Media Player
   You return to the album folder window in the My Music folder.

9. Click the **Back button** 🔙 Back on the Standard Buttons toolbar twice, click the artist folder to select it (if necessary), click **Delete this folder** in the task pane, click **Yes** to confirm the folder deletion, then close all remaining open windows

FIGURE L-17: Album music tracks and new playlist

Album name

Artist name

New playlist

Copied music tracks

FIGURE L-18: Contents of new playlist

New playlist

Click list arrow to select a playlist quickly

Music tracks in the new playlist

Changing multimedia AutoPlay settings

When you insert a CD into your CD-ROM drive, Windows looks on the CD to determine its content type, then checks AutoPlay settings to determine what it should do next. For music CDs, the default AutoPlay setting is to open Windows Media Player and play the first track; your settings might differ. If you have CDs with music files, pictures, video files, or mixed content, you can change the action Windows takes when it detects the content on the CD. You can have Windows play the first file using Windows Media Player, open the first folder to view files using Windows Explorer, or take no action. To change how your computer handles multimedia content, right-click the CD-ROM drive icon in My Computer, click Properties on the shortcut menu, click the AutoPlay tab, click the content type you want to change, then click the action you want Windows to perform when it detects the media type you selected, then click OK.

Practice

► Concepts Review

Label each element of the screen shown in Figure L-19.

FIGURE L-19

1. Which element points to Filmstrip view?
2. Which element allows you to create a playlist?
3. Which element points to thumbnails?
4. Which element transfers music to the My Music folder?
5. Which element takes a picture?
6. Which element points to music in a playlist?
7. Which element scans a picture?

Match each term with the statement that describes its function.

8. Playlist
9. Filmstrip
10. Thumbnails
11. Web Publishing
12. Annotation

a. A picture view best for a few files
b. A view that displays a miniature image of pictures
c. A customized list of media files
d. An action that adds drawing and text to a picture
e. A process that copies files to a Web site

Select the best answers from the following lists of choices.

13. Which of the following devices is like a photocopy machine?

a. Digital still camera

b. Digital video camera

c. Scanner

d. Portable

14. Which of the following picture types allows you to adjust color contrast?

a. Color picture

b. Grayscale picture

c. Black and white picture or text

d. Custom

15. Where does the Scanner and Camera Wizard store files by default?

a. My Computer

b. My Pictures

c. My Documents

d. My Network Places

16. Which of the following folder views is designed for pictures?

a. Filmstrip

b Tiles

c. Icons

d. List

17. Which of the following folder views displays pictures as a photo album?

a. Filmstrip

b Tiles

c. Icons

d. Thumbnails

18. Which of the following is NOT a folder template?

a. Picture (best for fewer files)

b. Documents (best for many files)

c. Videos

d. Music (best for audio files and playlists)

19. Which of the following is NOT a picture task in the My Pictures folder?

a. E-mail this picture

b. View as a slide show

c. Set as desktop background

d. Order prints online

▶ Skills Review

1. Take pictures from a digital camera.

 If you don't have a digital video or still camera attached and installed on your computer, skip to Step 2.

a. Open the Scanners and Cameras window, then start the digital video camera and take some pictures.

b. Deselect the pictures you don't want to save.

c. Save the picture you do want in a folder named **Class Pictures** and delete any remaining pictures on the device.

d. Finish the wizard, view the pictures, then delete the Class Pictures folder.

2. Get pictures from a scanner.

 If you don't have a scanner attached to and installed on your computer, skip to Step 3.

a. In the Scanners and Cameras window, start the scanner.

b. Place the picture you want to scan on the scanner, select a picture type option, then preview the scan.

c. Resize the scan area as necessary.

d. Save the picture you want to keep with the TIF format in a folder named **Class Pictures**.

e. Finish the wizard, view the pictures, then delete the Class Pictures folder.

3. View pictures.

a. Create a folder called **Class Pictures** in the My Documents folder.

b. Copy at least two pictures (one being in the TIF format) of your own into the Class Pictures folder.

c. Open the folder and view the pictures as a slide show, then open a picture in the Windows Picture and Fax Viewer.

d. Display the picture in TIF format, then annotate the picture with drawings or text.

   e. Save the annotated picture with a new name in the Class Pictures folder.

   f. Close the Windows Picture and Fax Viewer, then close the Class Pictures folder.

4. Make a photo album.

   a. In the My Documents folder, display folder properties for the Class Pictures folder.

   b. Display the Customize tab, then select Photo Album (best for fewer files) from the folder type template list arrow.

   c. Apply this template to all subfolders.

   d. Open the Class Pictures folder and view the pictures in Filmstrip view, then close the Class Pictures folder.

5. Format and print photos.

   a. In the My Document folder, open the Class Pictures folder.

   b. Click Print pictures in the task pane, then clear the check boxes for all pictures except one.

   c. Select a printer if necessary and make sure your paper type matches the paper in the printer.

   d. Select a page layout for the pictures, then finish the wizard.

6. Send a photo in an e-mail.

   a. In the Class Pictures folder, select a file, then click E-mail this file in the task pane and make all of the pictures smaller.

   b. Maximize the e-mail message window, type the e-mail address of someone you know and any necessary message text, then send the e-mail.

7. Publish files on the Web.

   a. In the Class Pictures folder, select a file, then click Publish this file to the Web in the task pane.

   b. Clear the check boxes for all pictures, except one.

   c. Publish the file to a personal Web site on MSN Communities. (Sign in with your .NET Passport as instructed.)

   d. Finish the wizard, view the picture in your Web browser, then close your Web browser.

   e. Delete the Class Pictures folder and close all remaining open windows.

8. Copy and play music from a CD.

   a. Insert a music CD to open Windows Media Player and play the first track, then click Copy from CD on the taskbar.

   b. Clear the check boxes of the music track you don't want to copy, then click Copy Music.

   c. Do not protect content. Close Windows Media Player when the music is copied.

   d. Open the artist folder in the My Music folder, play the music, then close all open windows.

9. Create a playlist.

   a. Open Windows Media Player and display the Media Library.

   b. Create a new playlist called **Class Playlist**. Add the music you copied to your computer to the playlist.

   c. Play the music from the playlist, stop it, then delete it from the Media Library.

   d. Close Windows Media Player, then delete the artist folder in My Music.

► Independent Challenge 1

You are a creative consultant for Home Memories, a scrap booking company. As part of your in-home demonstration to promote scrap booking and the business, you want to take digitized photos using a digital still or video camera or scan photos from a scanner and print them using a multipicture layout.

   a. Use a digital still or video camera or scanner that is attached to your computer to store photos in a folder in My Pictures.

   b. Use the Photo Printing Wizard to print your pictures in a multipicture layout.

   c. When you finish printing, delete the folder with your stored photos.

► Independent Challenge 2

As the coordinator for your family's next reunion, you want to send an e-mail and a family photo from the last reunion to everyone involved. To make it easier for family members to view and include their own family pictures, you want to publish files on a personal Web site on MSN Communities.

a. Open My Pictures and select a picture, preferably a family picture if available.

b. Click Publish this file to the Web in the task pane, then clear the check boxes for all pictures, except one.

c. Publish the file to a personal Web site on MSN Communities. (Sign in with your .NET Passport as instructed.)

d. Finish the wizard, then view the picture in your Web browser.

e. Print the screen. (Press [Print Screen] to make a copy of the screen, open Paint, click Edit on the menu bar, click Paste to paste the screen into Paint, then click Yes (if necessary) to paste the large image. Click the Text button on the Toolbox, click a blank area in the Paint work area, then type your name. Click File on the menu bar, click Page Setup, change 100% normal size to 50% in the Scaling area, then click OK. Click File on the menu bar, click Print, then click Print.) When you finish, close your Web browser.

f. Select a picture, click E-mail this file in the task pane, then make all of the pictures smaller.

g. Type the e-mail address of someone you know and message text about the date, time, and activities planned for the reunion. Also include the Web address, www.msnuser.com\mywebdocuments, then send the e-mail.

► Independent Challenge 3

You are a college student majoring in music. As part of your studies, you need to listen to different types of music and identify the unique parts of each one. You want to copy music tracks from different CDs onto your computer and then create a playlist to make it easier to categorize the music tracks and listen to them.

a. Insert a music CD into the CD-ROM drive and copy selected tracks to a folder called **Music Major**. Do this for multiple CDs if you have them available.

b. Create a playlist called **Music Major Playlist**, then add the copied music tracks to the playlist.

c. Display the playlist, then print the screen. (See Independent Challenge 2, Step e for screen printing instructions.)

d. Play the music tracks from the playlist, then delete it.

e. Close Windows Media Player, then delete the Music Major folder in the My Music folder.

► Independent Challenge 4

You are an assistant to a movie producer at a small international company that creates short digital films. Your boss continually reviews digital portfolios with music, videos, and DVDs to find talent for upcoming projects. Your boss asks you to create a playlist with video and music tracks in Windows Media Player, which will make the reviewing process easier.

a. Open Windows Media Player, find at least two videos and music tracks on WindowsMedia.com, then add them to Media Library. (*Hint:* Play the media, then use the Add to Media Library command on the File menu.)

b. Create a playlist called **Media Review Playlist**, then add the videos and music tracks to the playlist. The videos appear in the Media Library under Video in All Clips.

c. Display the playlist, then print the screen. (See Independent Challenge 2, Step e for screen printing instructions.)

d. Play the videos and music tracks from the playlist, delete it, then close Windows Media Player.

► Visual Workshop

Re-create the screen shown in Figure L-20, which displays the Windows Media Player window in the Media Library with a playlist for an artist with at least one music track copied from two different albums. Your artist and albums will differ. Print the screen. (See Independent Challenge 2, Step e for screen printing instructions.)

FIGURE L-20

Unit
M

Creating
Movies Using Movie Maker

Objectives

► **Plan a Movie Maker video**
► **Start Movie Maker and view a project**
► **Import and view video clips**
► **Organize and remove clips and collections**
► **Create a Movie Maker project file**
► **Trim clips in Timeline view**
► **Create transitions between clips**
► **Add a soundtrack**
► **Save and view your movie**

Microsoft Windows Movie Maker lets you create movies with images and sounds that you can view on your computer, send to others in e-mail, or make available on the World Wide Web. You can use video recorded by a video or Web camera, images taken with a still camera, or any sounds, music, or narration recorded by a microphone to create home movies or business productions with professional results. Movie Maker provides you with the tools you need to import footage from video cameras and VCRs or directly from digital video cameras, store and organize the media on your computer, and produce polished movies that you can view and share with family, friends, and business associates using Windows Media Player. John Casey, the owner of Wired Coffee Company, is considering using Movie Maker to create a marketing video for the Wired Coffee Web site. While he waits for a videographer to supply video footage, he decides to create a movie using video and audio clips he found on the Web.

Planning a Movie Maker Video

Movie Maker lets you combine video, audio, and image files to create movies you can show on your computer, e-mail to others, or place on a Web page. You save the movie you create as a file, just as you would save a word processing or spreadsheet file, and you can play and view it at any time. However, movies and their accompanying files are larger than most other documents you create—usually exceeding 5 MB. Before you begin, it's a good idea to plan your content. ✎ John reviews the steps involved in planning a Movie Maker video.

Before he creates the video, John will do the following:

► Decide the purpose of the movie

Your movie might be a promotional piece or catalog for business use, or a vacation movie to share with family and friends. Your purpose determines the subject, type, and quality of the **source material**, which is the video and audio material you will use. John decides to create a short movie about the sun and planets using video clips from the NASA Web site and some audio files from his CD collection to learn how to use Movie Maker.

► Determine how to share the movie with others

You might want to show your movie on a computer projection screen at a meeting, send it as an attachment in an e-mail message, or place it on a Web site. When you place a movie on a Web site, viewers might **download** it, which means to transfer it to their computers and store it for future viewing. If your movie is very long or has many high-quality images, the movie file will be large and will take a long time to download. Because the NASA video clips are high-quality and therefore large, John decides to limit the length of his movie to about one minute to keep the file size small.

► Choose source material

If you have a digital video or digital Web camera, you can record or capture digital images directly into Movie Maker on your computer. To use existing video or audio segments, called **clips**, you must **import** them, or bring them into, Movie Maker. You can also import clips from videotape, but your computer must have a video capture card to convert clips from analog to digital format. You can start the System Information accessory on the System Tools submenu to determine whether you have a video capture card installed on your computer. John plans to import the NASA video clips and background music audio files into Movie Maker.

► Sketch the movie

Before putting your movie together in Movie Maker, it's important to make a sketch of your movie that shows the order of the audio and video components. What audio clips do you want to play with what video clips? Figure M-1 shows John's sketch. It starts with a clip of the Earth and Venus, then transitions to a clip of the spinning sun, followed by some footage of a quake on the sun, and ends with a shot of Apollo orbiting the Earth. John's sketch also shows his soundtrack, which starts with an Earth song and transitions to other space sounds.

► Review the process used to create a movie

Figure M-2 shows the process you use to create a movie. First, you bring clips of source material into a Movie Maker project file. A **project file**, which is the working copy of your movie, is a Movie Maker document with the filename extension .MSWMM. You then use the project file to: set the order of your movie segments; **trim** (delete) portions of clips you don't want to use; specify how clips display from one to the next, called **transitions**; and, lastly, preview your work. Finally, you save your project file as a movie with the filename extension .WMV and display the completed movie using the Windows Media Player program. John will bring his video and audio clips into a Movie Maker project file and edit them to create his movie. When the movie looks the way he wants, he will save it as a .WMV file and transfer, or upload it, to his Web site.

FIGURE M-1: Sketch of John's movie plan

FIGURE M-2: Movie creation process with Movie Maker

Windows XP

Starting Movie Maker and Viewing a Project

Movie Maker is a Windows accessory program, so to start it you must first open the Accessories menu on the All Programs menu. To work on an existing Movie Maker project, you must open the appropriate project file. You can view a project in one of two views: **Storyboard view**, which shows the order of your clips, and **Timeline view**, which shows the duration of each clip and the types of transitions between them as well as the sound track. John wants to view an existing project to get acquainted with the main screen elements of Movie Maker.

QuickTip

When Windows Movie Maker starts for the first time, an informational tour will automatically start.

1. Click the **Start button** on the taskbar, point to **All Programs**, point to **Accessories**, then click **Windows Movie Maker**
   The Movie Maker program starts. Depending on previous use of the program, you may see clips in the large area in the center of the screen known as the Collections area, and folders in the Collections pane on the left side of the screen where you store the clips.

2. Click the **Open Project button** on the Standard toolbar
   The Open Project dialog box opens, displaying the contents of the My Videos folder.

Trouble?

If an error message appears asking for missing linked files, click Browse in the message box, then look in the drive and folder where your Project Files are located.

3. Click the **Look in list arrow**, navigate to the drive and folder where your project files are stored, click **MM M-1.mswmm**, click **Open**, then maximize the project window if necessary
   The project opens, showing movie clips at the bottom of the screen and a frame of the first clip on the right side of the screen in the monitor. Below the monitor is the **Monitor bar**, which contains buttons to control the playback and navigation of the movie, which are similar to those on a VCR. See Figure M-3 to identify the names and functions of the major screen elements. The monitor and workspace show the open project in Storyboard view. You use Storyboard view to set the order of your clips.

4. Click the **Timeline button** in the workspace
   The workspace now displays the Timeline view of your project, as shown in Figure M-4. The timeline lets you measure the relative length of each video clip in seconds. At the bottom of the workspace is the **Audio bar**, which contains audio clips for the sound track. You use Timeline view to set the timing and length of your clips as well as the transitions between them.

5. Click the **Zoom In button** in the workspace
   The timeline increments expand, giving you a closer view of your movie project clips.

6. Click the **Zoom Out button** in the workspace
   The timeline increments return to their original size.

7. Click the **Storyboard button** in the workspace
   Your movie returns to Storyboard view, displaying the clips without their durations or the sound track.

8. Click the last frame in the Storyboard, then click the **Play button** on the Monitor bar
   The individual video clip plays with its accompanying soundtrack.

9. Click **Play** on the menu bar, then click **Play Entire Storyboard/Timeline** to preview your movie
   The entire movie plays with its accompanying soundtrack. As each clip plays on the monitor, the corresponding clip on the storyboard is highlighted in white.

FIGURE M-3: Movie Maker window with open project in Storyboard view

Menu bar
Location toolbar
Standard toolbar
Collections toolbar

Collections pane; your collections might differ

Workspace in Storyboard view

Project toolbar
Monitor
Seek bar
Monitor bar
Collections area

Timeline button

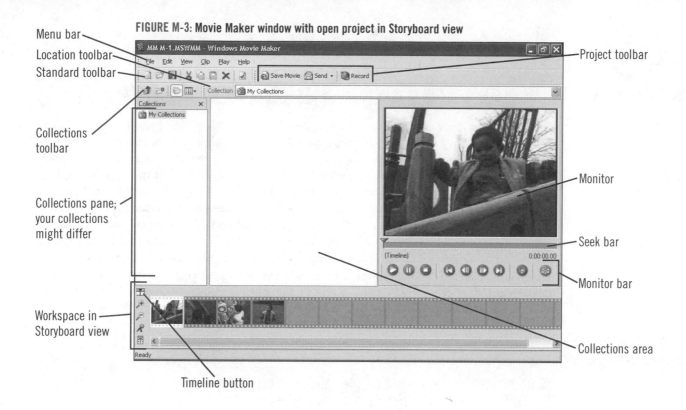

FIGURE M-4: Workspace in Timeline view

Timeline

Video clips

Storyboard button
Zoom In button
Zoom Out button
Audio bar

Sources of video and sound clips

If you want to use existing video and audio clips in your movie instead of recording them yourself, you can obtain them from various companies that specialize in video processing, or download them from the World Wide Web. Commercial CDs are excellent sources for audio clips. If you record clips from any commercial source, however, be sure you are aware of copyright restrictions that regulate how you may or may not use the content. For more information, see the Movie Maker Help file topic, "Using content legally."

Importing and Viewing Video Clips

Before you can use video or audio source material in your movies, you must first bring them into Movie Maker from a file on your computer or directly from a digital source connected to your computer, such as a digital video camera or microphone. To bring in video or audio clips or still pictures that are already in a digital file, you use the Import command on the File menu. Table M-1 shows which file formats (identified by filename extensions) you can import to Movie Maker. If your video, audio, or pictures are not in digital format, such as video footage from video cameras and VCRs, photograph prints, or music on tape cassette, you will need additional hardware on your computer, such as a video capture card or scanner, to transfer the media to your computer and create digital files. When you bring clips into Movie Maker, the program creates a collection folder on the left side of the screen in the **Collections pane**, which contains the video or audio clip you imported. The contents of the selected collection folder appear in the right pane of the **Collections area**. You can store more than 20 hours of video for each gigabyte of hard disk space on your computer. ✎ To create his movie about the sun and planets, John decides to import some .avi video clip files he recently downloaded from the NASA Web site into a collection folder.

Steps

1. **Click File on the menu bar, then click Import**
   The Select the File to Import dialog box opens.

2. **Click the Look in list arrow, then navigate to the drive and folder where your Project Files are located**
   A selection of video and audio clips appears in the Select the File to Import dialog box.

QuickTip
To select multiple files in nonconsecutive order in the Select the File to Import dialog box, press and hold [Ctrl], then click each file you want to select.

3. **Press and hold [Shift], click the file MM M-2.avi, click the file MM M-5.avi to select the files MM M-2.avi, MM M-3.avi, MM M-4.avi, and MM M-5.avi, then release [Shift] and the mouse button**
   Pressing [Shift] allows you to select multiple files in consecutive order in the Select the File to Import dialog box and in any dialog box where you are selecting files to open or import.

4. **Make sure that the Create clips for video files check box is selected**
   Selecting the Create clips for video files check box makes a collection of clips easier to work with. It ensures that Movie Maker automatically breaks video files into separate clips every time it detects a completely new frame. In this case, however, each file contains only one clip.

5. **Click Open**
   When Movie Maker imports video files, a collection folder with the name of each imported file is created on the left side of the screen under My Collections, and the clips the selected collection contains appear on the right side of the Collections area. When you import audio or picture files, the new clips are placed in the currently selected collection and are not automatically placed in new collections.

6. **In the Collections pane click the MM M-2 collection, then click the Clip 1 video clip in the Collections area**
   The first frame of the selected clip appears in the monitor, and the clip name appears below the Seek bar, as shown in Figure M-5.

QuickTip
To play or pause a clip quickly, press [Spacebar]. You can also drag any clip from the Collections area to the monitor to begin playing that clip.

7. **Click Play button ⊙ on the Monitor bar**
   As the clip plays, the triangle in the Seek bar moves right to show its progress, and the timer below the Seek bar shows how much time has elapsed. You can click other Monitor bar buttons below the Seek bar or drag the triangle in the Seek bar to control the playback of the movie.

8. **Play each clip in the collections you imported**
   Now you are familiar with the content of all the clips for the movie.

FIGURE M-5: Selected clip in MM M-2 collection

Imported clip in MM M-2 collection

Imported clips in collections

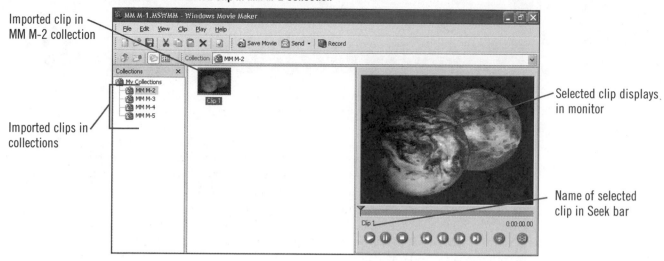

Selected clip displays in monitor

Name of selected clip in Seek bar

TABLE M-1: File types Movie Maker can import

file type	file extensions
Video	.asf, .avi, .wmv
Movie Maker	.mpeg, .mpg, .mlv, .mp2, .mpa, .mpe
Audio	.wav, .snd, .au, .aif, .aifc, .aiff, .wma, .mp3
Windows media	.asf, .wm, .wma, .wmv
Still images	.bmp, .jpg, .jpeg, .jpe, .jfif, .gif, .dib
PowerPoint files and slides	.ppt

CLUES TO USE

Recording video and sound clips directly in Movie Maker

You can record your own video source material from an analog or digital video camera, videotape, or television directly in Movie Maker. Similarly, you can record audio source material from radio, audio or video tape, or a CD. In the recording process, Movie Maker converts the material to Windows Media format. To record video or audio, click the Record button 🔲 on the Project toolbar, specify if you want to record audio or video, specify the device and quality setting, select whether you want to set a record time limit or the Create clips option, then click Record. When you select the Create clips option,

Movie Maker automatically creates separate clips every time an entirely different frame is detected, which is helpful when you want to find specific parts of a movie. To end the recording, click Stop, then save the media file with a name in the Save Windows Media File dialog box. If you selected the Auto generate file option in the Options dialog box (click View on the menu bar, then click Options), the Windows Media File dialog box doesn't appear, and a new file is automatically created and saved in the specified location.

Windows XP

Organizing and Removing Clips and Collections

As you continue to collect video and sound clips for use in different movie projects, the number of clips in a collection and in Movie Maker can grow rapidly and become hard to manage. You can use the same management techniques you use in My Computer and Windows Explorer to help you organize and remove clips and collections. Once you have clips in your collections, you can rename the clips and collections as you would a file or folder and use them to create a movie. When you no longer need individual video and sound clips or entire collections, you can remove them from Movie Maker. When you remove video and sound clips and collections, they are only deleted from Movie Maker; the original video and sound files, which you imported into Movie Maker, are not deleted and remain unchanged on your hard drive. ✒ John wants to organize clips and collections and remove any collections he no longer needs.

1. In the Collections pane, right-click the **MM M-2** folder, click **Rename**, type **Space Videos**, then press **[Enter]** to change the name of the collection
   Now the collection has a meaningful name, making it easier to identify.

2. Right-click the filename under the clip in the Collections area, click **Rename**, type **EarthVenus**, then press **[Enter]** to change the name of the clip
   Now the clip in the Space Videos collection has a meaningful name.

QuickTip

To create a new collection folder in a folder, select any folder in the Collections pane, click the New Collection button 📁 on the Collections toolbar, type a name, then press [Enter].

3. Rename the clips (but not the collections themselves) in **MM M-3** as **Sun**, **MM M-4** as **Apollo**, and **MM M-5** as **Quake**, then drag each clip to the Space Videos collection in the Collections pane
   Now all the clips have meaningful names, and they are organized in a collection folder.

4. In the Collections pane, right-click the **MM M-3** folder, click **Rename**, type **Space Sounds**, then press **[Enter]** to change the name of the collection

5. In the Collections pane, click the **Space Videos** collection
   The Space Videos collection appears with the organized clips in the Collections area, as shown in Figure M-6.

6. In the Collections pane, click the **MM M-4** collection
   The collection is empty.

QuickTip

To delete a video or sound clip, click the clip you want to remove in the Collections area, click the Delete button ✖, then click Yes.

7. Click the **Delete button** ✖ on the Standard toolbar, then click **Yes** to confirm the deletion
   You deleted the MM M-4 collection folder.

8. In the Collections pane, click the **MM M-5** collection if necessary, click the **Delete button** ✖ on the Standard toolbar, then click **Yes** to confirm the deletion
   You deleted the MM M-5 collection folder. Compare your screen to Figure M-7.

FIGURE M-6: Movie Maker window with organized clips and collections

Renamed collections

Renamed clips moved into Space Videos collection

FIGURE M-7: Movie Maker window with deleted collections

MM M-4 and MM M-5 collections deleted

Learning more about Movie Maker on the Web

You can learn more about Movie Maker by visiting the Windows Movie Maker Web site on the Web. The Microsoft Web site provides the latest information about using Movie Maker to create, edit, and share movies. You can find out the information you need to use Windows Movie Maker for Windows XP with analog and digital video equipment, and how to transfer video footage from a VCR or video camera directly to your computer. To access the Web site, click Help on the menu bar, then click Windows Movie Maker on the Web. You need an Internet connection to access the Web site.

Windows XP

Creating a Movie Maker Project File

When you start Movie Maker, a new, untitled project automatically opens. To create a movie, you drag video and audio clips from your Collections area to the project file's storyboard. You can then arrange the clips in any order you want by dragging them on the storyboard. After you preview your project and are satisfied with the results, you save it as a movie file that you can send to others and play using Windows Media Player. ✎ John decides to create a project file using the planet images he imported.

Steps

1. **Click the New Project button ▢ on the Standard toolbar, then click No if you are asked to save the current project in the workspace**
   The first project you opened closes, and a new project opens. The title bar reads "Untitled," and the storyboard and monitor are empty, verifying that you are viewing a new project. The collections in Movie Maker remain the same. They are independent of the current project.

2. **In the Collections pane, click the Space Videos collection**
   The clips display in the Collections area.

3. **Position the mouse pointer over the EarthVenus clip in the Collections area, then drag it to the first frame of the storyboard, releasing the mouse button when the pointer becomes ▨**
   As you drag the EarthVenus clip, a dark gray bar appears on the left side of frame one to indicate the new location of the clip. The EarthVenus clip appears on the storyboard as shown in Figure M-8. When you place clips on the storyboard, the program saves a reference to the clip's location, but it does not save the clip itself in the project file. Do not rename, move, or delete clips from your hard disk that you use in your project files. If you send your project file to someone, be sure to include the source material clips as well.

> **QuickTip**
>
> If you drag the wrong clip to the storyboard, select it, then press [Delete]. The clip remains in the Collections area and on your hard drive.

4. **Drag the Sun clip to the second frame of the storyboard, drag the Apollo clip to the third frame of the storyboard, then drag the Quake clip to the fourth frame of the storyboard**
   After you drag a clip to the storyboard, notice that its name appears under the Seek bar. If you click the Play button, only the selected clip plays.

5. **Click the blank gray area of the storyboard to the right of the last clip**
   The first frame appears in the monitor and "(Timeline)" appears under the Seek bar instead of a selected clip name. If you play the video now, all of the clips in the storyboard will play.

6. **Click the Play button ◉ on the Monitor bar, then let the entire movie play**
   As the movie plays, information about its duration and progress appears in the time indicator below the Seek bar.

7. **Drag the Apollo clip in frame three of the storyboard to the right of the Quake clip in frame four**
   As you drag the clip, a dark gray bar appears between frames to indicate the new location of the clip. The clips are reordered in Storyboard view, as shown in Figure M-9.

8. **Click Play on the menu bar, then click Play Entire Storyboard/Timeline**
   The project plays the clips in the new order you specified.

9. **Click the Save Project button 🖫 on the Standard toolbar, click the Save in list arrow in the Save Project dialog box, navigate to the drive and folder where your Project Files are located, name the project Planets, then click Save**

FIGURE M-8: EarthVenus clip in Storyboard view

EarthVenus is the first clip in the movie

First frame

FIGURE M-9: Reordered clips in Storyboard view

Fourth frame; last one in movie

Apollo clip moved to end of movie

Creating a slide show

You can use Movie Maker to create slide shows by using still images that you create using a digital camera, Web camera, or scanner instead of video clips. The images must be saved in one of the formats listed for still images in Table M-1. You can import them into Movie Maker and create transitions between them, just as you would in a movie. To specify how long you want to display an image, click View on the menu bar, click Options, then under General in the Options dialog box, enter a number in the Default imported photo duration (seconds) text box. You can change the durations for individual pictures in Timeline view. You can also add sound clips to create a sound track that plays as your pictures appear on the screen. Portrait-oriented pictures in Movie Maker are the same height as landscape-oriented pictures, and Movie Maker inserts a black background on either side of each one.

Windows XP

Trimming Clips in Timeline View

Frequently, the clips you record or import into Movie Maker run longer than you want them to in your final movie. You can easily trim clips in Timeline view by playing the clip and setting the **start trim point** and **end trim point**. The portion between the trim points remains in your movie. The frames before and after the trim points are deleted from your movie, but the original clip in your collection is not affected and retains its original length. You can trim a clip as it plays, or you can pause and set the trim points. You can use the Start Trim Point and End Trim Point commands on the Clip menu, although it's often faster to use the timeline **trim handles** (small triangles above the selected clip) or keyboard shortcuts. ✍ John wants a shorter Sun clip in his movie, so he trims it.

1. With the Planets project open, click the **Timeline button** ⊞ on the left side of the storyboard, then click the **Zoom In button** 🔍 in the workspace
   The project appears in Timeline view with the timeline increments expanded, in which you can trim clips.

2. In the timeline, click the **Sun** clip (the second clip in the movie), then view its length in the timeline
   The Sun clip is selected. Notice that the timeline above the selected clip is now highlighted, and that the numbers indicate that the clip runs from about 12 seconds to about 1 minute, 10 seconds, for a duration of just under one minute as shown in Figure M-10. The name of the clip appears repeatedly between its start and end points.

3. Click **Clip** on the menu bar, then click **Set Start Trim Point**
   You set the start trim point at the beginning of the Sun clip.

4. Click the **Play button** ▶ on the Monitor bar, wait until the time display below the monitor approaches 40 seconds, then click the **Pause button** ⏸ on the Monitor bar
   A thin black line appears in the timeline at about 52 seconds indicating the current position in the movie.

5. Click **Clip** on the menu bar, then click **Set End Trim Point**
   The timeline above the Sun clip starts at about 12 seconds and ends at about 52 seconds. The clip's length is reduced to about 40 seconds. If you don't set the end trim point at exactly 40 seconds, don't worry; you'll have a chance to correct it in the next two steps.

6. With the Sun clip still selected, place the pointer over the **End trim handle** ◣ above the clip, until the pointer becomes ↔
   The Screen Tip reads End Trim. See Table M-2 for a summary of the mouse pointers available in Timeline view.

7. Drag the **End Trim handle** slowly to the left, from 52 seconds until the end point is at about 32 seconds, as shown in Figure M-11

8. With the Sun clip still selected, click the **Play button** ▶ on the Monitor bar
   The shortened clip plays for the duration you set.

QuickTip

To split a clip in two, select the clip, play it to the point where you want to break it, press the Pause button ⏸ on the Monitor bar, then click the Split Clip button ▦ on the Monitor bar.

Trouble?

If you didn't pause the clip near 40 seconds, use the Previous Frame ◀‖ or Next Frame ‖▶ button on the Monitor bar to get as close as possible to 40 seconds.

QuickTip

To restore a clip on the storyboard to its original length, click Clip on the menu bar, then click Clear Trim Points.

FIGURE M-10: Selected clip in Timeline view

Sun clip occupies about a minute of movie time

Split Clip button

Selected Sun clip in Timeline view

Clip name is repeated for clip duration

FIGURE M-11: Trimming a clip using trim handles

Trimmed clip now takes about 20 seconds of movie time

Shows length of selected clip as it plays

Start trim handle

End trim handle with pointer

TABLE M-2: Pointers in Timeline view

pointer	use to
↖	Select or drag clips to new locations
↑	Set play indicator in the location you click
↔	Drag play indicator or drag trim handles

Creating Transitions between Clips

Transitions are the way your movie clips change from one to the next. The default transition is a **straight cut**, where one clip ends and the next one starts immediately. You can achieve smoother, more gradual transitions by creating **cross-fades**, in which one clip slowly disappears while the next clip slowly appears. To create transitions, drag a clip so that it overlaps the clip to its left. The amount of overlap determines the length of the transition. A large overlap creates a long transition; a smaller overlap creates a shorter one. ◄◄◄ John decides that his movie would be more effective if he had short transitions between each of his clips.

Steps

1. With the Planets project open in Timeline view, click the **Zoom In button** 🔍 in the workspace

   The EarthVenus and Sun clips appear on the screen in the timeline with the Sun clip selected.

2. Position the pointer ↳ in the timeline over the Sun clip picture, then drag the **Sun** clip to the left, about an inch to the point shown in Figure M-12

   As you drag the mouse button, the pointer changes to ↳. After you release the mouse button, notice that most of the Sun clip picture in the timeline now overlaps the end of the EarthVenus clip. The overlap area appears, as shown in Figure M-13. This creates a cross-fade transition. The timeline indicates that the cross-fade lasts for about a second and a half. When you play the video, both images appear simultaneously on the screen for the transition time as the first fades into the second.

3. Position ↑ on the timeline just before the cross-fade area to place the play indicator there, click the **left mouse button**, click the **Play button** ▶ on the Monitor bar, watch the transition on the monitor, then click the **Stop button** ⏹ on the Monitor bar

4. Position the pointer over the **Play indicator** ▼ on the timeline (which changes to ↔, then drag the **Play indicator** back before the cross-fade area

   See Table M-3 for a list of monitor navigation shortcuts.

5. Repeatedly click the **Next Frame button** ⏯ on the Monitor bar while watching the monitor

   You see the transitions occur frame by frame.

6. Drag the **Sun** clip to the point shown in Figure M-14 (about an inch further to the left)

   The transition now takes about three seconds, so it's more gradual than before. Figure M-14 shows the longer transition.

7. Scroll to the left in the workspace using the horizontal scroll bar, then create transitions of about 3 seconds in length between the Quake and Sun clips and the Apollo and Quake clips

   The Apollo clip now ends at around 40 seconds.

8. Click **Play** on the menu bar, click **Play Entire Storyboard/Timeline**, then view the movie and the transitions

   The play indicator returns to the EarthVenus clip, and the entire movie plays on the monitor.

FIGURE M-12: **Transition between two clips in process**

Drag clip to here

FIGURE M-13: **Transition between two clips completed**

Overlap area indicates cross-fade   End of cross-fade

FIGURE M-14: **More overlap creates longer transition**

Drag clip to here   Sun clip overlaps with EarthVenus
                           clip for about 4 seconds

TABLE M-3: **Monitor navigation shortcuts**

to	do this
Play clip	Click ▶ or press [Spacebar]
Pause a playing clip	Click ⏸ or press [Spacebar]
Return to beginning of project	Double-click ⏹
Play clip frame by frame	Click ◀‖ or ‖▶
Move play indicator to next or previous clip	Click ▶▶ or ◀◀

Adding a Soundtrack

With Movie Maker, you can put two types of sounds in your movies: sounds that are part of a video clip, and separate sounds, such as music or narration, that appear on the Audio bar of the timeline. You can import and edit sound clips in the soundtrack the same way you edit video clips using the Audio bar. Remember that if you use a clip from a CD, you must obtain permission from the publisher. John already recorded a sound clip that he wants to use with his movie of space videos, so he imports it into his collections and adds it to his movie.

1. **With the Planets project open, click the Space Sounds collection in the Collections pane**
   You want to add some sound files to the Space Sounds collection.

2. **Click File on the menu bar, then click Import**
   The Select the File to Import dialog box opens.

3. **Click the Look in list arrow, navigate to the drive and folder where your Project Files are located if necessary, press and hold [Ctrl], click the sound files MM M-14.wma, MM M-15.wma, and MM M-16.wma, then click Open**
   All the sound files appear in the Space Sounds collections.

4. **Drag the MM M-14 sound clip from the Collections area to the left edge of the Audio bar, below the EarthVenus clip**
   See Figure M-15. As you drag the sound clip on the Audio bar, a small dark gray bar appears to indicate the new location of the clip, and the pointer changes to ⬚. The name of the clip appears in the Audio bar. Its duration is approximately 25 seconds.

5. **Use the horizontal scroll bar to display the end of the last clip, drag the MM M-15 sound clip from the Collections area to the right of MM M-14 on the Audio bar, then drag MM M-16 from the Collections area to the right of MM M-15**
   Now all the sound files are on your Audio bar.

Trouble?

Depending on the exact locations of your transitions, your results may vary.

6. **Drag the MM M-15 sound clip in the Audio bar to the left and over the MM M-14 sound clip, so that they overlap to the beginning of the Quake video clip**
   You created a transition where the two sound clips overlap. During the audio transitions, both sound clips play at once; you cannot produce a cross-fade transition using sounds.

7. **Use the horizontal scroll bar to display the end of the last clip, click the MM M-16 sound clip in the Audio bar to select it if necessary, then drag the End Trim handle of MM M-16 to adjust the sound length to the end of the video**
   Compare your screen to Figure M-16.

8. **Click Play on the menu bar, click Play Entire Storyboard/Timeline, then watch the monitor to see how the audio clips coordinate with the video clips**

9. **Click the Save Project button 💾 on the Standard toolbar to save the project**

Adjusting audio levels

With Movie Maker, you can play a video clip sound and soundtrack simultaneously and have one play louder than the other. For example, a video clip of an airplane might have airplane engine noises as part of the video clip. You can add a soundtrack from a CD or a narration that plays louder than the engine noises. To adjust the balance between the video clip sound and the soundtrack you created, click the Set audio levels button 🎚 in the workspace. In the Audio Levels dialog box, drag the slider towards the Video track or the Audio track to increase the volume, then click the Close button in the dialog box.

FIGURE M-15: **Sound files in Audio bar**

Sound file in
Collections area

Sound file in
Audio bar

FIGURE M-16: **Audio clip adjusted to end of last video clip**

Depending on the
exact locations of
your transitions, your
results may vary

Audio clip and Video
clip end at the
same time

Sound clip overlap

Adding narration

If you have a microphone attached to your computer, you can record a narration to accompany your movie. Your narration is saved as a .wav sound file directly in your Collections area so that you can place it in the Audio bar like any other audio clip. To record a narration, make sure you are in Timeline view, click File on the menu bar, then click Record Narration. In the Record Narration Track dialog box shown in Figure M-17, click Change to choose the capture device you are using. In the Configure Audio dialog box, click the Input line list arrow, click Line or Line In, then click OK. In the Record Narration Track dialog box, click Record, then start narrating. When you finish speaking, click Stop. In the Save

Narration Track Sound File dialog box, name the narration file, then click Save. Drag the narration to the appropriate location on the Audio bar.

FIGURE M-17: **Record Narration Track dialog box**

Click button to select
another capture device

Click button to begin
recording your narration

Saving and Viewing Your Movie

Once your movie looks and sounds the way you want, you can save it in .WMV format using the Save Movie command on the File menu. Use the .WMV file to play your movie in Windows Media Player, e-mail it to others, or place it on the Web. In the Save Movie dialog box, you can choose three levels of quality: low, medium, and high. In choosing movie quality, consider how you will distribute the movie. The higher the playback quality, the larger the file size, which increases the download time when you play back the movie over the Web. In the Save Movie dialog box, you can also specify the information viewers see when they play your movie in Windows Media Player.　　John wants to save his movie so that he can place it on his Web site to share it with friends and family.

1. With the Planets project open, click the **Save Movie button** 📄 on the Project toolbar
   The Save Movie dialog box opens.

2. Click the **Setting list arrow**, then click **Medium quality (recommended)** if necessary
   The Medium quality option strikes a good balance between quality video output and file size.

3. Click in the **Title text box**, type **Found in Space**, press **[Tab]**, type your name, press **[Tab]** three times to place the insertion point in the Description text box, then type **NASA shots with music**
   The information is filled in for the Save Movie dialog box, as shown in Figure M-18. The information you entered in the text boxes in the Save Movie dialog box appears when your movie plays in Windows Media Player.

4. Click **OK**
   The Save As dialog box appears.

5. Click the **Save in list arrow**, navigate to the drive and folder where your Project Files are located, type **Space Movie.wmv** in the File name text box, then click **Save**
   The Creating Movie dialog box opens, displaying a progress meter while the movie is created. Upon completion, a dialog box appears, telling you that the movie has been saved and asking if you want to watch it now.

6. Click **Yes**
   Your movie plays, including video and sound. Notice that the information you entered in the Save Movie dialog box appears here.

7. Use the **Play/Pause button** and the **Volume control slider** on the Seek bar, as shown in Figure M-19, to adjust settings and view the movie again, then click the **Close button** in the Windows Media Player

8. In the Collections pane, click the **Space Sounds** collection, click the **Delete button** ✗ on the Standard toolbar, click **Yes** to confirm the deletion, then delete the Space Videos collection
   You deleted the specified collections.

Trouble?
If you are asked to save the project, click Yes.

9. Click the **Close button** in Movie Maker if necessary, click **Yes** to create a backup of your collections file, name the back-up file **Space Project Backup**, then save it to the drive and folder where your Project Files are located

FIGURE M-18: **Save Movie dialog box**

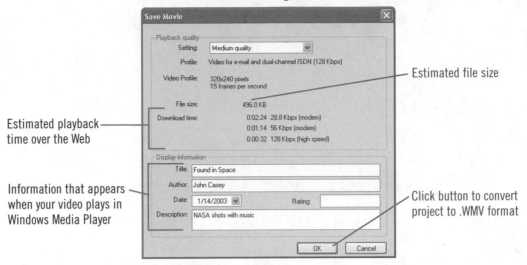

Estimated file size

Estimated playback time over the Web

Information that appears when your video plays in Windows Media Player

Click button to convert project to .WMV format

FIGURE M-19: **Your movie in Windows Media Player**

Title you assigned in Save Movie dialog box

Click button to stop

Click button to pause or play

Drag slider to adjust volume

CLUES TO USE

Sending a movie in an e-mail message

After you create a movie, you can send it in an e-mail message by clicking the Send button ✉ on the Project toolbar, then clicking E-mail. In the Send Movie Via E-mail dialog box, select a movie quality option, enter the display information that you want to appear when your movie is played, then click OK. In the Name the movie to send dialog box, enter a file name for the movie, then click OK. Movie Maker creates your movie, then asks you to select your e-mail program, such as Outlook Express. Double-click your e-mail program in the list, address your e-mail message, then click the Send button. When sending an e-mail with a movie attached, be aware that some ISPs limit the size of incoming messages and that large e-mails take longer to send and receive. If your e-mail program is not in the list, click As an attachment in another e-mail program. This compresses and saves the file to your hard disk, where you can manually attach the movie file to an e-mail message using your e-mail program.

Practice

▶ Concepts Review

Label each element of the screen shown in Figure M-20.

FIGURE M-20

1. Which element points to the timeline?
2. Which element points to the monitor?
3. Which element points to the Seek bar?
4. Which element points to the Collections pane?
5. Which element points to the Collections area?
6. Which element points to the Audio bar?
7. Which element points to the Monitor bar?
8. Which element points to the Start trim handle?

Match each of the terms with the statement that describes its function.

9. **Clip**
10. **Collection**
11. **Storyboard**
12. **Timeline**
13. **Cross-fade**

a. View most convenient for changing clip order
b. Audio or video segment
c. View most convenient for adding transitions
d. Group of clips
e. Method of changing from one clip to the next in a movie

Select the best answers from the following lists of choices.

14. Before you can use a pre-existing video clip in Movie Maker, you must first _____ it.
   a. Record
   b. Import
   c. Collect
   d. Transition

15. A "working copy" of a movie is called a
   a. Storyboard.
   b. Timeline.
   c. Project.
   d. Clip.

16. To trim clips, you must ensure that Movie Maker is in which view?
   a. Project
   b. Timeline
   c. Trim
   d. Storyboard

17. Which one of the following is a video format that Movie Maker can import?
   a. .avi
   b. .mswmm
   c. .wav
   d. .jpeg

▶ Skills Review

1. **Plan a Movie Maker video.**
   a. Write the basic steps in planning a Movie Maker video without referring to the unit material.
   b. Compare your results to page M-2.

2. **Start Movie Maker and view a project.**
   a. Start the Movie Maker program.
   b. Open the Project File MM M-7.mswmm (locate the file if necessary), and play it in Storyboard view.
   c. Display and play the project in Timeline view.
   d. Zoom in, then zoom out, then redisplay the project in Storyboard view.

3. **Import and view video clips.**
   a. Import and view the following picture from your Project Files: MM M-8.jpeg, MM M-9.jpeg, MM M-10.jpeg, and MM M-11.jpeg. (*Note:* Because the files are still images, you can import them into the same collection.)

4. **Organize and remove clips and collections.**
   a. Rename the clips Wagon, Horse, Shed, and Bales, respectively.
   b. Create a collection called **Country Pictures**, then move all the pictures into the collection.
   c. Create another collection called **Country Sounds**.

5. **Create a Movie Maker project file.**
   a. Create a new Movie Maker project. Since you are using still photographs, your project is a slide show.
   b. Drag the Bales, Shed, Horse, and Wagon photos into the first four positions in the Storyboard.
   c. Save the project as **Wyoming**, then play it in Storyboard view.
   d. Change the order of the clips so that the Shed picture is the last clip in the slide show, then save the project.

6. **Trim clips in Timeline view.**
   a. View the project in Timeline view.
   b. Extend the Wagon clip to 6 seconds using the End Trim marker. (Because these are still images, you can extend the length of time they display on screen. You cannot do this with video images, which have fixed lengths.)
   c. The Horse, Shed, and Bales clips should default to 5 seconds each. Play each clip to verify its length, then play the entire Timeline.

7. Create transitions between clips.

    a. Set the Horse clip so it overlaps the Wagon clip for about 2 seconds.

    b. Set transitions of about 1 second for the remaining clips, then save the project.

8. Add a soundtrack.

    a. Import the sound file MM M-12.wma into the Country Sounds collection, then add the file as the soundtrack.

    b. Play the slide show with its soundtrack, then save the project.

9. Save and view your movie.

    a. Save your movie with the filename **Wyoming**, setting the following information to display: Title: Out West; Author: Your name; Description: Pictures of last year's trip.

    b. View the movie in Windows Media Player.

    c. Remove the clips and collections you created, close Movie Maker, then back up the remaining collections if necessary.

▶ Independent Challenge 1

You work for the National Aeronautics and Space Administration (NASA) as the educational outreach liaison for the state of Florida. Your job is to organize field trips to Cape Canaveral and to visit schools across the state to stimulate student interest in NASA programs. You plan to create a movie to show in classrooms and to place on the NASA Educational Outreach Web site. Your manager asks you to create a sample movie using Movie Maker.

    a. Start Movie Maker and create a new project if necessary.

    b. Import the following clips in your collections area: MM M-2.avi, MM M-3.avi, MM M-4.avi, MM M-5.avi. View each one, then rename the clips as follows: the clip in the collection MM M-2 to EarthVenus; MM M-3 to Sun; MM M-4 to Apollo; and MM M-5 to Quake.

    c. Rename the MM M-2 collection as **NASA Videos**, move all the video clips into the NASA Videos collection folder, then delete the empty collection folders.

    d. Create a collection named **NASA Sounds**, then import the audio file MM M-13.wma into the Collections area.

    e. Create a movie project in Storyboard view by dragging the clips into the following frames: Quake into Frame 1, Apollo into Frame 2, EarthVenus into Frame 3, and Sun into Frame 4. Save the project as **NASA**.

    f. In Timeline view, trim the Sun clip to 10 seconds. Play the clip to verify its length, making necessary adjustments.

    g. Create a transition of approximately 2 seconds between each clip. Play each transition frame by frame, and verify the length of each in the timer below the Seek bar.

    h. Add the sound clip MM M-13.wma to the sound track. Position it in the middle of the movie so that the show starts in silence, plays the audio clip in the middle, and ends in silence. (You will have approximately 7 or 8 seconds of silence at the beginning and the end of the movie.)

    i. Preview the entire movie in the monitor.

    j. Save the project as a movie. Save it with medium quality, title it **Journey**, add your name as the author, then add the description **Apollo shots with drum**. Name the movie file **Education**. Open and play the movie in Windows Media Player.

    k. Delete the collections you created, then close Movie Maker.

▶ Independent Challenge 2

The owner of Wee Folks Preschool wants to produce an advertising movie for its Web site. She asks you to bid on the job. As part of your bid, you prepare a sample movie using the Movie Maker sample files and an added sound track.

    a. Start Movie Maker and create a new project if necessary.

    b. Import the Windows Movie Maker Sample File.wmv from the My Videos folder in the My Documents folder or from the drive and folder where your Project Files are located.

c. Create a **Sounds** collection, then import the sound files Play1 and Play2 from the folder where your Project Files are located into the new collection.

d. Create a movie approximately 20 seconds long, using the sample files and the Play1 and Play2 clips. You may add any other sound clips you like.

e. Adjust clip lengths and transitions in any way you think would be effective. Adjust the audio levels using the Set audio levels button in the workspace to change the audio balance between the sound in the video and the sound in the Audio bar. Save the project as **Wee Folks**.

f. Save the project as a movie named **Wee Folks Sample**. Assign the piece an appropriate title and description, and be sure to include your name as the author. View the movie in Windows Media Player.

g. Delete the collections you created, then close Movie Maker.

▶ Independent Challenge 3

You are planning to set up a Web site for your upcoming family reunion on the free server space from your Internet Service Provider (ISP). You want to use Movie Maker to create a slide show of interesting family pictures and place it on the site. Keep in mind, however, that your ISP limits your site to 5 MB, so you have to monitor the sizes of your graphics and the movie.

a. Choose five appropriate pictures in JPEG format to include in your show. If necessary, scan them from hard copy using a scanner. Make sure each image is under about 400 KB. You may need to reduce the resolution to achieve this. If you do not have access to any photographs in JPEG format or cannot get to a scanner, use the files MM M-8.jpeg, MM M-9.jpeg, MM M-10.jpeg, and MM M-11.jpeg in the folder where your Project Files are located.

b. Create a **Slides** collection, then move all photographs into it.

c. Set up the slide show as a Movie Maker project, adjusting clip locations, display times, and transitions in any way you feel is effective, then save the project as **Reunion**.

d. Record a sound track from a CD. Make the sound clip about 20 seconds long, and include it in your slide show. If you cannot record sound clips, use one of your own or one or more of the sound clips from the folder where your Project Files are located.

e. If you have a microphone, add narration to the slide show. If not, continue to the next step.

f. Save the project as a movie, using appropriate title and descriptive information, then save the movie as **Family Reunion**. Play it in Windows Media Player. Delete the collections you created, then close Movie Maker.

Independent Challenge 4

You are being considered for a job as a junior product manager at the Blythe International Advertising Agency, which prepares custom marketing videos for clients worldwide. As part of the selection process, the marketing director asks you to submit a short movie created in Movie Maker that shows your skills. You can choose the subject.

a. Locate approximately five .avi files and two or three sound files. If you have a video capture card, create your own .avi files from videotape; if you have access to a digital video camera, create and record clips directly into Movie Maker. Or go to a search engine such as Alta Vista, Yahoo!, Excite, or Infoseek, and search for keywords such as "video," "sound files," or ".avi." You may also add still images in JPEG or other acceptable formats. Be aware of the size of any clips you create or download.

b. Plan and create a movie, using trimming, transitions, sound files, and/or narration. Save the project file as **Blythe**.

c. Preview the movie in the monitor.

d. When you are satisfied with its contents, save the project as a movie named **Blythe Sample**. View it in Windows Media Player.

Visual Workshop

Using the skills you learned in this unit, create the project shown in Figure M-21. Save the project as **Odyssey**. (*Hint*: You can use the Copy and Paste commands to copy any sound or video file.) All necessary files are in the folder containing your Project Files. The three video clips you need are MM M-2.avi (EarthVenus), MM M-3.avi (Sun), and MM M-4.avi (Apollo). The sound clip you need is MM M-6.wma. Save the project as a movie named **Space Odyssey**.

FIGURE M-21

Managing

Hardware

- ► **Understand plug and play hardware**
- ► **Install a printer**
- ► **View printer properties**
- ► **Manage printers and print jobs**
- ► **Install hardware devices**
- ► **View system hardware**
- ► **View hardware settings**
- ► **Remove hardware devices**

A **hardware device** is any physical device that you plug into and that is controlled by your computer. This device can be, for example, a network or sound card that you install inside your computer, or it can be a printer or a scanner that you plug into the outside of the computer. Windows XP makes it easy to manage your hardware. In this unit, you learn how to install hardware automatically with Windows plug and play, install a printer using the Add Printer Wizard, manage printers and print jobs, view hardware properties with the Device Manager, and remove hardware from the computer quickly and easily. John Casey, owner of Wired Coffee Company, uses Windows to install, manage, and remove different computer hardware devices and to learn about plug and play hardware in the process.

Understanding Plug and Play Hardware

Windows XP includes plug and play support for hardware, making it easy to install and uninstall devices quickly. With **plug and play** support, you simply plug the device in, and Windows sets the device to work with your existing hardware and resolves any system conflicts. When you install a hardware device, Windows installs related software, known as a **driver**, that allows the hardware to communicate with Windows and other software applications. Plug and play automatically tells the device drivers where to find the hardware devices. Plug and play matches up physical hardware devices with the software device drivers that operate them and establish channels of communication between each physical device and its driver. With plug and play, you can be confident that any new device will work properly with your computer and that your computer will restart correctly after you install or uninstall hardware. ◀━━ John wants to install a new printer, so he decides to learn about plug and play devices. Plug and play supports only those devices that indicate that they are plug and play compatible, as shown in Figure N-1.

In order to install a plug and play device, you need to do the following:

► Gather your original Windows XP CD-ROMs, the hardware device that you want to install, and the disks that come with the device if available.

► Turn off your computer before you physically install a hardware device, such as a network card or a sound card, inside your computer. To install a hardware device that plugs into the outside of your computer, such as a scanner or printer, you can use the Add Hardware utility program in the Control Panel without turning off your computer.

► Follow the manufacturer's instructions to plug the new device into your computer.

► Turn on your computer or start the Add Hardware utility program in the Control Panel. Windows tries to detect the new device and install the device drivers. If Windows doesn't recognize the new hardware device, the device might not be plug and play compatible or installed correctly. Turn off your computer, check the device documentation and installation carefully, then turn on your computer again. If the device driver is not available on your computer, Windows asks you to insert into the appropriate drive the Windows XP installation CD-ROM or the disk that comes with the device from the manufacturer.

► Follow the instructions on the screen until a message indicates that you are finished. Windows automatically notifies all other devices of the new device so there are no conflicts and manages the power requirements of your hardware and peripherals by shutting them down or conserving power when you are not using them. And, if you are working in another program when you install or uninstall a device, plug and play lets you know that it is about to change your computer configuration and warns you to save your work.

FIGURE N-1: **Computer with attached printer via a cable**

CLUES TO USE

Understanding printers

Although there are many different kinds of printers, there are two main categories: ink- or bubble-jet, and laser. An ink-jet printer works by spraying ionized ink at a sheet of paper. Ink-jet printers are less expensive and considerably slower than laser, but still produce a good quality output. A laser printer utilizes a laser beam to produce an image on a drum, which is rolled through a reservoir of toner and transferred to the paper through a combination of heat and pressure. Laser printers are faster and produce a higher quality output than ink-jets, but are also more expensive. Printers are classified by two main characteristics: resolution and speed. Printer resolution refers to the sharpness and clarity of a printed page. For printers, the resolution indicates the number of dots per inch (dpi). For example, a 300-dpi printer is one that is capable of printing 300 distinct dots in a line one-inch long, or 90,000 dots per square inch. The higher the dpi, the sharper the print quality. Printer speed is measured in pages per minute (ppm). The speed of printers varies widely. In general terms, ink-jet printers range from about 4 to 10 ppm, while laser printers range from about 10 to 30 ppm. The speed depends on the page's contents: if there is just text or the page has only one color, the ppm is in the high range, but when a page contains graphics and/or has multiple colors, the ppm rate falls to the low range.

Installing a Printer

To install a printer, you do not need to shut down your computer. Simply attach the printer cable to the appropriate connector on your computer, according to the manufacturer's instructions, and plug in the power cord. If you connect your printer to your computer through a USB port, Windows automatically detects the new hardware device and installs the printer, and you are ready to print. Otherwise, you can use the Add Printer Wizard in conjunction with the Found New Hardware Wizard to detect and install the printer. If the Found New Hardware Wizard doesn't detect your printer, you can also use the Add Printer Wizard to manually perform the task. The Add Printer Wizard asks you a series of questions to help you install either a network or local printer, establish a connection, and print a test page. If the printer does not work properly, Windows starts an automated troubleshooter to help you fix the problem. John purchased a new HP OfficeJet printer. In this lesson you don't actually install a new printer, but you step through the wizard to learn how it installs the appropriate software.

Steps

QuickTip

If your Start menu command is not available, double-click the Add or Remove Programs icon 🗊 in the Control Panel to install Fax Services.

1. **Click the Start button on the taskbar, then click Printers and Faxes**
   The Printers and Faxes window opens, as shown in Figure N-2, in Tiles view.

2. **In the task pane, click Add a printer, then click Next in the wizard dialog box**
   The next wizard dialog box asks you to specify whether you are installing a local or network printer. A **local printer** is a printer that is directly connected to your computer, and a **network printer** is one that is connected to a network to which you have access.

QuickTip

If you were actually installing a printer, you would turn on the detection feature so that the Found New Hardware Wizard could automatically complete the installation for you.

3. **Click the Local printer attached to this computer option button if necessary, click the Automatically detect and install my Plug and Play printer check box to deselect it if necessary, then click Next**
   The next wizard dialog box asks which port you want to use with this printer. A **port** is the location on the back of your computer where you connect the printer cable. You can connect the cable to either a printer port, which is labeled LPT1 or LPT2, to a communications port, which is labeled COM1 or COM2, or to a Universal Serial Bus port, which is labeled USB.

4. **Click the Use the following port option button if necessary, make sure the recommended port is selected in the list box, then click Next**
   The next wizard dialog box asks you to select a printer.

Trouble?

If an HP OfficeJet printer is already installed on your computer, select another printer, or click the "Keep existing driver (recommended) option button if necessary, then click OK.

5. **Press [H], click HP in the Manufacturer list if necessary, click HP OfficeJet in the Printers list, as shown in Figure N-3, then click Next**
   The next wizard dialog box asks you to type a name for the printer and whether you want the printer to be the default printer. HP OfficeJet appears as the printer name, and the No option is selected. If you have access to several printers, the default printer is the printer that you use most often. When you start a print job without specifying a particular printer, the job is sent to the default printer. A black dot with a checkmark appears, as shown in Figure N-4.

6. **Click Next, click the Do not share this printer option button if available, then click Next**
   The next wizard dialog box asks if you want to print a test page.

Trouble?

If the Windows XP installation CD-ROM is not available, click Cancel, then click OK in Step 7 to cancel the operation. For the remaining lessons, you will need to use a printer that is currently installed on your computer.

7. **Click the No option button, click Next, then click Finish**
   Since the printer is not connected, you do not need to print a test page. Normally, printing a test page is important to make sure the printer is working properly. Windows XP may need to install a printer driver from the CD-ROM to complete the printer installation.

8. **If necessary, insert the Windows XP installation CD-ROM into the appropriate drive, click OK, then click the Close button in the Windows XP CD-ROM window**
   The printer icon appears in the Printers and Faxes window, as shown in Figure N-4.

FIGURE N-2: Printers and Faxes window

Your window name might differ

Click link to install a printer

Network printer

Your selection of printers and faxes will differ

Number of documents to be printed

Printer status information

FIGURE N-3: Add Printer Wizard dialog box

List of available printer manufacturers; your list might differ

Selected printer

List of printers for the selected manufacturer

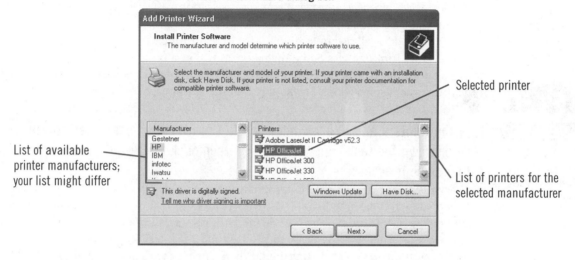

FIGURE N-4: Printers and Faxes window with new printer

Checkmark indicates default printer

Icon for local OfficeJet printer

Understanding USB ports

A printer port is called a parallel port, which sends more than one byte simultaneously. A communications port is called a serial port, which sends information one byte at a time. The USB port is a new technology that is expected to replace parallel and serial ports. A USB (Universal Serial Bus) port is an external hardware interface on the computer that allows you to connect a USB device. A single USB port can be used to connect up to 127 peripheral devices, such as mice, modems, and keyboards, and supports data transfer rates of 480 Mbs (480 million bits per second). USB also supports plug and play installation and hot plugging, which is the ability to add and remove devices to a computer while the computer is running and have the operating system automatically recognize the change.

Viewing Printer Properties

After you install a printer, the printer appears in the Printers and Faxes window and in a program's Print dialog box, where you can view and change printer properties and personal preferences. Viewing printer properties gives you information about a printer's computer connection or network location, sharing options, related software drivers, color management options, graphics settings, installed fonts, and other advanced settings, such as spooling. **Spooling**, also known as **background printing**, is the process of storing a temporary copy of a file on the hard disk and then sending the file to the print device. Spooling allows you to continue working with the file as soon as it is stored on the disk instead of having to wait until the file is finished printing. In addition to printer properties, you can also view and change personal printer preferences, such as orientation, page order, pages per sheet, paper size, paper tray selection, copy count, and print quality and color. When you change personal printing preferences from the Printers and Faxes folder, the default settings are changed for all documents you print to that printer. When you change personal preferences from the Print or Pages Setup dialog boxes within a program, the settings are changed for individual documents. ✐ John wants to view the printer properties and personal preferences of the printer he just installed to make sure that the settings are correct.

Steps

Trouble?

If a connected printer is not available, click the HP OfficeJet icon, then skip Steps 5 and 6 in this lesson.

1. **In the Printers and Faxes window, click a printer icon connected to your computer, scroll down the task pane if necessary, then click the Details down arrow ⊗ in the task pane if necessary**
   Every installed printer on your computer is represented by an icon in the Printers window. When you select a printer icon, status information for that printer appears in the Details section of the task pane, as shown in Figure N-5, such as number of documents to be printed, and whether the printer is ready to print. When a printer icon in the window appears with a cable, it indicates a network printer. When a printer icon appears without a cable, it indicates a local printer. When a printer icon appears with a hand, it indicates a **shared printer**, a printer that is directly connected to your computer and is shared with other network users.

QuickTip

To troubleshoot a printer, click Troubleshoot printing in the task pane if available, then follow the instructions.

2. **In the task pane, click Set printer properties**
   The Printer Properties dialog box opens displaying the General tab, as shown in Figure N-6. Table N-1 describes the Printer Properties tabs in the dialog box; your tabs might differ.

3. **Click Printing Preferences**
   The Printing Preferences dialog box opens, displaying your printer's specific options. When you change these printing preferences, the default settings are changed for all documents you print to this printer.

4. **Click each available tab to display your printer's specific options, then click OK**
   Tabs and options vary from printer to printer.

5. **Click Print Test Page**
   A dialog box opens, asking if the test page printed correctly. The test page looks fine.

6. **Click OK to close the dialog box**

7. **Click the Ports tab**
   The Ports tab shows a printer's local connection.

8. **Click the Advanced tab**
   The Advanced tab shows a printer's current driver and gives you specific printing choices, such as print spooling to speed up printing.

9. **Click OK to close the Printer Properties dialog box**

FIGURE N-5: Printers and Faxes window

Default printer shared with network users

Printer connected over a network

Status information for selected printer

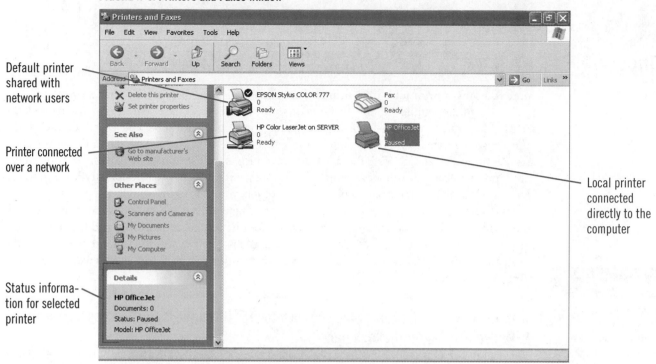

Local printer connected directly to the computer

FIGURE N-6: HP OfficeJet Properties dialog box with General tab

Your tabs might differ

Click button to change printer paper and layout preferences

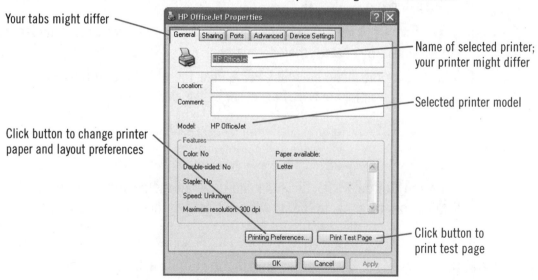

Name of selected printer; your printer might differ

Selected printer model

Click button to print test page

TABLE N-1: Tabs in the Printer Properties dialog box

tab	description
General	Lists general information about the printer and allows you to print a test page
Sharing	Allows you to share the printer over a network
Ports	Lists the printer's connection port and software drivers
Advanced	Lists software drivers and allows you to change printer options
Device Settings	Allows you to change printer device and related settings

Managing Printers and Print Jobs

After you send a print job to the printer from the Print dialog box in a program, or drag files in the My Computer window to the printer icon in the Printers and Faxes window, you can check the status. To check the status of a printer or manage multiple print jobs, you can double-click the appropriate printer icon in the Printers and Faxes window or on the taskbar in the notification area. A window opens showing the **print queue**, which is the list of files to be printed. You can use this window to cancel print jobs, temporarily pause print jobs, view printer properties, and so on. If you are having problems with a printer or print job, you can **defer**, or halt, the printing process to avoid getting error messages. With deferred printing, you can send a job to be printed even if your computer is not connected to a printer. To do this, you pause printing, and the file waits in the print queue until you turn off pause printing. John wants to learn how to manage the printer and print jobs. Because you are not actually printing to a real printer, you will use deferred printing in this lesson.

Steps

QuickTip

To get more information about a printer from the manufacturer, select the printer in the Printers window, then click Go to manufacturer's Web site in the task pane.

1. In the Printers and Faxes window, click the **HP OfficeJet icon** if necessary, then click **Pause printing** in the task pane

   In Tiles view, the HP OfficeJet icon displays the status change from ready to paused. Pause printing prevents the computer from attempting to send a print job to the printer, which is useful when your printer is turned off or not connected to your computer as in this example.

2. Click the **Start button** on the taskbar, point to **All Programs**, point to **Accessories**, then click **Paint** to open the program

3. Click **File** on the menu bar, click **Open**, navigate to the drive and folder where your Project Files are located, then double-click **Burst Sign** to open it

4. Click **File** on the menu bar, click **Print**, click the **HP OfficeJet icon** in the Print dialog box as shown in Figure N-7 if necessary, then click **Print**

   The file is sent to the HP OfficeJet printer, and a printer icon 🖨 appears in the notification area on the taskbar, indicating that print jobs are pending. Since you paused the printer, nothing prints; the job simply waits in the print queue until you either delete the job or connect a printer to your computer. In Tiles view, the number of files to be printed changes from 0 to 1.

5. Open the **Coffee Roast** file from the drive and folder where your Project Files are located, print the file to the HP OfficeJet printer, then Close the Paint window

   The Coffee Roast file is sent to the HP OfficeJet printer. In Tiles view, the number of files to be printed changes from 1 to 2. You want to check the status of your print jobs.

QuickTip

To view jobs sent to a network printer, you need to go to the computer that is physically connected to the printer and double-click the printer's icon in the Printers window.

6. Double-click the **HP OfficeJet icon** in the Printers and Faxes window

   The HP OfficeJet window opens, as shown in Figure N-8. The HP OfficeJet window displays the printer status in the title bar and the print jobs currently in the queue. The files are listed in the order in which they will be printed.

7. In the HP OfficeJet window, right-click **Burst Sign**, then click **Pause**

   The printing status of the selected file is changed to paused. When you want to print the paused file, right-click the file, then click Resume.

QuickTip

To delete a single file from the print queue, select the file, click Document on the menu bar, then click Cancel.

8. Click **Printer** on the menu bar, click **Cancel All Documents**, click **Yes** to confirm the cancellation, then click the **Close button** for all open windows

   All print jobs are deleted from the queue.

FIGURE N-7: **Printing a file to a paused printer**

Selected printer

Printer paused

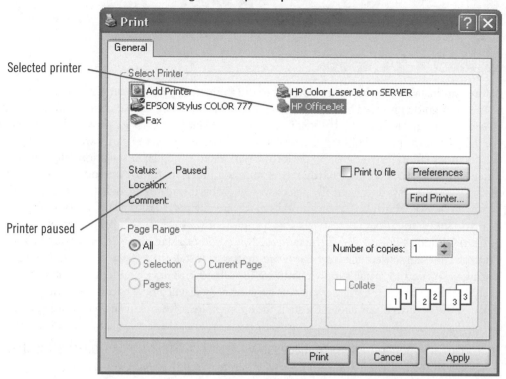

FIGURE N-8: **HP OfficeJet window**

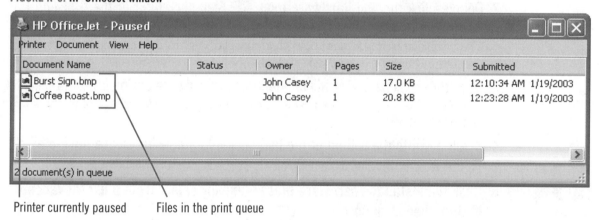

Printer currently paused   Files in the print queue

Adding a separator page to print jobs

When you work in a network environment in which many different users print their jobs on the same printer, adding a separator page to your files can be helpful. A separator (or banner) page lists the name, author, date, and time of the print job. You can only set up separator pages to a network printer with an administrator's permission. To add a separator page to print jobs, right-click the network printer icon in the Printers and Faxes window, then click Properties. In the Properties dialog box, click the Advanced tab, then click Separator Page. In the Separator Page dialog box, click Browse, select one of the separator files that Windows provides in the System32 folder or navigate to and select a custom separator page, then click Open. Click OK in the Separator Page and the Properties dialog boxes. The separator files provided by Windows might not work with some printers. To turn off the Separator Page feature, delete the filename and path in the Separator Page dialog box.

Installing Hardware Devices

Before you install a new hardware device, be sure to carefully read the product documentation and installation guide provided by the manufacturer. If the hardware device comes with an installation CD-ROM, it is recommended that you not use the Add Hardware Wizard provided by Windows and use the manufacturer's CD-ROM and related instruction to install the hardware instead. If the product documentation instructs you to perform a typical plug and play installation, turn off your computer, physically connect your hardware to your computer, then turn on your computer again. In most cases, Windows automatically detects your new hardware device and starts the Add Hardware Wizard. The Add Hardware Wizard installs hardware devices by asking you a series of questions to help you set up the necessary software for the new hardware device to work properly on your computer. If Windows doesn't detect the new hardware, you can start the Add Hardware Wizard in the Control Panel and select the new hardware device to install it.   John uses the Add New Hardware Wizard to install support software for a hardware device, a digital camera, he just connected to his computer. In this lesson you don't actually install a new hardware device, but you step through the wizard to learn how it installs the appropriate software for the hardware device.

Steps

1. Close all open programs if necessary, click the **Start button** on the taskbar, click **Control Panel**, then click **Switch to Classic View** if necessary
   The Control Panel window opens.

2. Double-click the **Add Hardware icon** , then click **Next** in the first Add Hardware Wizard dialog box
   The wizard searches for any new plug and play devices that are on your system. When it doesn't find one, the wizard asks if the hardware device is connected to your computer.

3. Click the **Yes, I have already connected the hardware option button**, then click **Next**
   The wizard asks you to add a new device or to select the installed device to check properties or troubleshoot.

4. Scroll down to the bottom of the list, click **Add a new hardware device** as shown in Figure N-9, then click **Next**

5. Click the **Install the hardware that I manually select from a list (Advanced) option button**, then click **Next**
   The wizard asks you to select the type of hardware for which you want to install the support software.

6. Click **Imaging devices** as shown in Figure N-10, then click **Next**
   The wizard asks you to select the make and model for the new hardware. Devices are listed alphabetically. The currently selected manufacturer is Agfa, and the model is Agfa ePhoto 1280 Digital Camera.

7. Click **Next** to accept the current selection, click **Automatic port detection** if necessary, then click **Next**
   The wizard asks you to enter a name for the device.

8. Click **Next** to accept the default device name, then click **Finish** to install the software

9. If necessary, insert the required Windows XP installation CD-ROM in the appropriate drive, click **OK**, then click the **Close button** in the Windows XP CD-ROM window
   Windows needs to install the appropriate driver to complete the installation. You then return to the Control Panel.

QuickTip

Because an actual hardware device is not connected to your computer, you want this feature to be active; if you were actually installing a hardware device, you would let Windows search for the new hardware device.

Trouble?

If the Windows XP installation CD-ROM is not available, click OK, then click Cancel.

FIGURE N-9: Add Hardware Wizard dialog box

Click to add a new device

Click any existing device
to troubleshoot it

FIGURE N-10: Choosing a hardware device to install

Selected device type
for installation

Click item to select the type of
device you want to install

Installing a scanner or digital camera

Installing a scanner or digital camera is easy with plug and play: plug the scanner or camera into your computer, then, if Windows detects the plug and play device, the Scanner and Camera Installation Wizard automatically starts. If Windows doesn't detect the device, you can click Add an imaging device in the task pane in the Scanners and Cameras window to start the wizard, select the device, and install it. The Scanner and Camera Wizard is designed specifically for installing imaging devices, but it works in a similar way as the Add Hardware Wizard. To open the

Scanners and Cameras window, click the Start button on the taskbar, click Control Panel, then double-click the Scanners and Cameras icon 🖼. After you install your scanner or digital camera, you can test it to make sure it works properly. With the scanner or camera connected to your computer, right-click the scanner or camera you want to test, click Properties, click the General tab in the Properties dialog box, then click Test Scanner or Test Camera. A message appears, telling you the results of the test.

Windows XP

Viewing System Hardware

When you install a new operating system, such as Windows XP, it is important to make sure that you are using the latest software drivers with your system hardware. If you are not using the latest software drivers, your hardware devices might not work to full capacity. You can view your system hardware using a Windows utility called the Device Manager. With the Device Manager, you can determine the software driver versions being used with your system hardware, update the software driver with a newer version, roll back to a previous driver version if the device fails with the new one, or uninstall a driver. After viewing your software driver version numbers, you can contact the manufacturer or visit their Web site to determine the latest versions. Most manufacturers allow you to download drivers from their Web sites for free. ✒ John wants to make sure that he is using the latest software driver version numbers.

QuickTip

If a specific device conflicts with some other device, its icon is marked by an exclamation point within a yellow circle 🟡, as shown in Figure N-11.

1. **In the Control Panel, scroll if necessary, double-click the System icon 🖥, click the Hardware tab in the System Properties dialog box, then click Device Manager**
   The Device Manager window opens, as shown in Figure N-11. Device Manager provides you with a list of the hardware types, also known as **hardware classes**, which are attached to your computer. To see the specific devices within a hardware type, you click the Expand indicator ⊞ next to the hardware device type. Once you select a specific device within a hardware device type, you can investigate the properties of the hardware device. On your computer, you use an older display adapter, a hardware device that allows a computer to communicate with its monitor, so you decide to learn about its properties.

2. **Click the Expand indicator ⊞ next to the Display adapters icon**
   The display expands to show the name of the display adapter attached to your computer.

QuickTip

To disable a hardware device, click the hardware device in the Device Manager, click the Disable button 🖥 on the toolbar, then click Yes. To enable the device, click the Enable button 🖥 on the toolbar.

3. **Click the display adapter type that is connected to your computer, then click the Properties button 🖥 on the toolbar**
   The Properties dialog box for your display adapter type opens with the General tab, showing identification and status information about the display adapter. The other tabs available on the Properties dialog box are Driver and Resources. The Driver tab lists the software drivers related to the hardware device and other options, while the Resources tab lists the memory settings related to the hardware device.

4. **Click the Driver tab**
   The Driver tab appears, displaying driver information, such as manufacturer name, date published, and version number, as shown in Figure N-12. You can also click Driver Details to learn more about the current version of the software driver, click Update Driver to install the latest driver for the display adapter that is connected to your computer, click Roll Back Driver to revert back to the previous driver installed, or click Uninstall to remove a driver.

5. **Click Driver Details**
   Details for the current driver are shown in the Driver File Details dialog box, including the driver file version number.

QuickTip

To view hardware devices by what they connect to, click View on the menu bar, then click Devices by connection.

6. **Click OK to close the Driver File Details dialog box, then click OK to close the display adapter Properties dialog box**
   You return to the Device Manager window.

7. **Click the Collapse indicator ⊟ next to the Display adapters icon**
   The list of display adapters collapses. Leave the Device Manager open as you continue to the next lesson.

FIGURE N-11: **Device Manager window**

Click the Expand indicator to display a specific device

Exclamation mark indicates a hardware device conflict

Hardware types attached to your computer; your list might differ

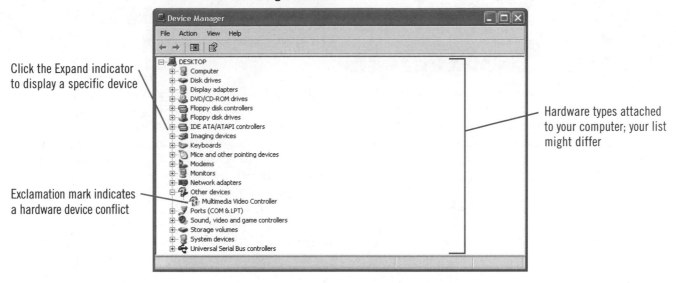

FIGURE N-12: **Display Adapter Properties dialog box**

Selected display adapter device

Driver information

Driver-related commands

CLUES TO USE

Getting system information

If you encounter a system problem, you may need to give information to a support technician. Support technicians require specific information about your computer so that they can resolve your system problem. In Windows XP, you can use System Information to quickly collect and display your system configuration data, as shown in Figure N-13. To open the System Information window, click the Start button on the taskbar, point to All Programs, point to Accessories, point to System Tools, then click System Information. For information about working in the System Information window, click Help on the menu bar, then click Contents.

FIGURE N-13: **System Information window**

Viewing Hardware Settings

Windows XP

One reason you might want to view hardware settings is if you plan to install any legacy hardware. **Legacy hardware** is any device not designed for Windows XP plug and play support. If you have a hardware device that is not designed for Windows XP plug and play, it is important to find out current hardware resource settings to avoid conflicts during installation, such as having two devices with the same resource settings. Before you actually place a legacy hardware device in your computer, you should browse through the devices currently attached to your computer system and ensure that your computer has the available resources to install the hardware device. With the Device Manager, you can view the device resources that are being used with your system hardware and determine whether your computer has the available resources to install a legacy or plug and play hardware device. Generally, you cannot install non plug and play hardware without performing some manual setup with the Device Manager. ◄▬▬ John has an old scanner and wants to examine current hardware resource settings to determine whether he can install the legacy hardware.

QuickTip

To scan for any hardware changes in the Device Manager, click the Scan for hardware changes button 🖳 on the toolbar.

1. In the Device Manager window, click **View** on the menu bar, then click **Resources by connection**

   The resources installed on the computer appear in a tree structure sorted by connection.

2. Click the **Expand indicator** ⊞ next to the Interrupt request (IRQ) icon

   The Device Manager displays the resource settings currently in use and the hardware that is using each resource, as shown in Figure N-14. Each installed device requires a communication line called an **interrupt request line (IRQ)**, which allows the physical hardware device to communicate with your computer's software. For example, when you press a key on your keyboard, a signal is sent from the keyboard (a hardware device) through an IRQ to Windows (computer software), which then performs an action. Two devices attempting to share an IRQ create an IRQ conflict, and neither device will work properly.

QuickTip

To get additional information about Device Manager, click the Help button 📝 on the toolbar.

3. Drag the **scroll bar** to the bottom of the dialog box if necessary

   Take note of the available IRQs on your computer. Any IRQ number between 0 and 15 that is not listed is available. When you install a legacy hardware device, the device's instructions might ask you to provide an IRQ setting. When prompted by the device instructions, provide an IRQ that is not already in use. Instead of writing down your computer resource information on paper, you can print a system summary report.

4. Click **Action** on the menu bar, then click **Print**

   The Print dialog box opens with the System summary report type selected by default, as shown in Figure N-15. Table N-2 describes the report options available in the Print dialog box.

Trouble?

If you are working in a lab, check with your instructor before printing.

5. In the Select Printer box, click a connected printer, then click **Print**

   Figure N-16 shows the first part of the summary report. If you are having trouble installing a hardware device, a technical support person might ask you questions that this summary report will help you answer. Leave the Device Manager open as you continue to the next lesson.

TABLE N-2: Print dialog box report types

report types	description
System summary	Prints general system, IRQ, port, memory, and DMA channel usage information about your computer
Selected class or device	Prints device type, resource, and driver information for a selected class or device
All devices and system summary	Prints general system, IRQ, port, memory, DMA channel usage, and driver information for all devices

FIGURE N-14: Device Manager window in Resources by connection view

IRQs 2, 5, and 7 are available; yours might differ

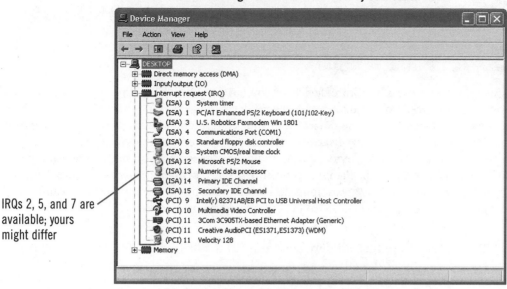

FIGURE N-15: Printing a hardware summary report

Click icon to select a different printer

Click option to select a report type

FIGURE N-16: Summary report

Note system summary information

Note IRQ usage summary information

Your report might look different

Removing Hardware Devices

Windows XP

If you no longer use a hardware device, or you have an older hardware device that you want to upgrade, you need to remove the hardware device drivers and related software before you remove the physical hardware device from your computer. With the Device Manager, you can quickly and easily remove hardware devices and any related device drivers. Before you remove a legacy device, printing the device settings is a good idea in case you need to reinstall the device later. Just as you can use the Printers window to install a printer, you can remove a printer in the Printers window as well. ◄— John decides not to connect the digital camera and printer he installed to his computer after all, so he wants to delete both of them.

1. In the Device Manager window, click **View** on the menu bar, then click **Devices by type**
   The devices installed on the computer appear in a tree structure sorted by type.

2. Click the **Expand indicator** ⊞ next to the Imaging devices icon
   The imaging devices currently installed on the computer appear under the Imaging devices icon.

   QuickTip

   To print out device settings, select the device in the Device Manager, click the Print button 🖨 on the toolbar, then click Print.

3. Click **Agfa ePhoto 1280 Digital Camera** to select the device you want to remove, as shown in Figure N-17

4. Click the **Uninstall button** 🗙 on the toolbar
   The Confirm Device Removal dialog box opens.

5. Click **OK** to remove the device, click the **Close button** in the Device Manager window, then click **OK** in the System Properties dialog box to close it
   You return to the Control Panel window.

6. Double-click the **Printers and Faxes icon** 🖨 (Professional or Home edition with Fax Services installed) or the **Printers icon** 🖨 (Home edition without Fax Services installed), then click the **HP OfficeJet icon**
   The HP OfficeJet icon appears highlighted in the Printers window, as shown in Figure N-18.

   Trouble?

   If a printer contains a print job, the Delete command does not work. You need to purge all print jobs before you can delete a printer.

7. In the task pane, click **Delete this printer**
   The Printers dialog box appears, asking if you want to delete the printer.

8. Click **Yes** to confirm the deletion, then click **Yes** if the default printer message box appears
   This removes the HP OfficeJet icon from the Printers window.

9. Click the **Close button** in the Printers and Faxes window

CLUES TO USE

Using the hardware troubleshooter

A hardware conflict can occur when two or more devices try to use the same IRQ. In many cases, one of the devices will not work. If you have a conflict, you can use the hardware troubleshooter to help you fix the problem. To use the troubleshooter, open the Properties dialog box from the Device Manager for the hardware device that is not working, then click Troubleshoot on the General tab. When the Help and Support Center window opens, answer the questions provided and follow the instructions to help you fix the problem.

FIGURE N-17: Device Manager window

Uninstall button

Selected device
for deletion

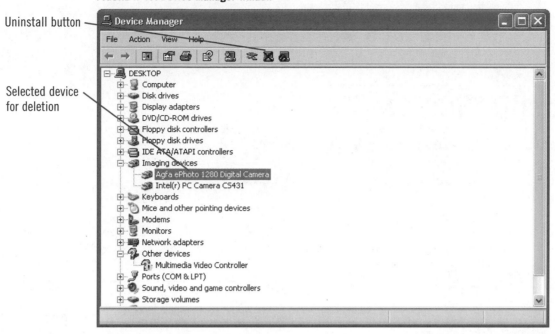

FIGURE N-18: Printers and Faxes window

Selected printer for deletion

Practice

► Concepts Review

Label each element of the screen shown in Figure N-19.

FIGURE N-19

1. Which element points to a local printer?
2. Which element points to a shared printer?
3. Which element points to a network printer?
4. Which element points to the default printer?
5. Which element points to a hardware device?
6. Which element points to a hardware device with a conflict?
7. Which element points to the number of files to be printed?

Match each of the terms with the statement that describes its function.

8. **Driver**
9. **Plug and play device**
10. **Port**
11. **Device Manager**
12. **Legacy device**
13. **IRQ**

a. Location on a computer where you connect a cable
b. Location where you work with device drivers
c. Hardware designed for Windows XP
d. How hardware communicates with Windows and other software
e. How a device communicates with a dedicated line
f. Hardware designed for pre-Windows XP

Select the best answer from the list of choices.

14. **Which of the following is a way to print a document?**
    a. Select the Print command from a program.
    b. Right-click a document, then click Print.
    c. Drag a document to the printer icon.
    d. All of the above.

15. **When right-clicking a printer icon, which of the following can you NOT do?**
    a. Open the printer's window.
    b. Set the printer as the default printer.
    c. Delete the printer.
    d. Close the printer's window.

16. **Which tab in the Printer Properties dialog box do you click to check printing preferences?**
    a. The General tab
    b. The Ports tab
    c. The Advanced tab
    d. The Device Settings tab

17. **Which of the following commands is NOT a way to stop a print job that is currently in progress?**
    a. Purge Print Jobs
    b. Pause Printing
    c. Cancel Printing
    d. Stop Printing

18. **Which tab in the System Properties dialog box do you click to open the Device Manager?**
    a. The General tab
    b. The User Profiles tab
    c. The Hardware tab
    d. The Advanced tab

19. **Which of the following is NOT a system report?**
    a. System summary
    b. All device and system summary
    c. Class or device summary
    d. Selected class or device

20. **What does IRQ stand for?**
    a. Interrupt result queue
    b. Interrupt request queue
    c. Interrupt request line
    d. Interrupt result line

Skills Review

---

1. **Install a printer.**
    a. Open the Printers and Faxes window (Professional or Home edition with Fax Services installed) or the Printers window (Home edition without Fax Services installed).
    b. Click Add a printer to start the Add Printer Wizard, then click Next.
    c. Click the Automatically detect and install my Plug and Play printer check box to deselect it if necessary, then click Next.
    d. Select an open port (COM or LPT), then click Next.
    e. Click Xerox as the manufacturer, click Xerox Document Centre 220 as the model, then click Next. (If necessary, click the Keep existing driver (Recommended) option button when prompted, then click OK.)
    f. Use the default printer name, click the No option button if necessary, click Next, click the Do not share this printer option button if available, then click Next.
    g. Click the No option button, click Next, then click Finish.
    h. If necessary, insert a Windows XP CD-ROM into the appropriate drive, click OK, then close the Windows XP CD-ROM window.

2. **View printer properties.**
    a. Select a printer icon for an available printer in the Printers and Faxes window.
    b. View printer properties.
    c. View printer preferences.
    d. Print a test page.
    e. Display the available tabs to view the various printer properties.
    f. Close the printer Properties dialog box.

3. **Manage printers and print jobs.**
    a. Right-click the Xerox Document Centre 220 icon, then click Pause Printing.
    b. Start Paint.
    c. Open the Burst Sign file from the drive and folder where your Project Files are located.
    d. Print the file to the Xerox Document Centre 220 printer.
    e. Open the Coffee Roast file from the drive and folder where your Project Files are located, then print the file to the Xerox Document Centre 220 printer.
    f. Close Paint.
    g. Double-click the Xerox Document Centre 220 icon in the Printers and Faxes window.
    h. Click Printer on the menu bar, then click Cancel All Documents, then click Yes.
    i. Close all of the open windows.

4. **Install a hardware device.**
    a. Open the Control Panel.
    b. Start the Add Hardware Wizard, then click Next.
    c. Click the Yes, I have already connected the hardware option button, then click Next.
    d. Scroll down, click Add a new hardware device, then click Next.
    e. Click the Install the hardware that I manually select from a list (Advanced) option button, then click Next.
    f. Click Infrared devices, then click Next.
    g. Click (Standard Infrared Port) as the manufacturer if necessary, click Serial Cable using IrDA Protocol as the model, then click Next.
    h. Click Next, select a port, click Next, then click Finish.
    i. If necessary, insert a Windows XP disk or CD-ROM, click OK, then close the Windows XP CD-ROM window.
    j. Click No if prompted to restart your computer.

5. View system hardware.

  a. Double-click the System icon in the Control Panel.

  b. Open the Device Manager.

  c. Click the Expand indicator next to the Infrared devices icon.

  d. Click Serial Cable using IrDA Protocol.

  e. Click the Properties button on the toolbar.

  f. Click the IrDA Settings tab, then click the Driver tab.

  g. Click OK.

  h. Click the Collapse indicator next to the Infrared devices icon.

6. View hardware settings.

  a. In Device Manager, click View on the menu bar, then click Resources by connection.

  b. Click the Expand indicator next to the Interrupt request (IRQ) icon.

  c. Click an IRQ in the list.

  d. Click Action on the menu bar, then click Print.

  e. Click the Selected class or device option button, then click Print.

7. Remove hardware devices.

  a. In Device Manager, click View on the menu bar, then click Devices by type.

  b. Click the Expand indicator next to the Infrared devices icon.

  c. Click Serial Cable using IrDA Protocol.

  d. Click the Uninstall button on the toolbar, click OK, click Yes to restart the computer if necessary, then reopen the Device Manager after restarting if necessary.

  e. Click the Close button in the Device Manager, then click OK to close the System Properties dialog box.

  f. In the Control Panel, double-click the Printers and Faxes icon (your icon name might differ with the Home edition).

  g. Click the Xerox Document Centre 220 icon.

  h. Click Delete this printer in the task pane, click Yes, then click Yes in the default printer message box if necessary.

  i. Close the Printers and Faxes window.

▶ Independent Challenge 1

You are an administrator at the U.S. Geological Survey and are in charge of creating earthquake reports on seismic activity in California. Your boss recently approved the purchase of a new color printer to help you create better reports. You want to install the color printer on your computer.

  a. Install a printer using the Add Printer Wizard.

  b. Assume the following about the installation: the printer is local, use an open port (LPT or COM), the manufacturer is Tektronix, and the printer model is Tektronix Phaser II PX.

  c. Do not set the printer as default or make it shared, and do not print a test page.

  d. Open the Printer Properties dialog box, then verify that the port and printer assignments are correct.

  e. Print the Printer Properties dialog box. (Press [Print Screen] to make a copy of the screen, open Paint, click Edit on the menu bar, click Paste to paste the screen into Paint, then click Yes to paste the large image if necessary. Click the Text button on the Toolbox, click a blank area in the Paint work area, then type your name. Click File on the menu bar, click Page Setup, change 100 % normal size to 50% in the Scaling area, then click OK. Click File on the menu bar, click Print, then click Print.)

  f. Delete the printer you just added.

  g. Close all open windows.

► Independent Challenge 2

You are the director of a youth center called Hosanna Homes for troubled teens. Half of your funding comes from the state, and the other half comes from donations. At the end of the month, you need to send a report to the state indicating the status of each teen at the home. You also send a report to donors to let them know what happened during the month. For this challenge, create several reports, print the documents, and manage the print jobs.

a. Use a real, working printer that is attached to your computer.

b. Pause printing. Get permission from your instructor or technical support person to do this.

c. Assume the following information about the youth center:

> Hosanna Homes ID: 251523
> 35 Live Oak Ranch Road
> Livermore, TX 82510

d. Using WordPad, create a file named **June State** on the drive or folder where your Project Files are located, then enter the following information:

> **State of Texas Protective Services**

Name	Age	Level	Number of Days
Maura Colligan	16	4	30
Brian Hubbard	17	5	30
Jill Meyer	16	3	30
David Smith	17	4	30
Earl Todd	15	1	16

e. Print the document on the chosen printer.

f. Open a new WordPad window, and create a file named **June Donor** on the drive where your Project Files are located, then enter the following information:

> **Dear Donor,**
> **During the month, Hosanna Homes received a new teenager at the ranch. His name is Earl Todd. He is 15 years old. His hobbies are playing football and basketball, and drawing sports pictures.**
> **Hosanna Homes is in need of sports and recreational equipment. If you or anyone you know has any equipment to donate, please contact me at the main office.**
> **Thank you for all your support.**
> *Your name*, Director

g. Print the document using the chosen printer.

h. Open the printer window, then cancel the print job June State.

i. Choose the Pause Printing command to turn off Pause Printing, and print the job June Donor.

j. Check the status of the printer.

k. Open the file **June State** in the WordPad window, change the number of days for Earl Todd from 16 to 18, then save the file.

l. Print the file, then close all open windows.

Independent Challenge 3

You are the owner of Lasting Impressions, a photography studio that specializes in wedding and location photography. To increase revenues and streamline production, you want to add the ability to take digital wedding photos for your photography clients. Before you invest in the hardware and software needed, you decide to install a digital camera and check your computer's hardware properties for the device.

a. Open the Control Panel.

b. Open the Scanners and Cameras window.

c. Click Add an imaging device in the task pane.

d. Install a Kodak digital camera.

e. Display the properties for this device.

f. Print the screen. (See Independent Challenge 1, Step e for screen printing instructions.)

g. Remove the Kodak digital camera.

h. Close all open windows.

▶ Independent Challenge 4

You are an engineer at Denson Engineering, an international company that specializes in technical drawings. You want to install a special hardware device to create 35mm slides for a technical presentation that you developed with some of your drawings. During the installation of the legacy hardware, you encounter some problems. When you call technical support, the representative asks you to print a resource summary report to help diagnose the problems.

a. Open the Control Panel.

b. Open the System Properties dialog box.

c. Open the Device Manager window and choose to view devices by type if necessary.

d. View the IRQ resources.

e. Print a resource summary report for a selected IRQ resource.

f. Close the Device Manager window, then click Cancel in the System Properties dialog box.

g. Close all open windows.

► Visual Workshop

Display information about a keyboard, as shown in Figure N-20. Your results will differ from the ones shown here. Print the screen. (See Independent Challenge 1, Step e, for screen printing instructions.)

FIGURE N-20

Backing

Up Your Files

Objectives

► **Develop a backup strategy**
► **Copy files to a hard drive**
► **Start Backup**
► **Select files for a backup**
► **Perform a normal backup**
► **View and print a backup report**
► **Perform an incremental backup**
► **Restore a backed up file**
► **Delete a backup set**

Making backup copies of your files is an important task to perform on a regular basis, so you don't lose valuable data if your computer encounters problems. The term **back up** (or **backup**, when referring to the noun or adjective) usually refers to the process of using a special software program designed to read your data quickly, compress it into a small, efficient space, then store it on a medium, such as a set of disks or a tape cartridge. Windows XP Professional includes a program called Backup. Using Backup has several advantages over simply copying files to a floppy disk, including compressing files as they are copied so that you can fit more onto a floppy disk, and splitting a large file across two or more floppies, something you cannot do with the Copy command. Also, in an emergency, Backup offers several data-recovery aids to help you locate and restore important files quickly. John Casey, the owner of Wired Coffee Company, uses Backup to back up important files on a floppy disk.

Developing a Backup Strategy

With Backup, you can back up files from a local or network hard drive to a floppy disk, a zip disk, a network drive, or a tape drive that is attached to your computer, as shown in Figure O-1. This unit assumes you are using a floppy disk as your backup medium and focuses primarily on backup strategies using floppies. Before you back up files, it is a good idea to develop a backup strategy. A **backup strategy** is a method for regularly backing up your work that balances trade-offs between safety, time, and media space. For example, if safety were your only concern, you could back up your entire hard drive every hour. But you would not have any time to work, and you would spend a fortune on backup tapes. If spending minimal time and money on backups were your only concern, you might back up only a few crucial files once a month. The best choice is a balance between the two extremes. The **backup medium** that you use to store backed up files from a hard drive is usually a set of floppy or zip disks, or a tape cartridge designed to store computer data. Zip disks and tape cartridges are large capacity backup media that require special hardware on your computer, such as a zip or tape drive. This extra expense may be worthwhile if you depend on your computer for business. John wants to explore the different methods of backing up files in order to develop a backup strategy. See Table O-1 for a description of a sample weekly backup strategy.

These are some of the different methods for backing up files with Backup:

► A **normal backup** copies all selected files to the backup medium, regardless of when the files were last changed, and clears the archive attribute for each file in order to mark the file as backed up. An **archive attribute** is an internal Windows file marker indicating whether a file needs to be backed up.

► An **incremental backup** copies only the files that have changed since your most recent normal or incremental backup. It also clears the archive attribute for each file that is backed up. Therefore, the first incremental backup after a normal backup copies all files that have changed since the normal backup, and the second incremental backup copies only those files that have changed since the first incremental backup, and so on.

► A **differential backup** copies only the selected files that have changed since your most recent normal or incremental backup. Unlike incremental backups, however, the archive attribute is not cleared during a differential backup. Therefore, successive differential backups copy all the files that have changed since the last normal or incremental backup, not just the ones that have changed since the last differential backup. The first differential backup after a normal backup copies all files that have changed since the normal backup, and the second differential backup copies all the files that have changed since the normal backup, including all files that changed from both differential backups. Since differential backups copy more changed files, they take longer than incremental backups and require more disk or tape space.

► A **copy backup** copies all selected files, like a normal backup, but it does not clear the archive attribute. Therefore, you can use it to perform a special backup without affecting your normal backup routine.

► A **daily backup** copies all selected files that were changed on the day the backup is done. It does not clear the archive attribute. You can use daily backups to save your day's work without affecting your normal backup routine.

FIGURE O-1: Computer with floppy, zip, and tape drives

Backup
tape drive

Floppy drive

Zip drive

Tape drive is attached to
the computer externally;
yours might be internal

TABLE O-1: Example of a weekly backup strategy

day	tasks to do
Monday, Week 1	Label your medium (floppy disk or tape). If your backup requires more than one medium, label and number all the media in advance, so you can recognize them easily. Insert your first medium into the backup device and perform a normal backup with the Back up everything on this computer option.
Tuesday, Week 1	Reinsert the medium you used for the normal backup and perform an incremental backup. The incremental backup is appended automatically to the normal backup.
Wednesday through Friday, Week 1	Perform incremental backups. Each subsequent incremental backup is appended to the previous backup. If you need more than one medium, you will be prompted to insert another one. After your Thursday backup, you will have a complete rotation set.
Monday through Friday, Week 2	Repeat the cycle with a second set of media. If you need to perform a special backup of selected files, insert a different medium, perform a copy backup, re-insert the previous medium, then continue the normal cycle.
Monday through Friday, Week 3	Repeat the cycle with the first set of media; continue rotating. If you need to backup only the files that have changed during a day, insert a different medium, perform a daily backup, re-insert the previous medium, then continue the normal cycle.

Rotating your backups

For extra security, it is a good idea to rotate backup tapes or disks. For example, if you do a complete normal backup once a week and incremental backups on the intervening days, you might want to keep one week's worth of backup on one tape or set of disks and then use a different tape or set of disks the following week. If your original storage medium and your backup tape or set of disks are both damaged, you will still be able to restore files from the previous time period's backup. The files you restore probably will not be the most current versions, but you will be better off than if you had to re-create everything from scratch. If possible, store your backup tape or disks away from your computers. That way, if you experience a fire or theft, you will not necessarily lose both the original files on your computer and your backups.

Windows XP

Copying Files to a Hard Drive

Backup is designed to back up the contents of a hard drive (or several hard drives) onto a backup medium. However, Backup cannot back up files from one floppy disk to another. In order for you to have files to use while performing the back up, this unit begins by having you copy the files from the folder where your Project Files are located to a hard disk. As you proceed through the lessons, you will back up the files you copied onto the hard disk to a different blank floppy disk. If you do not have access to a hard drive, you might not be able to complete this unit; if this is the case, check with your instructor or technical support person about backing up different files that are already on a network drive. ⮂ John prepares to back up his files. In this lesson, you will copy the files in the folder where your Project Files are located to the C: drive (your hard drive might be different), so you can begin to back them up in the next lesson. First you'll create a new folder for the files in the My Documents folder.

Steps

1. Click the **Start button** on the taskbar, point to **All Programs**, point to **Accessories**, then click **Windows Explorer**
   The Windows Explorer window opens.

QuickTip
If the Collapse indicator ⊟ is next to the icon, the folder is already expanded.

2. In the left pane of Windows Explorer, locate the My Documents folder icon, then, if the **Expand indicator** ⊞ appears next to the icon, click ⊞ to expand the folder

3. In the left pane of Windows Explorer, click the **My Documents folder icon** if necessary, click **File** on the menu bar, point to **New**, click **Folder**, type **John's Backup**, then press **[Enter]**
   The new John's Backup folder appears in the list of folders and files in the My Documents folder. You will use this folder to store your Project Files temporarily.

4. In the left pane of Windows Explorer, click ⊞ next to the My Computer icon, click ⊞ next to the drive icon containing your Project Files, then click the **folder** containing your Project Files
   Windows Explorer displays the contents of the Your Project Files disk, which in this case is a floppy disk, in the right pane, as shown in Figure O-2.

5. Click **Edit** on the menu bar, then click **Select All**
   All the files in the folder containing your Project Files are selected.

QuickTip
To copy files quickly from one disk to another, such as from a floppy disk to a hard disk, you drag the selected files from the right pane of Windows Explorer to a folder or disk in the left pane.

6. Click **Edit** on the menu bar, click **Copy To Folder**, click ⊞ next to the My Documents icon in the Copy Items dialog box if necessary, then click the **John's Backup folder**
   The Copy Items dialog box appears, as shown in Figure O-3.

7. Click **Copy**
   The selected files are copied to the John's Backup folder.

8. In the left pane of Windows Explorer, click the **John's Backup folder icon**
   Windows Explorer displays the files in John's Backup folder in the right pane, as shown in Figure O-4. You are now ready to use Backup.

9. Click the **Close button** in the Windows Explorer window

FIGURE O-2: Windows Explorer

Your list might be different

Contents of Project Files folder

New folder on hard drive in the My Documents folder

FIGURE O-3: Copy Items dialog box

Click to select John's Backup folder

FIGURE O-4: Windows Explorer with John's Backup folder

Contents of the newly created John's Backup folder

Starting Backup

Now that you have files on the hard drive to back up, you can use Backup. Because backups take time each time you perform them, you should back up only the files that change on a regular basis, and only back up all of the files on your computer at less frequent intervals. For example, because software program files don't change, you can easily reinstall them from their original program CDs or disks, so you do not need to back them up as often as your personal document files, which might change on a daily or weekly basis. Ask yourself how much work you can afford to lose. If you cannot afford to lose the work accomplished in one day, then you should back up once a day. If your work does not change much during the week, back up once a week. When you start the Backup Utility, either the Backup or Restore Wizard dialog box opens (known as Wizard Mode), in which you can back up or restore files, or the Backup Utility window opens (known as Advanced Mode), displaying the Welcome tab, in which you can start the Backup Wizard or Restore Wizard separately, or manually perform your own back up or restore files. ➤ John starts Backup to do a normal backup of his important files on the hard drive to a floppy disk.

STOP *To complete the remaining lessons in this unit you may need to install Backup. See the Read This Before You Begin for installation instructions. To finish a complete backup, you need to complete the next three lessons in order and have a blank floppy disk or your Project Disk available.*

Trouble?

If the Backup or Restore Wizard dialog box opens, click the Advanced Mode link to open the Backup Utility window.

QuickTip

You can only back up the System State data on a local computer. You cannot back up the System State data on a remote computer using a communication line.

1. Click the **Start button** on the taskbar, point to **All Programs**, point to **Accessories**, point to **System Tools**, then click **Backup**
   The Backup Utility window opens with the Welcome tab, as shown in Figure O-5, which contains options to create a new backup, restore backed up files, or create a recovery disk.

2. Click the **Backup Wizard (Advanced) button** 🖳
   The Backup Wizard dialog box opens.

3. Click **Next**
   The next Backup Wizard dialog box, shown in Figure O-6, allows you to choose the items you want to back up. You can back up every file on your computer, selected files, drives, or network data, or only the System State data. The **System State data** is a collection of Windows operating system-specific data, such as the registry and boot files, that have been customized during normal usage for your computer. When you back up your System State data and restore it after a system problem, you bring back your customized version of the files instead of the general System State data reinstalled with the Windows XP CD.

4. Click the **Back up selected files, drives, or network data option button**

5. Click **Next**
   Leave the Backup Wizard dialog box open and continue to the next lesson, in which you will select the files to back up.

CLUES TO USE

Creating an Automated System Recovery disk

In the event of a major system failure in which you cannot start your Windows XP computer, you could lose important data and waste a lot of time trying to fix your computer. To avoid these disastrous results and prepare for possible problems in the future, you can use the Automated System Recovery Preparation Wizard to help you create a backup of your system files and an Automated System Recovery (ASR) disk to restore your system. To protect your computer, start the Backup program, click the Automated System Recovery Wizard button on the Welcome tab, read the wizard welcome screen, click Next, select a backup type and enter a backup name and location (use a tape or network location, not a floppy disk), click Next, then click Finish. The Backup program backs up your system files, then asks you to insert a disk to complete the ASR process. The ASR disk doesn't backup your personal data files, so it is a good idea to use the Backup Wizard in addition to creating a separate backup of your personal data files, so they can be restored, too.

FIGURE O-5: Backup Utility window with the Welcome tab

Click button to create a backup

Click button to restore backup files

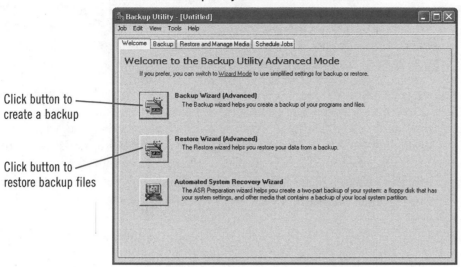

FIGURE O-6: Choosing what to back up

Click option to back up selected files

Understanding permissions to back up files and folders

You must have certain permissions to back up files and folders. If you are an administrator or a backup operator in a local group using Windows XP Professional, you can back up any file and folder on the computer to which the local group applies. However, if you are not an administrator or a backup operator, and you want to back up files, then you must be the owner of the files and folders you want to back up, or you must have one or more of the following permissions for the files and folders you want to back up: Read, Read and Execute, Modify, or Full Control. You can also restrict access to a backup file by selecting the Allow only the owner and the Administrator access to the backup data check box in the Backup Job Information dialog box. If you select this option, only an administrator or the person who created the backup file will be able to restore the files and folders. To add a user to the Backup Operators group, double-click the Administrative Tools icon 🖼 in the Control Panel, double-click the Computer Management icon 🖳 in the Administrative Tools window to open the Computer Management Window, click the Expand indicator ➕ next to Local Users and Groups in the console tree, click Groups in the console tree, double-click Backup Operators in the details pane, click Add in the Backup Operators Properties dialog box, type the domain and user name of the person you want to make a backup operator in the form \\Domain\user name, then click OK. For more information about using Computer Management, see Unit P, Administering Your Computer.

Selecting Files for a Backup

Windows XP

When backing up only some of the files on your disk, you need to display and then select the folders and files that you want to back up in the Backup Utility window. Working in this window is similar to working in Windows Explorer. To display or hide the folders located on your hard drive, click the Expand indicator ⊞ or the Collapse indicator ⊟ to the left of the drive or folder icon. In addition, there is a check box to the left of each storage device, folder, or file on your computer. After using ⊞ and ⊟ to display and hide the appropriate files, you click this check box to select the folders and files you want to back up. ✐ John needs to select the files he wants to back up.

Steps

1. **In the Backup Wizard dialog box, click the Expand indicator ⊞ to the left of the My Documents icon in the Items to back up list**
   The My Documents icon expands to display all the folders and files it contains. See Table O-2 for information concerning the display of drives and folders.

2. **In the Items to back up list, click the John's Backup folder icon (but do not click the check box)**
   The files stored in the John's Backup folder appear in the right pane. To back up all the files in a folder, click the check box next to the folder in the left pane. To back up a specific file, click the check box next to the file in the right pane.

3. **In the Items to back up list, click the John's Backup folder check box to select it**
   The files in the John's Backup folder appear checked, indicating that they will be backed up, as shown in Figure O-7. The gray checked box beside the My Documents icon indicates that only some of the folders and files in that drive are selected.

4. **Click Next, then type Backup in the Type a name for this backup text box if necessary**
   The Backup Wizard asks you to select a backup destination, as shown in Figure O-8 (the place where you will store your backed up files). If you don't have a tape device installed on your computer, the backup media type File is selected by default and grayed out. The default destination for the backup is the 3 ½ Floppy (A:) drive; your drive might be different. The default backup file name is "Backup." The Backup file is saved with the .bkf extension, which is the extension for all backup files.

Trouble?

If you are not backing up your files to a floppy disk, click Browse, navigate to the drive and folder where your Project Files are located in the Save As dialog box, then click Save.

5. **If necessary, insert a floppy disk or your Project Disk into the appropriate drive on your computer to save the backup file**

6. **Click Next**
   The Backup Wizard dialog box displays the current backup settings. In the next lesson, you will actually perform the backup.

CLUES TO USE

Backing up and restoring files on different disk file systems

You can use Backup to back up and restore data on either FAT or NTFS volumes. However, if you have backed up data from an NTFS volume used in Windows XP, it is recommended that you restore the data to an NTFS volume used in Windows XP instead of Windows 2000, or you could lose data as well as some file and folder features. For more information about FAT and NTFS disk file systems, see Unit P, Administering Your Computer.

FIGURE O-7: Choosing items to back up

Gray check mark indicates partial contents of folder selected

Your list might differ

Click icon to display folder contents

Click check box to select folder contents for backing up

FIGURE O-8: Choosing where to store the backup

Backup file name

Click to change the backup location and filename

TABLE O-2: Displaying drive and folder contents

folder selection	item	function
⊞	A plus sign to the left of a drive or folder	All the folders it contains are hidden
⊟	A minus sign to the left of a drive or folder	All the folders it contains are displayed
	No sign to the left of a drive or folder	The folder does not contain any subfolders, although it may contain files
☑	A blue checked box to the left of a drive or folder	All the folders and files it contains are selected for backup
☑	A gray checked box to the left of a drive or folder	Only some of the folders and files it contains are selected for backup
☐	An unchecked box to the left of a drive or folder	None of the folders and files it contains are selected for backup

Performing a Normal Backup

Once you have selected the files that you want to back up and the destination where you want to store them, you are ready to perform the backup. During the backup, Backup compresses the files you selected and copies them to a floppy or other backup location. When a file does not fit on a floppy, Backup splits the file, fitting what it can on the current floppy and then prompting you to insert the next floppy. Depending on the number and size of your files and the backup device you are using, the backup can take a few minutes to a few hours to complete. If you are planning to back up large amounts of information, such as your entire hard drive, it is best to start the backup at the end of the day and use a tape or zip drive if possible so you do not have to swap multiple floppy disks. When you perform a backup, Backup creates a **backup set**, also known as a **backup job**, which contains the compressed copies of the files you backed up. The backup job is stored in the backup file you specified in the previous lesson (in this case, Backup.bkf on the floppy drive). You can store more than one backup job in a specified backup file. ➤ John is ready to select backup options, enter a name for the backup job, then start the backup.

1. **In the Backup Wizard dialog box, click Advanced**

   The Backup Wizard asks you to select the type of backup operation to perform, as shown in Figure O-9. The Normal backup option is selected by default.

2. **Click Next**

   The Backup Wizard asks you to select options that will compare original and backup files after the backup, and compress the backup data. This is done to verify that the data was successfully backed up and to compress the backed up data to save space. The wizard also asks you to enable or disable **volume shadow copy**, which is the ability to backup files even though they are in the process of being written to, such as a database that is continually open and updated.

QuickTip

If the Use hardware compression option is grayed out, the hardware, such as a FAT disk, is not available to perform hardware compression.

3. **Click the Verify data after backup check box to select it**

4. **Click the Disable volume shadow copy check box to select it, then click Next**

   The Backup Wizard asks you to choose whether to append this backup to the media or replace the data on the media with this backup.

5. **Click the Append this backup to the existing backups option button if necessary, then click Next**

   The Backup Wizard asks you to select the option to run the backup now or schedule it for later.

QuickTip

To schedule a backup using a calendar, click the Schedule Jobs tab, select the day, click Add Job, then follow the Backup Wizard instructions.

6. **Click the Now option button if necessary, then click Next**

   The Backup Wizard displays a summary of the current backup settings, as shown in Figure O-10.

7. **Click Finish**

   The Backup Progress dialog box opens with a progress meter that indicates the current backup status. If the backup requires more than one floppy disk, a dialog box appears asking you to insert another disk. Upon completion, the Backup Progress dialog box indicates that the operation is complete, as shown in Figure O-11.

8. **Click Close**

   The Backup Utility window appears.

FIGURE O-9: Choosing the type of backup

Click list arrow
to select the
type of backup

FIGURE O-10: Completing the Backup Wizard

Summary of
backup settings

Click button to
finish the backup

FIGURE O-11: Backup Progress dialog box

Click to view or
print a report

Backup status
is completed

Number of files
backed up

Viewing and Printing a Backup Report

After performing a backup, Backup creates a report with status information about the backup. The backup report is created in Notepad (a text-editing program that comes with Windows XP) and saved in the Backup program folder on your hard drive. Each time you perform a backup, the report information is added to the beginning of the backup report file in order to create a backup history. To make it easier to manage your backup jobs, it is important to view and print a backup report after each backup so you can have a hard copy reference of the files backed up and make sure no errors occurred. To customize your report, you can use the Report tab in the Backup Job Options dialog box to specify the items you want to include in your backup report. ✒️ John wants to view the backup report, change a report option, and then print a copy. Then he will make a change to one of the files he has backed up.

1. Click **Tools** on the Backup Utility menu bar, then click **Report**

   The Backup Reports dialog box opens with a list of backup reports performed on this computer, identified by report date, time, and backup job name. When you perform a backup immediately, instead of scheduling it for later, Backup uses "Interactive" for the backup job name instead of the backup job name you assigned.

QuickTip

Each time you start and exit Backup, a new backup report file is created in Notepad.

2. Click the backup report with the current time and date you just created (the top entry), then click **View**

   Notepad opens, as shown in Figure O-12. The report lists: the type of operation and the media name; the backup set number, description, and type; the backup job start time, end time, date, number of processed files, size (in bytes) of the processed files; and the backup time. Notice that the report does not include names of the files that were backed up.

3. Click **File** on the menu bar, click **Print**, then click **Print** in the Print dialog box

4. Click the **Close button** in the Notepad window, then click **Cancel** to close the Backup Reports dialog box

   The Backup Utility window remains open.

5. Click **Tools** on the Backup Utility menu bar, click **Options**, then click the **Backup Log tab** in the Options dialog box

   The Options dialog box opens with the Backup Log tab displayed, as shown in Figure O-13. See Table O-3 for a description of the Options dialog box tabs.

6. Click the **Detailed option button**, then click **OK**

   Now when you perform the incremental backup in the next lesson, the report will list the files that were backed up.

7. Leave the Backup Utility window open, click the **Start button** on the taskbar, point to **All Programs**, point to **Accessories**, click **WordPad**, then open the document **WIN O-1** from the John's Backup folder in the My Documents folder on your hard drive

   Make sure you open the document from the correct location (the John's Backup folder in the My Documents folder on the hard drive), not from the folder where your Project Files are located. The WordPad window appears with the WIN O-1 document. This is the file you will change for the backup in the next lesson.

8. In the first paragraph, select the word **November**, then type **October**

9. Click the **Save button** 💾 on the toolbar, then click the **Close button** in the WordPad window

   Leave Backup open, then continue to the next lesson.

FIGURE O-12: **Backup report in Notepad**

Backup file

Number of files
backed up

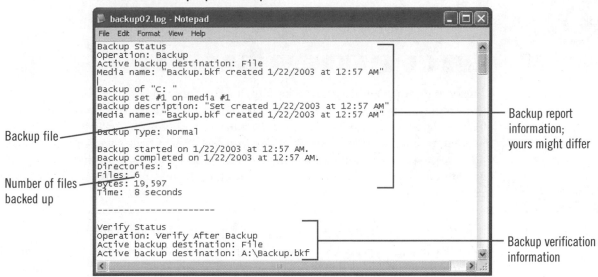

Backup report
information;
yours might differ

Backup verification
information

FIGURE O-13: **Options dialog box**

Click option to
include filenames in
the backup report

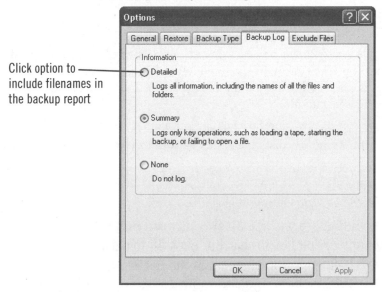

TABLE O-3: **Options dialog box tabs**

tab	description
General	Allows you to verify that data is successfully backed up, specify how to handle media that already contain backups, and select different types of alert messages
Restore	Allows you to specify how to restore files
Backup Type	Allows you to specify the default backup type when you start a backup
Backup Log	Allows you to specify the items you want to include in your backup report
Exclude Files	Allows you to add or remove files of a specified type to or from a backup

Performing an Incremental Backup

When you perform an incremental backup, it affects only the files that have changed since the last backup. This saves you from having to redo the entire backup every time. Files created after the date of the initial incremental backup set and files that have been renamed are not included in the incremental backup unless you select them before you start the backup operation. ✎ John completed a complete backup of all his files, but it does not include the current version of the file he just changed. John performs an incremental backup to include the change he just made to the WIN O-1 file.

Steps

1. **In the Backup Utility window, click the Backup tab if necessary**
   The Backup tab appears. If you have already performed a backup and want to use similar settings, you can use the Backup tab to perform a quick backup. The Backup tab allows you to select the files you want to back up, change backup options, then start the backup process.

2. **Click the Expand indicator ⊞ to the left of the My Documents icon, then click the John's Backup folder check box to select it**
   The Backup Utility window appears with John's Backup folder selected, as shown in Figure O-14. When a folder is selected with a blue check mark, all the files in the folder are selected.

3. **Click Start Backup**
   The Backup Job Information dialog box opens. When you perform a backup, Backup creates a **backup job**, also known as a **backup set**, which contains the compressed copies of the files you backed up. The backup job is stored in the backup file you specified in the previous lesson (in this case, Backup.bkf on the floppy drive). You can store more than one backup job in a specified backup file.

4. **In the Backup description text box, insert your name before the current description**
   This new job name will distinguish this backup from the complete backup you performed earlier.

5. **Click Advanced**
   The Advanced Backup Options dialog box opens.

QuickTip

To compress backup data to a tape, click the If possible, compress the backup data to save space check box to select it in the Advanced Backup Options dialog box.

6. **Click the Backup Type list arrow, click Incremental, click the Disable volume shadow copy check box to select it, click OK to close the Advanced Backup Options dialog box, then click Start Backup in the Backup Job Information dialog box**
   The Backup Progress dialog box opens with a progress meter indicating current backup status. The file that changed since the last backup is backed up. Upon completion, a message dialog box opens indicating that the operation is finished.

QuickTip

To start a new report document, use the Search command on the Start menu to find the report document, then rename it. Backup creates a new report document during the next backup.

7. **In the Backup Progress dialog box, click Report, then drag the scroll box to the bottom of the Notepad window**
   Notepad opens with the backup report, as shown in Figure O-15. Each time you perform a backup, the backup report information is appended to the end of the report. The name of the changed file appears in the backup report.

8. **Click the Close button in the Notepad window, then click Close to close the Backup Progress dialog box**
   The Backup Utility window appears, in which you want to restore the report options to their original settings.

9. **Click Tools on the menu bar, click Options, click the Backup Log tab in the Options dialog box, click the Summary option button, then click OK**
   The report options are restored to the Summary option, which is the default setting.

FIGURE O-14: Backup Utility window with Backup tab

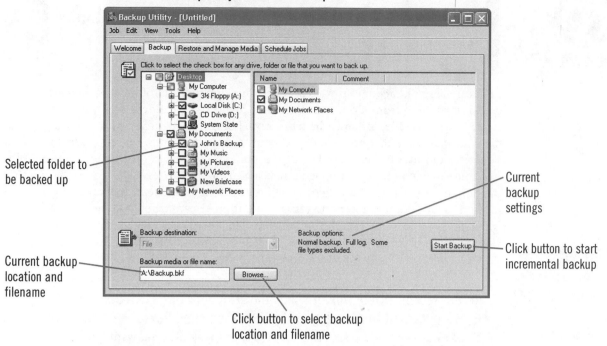

Selected folder to be backed up

Current backup settings

Current backup location and filename

Click button to start incremental backup

Click button to select backup location and filename

FIGURE O-15: Backup report in Notepad

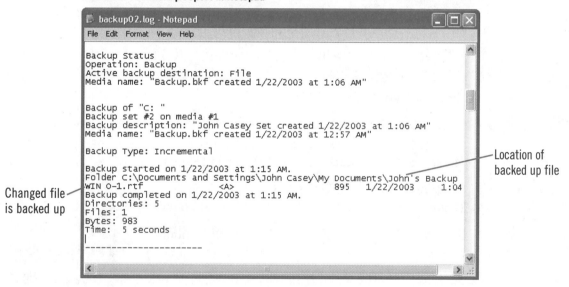

Changed file is backed up

Location of backed up file

CLUES TO USE

Using a tape drive to back up files

Using a tape drive can make backing up large amounts of information, such as an entire hard drive, fast and easy. A tape drive is a hardware device that reads data from and writes onto a tape. Before you use a tape drive with Backup, make sure the tape drive is compatible with Backup. For a complete list of compatible tape drives, click Help Topics on the Help menu in the Backup Utility window. After connecting the tape drive to your computer and loading a tape cartridge into the tape drive, you can click the Restore and Manage Media tab, then right-click the tape media to restore the tape tension, format or erase a tape cartridge to back up your files. To format a tape cartridge, you need to have a DC-2000-type tape drive, which requires that you format a tape before you use it.

Restoring a Backed Up File

The real value in backing up your files becomes apparent if you lose or damage some files or need information from a document that has changed a great deal over time. You can restore a single file, several files, or an entire hard drive. Using the Restore Wizard, you can specify which files you want to restore and where you want them to be placed. When you create a backup set, a **catalog**, or index of the backed up files, is built and stored on the backup medium. When you store the catalog on the backup medium, it speeds up the process when you want to restore files. Instead of re-creating the catalog, the Restore function opens the catalog on the backup medium. However, if you want to restore data from several tapes, and the tape with the catalog is missing, or you want to restore data from media that is damaged, you should not select the Use the catalogs on the media option. ➤ A coworker at Wired Coffee needs the original WIN O-1 file, so he asks John to restore that file onto the hard drive.

Steps

1. In the Backup Utility window, click the **Welcome tab**, click the **Restore Wizard (Advanced) button** 🖺, then click **Next**
   The Restore Wizard opens, asking you to specify the files you want to restore.

2. In the Items to restore list, click the **Expand indicator** ➕ to the left of the File icon 💿, click ➕ to the left of the Backup.bkf icon, then click the **Backup.bkf icon** 💾
   The Restore Wizard appears with a list of backup sets in the Backup.bkf file, as shown in Figure O-16. Your hard drive disk letter might differ.

3. In the Items to restore list, click the hard drive (C:) icon for Set 1, click ➕ to the left of the hard drive (C:) icon for Set 1, then click ➕ to the left of each folder icon until John's Backup folder appears

4. In the Items to restore list, click the **John's Backup folder** (scroll to see it if necessary), then click the **WIN O-1 file check box** to select it in the right pane
   The selected file appears checked, as shown in Figure O-17.

5. Click **Next**, then click **Advanced**
   The Restore Wizard asks you to select a destination for the restored files and folders.

6. Click **Next** to restore the file in its original location
   The Restore Wizard asks you to choose how you want to restore files that are already on disk.

7. Click the **Replace existing files option button** if necessary, then click **Next**
   The Restore Wizard asks you to select the advanced options you want to use.

8. Click **Next**, then click **Finish**
   The Restore Progress dialog box opens with a progress meter indicating current status. Upon completion, the Restore Progress dialog box indicates that the operation is complete. Notice the number of files processed, or restored, is one.

9. Click **Close** to return to the Backup Utility window
   The previous version of the WIN O-1 file is restored. John could check this by opening the restored file in WordPad.

FIGURE O-16: Restore Wizard dialog box with backup sets

Backup file; your hard disk might differ

Hard disk for backup set 1

Hard disk for backup set 2

Backup set 1

Backup set 2

FIGURE O-17: Restore Wizard dialog box with selected file to restore

Your list of folders might differ

Click check box to select the file you want to restore

John's Backup folder; you might need to scroll to view the folder name

CLUES TO USE

Excluding file types from a backup

When you want to backup all but a few files of a specific type on your computer, it is more efficient to back up all the files on your computer and then exclude the ones you don't want to back up instead of selecting each individual file you want to back up. To exclude file types from a backup, click Tools on the Backup Utility menu bar, click Options, click the Exclude Files tab, then click Add new under the Files excluded for all users list if you want to exclude files that are owned by all users, or click Add new under the Files excluded for user list if you want to exclude only files that you own. In the Add Excluded Files dialog box, click the file type to exclude in the Registered file type list, or type a period and then the one, two, or three letter file extension in Custom file mask text box to exclude a custom file type. Type a path in the Applies to path text box if you want to restrict the excluded file type to a specific folder or hard disk drive, then click OK. If you restrict excluded files to a specific path or folder, the files will be restricted from all subfolders of that path unless you click the Applies to all subfolders check box to deselect it.

Deleting a Backup Set

Each time you perform a backup, Backup creates a backup set containing the backed up files. You can store more than one backup set in a backup file. After backing up files for a while, you might find a number of unneeded backup sets accumulating in a backup file. You can delete these sets quickly and easily from the backup file within Backup. When you delete a backup set, only the backup set is deleted, but the backup file, such as Backup.bkf, remains in the backup location. If you want to delete the backup file, drag the file icon into the Recycle Bin as you would any other Windows file. ◀━━ John deletes old backup sets from Backup and deletes the backup file using Windows Explorer.

1. In the Backup Utility window, click the **Restore and Manage Media tab**
   The current list of backup files appears in the Backup Utility window.

2. Right-click the **Backup.bkf icon** as shown in Figure O-18, then click **Delete catalog** on the shortcut menu
   Both backup sets in this catalog are deleted.

3. Click the **Close button** in the Backup Utility window

4. Click the **Start button** on the taskbar, point to **All Programs**, point to **Accessories**, then click **Windows Explorer**
   You can use Windows Explorer to delete the John's Backup folder and backup files in order to restore your drives to their original state.

5. Click the **Expand indicator** ⊞ next to the My Documents folder if necessary, click the **John's Backup folder**, press **[Delete]**, then click **Yes** in the Confirm Folder Delete dialog box

6. Click ⊞ next to the My Computer icon, locate the drive containing your Project Files with the backup file, then click the **drive icon**
   Windows Explorer displays the contents of the floppy disk in the right pane.

7. Click the **Backup file**, press **[Delete]**, then click **Yes** to confirm the deletion

8. Click the **Close button** in the Windows Explorer window
   Now the backup jobs and John's Backup folder are deleted.

FIGURE O-18: Backup Utility window with the Restore and Manage Media tab

Backup file with
two backup sets

Click command
to delete the
backup file

Scheduling a backup

Scheduling backups according to a backup strategy can help you perform backups on a regular basis and protect your data. Typically, late at night or on weekends, when nobody is around, is a good time to perform backups. Backup makes it easy to schedule backups any time you want to perform them. You can schedule a backup to run once, every day, every week, or every month. You can also set additional options that start or stop the backup if the computer is idle, meaning that it is not processing any tasks. To schedule a backup, click the Schedule Jobs tab in the Backup Utility window, shown in Figure O-19. Double-click the day in which you want to perform the backup to start the Backup Wizard, follow the step-by-step instructions to select what to back up, where and how to back it up, and any backup options you want until the wizard asks you when to back up the files. Enter the job name you want for the backup, click Set Schedule to open the Schedule Job dialog box displaying the Schedule tab, click the Schedule Task list arrow, select a backup interval, click the Start time up or down arrow to specify a backup time, then

click OK to return to the Backup Wizard. Click Next, enter a password twice as indicated, click OK, then click Finish. A backup schedule icon 📇 appears in the Schedule Jobs tab on the backup date. On the scheduled day and time, the Task Scheduler starts Backup and performs the backup operation.

FIGURE O-19: Backup Utility window with the Schedule Jobs tab

Practice

► Concepts Review

Label each element of the screen shown in Figure O-20.

FIGURE O-20

1. Which element indicates that all the folders and files the folder contains are selected for backup?
2. Which element indicates that the file is selected for backup?
3. Which element indicates that only some of the folders and files the folder contains are selected for backup?
4. Which element indicates that none of the folders and files the folder contains are selected for backup?
5. Which element indicates that all the subfolders the folder contains are displayed?
6. Which element points to the current location of the backup file?

Match each of the terms with the statement that describes its function.

7. A backup option   a. Backs up files
8. Backup Wizard   b. Retrieves files
9. Normal backup   c. Clears archive attributes
10. Restore Wizard   d. Saved in backup file
11. A backup set   e. Verifies a backup
12. Differential backup   f. Does not clear archived attributes

Select the best answer from the list of choices.

13. **Which of the following is NOT a feature of Backup?**
    a. Compresses files as it copies them
    b. Backs up floppy to floppy
    c. Splits large files across two or more floppies
    d. Automatically detects tape drives
14. **Which of the following is something you CANNOT do with Backup?**
    a. Back up files
    b. Modify files
    c. Verify files
    d. Restore files
15. **A gray checkmark next to a folder indicates that**
    a. All of the folders and files are selected.
    b. Some of the files are selected.
    c. Some of the subfolders and files are selected.
    d. All of the files are selected.
16. **Which backup type copies only files that have changed since the last backup?**
    a. Daily
    b. Normal
    c. Incremental
    d. System State data

▶ Skills Review

1. **Copy files to a hard drive.**
   a. Start Windows Explorer, then in the My Documents folder, create a new folder called **Backup Files**.
   b. In the Folders list, display the drive and folder where your Project Files are located.
   c. Copy all the files in your Project Files folder to the Backup Files folder, then close Windows Explorer.
2. **Start Backup.**
   a. Start Backup. If the Backup or Restore Wizard opens, click the Advanced Mode link.
   b. Click the Backup Wizard (Advanced) button, then click Next.
   c. Click the Back up selected files, drives, or network data option button, then click Next.
3. **Select files for a backup.**
   a. In the Items to back up list, click the Expand indicator to the left of the My Documents icon.
   b. Click the Backup Files folder icon, click the Backup Files folder check box to select it, then click Next.
   c. If necessary, insert a floppy disk or your Project Disk into the appropriate drive on your computer.
   d. Type **WiredBackup** as the backup name, then click Next.
4. **Perform a normal backup.**
   a. In the Backup Wizard dialog box, click Advanced, select the Normal backup type if necessary, then click Next.
   b. Select the Verify data after backup check box, select the Disable volume shadow copy check box, click Next, click the Append this backup to the existing backups option button if necessary, then click Next.
   c. Click the Now option button if necessary, click Next, click Finish, then click Close in the Backup Progress window when done.
5. **View and print a backup report.**
   a. Click Tools on the menu bar, then click Report.
   b. Click the backup report with the current time and date you just created, then click View.
   c. Drag the scroll box to the bottom of the Notepad window to read the report status, close Notepad, then click Cancel.
   d. Click Tools on the menu bar, click Options, then click the Backup Log tab.
   e. Click the Detailed option button, then click OK.
   f. Start Paint, then open the file Wired Coffee Logo from the Backup Files folder.
   g. Add the text **Great Coffee!** to the image, save the file, then close Paint.
6. **Perform a differential backup.**
   a. Click the Backup tab in the Backup Utility dialog box. Click the Expand indicator to the left of the My Documents icon, click the Backup Files folder check box to select it, then click Start Backup.
   b. In the Backup description text box, insert the text **Wired Coffee** before the current description.

   c. Click Advanced, click the Backup Type list arrow, then click Differential.

   d. Click the Disable volume shadow copy check box to select it, click OK, then click Start Backup.

   e. Click Report, then drag the scroll box to the bottom of the Notepad window to read the report status.

   f. Click the Close button in the Notepad window, then click Close in the Backup Progress dialog box.

   g. Click Tools on the menu bar, click Options, click the Backup Log tab, click the Summary option button, then click OK.

7. Restore a backed up file.

   a. Click the Welcome tab, click the Restore Wizard (Advanced) button, then click Next.

   b. Click the Expand indicator to the left of the File icon, click the Expand indicator to the left of the WiredBackup.bkf icon, then click the WiredBackup.bkf icon.

   c. Click the hard drive icon for Set 1, click the Expand indicator to the left of the hard drive icon for Set 1, then click the Expand indicator to the left of each folder icon until the Backup Files folder appears.

   d. Click the Backup Files folder, then click the Wired Coffee Logo file check box in the right list box.

   e. Click Next, click Advanced, click Next, click the Replace existing files option button if necessary, then click Next.

   f. Click Next, click Finish, then click Close.

8. Delete a backup job.

   a. Click the Restore and Manage Media tab. Right-click the WiredBackup.bkf icon, then click Delete catalog.

   b. Click the Close button in the Backup Utility window.

   c. Start Windows Explorer, then delete the Backup Files folder in the My Documents folder.

   d. Delete the WiredBackup.bkf file on the floppy disk, then Close Windows Explorer.

▶ Independent Challenge 1

You are the manager of the computer systems division for Global Telecommunications, Inc. (GTI), a worldwide manufacturer and distributor of telephone systems. To help safe guard the computer systems, you want to create a consistent backup strategy that systems administrators at each location can implement.

   a. Use WordPad to create a document that explains a strategy and the necessary steps for backing up network drives. Save the file as **Backup Strategy** to the drive and folder where your Project Files are located.

   b. Implement the backup strategy. Take at least one print screen of a wizard dialog box or the Backup Utility window as you go through the material, and insert the picture in the WordPad document. To take a print screen of the current window and then insert it into the WordPad document, press [Alt][Print Screen], switch to the WordPad document, click where you want the picture, then click the Paste button on the WordPad toolbar.

   c. Save the document, print it, then close WordPad.

▶ Independent Challenge 2

You are an associate at Andersen, Williams & Barnes law firm. You are creating a California corporation, and need to fill out corporation forms for the state, create bylaws, and hold board meetings.

In this challenge, you will create your own information. Assume the following facts about the corporation:

- Corporation name: IntSoft, Inc.
- Business: Develop testing tools for Windows software developers
- Ownership: Dorian Golu, 6,000 shares (60%); and John Yokela, 4,000 shares (40%)
- Address: 722 Main Street, Suite 100, Silicon Valley, CA 90028

   a. Using Windows Explorer, create a folder named **IntSoft 02** in the My Documents folder.

   b. Using WordPad, create the following documents in the IntSoft 02 folder:

- A document stating the above information called **INTA0I**

- Board meeting minutes, called **INT BM 001**, stating all the steps to create the corporation have been taken
- A bill for services called **INT Bill 001**

c. Start Backup, then insert a floppy disk into the appropriate drive.

d. Start the backup, create a new backup job, then back up the selected files that you created in WordPad.

e. Back up the files to a floppy disk as **Important**.

f. Select the files that you created with WordPad, then perform the normal backup, disable volume shadow copy, and print a report if necessary.

g. Add billing information to INT Bill 001, save the document, then perform an incremental backup and disable volume shadow copy.

h. Add **INT BKUP** to the backup description, then restore the changed file and verify that the incremental backup stored the latest version.

i. Delete the backup jobs, then using Windows Explorer, delete the IntSoft 02 folder and the backup file on the floppy disk or your Project Disk.

► Independent Challenge 3

You are a graphic artist for Zero Gravity Designs, Inc., a company that specializes in logos. A real estate developer asks you to create a logo for his company, called Syntec, Inc.

a. Using Windows Explorer, create a folder named **Syntec** in the My Documents folder.

b. Using Paint, create at least three Paint documents with different logo designs, then save them in the Syntec folder.

c. Start Backup, then insert a floppy disk into the appropriate drive.

d. Start the backup, create a new backup job, then back up the selected files that you created in Paint.

e. Back up the files to a floppy disk as **Syntec Files**.

f. Select the files that you created with Paint, then perform the normal backup and disable volume shadow copy.

g. Revise at least two designs, save the documents, then perform an incremental backup and disable volume shadow copy.

h. Add **SYN BKUP** to the backup description, print a report if requested by instructor, then delete the backup jobs.

i. Using Windows Explorer, delete the Syntec folder and the backup file on the floppy disk or your Project Disk.

► Independent Challenge 4

You own a company called Safety One, Inc., that specializes in gun safety training programs for police academies and the general public. You need to create a class outline and a letter for an introductory gun safety class.

a. Using Windows Explorer, create a folder named **Safety 1** in the My Documents folder.

b. Using WordPad, create the following documents in the Safety 1 folder:

- An outline called **GS 101 Outline** for the Gun Safety 101 class
- A letter called **GS Comments** to friends at the police department asking for comments on the outline

c. Start Backup, then insert a floppy disk or your Project Disk into the appropriate drive.

d. Start the backup, create a new backup job, then back up the selected files that you created in WordPad.

e. Back up the files to a floppy disk or your Project Disk as **Safety One**.

f. Select the files that you created with WordPad, then perform the normal backup, disable volume shadow copy, and print a report if requested by your instructor.

g. Revise the GS 101 Outline document, then save the document.

h. Perform a differential backup, disable volume shadow copy, then add **SO BKUP** to the backup description.

i. Restore the GS 101 Outline document from the backup job, print a report if requested by your instructor, then delete the backup jobs.

j. Using Windows Explorer, delete the Safety 1 folder and the backup file on the floppy disk or your Project Disk.

▶ Visual Workshop

Re-create the screen shown in Figure O-21, which displays the Notepad window with a backup report. Your hard drive folders and backup location might be different. Print the report in Notepad or print the screen. (Press [Print Screen] to make a copy of the screen, open Paint, click Edit on the menu bar, click Paste to paste the screen into Paint, then click Yes to paste the large image if necessary. Click the Text button on the Toolbox, click a blank area in the Paint work area, then type your name. Click File on the menu bar, click Page Setup, change 100 % normal size to 50% in the Scaling area, then click OK. Click File on the menu bar, click Print, then click Print.) Upon completion, delete the backup catalog in the Backup Utility window, then delete the backup file in My Computer in which you stored the file.

FIGURE O-21

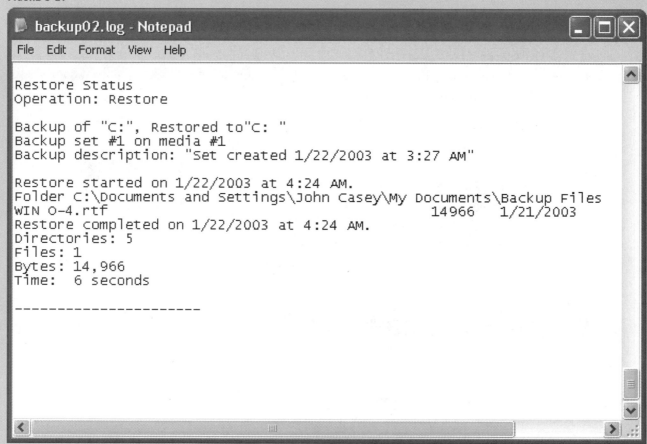

```
Restore Status
Operation: Restore

Backup of "C:", Restored to"C: "
Backup set #1 on media #1
Backup description: "Set created 1/22/2003 at 3:27 AM"

Restore started on 1/22/2003 at 4:24 AM.
Folder C:\Documents and Settings\John Casey\My Documents\Backup Files
WIN O-4.rtf                                    14966   1/21/2003
Restore completed on 1/22/2003 at 4:24 AM.
Directories: 5
Files: 1
Bytes: 14,966
Time:  6 seconds

----------------------
```

Administering
Your Computer

► **Explore Windows administrative tools**

► **Monitor activity with Event Viewer**

► **Manage an event log**

► **Create a performance chart**

► **Set up an alert**

► **View Computer Management tools**

► **Understand disk file systems**

► **Manage disks**

► **Monitor local security settings**

If you have purchased a computer and set it up in your home, you are that computer's administrator. Computers on a network in an institution, such as at a university, are called clients. The clients are managed by one or more system or network administrators, who have the task of ensuring that the network and its services are reliable, fast, and secure. Although most network administration takes place on the server end, clients must also be administered. Windows XP includes administrative tools that make it easy to ensure that client computers are operating as they should. ◄━━ John Casey, owner of Wired Coffee Company, is considering setting up a few computers for patrons to use while relaxing at Wired Coffee. He wants to understand more about how those computers would need to be administrated and secured. He asks his system administrator, Margaret Kolbe, to assist him in understanding Windows XP administrative tools.

Exploring Windows Administrative Tools

Windows XP offers a set of administrative tools that help you administer your computer and ensure it operates smoothly. The Administrative Tools window, opened from the Control Panel, provides tools that allow you to configure administrative settings for local and remote computers as shown in Table P-1. If you are working on a shared or network computer, you might need to be logged on as a computer administrator or as a member of the Administrators group in order to view or modify some properties or perform some tasks with the administrative tools. You can open User Accounts in the Control Panel to check which account is currently in use or check with your system administrator to determine whether you have the necessary access privileges. Margaret explains that many Windows XP users won't ever have to open the Administrative Tools window, but that computers open to the public or on a network will probably require more maintenance. She suggests, therefore, that John open this window to see the tools available to him.

Steps

> **(stop)** *If you are working on a shared or network computer, you might not be able to work through all the steps in this unit; however, you can read the lessons without completing the steps to learn what is possible as a system administrator.*

1. Click the **Start button** on the taskbar

Make a note of the name that appears at the top of the Start menu, which identifies the account currently logged onto your computer.

2. Click **Control Panel**, then click **Switch to Classic View** if necessary

The Control Panel window opens, displaying the available administrative tools.

3. Double-click the **User Accounts icon** 🖳

The User Accounts window opens, displaying a list of user accounts at the bottom of the window. If the name at the top of the Start menu matches the name associated with the computer administrator account, you have the access privileges to use all the administrative tools.

4. Click the **Close button** in the User Accounts window

The Control Panel window appears.

5. Double-click the **Administrative Tools icon** 🖳

Figure P-1 shows the tools available on John's computer. Your Administrative Tools window might show other tools or fewer tools if your network administrator has installed additional administrative tools or removed tools.

> **Trouble?**
>
> If you are not logged on as a computer administrator, check with your instructor or network administrator to determine whether you need to log off and log on as a Computer administrator.

Accessing administrative tools from the Start menu

If you frequently use the Windows administrative tools, you can save time by adding a menu item to the Start menu, so you can bypass the Control Panel. To add the Administrative Tools menu item to the Start menu and the All Programs menu, right-click the Start button, then click Properties. In the Taskbar and Start Menu Properties dialog box, click the Start Menu tab if necessary, click Customize, click the Advanced tab in the Customize Start Menu dialog box, scroll to the bottom of the Start menu items list, click the Display on the All Programs menu and the Start menu option button under System Administrative Tools, then click OK twice. To access the Administrative Tools menu item, click the Start button on the taskbar. The Administrative Tools menu appears in the right column of the Start menu under the Control Panel menu item and includes a submenu of administrative tools.

FIGURE P-1: Viewing the Administrative Tools window

Available only in the Professional edition

Your list of administrative tools might differ

TABLE P-1: Administrative tools

icon	tool	description
	Component Services	Configures and manages system and application components
	Computer Management	Provides access to administrative tools to manage local and remote computers
	Data Sources (ODBC)	Enables programs to access, trace, and manage data in database management systems
	Event Viewer	Displays monitoring and troubleshooting messages from the system and other programs
	Local Security Policy	Modifies local security policy, such as user rights and audit policies; available only in the Professional edition
	Performance	Displays graphs of system processes and configures data logs and alerts
	Services	Displays, starts, and stops services provided to users by your computer

Network security

A network's security is measured by the degree to which data and resources on the computer are protected from system failure or unauthorized intrusion. One way a network administrator ensures security is by assigning rights to individual users or groups of users. For instance, a user on a client computer running Windows XP that has physical access to a network cannot access network files or resources until the administrator has granted rights to that computer and user. The ability to access administrative tools is assigned only to certain user groups, such as the Administrators group, to protect the unauthorized or accidental modification of important information. If you are a user, or member, in a group that does not have the right to use administrative tools, you might not be able to perform all the steps in this unit or even see some of the tools in Figure P-1. To check membership in a group (available in Windows XP Professional only), double-click the Computer Management icon in the Administrative Tools window, click the Expand indicator next to Local Users and Groups in the left pane, click the Groups folder, then double-click a group icon in the right pane to display a list of members in the Properties dialog box. To add members, click Add in the Properties dialog box, in the Select Users dialog box type the new member name or select one as indicated, then click OK twice.

Monitoring Activity with Event Viewer

Windows XP

Every time you start Windows, an event-logging service notes any unusual event that occurs, such as a failed logon, the installation of a new driver for a hardware device, the failure of a device or service to start, or a network interruption. For some critical events, such as when your disk is full, a warning message appears on your screen. Most events, however, don't require immediate attention, so Windows logs them in an event log file that you can view using the Event Viewer tool. Event Viewer maintains three logs: System, for events logged by Windows operating system components; Security, for security and audit events (such as who logged on); and Application, for program events. When you are troubleshooting problems on your computer, you can use the Event Viewer logs to monitor what activity took place. ✐ Margaret asks John to open Event Viewer to see what types of activities have been logged on the computer.

Steps

1. In the Administrative Tools window, double-click the Event Viewer icon 📖

The Event Viewer window opens. The left pane of the window displays the three types of logs maintained by your computer. From the Action menu, you can run commands to save a log to a file or open additional log files, for example, from other computers on the network.

QuickTip

Once you have selected a log from the left pane, click View on the menu bar to open a menu of viewing options, including the option of choosing which columns to display or the order in which they appear.

2. In the left pane, click System if necessary

The log for System events appears in the right pane of the Event Viewer window. Figure P-2 shows the System window for John's computer. Your log will show different events. You can click any column header to resort the list; by default, items are sorted by date, with the most recent events listed first. The first column, Type, identifies the nature or severity of the event: ⓘ indicates a normal event; ⚠ warns that the event might indicate a problem; and ❌ indicates a more serious error that resulted in the loss of a function or data. See Table P-2 for a description of each column.

3. Double-click an event in the right pane

The Event Properties window for the event you double-clicked opens, showing details of the event. Figure P-3 shows the Event Properties window for a system time error. Additionally, a description appears, and in some cases, a data section at the bottom of the window. Some events generate **binary data** that experienced computer technicians can evaluate to better interpret the event.

4. Click either the up arrow button ⬆ **or the down arrow button** ⬇

Another event description appears in the window.

5. Click OK to close the Event Properties window

QuickTip

If your Security log is blank, then you are not on a network, you don't have the rights to view this log, or there have been no security breaches. Skip Step 6.

6. Click Security in the left pane

If your computer has experienced any security events, such as a user trying to log on using an incorrect password, those events will be listed in the right pane.

7. Click Application in the left pane

The right pane lists all of the events associated with the operation of the various applications on your system. This could include the installation of new programs or errors that have caused your programs to fail.

8. Click System in the left pane to return to the System log

FIGURE P-2: System Event log

Three classes of
events tracked by
Windows

Icon indicates
event type

Events recorded
in the System log

FIGURE P-3: Viewing event details

Information from
the System log

Additional details
about the event

Click button to view the
previous event

Click button to view the
next event in the log

Click button to copy the
description of the event
to the Clipboard

TABLE P-2: Event Viewer columns

column	description
Type	Identifies the nature of the event, such as informational, a warning, or an error
Date and **Time**	Point when an event occurred, based on the computer's clock
Source	The object, such as the program, computer, or user, that logged the event
Category	Event classification if applicable, such as Logon/Logoff
Event	Number that identifies the specific event type; this number helps technical support personnel track events in the system
User	User associated with the event if applicable; the user is not responsible for most events, so the User entry is often N/A
Computer	Name of the computer where the event occurred

Managing an Event Log

Event logs grow in size as you work on your computer, but Event Viewer provides tools that help you view just the information you need and store the information you want to save for later. For example, you can apply a **filter** that allows you to view only events matching specified criteria, such as all events associated with a certain user. You can also search for a specific event using similar criteria. You probably don't want your active log to include events that happened long ago. With Event Viewer, you can **archive**, or save, your log periodically and then clear the archived events. Most administrators archive event logs on a regular schedule. ✏ Margaret wants John to explore filtering and locating events. John also wants to archive his System log and then clear the events to prevent the list from becoming too long. In this lesson, you will practice the first few steps of clearing a log, but you will not actually complete the procedure so as not to affect your system.

Steps

1. In the Event Viewer window, click **View** on the menu bar, then click **Filter**

The System Properties dialog box opens with the Filter tab active, as shown in Figure P-4. You can deselect the Event types check boxes to view only events of a certain type or from a specified time period, or you can view events from a specified source, category, user, computer, or ID number.

2. In the Event types section, deselect each check box except Error, then click **OK**

The System Properties dialog box closes, and only error events appear in the System log. Depending on your computer system, you might not have any error events.

3. Click **View** on the menu bar, click **Filter**, click **Restore Defaults** in the System Properties dialog box, then click **OK**

All events appear in the System log.

4. Click **View** on the menu bar, then click **Find**

The Find in local System dialog box, shown in Figure P-5, allows you to search through all types of events or only certain types. You can specify a source, category, ID, computer, user, or description when searching for a particular event. Once you've specified what you are looking for, you click the Find Next button.

5. Click **Close**

The Find in local System dialog box closes.

6. Right-click **System** in the left pane, then click **Save Log File As**

The Save "System" As dialog box opens.

7. Click the **Save in list arrow**, navigate to the drive and folder where your Project Files are located, type **System** in the File name text box, then click **Save**

You have saved the system event log in a file with an .evt extension.

8. Click the **Close button** in the Event Viewer window

The Event Viewer window closes, and you return to the Administrative Tools window.

FIGURE P-4: Filtering an event log

Filter by event type

Filter by a specific value

Filter by date

FIGURE P-5: Find in local System dialog box

Search for specific types of events

Search for a specific value

Click button to locate next event matching your criteria

Changing log settings

You can control how any log in the Event Viewer collects data by defining a maximum log size (the default is 512K) and instructing Event Viewer how to handle an event log that has reached its maximum size. Only users with administrative rights can change log settings. When the log—Application, Security, or System—is selected in the left pane of the Event Viewer window, you can click the Properties button on the toolbar to open the Properties dialog box, which allows you to change log settings. In addition to specifying a maximum log size, you can also choose from three log options when the log is full: new events can automatically overwrite the oldest events, new events can overwrite only events older than a specified number of days, or you can set Event Viewer not to overwrite events, in which case you must manually clear a full log before it can resume logging events.

Creating a Performance Chart

On a daily basis, your system generates a variety of performance data, such as your computer's memory or processor use, or the amount of congestion on a device. As the system administrator, you can use the Performance tool to create charts from the data that enable you to observe how a computer's processes behave over time. The types of performance data you monitor and record are called **performance objects**. Each performance object has a set of **counters** associated with it that provide numeric information. The Performance tool charts the numeric data gathered from the counters and provides graphical tools to make it easier to analyze and track the performance of your computer. ➤ Margaret helps John create a performance chart documenting the activities of the computer's processor.

Steps 1234

QuickTip

If the default counters don't track the data you want, you can delete them and add the ones you want at any time.

1. In the Administrative Tools window, double-click the **Performance icon** 📊, then click the **View Graph button** 📈 on the System Monitor toolbar in the Performance window if necessary

   The Performance window opens, as shown in Figure P-6, and begins charting the default counters listed at the bottom of the window. The right pane displays a chart of the object's performance. From the left pane you can create log files that record the performance values in text format.

2. Delete each counter by clicking the **Delete button** ✕ on the System Monitor toolbar, then click the **Add button** ✚ on the System Monitor toolbar

   Your chart will be difficult to read if you do not limit the number of counters shown on the chart. The Add Counters dialog box opens, displaying a list of performance objects and their counters that you can select to chart as shown in Figure P-7. You want to chart one of the counters associated with the computer's processor.

3. Click the **Performance object list arrow**, then click **Processor** if necessary

QuickTip

To see what a counter measures, click the counter in the Counter list, then click Explain.

4. Click **%Privileged Time** in the Select counters from list, then click **Add**

   The %Privileged Time counter monitors the percentage of the time the processor spends working with hardware, system memory, and other **privileged system components**, which are Windows operating system processes or tasks in progress. The Performance tool immediately begins charting this counter, though you may not be able to see the chart if the Add Counters dialog box obscures it on your screen.

QuickTip

To show accurate processor use in a performance chart, disable screen savers in the Control Panel, as they take up processor resources and give your chart a distorted view of processor performance.

5. Click **%Processor Time** in the Select counters from list, then click **Add**

   This counter measures the percentage of time that the processor is busy executing commands, known as a **non-idle thread**; it is a primary indicator of processor activity.

6. Click **%User Time**, then click **Add**

   The %User Time counter measures time spent on requests from user applications.

7. Click **Close** in the Add Counters dialog box

   A red bar moves across the screen, and the chart shows the performance of the three counters as colored lines on the chart.

QuickTip

To highlight a line, click the counter object at the bottom of the chart, then click the Highlight button 💡 on the System Monitor toolbar.

8. Double-click the time in the notification area of the task bar, click **Cancel** in the Date and Time Properties dialog box, then click the **Start button** on the taskbar twice

   Watch how the measure of processor time jumps up when activity occurs.

9. Click the **Freeze Display button** ⊗ on the System Monitor toolbar

   The performance counters stop tracking events.

FIGURE P-6: Charting system performance

View Graph button

Counter type

Statistics about the most recent reading for the selected counter

Color-coded lines distinguish each counter

Click buttons to add and delete counter objects

System Monitor toolbar

Your chart will differ

Performance object type

List of charted performance counters

FIGURE P-7: Selecting performance counters to chart

Type of performance object

Counter list; displays counters associated with the performance object

Click button to read an explanation of the selected counter

Baseline charts

Performance charts include statistics about each counter you select, but unless you know how your system should perform, these statistics might not be very meaningful. For this reason, administrators create baseline charts, charts made when the computer or network is running at a normal level. When there are problems, the administrator can create another performance chart that can be compared to the baseline chart. By regularly creating and comparing performance charts, administrators can anticipate and then prevent problems.

Setting Up an Alert

In addition to creating performance charts, you can use the Performance window to create user alerts. An **alert** is a warning that is automatically generated when a counter value exceeds or falls short of a threshold value you have specified. When an alert condition is met, the date and time of the event are recorded in the Application log, which you can view from the Event Viewer. For example, you can set the %User Time alert to monitor the percentage of elapsed time the computer spends running programs. Some programs require more processing time than others, which can slow down your computer. The %User Time alert can let you know if your programs are using too many resources and slowing down your computer. Your system can record up to 1,000 alert events, after which the oldest events are discarded as new events occur. Margaret guides John through setting up an alert to monitor the use of the computer's processor. The alert will occur whenever the percentage of the time the processor is in use exceeds a certain threshold, such as 75%.

Steps

1. In the Performance window, click the **Performance Logs and Alerts icon** in the left pane, then double-click **Alerts** in the list that opens in the right pane

2. Click **Action** on the menu bar, then click **New Alert Settings**
   The New Alert Settings dialog box opens. Each alert requires a specific name, so you first have to give it a name to identify it to the performance monitor.

3. In the Name box, type **Alert Test**, then click **OK**
   The Alert Test dialog box opens. From this dialog box, you specify which counters you want to track, and under what conditions the alert will be triggered.

> **QuickTip**
>
> To monitor additional counters, repeat Steps 4-7 for each counter.

4. Click **Add**
   The Add Counters dialog box opens.

5. If necessary, click the **Performance object list arrow**, then click **Processor**

6. Click **%Processor Time** in the Select counters from list, click **Add**, then click **Close**
   The Add Counters dialog box closes, and the Alert Test dialog box appears.

7. Click the **Alert when the value is list arrow**, click **Over** if necessary, then type **75** in the Limit text box
   An alert will be added to the alert log when processor time exceeds 75%, as shown in Figure P-8

> **QuickTip**
>
> To stop an alert, select the alert in the right pane, then click the Stop the selected alert button on the toolbar.

8. Click **OK**
   The Alert Test you just created appears in the right pane of the Performance window. The icon appears green when it is running and red when it is not.

9. Right-click the **Alert Test icon**, click **Delete**, click **OK** if the Performance Logs and Alerts message box opens, then click the **Close button** in the Performance window
   You return to the Administrative Tools window.

CLUES TO USE

Alert actions and schedules

The Action tab in the selected alert's Properties dialog box allows you to specify what action you want to take when your system triggers an alert. By default, the system logs an entry in the application event log when it triggers an alert. You can also specify that the system send a message to the network administrator, that performance data be collected, or that a specific program be run. To run a program, click the Browse button, specify the program path, then click OK. You can also schedule alerts using the Schedule tab in the selected alert's dialog box. Your system will scan for an alert at the times or intervals you specify.

FIGURE P-8: Creating a performance alert

Click the Action tab to choose an action when the alert condition is met

Click the Schedule tab to schedule a time to automatically check for alerts

Your path will vary

Threshold value

Click button to add additional counters

Managing your computer's performance

You can adjust Windows XP to improve its performance by changing the way Windows XP manages system processing and memory. You can set Windows XP to give a greater proportion of processor time to the program in which you are currently working, known as a foreground process. The greater the processor time, the faster response time you receive from the program in which you are currently working. If you have background processes, such as printing, that you want to run while you work, you might want to have Windows XP share processor time equally between background and foreground programs. To optimize performance for foreground and background processes, double-click the System icon in the Control Panel, click the Advanced tab in the System Properties dialog box,

click Settings in the Performance section, click the Advanced tab, then click the Programs option button if necessary to optimize for foreground processes, or click the Background services option button to optimize for background processes. When your computer is running low on RAM and more is needed immediately to complete your current task, Windows XP uses hard disk drive space to simulate system RAM. This is known as virtual memory. For processes that require a lot of RAM, you can optimize virtual memory use by allocating more available space on your hard disk drive. In the Virtual memory section, click Change, then enter the initial size and maximum size you want to allocate for virtual memory use.

Viewing Computer Management Tools

Computer Management consolidates administrative tools, including those you've already used, such as Event Viewer and Performance, into a single window that you can use to manage a local or remote computer. When you open Computer Management, the Computer Management window uses a two-pane view that is similar to Windows Explorer. The hierarchy of tools in the left pane of the Computer Management window is called a **console tree**, and each main category of tools is called a **node**. The three nodes in the Computer Management window (System Tools, Storage, and Services and Applications), allow you to manage and monitor system events and performance and to perform disk-related tasks. Each node contains **snap-in tools**, which come in two types: standalone or extension. Standalone snap-ins are independent tools, while extension snap-ins are add-ons to current snap-ins. To perform an administrative task, you might need to navigate the hierarchy before you select a tool in the console tree. The selected tool appears in the right pane, and you can use the toolbars and menus that appear to take appropriate action with the tool. ✎ Margaret asks John to practice using Computer Manager by viewing the Application log to see how his alert was monitored.

Steps

1. In the Administrative Tools window, double-click the **Computer Management icon** 🖥️
   The Computer Management window opens, displaying two panes, as shown in Figure P-9. The left pane lists the hierarchy of tools; you navigate the tools using Expand indicators ⊞ and Collapse indicators ⊟ to display and hide objects in the tool hierarchy.

2. Click **System Tools** in the console tree (the left pane)
   The snap-in tools associated with System Tools appear in the right pane. The detailed list displays the snap-in tool type and a description.

3. Click the **Expand indicator** ⊞ next to System Tools to view the tools in the System Tools node if necessary

4. Click ⊞ in the console tree next to Event Viewer to view the event logs if necessary

5. Click **Application** under the Event Viewer
   Application events appear in the right pane.

6. Double-click the first **Information event** in the Application log list.
   If you have been working through the lessons without pausing, the Application log should show two Information events related to the Alert Test event, as well as many others. Figure P-10 shows the first event; it notes that the conditions of the Alert Test have been met.

7. Click **Cancel** to close the Event Properties dialog box
   You return to the Computer Management window.

8. Click the **Collapse indicator** ⊟ in the console tree next to Event Viewer

QuickTip

Notice that the System Tools node lists the Performance Logs and Alerts tools a little further down, where you can make changes to current logs and alerts.

FIGURE P-9: **Computer Management window**

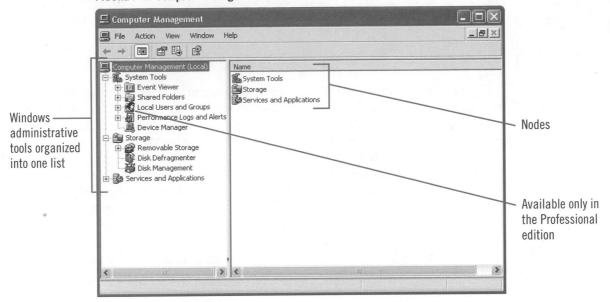

Windows administrative tools organized into one list

Nodes

Available only in the Professional edition

FIGURE P-10: **Viewing an alert event**

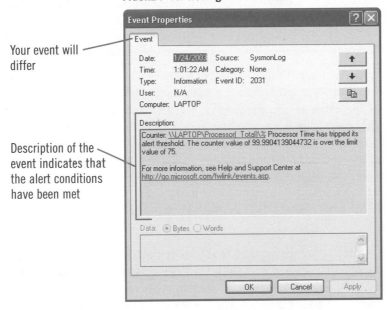

Your event will differ

Description of the event indicates that the alert conditions have been met

Understanding local users and groups

In Windows XP Professional, you can manage the access privileges and permissions of local user and group accounts. A local user account is an individual account with a unique set of permissions, while a group account is a collection of individual accounts with the same set of permissions. You can change local user and group accounts in the Computer Management window using the Local Users and Groups tool. This security feature limits individual users and groups from accessing and deleting files, using programs such as Backup, or making accidental or intentional system-wide changes. You can create or modify a user account, disable or activate a user account, identify members of groups, and add or delete members to and from groups. To perform these account tasks and many others, click the Expand indicator ⊞ next to Local Users and Groups in the Computer Management window, click the Users or Groups folder icon below it, then double-click an account icon or select a command on the Action menu.

Understanding Disk File Systems

A disk must be formatted with a **file system** that allows it to work with the operating system to store, manage, and access data. Two of the most common file systems are FAT (or FAT32, which is an improvement on FAT technology) and NTFS. Disks on DOS, Windows 3.1, or Windows 98 computers use the FAT file system, while disks on computers running Windows NT 4.0 and later (including Windows XP) can use either the NTFS or FAT system. NTFS is a newer file system that improves on some of the shortcomings of FAT disks that make them less desirable on a network. Table P-3 describes the improvements of the NTFS file system over the FAT file system. Which file system your disks are most likely to use and why depends on the type of disk, whether your computer is on a network, and your computer's role as a resource on the network. ◄—— Margaret explains the features of file systems to John.

Details

There are important differences between FAT and NTFS file systems:

► **FAT**

When you format a disk with the FAT file system, a formatting program divides the disk into storage compartments. First it creates a series of rings, called **tracks**, around the circumference of the disk. Then it divides the tracks into equal parts, like pieces of a pie, to form sectors, as shown in Figure P-11. The number of sectors and tracks depends on the size of the disk.

Although the physical surface of a disk is made of tracks and sectors, a file is stored in clusters. A cluster, also called an **allocation unit**, is one or more sectors of storage space. It represents the minimum amount of space that an operating system reserves when saving the contents of a file to a disk. Thus, a file might be stored in more than one cluster. Each cluster is identified by a unique number. The first two clusters, shown in yellow in Figure P-11, are reserved by the operating system. The operating system maintains a file allocation table (or FAT) on each disk that lists the clusters on the disk and records the status of each cluster: whether it is occupied (and by which file), available, or defective. Each cluster in a file "remembers" its order in the chain of clusters—and each cluster points to the next one until the last cluster, which marks the end of the file.

► **NTFS**

NTFS features a built-in security system that does not allow users to access the disk unless they have a user account and password with the necessary rights and permissions. NTFS protects disks from damage by automatically redirecting data from a bad sector to a good sector without requiring you to run a disk-checking utility. Given the reliability and the built-in repair mechanisms of NTFS disks, only rarely do they require maintenance. This is an example of **fault tolerance**, the ability of a disk to resist damage, which is a critical issue with disks on a network computer.

FIGURE P-11: Files stored in clusters

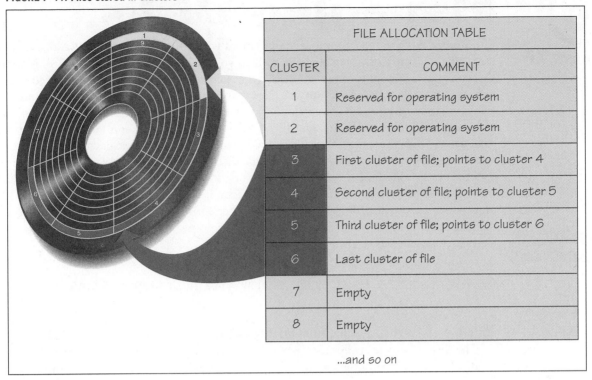

FILE ALLOCATION TABLE	
CLUSTER	COMMENT
1	Reserved for operating system
2	Reserved for operating system
3	First cluster of file; points to cluster 4
4	Second cluster of file; points to cluster 5
5	Third cluster of file; points to cluster 6
6	Last cluster of file
7	Empty
8	Empty

...and so on

TABLE P-3: NTFS improvements on the FAT file system

feature	FAT	NTFS
Security	Vulnerable to "hackers"—unauthorized users who break into other people's files	Includes built-in security measures that allow only people who have permission to access files
Recoverability	Likely to fail if a sector containing system data is lost because they store critical system files in single sectors	Highly reliable because it uses redundant storage—it stores everything in vital sectors twice, so if a disk error in a vital sector occurs, NTFS can access file system data from the redundant sector
File size	Designed for small disks (originally less than 1 MB in size); can handle a maximum file size of 4 GB	Handles files up to 64 GB in size

CLUES TO USE

Selecting a file system

NTFS does not support floppy disks, so all floppies are formatted with FAT. If you are running Windows XP on a stand-alone computer, you can choose either FAT or NTFS, but in most cases, the file system has already been determined either by the person who originally set up the computer or by the manufacturer from whom you purchased the computer. If your computer is a client on a Windows XP network, it is likely that your hard disk uses NTFS. Because NTFS is more suited to network demands, such as a high level of security and resistance to system failure, network administrators format network disks with NTFS whenever possible. Sometimes, however, users on a network want or need to use a non-Windows XP operating system. Also, a user might need a computer that is capable of running Windows XP or Windows 98/Me. The disks on that computer would then be formatted with FAT.

Managing Disks

The Storage node in the Computer Management window provides you with tools, such as Disk Defragmenter and Disk Management, to help you manage your disks. The Disk Management tool is a graphical tool for managing disks that allows you to partition unallocated portions of your disks into volumes. A **volume** is a fixed amount of storage on a disk. A single disk can contain more than one volume, or a volume can span part of one or more disks. Each volume on a disk is assigned its own drive letter, which is why the term volume is often synonymous with the term drive. Thus, the same physical disk might contain two volumes. Each volume can use a different file system, so you might have a single disk partitioned into two volumes, each with its own file system. Figure P-12 shows how you might partition a single hard disk in two different ways: first, with a single NTFS volume, and second, with one NTFS volume and one FAT volume, which can be helpful if you have a computer with two operating systems, Windows 98 on the FAT volume and Windows XP on the NTFS volume. Margaret suggests that John view the storage tools.

Steps

1. In the Computer Management window, click the **Expand indicator** ⊞ next to the Storage node if necessary

2. In the console tree, click **Disk Management**
   The disks on your computer appear in the right pane. The top right pane of the window displays your computer's volumes, and the bottom right pane offers a graphic display of the breakdown of space on each disk, allowing you to see how your disks are partitioned. Figure P-13 displays a computer with a hard disk and a CD-ROM disk, assigned to drive letter D. The hard disk, labeled Disk 0, has only one FAT drive, assigned to drive letter C:, and no unallocated space. The 0 in the label Disk 0 indicates the disk number, starting from 0, for each disk type disk on the computer. Hard and removable disks are one disk type, while CD-ROMs and DVDs are another.

3. Click the **Settings button** 🗔 on the toolbar
   The Settings dialog box opens, as shown in Figure P-14, allowing you to change the color or pattern of any disk region displayed in the Disk Management window. Refer to the Disk region list in Figure P-14 to identify the disk regions that you might see on your drives. System administrators use many of the items in this list to create drives that are extremely reliable for data storage.

4. Click **Cancel** to close the Settings dialog box

5. In the console tree, click **Disk Defragmenter**
   The Disk Defragmenter program window appears in the right pane. You can analyze and defragment a disk from the Computer Management window.

6. Click the **Close button** in the Computer Management window

Partitioning a disk

If you have a computer at home, its disks are most likely already partitioned, and partitioning those disks further can be laborious if there is no available free space (space that is not yet part of a partition). If, however, you have the necessary rights on a computer whose disk or disks have available unallocated space, you can partition your disk. You right-click an unallocated region of a disk in the Disk Management pane, then click Create Partition. You then follow the Create Partition Wizard directions that appear on your screen. This wizard helps you format your new drive, so you can store data on it.

FIGURE P-12: A hard disk, partitioned two different ways

C: drive NTFS volume (150 MB)

D: drive FAT volume (50 MB)

D: drive NTFS volume (100 MB)

FIGURE P-13: Viewing Disk Management information

Drive is formatted using the FAT32 file system

Two drives on the system

FIGURE P-14: Settings dialog box

These items can be displayed in the Computer Management window

Monitoring Local Security Settings

Using Windows XP Professional, you can view and monitor local security settings with the Local Security Settings tool to ensure that computer users are adhering to the organization's security policies. For example, you can set user account and password options to require computer users to create complex passwords of a specific length and change them on a regular basis. A **complex password** contains characters from at least three of the four following categories: uppercase (A through Z), lowercase (a through z), numbers (0 through 9), and nonalphanumeric (!, \$, *, etc.). In addition to setting security options, you can also **monitor**, or **audit**, the success or failure of security related events, such as account logon and logoff activities, user account changes, and program launches. When an event that you have chosen to audit is triggered, it appears in the Event Viewer in the Security node. ⟍⟍⟍ Margaret suggests that John learn how to view and monitor local security settings.

Steps 1234

 If you are using Windows XP Home edition, you will not be able to work through the steps in this topic. Read the topic without completing the steps.

1. In the Administrative Tools window, double-click the **Local Security Policy icon** 🗗
   The Local Security Settings window opens, with a two-pane view like Windows Explorer.

2. Click the **Expand indicator** ⊞ next to Account Policies, then click the **Password Policy folder**
   Password Policy displays current password policies and settings, as shown in Figure P-15.

3. In the right pane, double-click **Maximum password age**, then click **Cancel** to avoid making any changes
   The Maximum password age Properties dialog box displays a numeric box in which you can change the number of days until a password expires.

4. Click ⊞ next to Local Policies, then click the **Audit Policy folder**
   Audit Policy displays security events you can monitor in the Event Viewer.

5. In the right pane, double-click **Audit account logon events** to open its Properties dialog box, click the **Success check box** to select it, then click **OK**
   Audit account logon events policy changes to "Success," as shown in Figure P-16.

Trouble?

If Switch User is not available, click Logoff, close all programs if necessary, log on again, then open the Administration Tools window via the Control Panel and start Local Security Settings.

6. Click the **Start button** on the taskbar, click **Log Off**, click **Switch User**, then log on again with your account or the administrator account
   Logging off and on your computer triggers the local security policy event.

7. In the Local Security Settings window with Audit Policy selected, double-click **Audit account logon events** in the right pane to open its Properties dialog box, click the **Success check box** to deselect it, click **OK**, then click the **Close button** in the Local Security Settings window
   The audit policy is restored to its original settings, and the Local Security Settings window closes.

8. In the Administration Tools window, double-click the **Event Viewer icon** 🗐 to open the Event Viewer window, then click **Security** in the left pane
   The successful audit events appear in the Event Viewer, as shown in Figure P-17.

9. Scroll to the right and change column widths if necessary to display audit information, then click the **Close** button in the Event Viewer, Administrative Tools, and Control Panel windows

FIGURE P-15: Password policies with current settings

Security Settings categories

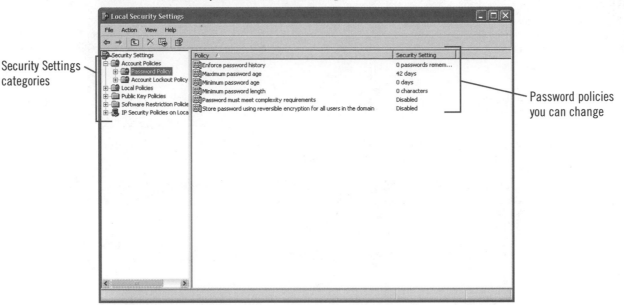

Password policies you can change

FIGURE P-16: Audit policies with current settings

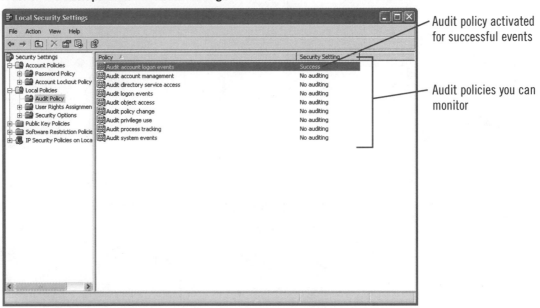

Audit policy activated for successful events

Audit policies you can monitor

FIGURE P-17: Event Viewer window with successful audit event

Successful audit event; your list might differ

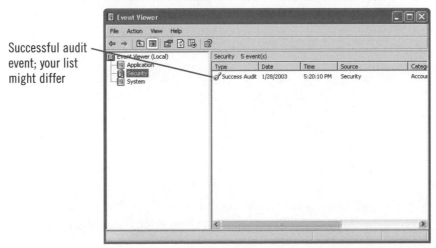

Practice

► Concepts Review

Label each element of the screen shown in Figure P-18.

FIGURE P-18

1. Which element points to the tool that displays monitoring and troubleshooting messages from the system and other programs?
2. Which element points to the tool that displays graphs of system processes and configures data logs and alerts?
3. Which element points to the tool that provides access to administrative tools to manage local and remote computers?
4. Which element points to the tool that limits users from accessing and deleting files, using programs, or making system-wide changes?
5. Which element points to the tool that manages volumes and creates partitions?

Match each of the terms with the statement that describes its function.

6. Performance Monitor	a. Allows you to examine System, Security, and Application logs
7. NTFS	b. Allows you to log an alert
8. Disk Management	c. Uses redundant storage
9. Volume	d. Allows you to create a partition
10. Counter	e. When a computer or network is running at a normal level
11. FAT	f. Storage space that can span one or more disks
12. Baseline	g. Designed for small disks
13. Event Viewer	h. Numerical information about the performance of an item on your computer

Select the best answer from the list of choices.

14. **The Computer Management window contains tools that allow you to:**
    a. Install new programs.
    b. Change your display settings.
    c. View but not change system information.
    d. Track performance data.

15. **If you want your computer to create an alert when your processor is running at 85%, which tool should you use?**
    a. Disk Administrator
    b. Event Viewer
    c. Performance Monitor
    d. User Manager

16. **If an alert threshold value is reached, Windows will:**
    a. Add an alert event to the Event Log.
    b. Send e-mail to the network administrator.
    c. Shut down the computer.
    d. Print a diagnostic report.

17. **To interpret a performance chart, an administrator should compare it to:**
    a. A Windows diagnostic report.
    b. The Event Viewer System log.
    c. A list of volumes in Disk Management.
    d. A baseline chart.

18. **What is a counter?**
    a. An object such as a processor or physical disk
    b. A program you can run when an alert reaches a threshold value
    c. A numeric value that measures the performance of an object
    d. A red bar on the Performance Monitor chart that indicates an object's status

19. **FAT stands for:**
    a. File allocation track.
    b. Format allocation track.
    c. File allocation table.
    d. Format allocation table.

20. **The Disk Management tool allows you to partition disks into:**
    a. Clusters.
    b. Volumes.
    c. Sectors.
    d. Tracks.

▶ Skills Review

1. **Explore Windows administrative tools.**
    a. Open the Control Panel, then double-click the Administrative Tools icon.
    b. Write down a sentence that describes each administrative tool.

2. **Monitor activity with Event Viewer.**
    a. Start Event Viewer, then click the Application icon in the left pane. If this log is empty, use another log, such as System.
    b. Double-click one of the entries to view a description of that event in the Event Properties window, click the up arrow or down arrow button to display other events, then click OK.

3. **Manage an event log.**
    a. In the Event Viewer window, click View on the menu bar, then click Filter.
    b. Deselect all the Event types check boxes except for Warning and Error, then click OK.
    c. View details on two of the events.
    d. Click View on the menu bar, click Filter, click Restore Defaults, then click OK.
    e. Click View on the menu bar, then click Find.
    f. Click the Event source list arrow, then click one of the programs in the list.
    g. Click Find Next. (The first event matching your criteria is selected in the event log; if you don't get a match, skip to Step i.)
    h. Double-click the event you just found, then click Cancel in the Event Properties window.
    i. Save the Application log as **Application** to the drive and folder where your Project Files are located, then close Event Viewer.

4. **Create a performance chart.**

   a. Start Performance, then click the View Graph button on the System Monitor toolbar if necessary.

   b. Click the Add button on the System Monitor toolbar, click the Performance object list arrow, then click Memory.

   c. Add the Available Bytes, and the Committed Bytes counters, then click Close.

   d. Allow the chart to generate for a few minutes, then identify which is greater, the number of available bytes or the number of committed bytes.

5. **Set up an alert.**

   a. Click the Expand indicator next to Performance Logs and Alerts in the left pane, then click the Alerts icon.

   b. Click Action on the menu bar, then click New Alert Settings.

   c. Type **Alert Check**, then click OK.

   d. Click Add, then select Processor in the Performance object list if necessary.

   e. Click %Processor Time in the Counter list, click Add, then click Close.

   f. Set the Alert when the value is option to Over, type 85 in the Limit text box, then click OK.

   g. Return to the Performance window and delete the alert you just created.

   h. Close Performance.

6. **View Computer Management tools.**

   a. Start Computer Management, then open the Event Viewer folder.

   b. Double-click Application in the right pane, double-click an event, then click OK.

   c. Open Device Manager, then open Disk Defragmenter.

7. **Manage disks.**

   a. In the Computer Management window, open Disk Management.

   b. Identify the number of FAT volumes you have and the number of NTFS volumes if any.

   c. Determine how physical disk space is used on your computer.

   d. Write down two reasons why your computer's disks might be configured the way they are (consider the advantages of NTFS over FAT in a network environment).

   e. Close Computer Management.

8. **View and save system information.**

   a. Start Local Security Settings. If you are using Windows XP Home edition, skip these steps.

   b. Open the Account Policies folder, then open the Password Policy folder.

   c. Double-click a policy to view its options, then click Cancel.

   d. Open the Local Polices folder, then open the Audit Policy folder.

   e. Open the Audit policy change policy, select the Success check box, then click OK.

   f. Open the Audit account management policy, select the Success check box, then click OK.

   g. Open each policy you just changed and deselect the Success check box, then click OK to restore settings.

   h. Close Local Security Settings.

   i. Start Event Viewer, click the Security icon in the left pane to view the Policy Change triggered events, then close Event Viewer, the Administrative Tools window and the Control Panel window.

► Independent Challenge 1

You own a small bakery, and you just purchased a computer with Windows XP to help manage inventory, payroll, and other accounting procedures. You decide to create a baseline chart using Performance that indicates how the computer performs in normal circumstances so you can monitor your system performance.

   a. Use Performance to create a chart with two Memory counters: %Committed Bytes In Use and Cache Bytes.

   b. Print the chart and put your name on the printout. (Press [Print Screen] to make a copy of the screen, open Paint, click Edit on the menu bar, click Paste to paste the screen into Paint, then click Yes to paste the large image if necessary. Click the Text button on the Toolbox, click a blank area in the Paint work area, then type your name.

Click File on the menu bar, click Page Setup, change 100% normal size to 50% in the Scaling area, then click OK. Click File on the menu bar, click Print, then click Print.)

c. Use the Explain button in the Add Counters dialog box to learn more about the two counters you charted. On the back of your printout, write a short description of both counters.

d. Close Performance.

 # Independent Challenge 2

You own a small résumé preparation business. You are considering buying a new hard disk for your Windows XP computer, which you use to produce and store clients' resumes. Before you shop, you want to produce documentation on your current disk setup so that you can take your findings to different computer vendors and provide the sales representatives with the information they need to advise you. You use both Disk Management and Event Viewer.

a. Open the Computer Management window, then open the Disk Management folder.

b. Create a printout of your disk configuration and put your name on the printout. (See Independent Challenge 1, Step b for print screen printing instructions.)

c. Open the Event Viewer folder and use the Find feature to view all events related with "disk."

d. Open the disk event, then create a printout of Event Properties dialog box. (See Independent Challenge 1, Step b for print screen printing instructions.)

e. Close Computer Management.

 # Independent Challenge 3

You are the systems administrator for the research and development (R&D) department at Herrera Pharmaceuticals. One of the R&D specialists has been having problems with her computer. You decide to start by examining the event logs, particularly the System log. You also want to check the log settings to make sure the log is collecting data properly.

a. Start Event Viewer, open the System log, then use the Filter feature to view only Error and Warning events.

b. Print the list and put your name on the printout. (See Independent Challenge 1, Step b for print screen printing instructions.)

c. Check Event Viewer settings using the Properties command on the Action menu. On the printout, write a summary of the current settings.

d. Save the System log as **Latest System** to the drive and folder where your Project Files are located.

e. Restore the default Filter settings, then close Event Viewer.

Independent Challenge 4

You and some fellow students at your university have joined forces with a supplier of sweaters, blankets, and other handmade wares from Peru to create an international import business. You've been using an older computer with Windows XP, and you are concerned because your computer runs rather slowly. You decide to run some tests on the processor and memory and gather some information about how you might improve your computer's performance.

a. Use Performance to create two charts, one on memory and one on your computer's processor. Use three counters for each chart. Use the Explain button in the Add Counters dialog box to learn more about the counters.

b. Print the charts. (See Independent Challenge 1, Step b for print screen instructions.) On the back of each printout, describe the counters and explain the chart results, then close Performance.

► Visual Workshop

This exercise can be completed by users of both Windows XP Professional and Home. Re-create and print the screen shown in Figure P-19, which displays a Performance chart. Your chart numbers will differ. Print the screen. (See Independent Challenge 1, Step c for print screen printing instructions.)

FIGURE P-19

This exercise can be completed only by users of Windows XP Professional. Re-create and print the screen shown in Figure P-20, which displays the Event Viewer window with the Security node selected in the left pane and audit events in the right pane. Your date, time, and user name will differ. Print the screen. (See Independent Challenge 1, Step c for print screen printing instructions.)

FIGURE P-20

Appendix

Objectives

► Identify New Features in Windows XP
► Identify Differences between Windows XP Home and Professional
► Prepare to Install Windows XP
► Install Windows XP
► Set Up a Computer for Multiple Users
► Manage Power Options on Portable Computers
► Improve the Font Display on Portable Computers
► Create a Home or Office Network
► Set Up to Use a Remote Computer
► Connect to a Remote Computer
► Send and Receive a Fax

This appendix provides information about new features in Windows XP, the differences between Windows XP Home and Windows XP Professional, and how to prepare and install the operating system software. For those users who want to share a computer at home or the office, you'll learn how to set up and use a computer for multiple users. If you use a portable computer, also known as a **laptop** or **notebook**, you can change computer power options to reduce the power consumption of your entire system or a specific device, and smooth out the edges of fonts on the screen to improve the font display. This appendix also shows you how to communicate remotely with others from your computer. You'll learn how to set up and create a home or office network, set up and connect to a remote computer, and send and receive faxes.

Identifying New Features in Windows XP

Windows XP comes with new features that make your computer significantly easier and faster to use than earlier versions of Windows. Windows XP makes it easier to open files and programs, find information, and accomplish other common tasks, such as send e-mail, browse the Internet, scan and view pictures, play music and videos, and change Windows XP settings. Windows XP design improvements include a two-column Start menu with frequently-used programs and files, similar windows grouped on the taskbar, a task pane with common commands that correspond to the current task, and Control Panel icons organized by category. If you share a computer with family and friends, Windows XP makes it easy to create individual accounts with customized settings for each user and provides a Welcome screen that allows you to switch between multiple accounts without having to exit programs and log off completely. Some of the main new features in Windows XP are shown in Figure AP-1 and are listed below.

Details

► Welcome screen and Fast User Switching

With the Welcome screen, you can share the same computer with family and friends and still maintain privacy and control over your personal files. You can use Fast User Switching to switch between users without having to close each other's programs.

► Enhanced Start menu and taskbar grouping

The Start menu organizes programs and frequently-used tasks. If you have many open files, programs, and windows, they are grouped together on the taskbar according to the program type.

► Task-focused design

The My Computer, My Documents, and other windows display a task pane on the left side of the window with commands and options associated with your current task or selection. The Control Panel also displays options by category in addition to the Classic view.

► Help and Support Center

This allows you to search multiple sources including the Microsoft Knowledge Base on the Internet, to print from the online documentation, and to access frequently-used help topics.

► System Restore

System Restore allows you to restore your computer to a previous version of the system.

► Search Companion

The Search Companion identifies the kind of help needed and retrieves relevant information.

► Windows Messenger

An easy way to communicate with your **buddies**, a list of contacts with whom you interact regularly, in real time using text, voice, and video.

► Remote Assistance

Gives a friend permission to connect to your computer over the Internet, observe your screen, and control your computer.

► Home Networking

You can set up a home network and share an Internet connection and other computer resources, such as a printer or fax.

► CD burning

With a CD recording device installed on your computer, you can create your own CDs by dragging a folder with the files and folders you want to save to the CD-R or CD-RW device icon.

► Enhanced Windows Media Player

You can play DVDs, create your own music CDs, and export videos to portable devices.

► Enhanced My Pictures and My Music folders

With My Pictures, you can order prints, view pictures, publish pictures to the Internet, and compress pictures. With My Music, you can view a list of music files, play music files, shop for music online, and perform file management tasks.

► Scanner and Camera Wizard

Walks you through scanning a single image, collection of images, and multi-page documents.

FIGURE AP-1: Main new features in Windows XP

Task pane

My Documents subfolders; yours might differ

Search Companion

Taskbar grouping

Start button

Enhanced desktop look

Enhanced Windows Media Player

Windows XP

Identifying Differences between Windows XP Home and Professional

Windows XP comes in three editions: the Home Edition for consumers, the Professional Edition for business and power users, and a 64-bit version for Intel Itanium processor-based systems, called Windows XP 64-Bit Edition. The Home Edition is a subset of the Professional Edition. In other words, the Home Edition contains all the same features contained in the Professional Edition. However, the Professional Edition also contains additional features, some of which are shown in Figure AP-2, that are geared toward the business world. Each edition allows users to install an upgrade version for those who already have Windows 98 or later installed on their computer, or a full version for those who have Windows 95 or Windows NT 3.51 or earlier or no operating system installed on their computer.

Windows XP Professional features not found in the Home Edition:

► **Slightly different user interface**

Windows XP Professional comes with a few user interface default settings that are different from those in Windows XP Home. See Table AP-1 for a list and description of the user interface differences.

► **Access a remote desktop**

You can access a Windows XP Professional remote desktop from any operating system that supports a Terminal Services client, such as Windows 98 or Me, and Windows XP Home.

► **Supports more than one microprocessor**

Windows XP Professional supports up to two microprocessors, while the Windows XP Home supports only one. This allows you to perform multiple tasks at the same time, such as printing large documents and calculating large amounts of numbers, more quickly.

► **Backup and Automated System Recovery**

With the Backup utility program, you can back up files to a disk or tape and create an Automated System Recovery disk to help you recover a system from a serious error, such as a system crash.

► **Internet Information Service**

You can set up a personal Web server using the Internet Information Services Web server software to use to publish Web pages.

FIGURE AP-2: Windows XP Professional desktop

Programs available only in the Professional version

Printers and Other Hardware in the Home version

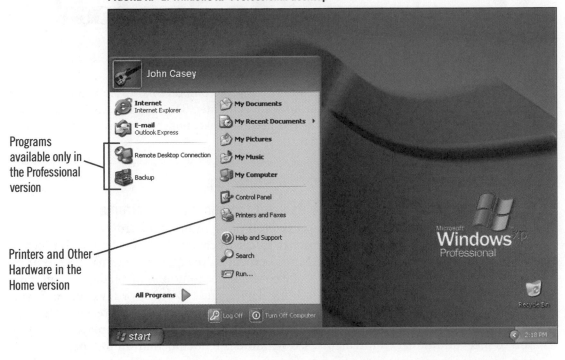

TABLE AP-1: User interface differences

user interface item	Windows XP Home	Windows XP Professional
Start menu	Printers and Other Hardware (not available unless enabled)	Printers and Faxes; My Recent Documents
Fax functionality	Not available unless you install it	Available
Guest account	Activated	Deactivated
Check box option on Screen Saver tab in the Display Properties dialog box	On resume, display Welcome screen	On resume, password protect

Preparing to Install Windows XP

Before you install Windows XP, you need to check your computer hardware and software and make several setup decisions that relate to your computer. The Windows XP Setup Wizard guides you through many of the choices you need to make, but there are some decisions and actions you need to make before you start the wizard.

To ensure a successful installation, do the following:

► Make sure your hardware components meet the minimum requirements
Your computer hardware needs to meet the following minimum hardware requirements: 300 megahertz (MHz) Pentium or higher microprocessor or equivalent recommended (233 MHz minimum), 128 MB of RAM recommended (64 MB minimum), 1.5 GB of free space on hard disk, Super VGA (800 × 600) or higher resolution video adapter and monitor, keyboard, mouse or compatible pointing device, and CD-ROM or DVD drive. Beyond the basic requirements, some software and hardware services, such as Internet access, networking, instant messaging, voice and video conferencing, and sound playback, call for you to meet additional requirements; see Windows XP documentation for specific details.

► Make sure your hardware and software are compatible
The Windows XP Setup Wizard automatically checks your hardware and software and reports any potential conflicts, but it is always a good idea to determine whether your computer hardware is compatible before you start the wizard. You can view the Hardware Compatibility List (HCL) at the Microsoft Web site at www.microsoft.com/hcl/, shown in Figure AP-3.

► Back up your files in case you need to restore your current operating system
If you're upgrading from an earlier version of Windows, you should back up your current files, so you can correct any problems that might arise during the installation. You can back up files to a disk, a tape drive, or another computer on your network. Check your current operating system help for instructions to back up your files.

► Make sure you have required network information
If you are connecting to a network, you need the following information from your network administrator: name of your computer, name of the workgroup or domain, and a TCP/IP address if your network doesn't use a DHCP (Dynamic Host Configuration Protocol) server. If you are not sure whether you are connecting to a workgroup or a domain, select the workgroup option. You can always connect to a domain after you install Windows XP Professional.

► Determine whether you want to perform an upgrade or install a new copy of Windows XP
After you start the Windows XP Setup Wizard, you need to decide whether to upgrade your current operating system, as shown in Figure AP-4, or to perform an entirely new installation, known as a **clean install.** You can upgrade from Windows 98, 98 SE, and Me to Windows XP Home Edition or Professional, and you can upgrade only from Windows 2000 Professional and Windows NT 4.0 Workstation to Windows Professional, but not to the Home Edition. Windows 98, 98 SE, and Me users can uninstall Windows XP, but this capability is not available to Windows NT 4.0 and Windows 2000 upgraders. Windows 95 and Windows NT 3.51 or earlier are not supported for upgrading, so those users will need to perform a clean install.

► Make sure you have the required product key information
On the back of the Windows XP CD-ROM packaging is a unique 25-character product key, such as KFEPC-12345-MHORY-12345-IROFE, that you need to enter during the Windows XP Setup Wizard installation to complete the process. Keep the product key in a safe place and do not share it with others. The unique product key allows you to activate and use Windows. Without the product key and activation, Windows XP will not work.

FIGURE AP-3: Microsoft Hardware Compatibility List Web site

Click button to check hardware compatibility

Your Web page might differ

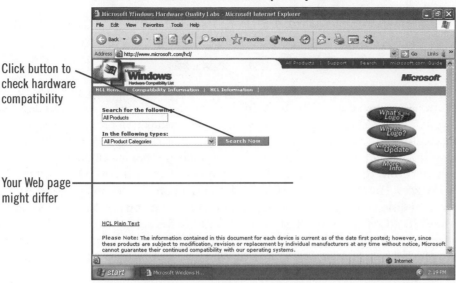

FIGURE AP-4: Selecting Windows XP installation type

Click list arrow to select installation type

Understanding activation and registration

When you install Windows XP, you are prompted to activate and register the product. Product activation and product registration are not the same. Product activation is required and ensures that each Windows product is not installed on more than the limited number of computers allowed in the software's end user license agreement. Activation is completely anonymous and requires no personal identification information to complete. To complete the activation process, you enter a unique 25-character product key, usually located on the back of the Windows XP CD-ROM packaging, during the Windows XP Setup Wizard installation process or when using the Activate Windows program located on the Start menu. You have a 30-day grace period in which to activate your Windows product installation. If the grace period expires, and you have not completed activation, all features will stop working except the product activation feature. In other words, you cannot perform any tasks on your computer, such as display the desktop, access any files on your hard disk, or send and retrieve e-mail. During the activation process, you can also register your copy of Windows XP. Product registration is not required, but completing the process, which includes providing contact information, ensures that you receive product update and support information from Microsoft.

Installing Windows XP

The Windows XP Setup Wizard guides you step-by-step through the process of installing Windows XP. When the installation is finished, you are ready to log on to Windows XP. Be aware that your computer restarts several times during the installation process. Depending on the type of installation you need to perform, either upgrade or clean, you start the Windows XP Setup Wizard in different ways. If you perform an upgrade or clean install on a Windows version, you simply start your computer and insert the Windows XP installation CD to start the Windows XP Setup Wizard. However, if you perform a clean install on a nonsupported operating system or a blank hard disk, you need to start your computer by inserting the Windows XP installation CD into the CD-ROM drive, which starts the Windows XP Setup Wizard. A clean install requires you to select additional options as you step through the wizard, but the steps are basically the same. The following procedure performs a Windows XP upgrade installation and is provided as a general guide; your installation steps might differ.

Steps

 If you do not wish to change your current setup, read this lesson without completing the steps. If you are in a lab, see your instructor or technical support person.

Trouble?

If Windows doesn't automatically detect the CD, click the Start button, click Run, in the Run dialog box click Browse, navigate to the CD-ROM drive, click Setup, click Open, then click OK.

1. Start your computer, then insert the **Windows XP CD** into your CD-ROM drive
If Windows automatically detects the Windows XP CD, the Welcome to Microsoft Windows XP setup screen opens, as shown in Figure AP-5.

2. Click **Install Windows XP**
The next setup screen asks you to select the type of installation.

3. Click the **Installation Type list arrow**, select an installation type, then click **Next**
The steps to upgrade are different than a new installation. In this example, you perform an upgrade. The next setup screen asks you to read and accept the **End User License Agreement** (EULA), a contract that gives you permission to use Windows XP and imposes certain restrictions, such as copying the software.

Trouble?

Your installation steps might differ.

4. Click the **I accept this agreement option button**, click **Next**, enter the 25-character product key as shown in Figure AP-6, then click **Next**
The next screen asks if you want to check system compatibility and get an upgrade report.

5. Click the **Show me hardware issues and a limited set of software issues (Recommended) option button**, click **Next** to display an upgrade report screen if issues arise, resolve any issues as directed, then click **Next** if necessary
The next setup screen appears, asking if you want to download the updated Setup files.

Trouble?

If there is a connection problem accessing the Setup files, click the option button to skip the process to get the updated setup file, then click Next.

6. Click the **Yes, download the updated Setup files (Recommended) option button**, click **Next**, select a network type, then click **Next** if necessary

7. When the Welcome to Microsoft Windows setup screen appears, click **Next** to activate Windows, click an activation option button, then click **Next**
When the activation process is complete, the Ready to register with Microsoft? screen appears.

8. Click a registration option button, click **Next**, then complete the registration, if necessary
When the registration process is complete, the User Accounts screen appears, where you can enter names for those who want to share the computer and personalize each user's settings.

9. Enter other user names to share the computer, click **Next**, assign account passwords and customize each user's desktop settings, click **Next**, then click **Finish**
The Welcome screen opens, where you can select a user account and password.

FIGURE AP-5: Welcome to Microsoft Windows XP setup screen

Click button to start the Windows XP Setup Wizard

Click buttons to perform other setup tasks; your options might differ

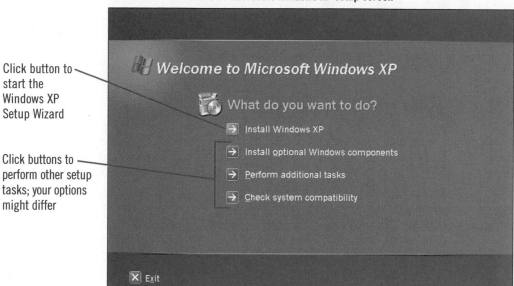

FIGURE AP-6: Product key setup screen

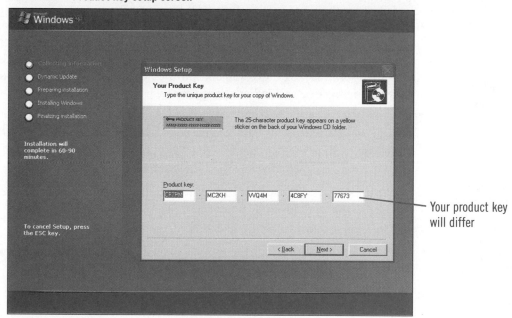

Your product key will differ

CLUES TO USE

Transferring files and settings from another computer

Instead of trying to re-create Windows settings manually from an old computer on a new Windows XP computer, you can use the Files and Settings Transfer Wizard. If you are connected to a computer over a network or a direct cable connection and want to transfer files and settings from that computer to your new Windows XP computer, you can use the Files and Settings Transfer Wizard to transfer settings for Windows, such as folder and taskbar options, desktop and display properties, and Internet Explorer browser and Outlook Express mail setup options, and files or entire folders, such as My Documents and Favorites. To start the Files and Settings Transfer Wizard, click the Start button on the taskbar, point to All Programs, point to Accessories, point to System Tools, then click Files and Settings Transfer Wizard. When the wizard dialog box opens, click Next, click the option button to identify this computer as new or old, click Next, then follow the instructions for the computer type selected.

App

Windows XP

Setting Up a Computer for Multiple Users

Windows XP allows you to share a computer at home or at the office without sacrificing privacy or control. You can use the User Accounts feature to store personalized settings for multiple users. Each person who uses a shared computer can customize the desktop, protect computer settings, and secure files, without affecting other users. You can set up a computer for multiple users by creating user accounts for each person. There are four types of user accounts: Computer Administrator, Standard, Limited, and Guest. The Computer Administrator account allows you to change all computer settings, such as install programs, make operating system changes, and create and modify user accounts. The Standard account, available only for users of Windows XP Professional in a network environment, allows you to install and uninstall programs and change your account picture and password. The Limited account allows you to change only your account picture and password. The Guest account allows nonregular users to access one account on your computer, so you don't have to create a new account every time you have a visitor. When you create more than one user account, a Welcome screen appears when you start Windows XP where you select the user account to open. Unless you protect a user account with a password, anyone can open it from the Welcome screen. A password helps you make sure your computer files stay private and secure. Once you create multiple accounts, you can use Fast User Switching when you choose the Log Off command on the Start menu to switch between users quickly, without having to close each other's programs each time you switch.

Steps

1. Click the **Start button** on the taskbar, click **Control Panel**, click **Switch to Classic View** if necessary, then double-click the **User Accounts icon** 🔧 in the Control Panel window
   The User Accounts window opens, as shown in Figure AP-7.

QuickTip

To change options for the Welcome screen or Fast User Switching, open User Accounts in the Control Panel, click Change the way users log on or off, select the options you want, then click Apply Options.

2. Under Pick a task, click **Create a new account**, type a name for the new account on the Name the new account page, then click **Next**
   The Pick an account type page opens.

3. Click the option button for the type of account you want, then click **Create Account**
   The new account appears in the User Accounts window.

4. Click the new user account you just created
   The Change account page opens, as shown in Figure AP-8.

5. Click **Create a Password**, type a new password, press **[Tab]**, type the new password again, press **[Tab]**, type a password hint, click **Create Password**, then click the **Close button** in the User Accounts window
   The new user account with a password is setup, and the User Accounts window closes.

QuickTip

To switch between users and still maintain open programs and settings quickly, click the Start button, click Log Off, then click Switch User.

6. Click the **Start button** on the taskbar, click **Log Off**, then click the **Log Off button** in the Log Off Windows dialog box
   Windows XP logs off, saves your settings, and displays the Welcome screen with the user accounts.

7. Click the Computer Administrator user account, type the password if necessary, then click the **Go button** 🢂 to display the desktop for the administrator

8. Click the **Start button** on the taskbar, click **Control Panel**, click **Switch to Classic View** if necessary, double-click 🔧, click the new user account you just created, click **Delete the account**, click **Delete Files**, click **Delete Account**, then click the **Close button** in all the open windows

FIGURE AP-7: User Accounts window

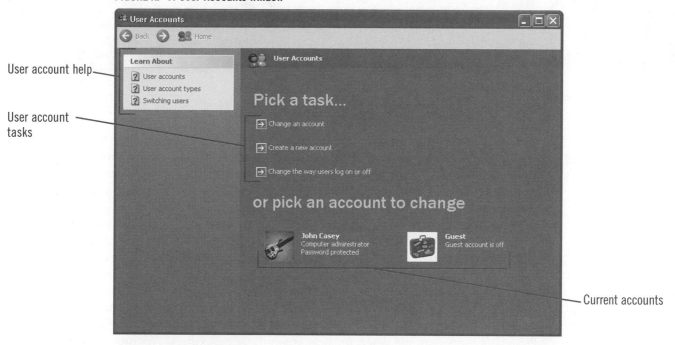

User account help

User account tasks

Current accounts

FIGURE AP-8: Changing a user account

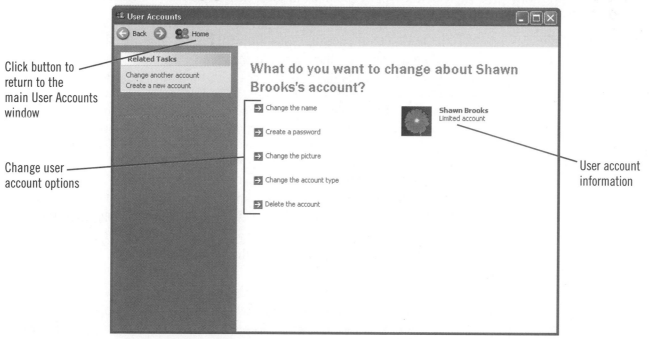

Click button to return to the main User Accounts window

Change user account options

User account information

Using the Guest account

The Guest account makes it easy for visitors to use a shared computer to create and print documents and graphics, check e-mail, and browse the Internet without making changes to other users' preferences and settings. The Guest account doesn't use a password and works like a Limited account. Before you can use the Guest account in Windows XP Professional, you need to activate it; the account is deactivated by default. To activate the Guest account, you need to log on as the computer administrator. In the User Accounts window, click the Guest account, then click Turn On the Guest Account. In Windows XP Home, the Guest account is active by default.

Managing Power Options on Portable Computers

You can change power options properties on your computer to reduce the power consumption of your entire system or of a specific device. For example, if you often leave your computer for a short time while working, you can set your computer to go into **standby**, a state in which your monitor and hard disks turn off after being idle for a set time. On standby, your entire computer switches to a low power state in which devices, such as the monitor and hard disks, turn off and your computer uses less power. When you bring the computer out of standby, your desktop appears exactly as you left it. Because standby does not save your desktop settings on disk, if a power failure occurs while your computer is on standby, you can lose unsaved information. If you are often away from your computer for an extended time or overnight but like to leave the computer on, you can set it to go into **hibernation**, a state in which your computer first saves everything in memory on your hard disk and then shuts down. When you restart the computer, your desktop appears exactly as you left it. Table AP-2 lists common tabs in the Power Options Properties dialog box and describes the power options each offers. This procedure modifies the power scheme for a portable or laptop computer to maximize battery life. However, you can perform these steps on any type of computer to conserve energy.

Steps

1. Click the **Start button** on the taskbar, click **Control Panel**, click **Switch to Classic View** if necessary, then double-click the **Power Options icon** 🔋 in the Control Panel window
   The Power Options Properties dialog box opens with the Power Schemes tab in front, as shown in Figure AP-9. A **power scheme** is a predefined collection of power usage settings. You can choose one of the power schemes included with Windows or modify one to suit your needs. The Power Options you see vary depending on your computer's hardware configuration. The Power Options feature automatically detects what is available on your computer and shows you only the options that you can control.

2. Click the **Power schemes list arrow**, then click **Portable/Laptop**
   Settings for the Portable/Laptop power scheme appear in the bottom section.

3. Click the **Turn off monitor list arrow**, click **After 1 min**, click **Apply**, then wait one minute without moving the mouse or pressing a key
   After a minute, the screen goes on standby and the screen is blank.

4. Move the mouse to restore the desktop
   The computer comes out of standby, and your desktop appears exactly as you left it.

5. Click the **Power schemes list arrow**, click **Always On**, then click **Apply**
   The Turn off monitor and Turn off hard disks options change to reflect power settings for this scheme. The power settings change to Never, the preset option.

6. Click the **Advanced tab**
   The Advanced tab appears, displaying settings to always display the Power Options icon on the taskbar and prompt for a password when your computer resumes from standby.

7. Click the **Always show icon on the taskbar check box** to select it, then click **OK**
   The Power Options icon appears in the notification area.

8. Double-click the **Power Options icon** 🔋 in the notification area (your icon might differ), then click the **Advanced tab** in the Power Options Properties dialog box

9. Click the **Always show icon on the taskbar check box** to deselect it, click **OK**, then click the **Close button** in the Control Panel window

FIGURE AP-9: Power Options Properties dialog box

Your tabs might differ

Click button to save customized power scheme

Click list arrow to change power schemes

Click list arrows to set monitor and hard disk power settings

Your tab might include additional options

TABLE AP-2: Common Power Options Properties tabs

tab	allows you to
Power Schemes	Change power settings for your monitor and hard disks
Advanced	Change user power options
Hibernate	Turn on and off hibernation; when the Hibernation option is turned on, you can select it when you shut down your computer
APM	Turn on or turn off Advanced Power Management (APM) support to reduce overall power consumption (available on most laptop and some desktop computers)
UPS	Select and configure an Uninterruptible Power Supply (UPS) device (available depending on the specific UPS hardware installed on your computer)
Alarms	Change settings for low battery notification alarms (available on most laptop computers)
Power Meter	Display power usage details for each battery in your computer (available on most laptop computers)

CLUES TO USE

Adding a secondary monitor to a portable computer

If you have a docked or undocked portable computer or desktop computer with two video ports on one video card, you can use DualView to add a secondary monitor and expand the size of your desktop. DualView is similar to the multiple monitor feature, but you cannot select the primary display, which is always the LCD display screen on a portable computer and the monitor attached to the first video out port on a desktop computer, and you don't need to purchase and install another video adapter on your computer. To install and use the secondary monitor using DualView, turn off your computer, plug the secondary monitor according to the manufacturer's instructions into the video out port on a portable computer or the second video out port on a desktop computer, turn on your computer (Windows detects the new hardware and installs necessary software), double-click the Display icon in the Control Panel, click the Settings tab, click the secondary monitor, click the Extend my Windows desktop onto this monitor check box to select it, then click OK.

Windows XP

Improving the Font Display on Portable Computers

If you have a portable computer or a flat screen monitor, you can improve the font display using ClearType. **ClearType** smoothes out the edges of fonts on the screen to look the same as fonts on the printed page. With ClearType, the letter "o" looks more like an oval, while without ClearType, the same letter "o" looks more like a square. ClearType is designed for flat screen monitors, so it might look slightly blurry on other computer monitors. If you are not using a flat screen monitor and still want to smooth out the edges of screen fonts, you can use the Standard option. When you use ClearType or Standard methods for smoothing screen fonts, you need to set the video card and monitor Color quality to at least 256 colors (8-bit). For better results, select a higher Color quality setting, such as High color (24-bit) or Highest color (32-bit).

Steps

1. Click the **Start button** on the taskbar, click **Control Panel**, click **Switch to Classic View** if necessary, then double-click the **Display icon** 🖥 in the Control Panel window
   The Display Properties dialog box opens.

2. Click the **Settings tab**
   Settings for screen resolution and color quality appear.

3. Click the **Color quality list arrow**, then click your highest color setting, which must be a color quality setting of at least 256 colors

4. Click the **Appearance tab**, then click **Effects**
   The Effects dialog box opens.

5. Click the **Use the following method to smooth edges of screen fonts check box** to select it
   A list box below the check box is activated.

6. Click the **list arrow** below the check box, then click **ClearType**
   The ClearType feature is selected, as shown in Figure AP-10.

7. Click **OK** to close the Effects dialog box

8. Click **OK** to apply the display property changes
   The screen fonts appear with smooth edges using ClearType, as shown in Figure AP-11.

9. Click the **Close button** in the Control Panel window
   The screen fonts appear with smooth edges using ClearType.

FIGURE AP-10: Effects dialog box with ClearType option selected

ClearType option selected

Dialog box text without ClearType screen fonts

FIGURE AP-11: Control Panel window using ClearType screen fonts

Smooth edges on the screen font using ClearType

CLUES TO USE

Changing Windows visual effects

Windows XP adds visual effects, such as a transition or shadow, to menus, windows, and other screen items by default to enhance the way they appear on the screen. For example, some of the visual effects include adding a transition effect, such as Fade or Scroll, when displaying menus and ScreenTips, showing shadows under menus or the mouse pointer, animating windows when minimizing and maximizing, or showing a translucent selection rectangle while you drag to select files and folders. If a visual effect doesn't appeal to you or slows your computer down, you can change or turn off the effect. You can change some visual effect options using Display Properties and others using System Properties in the Control Panel. To change

visual effects in Display Properties, double-click the Display icon in the Control Panel, click the Appearance tab, click Effects to display the Effects dialog box, select or deselect the options you want to turn on or off, then click OK twice. To change visual effects in System Properties, double-click the System icon in the Control Panel, click the Advanced tab, click Settings in the Performance area, click the Visual Effects tab, click the Custom option button, select or deselect the options you want to turn on or off, then click OK. Some visual effects options appear in both Display Properties and System Properties with slightly different names; you can change the common options in either place.

Windows XP

Creating a Home or Office Network

If you have several computers in your home or a small business, the Network Setup Wizard can help you connect them together to create a network, even if they don't all use Windows XP. In addition to Windows XP Home and Professional computers, the Network Setup Wizard also supports computers using Windows 98 and Windows Millennium (Me). You can set up the physical layout of your home or office network in several ways, such as using existing phone lines and cables in a home phoneline network; using a network hub and cables as shown in Figure AP-12; or with wireless technology in a peer-to-peer network, as shown in Figure AP-13. Before you can use the Network Setup Wizard to set up a Windows XP home or office network, you need to install necessary hardware such as network cards and a network hub and cables according to the manufacturer's documentation. You also need to turn on all computers, printers, and external devices, and establish a connection to the Internet if you want to share the single Internet connection with all the computers on the network.

Steps

Trouble?

If you are not logged on with a computer administrator account, the Network Wizard cannot set up a network. You need to log off your computer and log on again with a computer administrator account.

1. Click the **Start button** on the taskbar, point to **All Programs**, point to **Accessories**, point to **Communications**, then click **Network Setup Wizard**
   The Network Setup Wizard dialog box opens, displaying a welcome message.

2. Click **Next**, read the Before you continue message, make sure your hardware is installed and turned on, then click **Next**
   The next dialog box asks how your computer connects to the Internet and other computers.

3. Click the appropriate connection method option button, or if your connection method is not listed, click the **Other** option button, click **Next**, then click a connection method option button
   See Figure AP-14 to view the available connection methods in the two Network Setup Wizard dialog boxes. If you are not sure which network option to choose, you can click the View an example link below a connection option to see a picture of the network type.

Trouble?

If a network configuration is not recommended warning appears, click Next to enable the Internet Connection Firewall and continue.

4. Click **Next** to continue
   The next dialog box asks you to select your Internet connection. The following dialog box will ask you to give your computer a description and name. The name is a unique network identifier for the computer. The computer name is uppercase, is limited to 15 characters, and cannot contain spaces or any of the following special characters: ; : , " < > * + = \ | ?.

5. Click your connection, click **Next**, enter a description and name, then click **Next**
   The next dialog box asks you to give your workgroup network a name.

6. Enter a workgroup name, then click **Next** to continue
   The next dialog box asks you to review your network settings before you apply them.

7. Click **Next** to configure this computer for the network
   After the configuration is complete, the next dialog box asks you to select an option to help you run the Network Setup Wizard once on each computer you want connected. You can create a Network Setup Disk or use the Windows XP installation CD to install Windows XP networking support on Windows 98 and Windows Millennium (Me) computers.

8. Click an option, click **Next** to display the final dialog box or instructions based on the previous option, click **Next** if necessary, click **Finish**, then click **Yes** if necessary to restart your computer with the network
   After your computer restarts, you can open My Network Places, then click View workgroup computers in the Task pane to view the network.

FIGURE AP-12: Network using a network hub and cables

FIGURE AP-13:Network using wireless technology

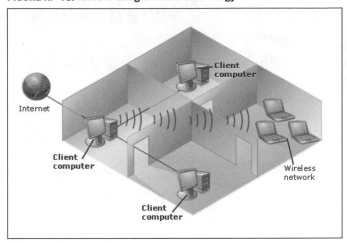

FIGURE AP-14: Network Setup Wizard connection types

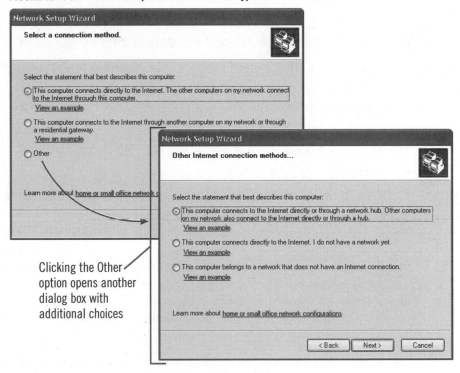

Clicking the Other option opens another dialog box with additional choices

Setting up the hardware for a home or office network

You can set up the hardware for your home or office network in several ways, such as a home phoneline network or peer-to-peer network using a network hub or wireless technology. Your network setup depends on the location of your computers and on the current hardware you have on your computer. If you want to connect computers together that are located in several different rooms, the best solution is to install a home phoneline network (HPN), which uses existing phone lines and telephone jacks and cable without a network hub and special cables stretched from room to room. If you set up an HPN, you need to install Home

Phoneline Network Adapter (HPNA) cards on each computer. If you want to connect computers that are located in different rooms near each other, the best solution is to install a peer-to peer network using a wireless network hub and wireless network interface cards installed in each computer. If you want to connect computers together that are located in the same room, the best solution is to install a peer-to-peer network using a network hub, a network cable such as category 5, and a network interface card (NIC) installed in each computer.

Windows XP

Setting Up to Use a Remote Computer

With Remote Desktop, available only with Windows XP Professional, you can connect to a computer at a remote location and have access to all of the programs, files, printers, and networked computers as if you are directly working on the remote computer. The Remote Desktop makes it easy to work at home with complete access to the office or to collaborate with co-workers at different locations on the same computer. For example, you can connect to your work computer and update a report or check mail from your computer at home as if you were still at the office. Before you can use the Remote Desktop, you need to set up a computer running Windows XP Professional, known as the **remote computer**, with a connection to a network or the Internet, and a second computer, known as the **home computer**, with the Remote Desktop Connection software installed and access to the remote computer using a network connection, modem, or Virtual Private Network (VPN).

Steps

If you are working on Windows XP Home, you will not be able to work through the steps in this topic. Read this lesson without completing the steps.

Trouble?

If you are not logged on as a computer administrator, the Network Wizard won't work. Log off and log on again with a Computer Administrator account.

1. Click the **Start button** on the taskbar, click **Control Panel**, click **Switch to Classic View** if necessary, then double-click the **System icon** 🖥️
The System Properties dialog box opens.

2. Click the **Remote tab**
The Remote tab allows you to determine how this computer can be used from remote locations.

Trouble?

If a warning message box opens telling you that some local user accounts might not have passwords, click OK, then add passwords with User Accounts in the Control Panel before the next lesson.

3. Click the **Allow users to connect remotely to this computer check box** to select it if necessary, then write down the name of the computer
The System Properties dialog box appears as shown in Figure AP-15. If you want to connect to a remote computer over a LAN, the computer name or IP address will work, but if you want to connect to a remote computer over the Internet, you need your computer's IP address, which is assigned to the network adapter card that connects to your network. To find out your IP address, open My Network Places, click View network connections in the task pane, select your network adapter icon, then view the Details section in the task pane.

4. Click **Select Remote Users**
The Remote Desktop Users dialog box appears, as shown in Figure AP-16.

5. If your remote user is not listed, click **Add** to open the Select Users dialog box, type a user name in the Enter the object names to select text box, or click **Advanced**, search for and select a name, then click **OK**

6. Click **OK** to close the Select Users dialog box if necessary
The Remote Desktop Users dialog box appears with the remote user's name.

7. Click **OK** to close the Remote Desktop Users dialog box, then click **OK** to close the System Properties dialog box
The Control Panel appears.

Trouble?

For information on setting up the home computer to use Remote Desktop, see the Clues in this lesson.

8. Click the **Close button** on the Control Panel window
You have completed the set up for the remote computer; make sure you leave it running. Now it's time to set up the home computer to use Remote Desktop.

FIGURE AP-15: System Properties dialog box with Remote tab

Computer name

Click link to
get help

Only available in
Professional Edition

FIGURE AP-16: Remote Desktop Users dialog box

Click button to add
more users

Current list of
remote users
allowed to connect
to this computer;
your list will differ

Setting up the home computer to use Remote Desktop

Before you can access a remote computer from a home computer, you need to install the Remote Desktop Connection software on the home computer. The home computer doesn't have to be running Windows XP Professional; it can have Windows 95, Windows 98, Windows Me, Windows NT 4, Windows 2000, or Windows XP Home. However, you do need the Windows XP Professional installation CD to install the Remote Desktop Connection software on the home computer. The software installation process doesn't change your operating system version, it only installs the remote connection software. To install the Remote Desktop Connection software on the home computer, insert the Windows XP Professional installation CD into your CD-ROM drive, click Perform additional tasks on the Welcome screen, then click Set up Remote Desktop Connection. When the InstallShield Wizard for Remote Desktop Connection dialog box opens, click Next, click the I accept the terms in the license agreement option button, click Next, enter your User Name and Organization name if necessary, click Next, click Install, then click Finish. After the installation is complete, click Exit to close the Welcome screen.

Windows XP

Connecting to a Remote Computer

After you set up the remote and home computers to use Remote Desktop, you are ready to connect to the remote computer from the home computer. When you connect to a remote computer from a home computer, Remote Desktop locks the remote computer so no one can use it. The home computer gains complete control of the remote computer as if you were working directly in front of it. At the top of the home computer screen is a yellow bar with the remote computer name in the middle called the **Remote Desktop Connection title bar**. The title bar also contains buttons on the right to minimize, restore down, and disconnect, and a toggle button on the left to pin or unpin the title bar to stay on top of any open windows. The next time you want to use the remote computer after using Remote Desktop, you need to sign in at the Welcome screen or press [Ctrl][Alt][Delete] to unlock it.

STOP **Before you can connect to a remote computer, you need to set up the remote computer with Windows XP Professional to allow other computers to connect to it and set up the home computer with the Remote Desktop Connection software for supported Windows operating system other than Windows XP. See the previous lesson for details.**

1. On the home computer, click the **Start button** on the taskbar, point to **All Programs** or **Programs**, point to **Accessories**, point to **Communications**, then click **Remote Desktop Connection**

   The Remote Desktop Connection dialog box opens.

2. Click **Options**

   The Remote Desktop Connection dialog box expands to display additional connection options, as shown in Figure AP-17. See Table AP-3 for a description of each tab in the Remote Desktop Connection dialog box.

Trouble?

If you don't know the remote computer's name, you can click the Computer list arrow, then click a recently used computer name or click <Browse for more...>.

3. In the Computer text box, type the computer name (or IP address if needed) of the remote computer to which you want to connect, then press **[Tab]**

   Now you need to enter the username and password, and domain name if necessary, to log on to the remote computer in the same way you log on to a network computer.

4. Type the user name in the User name text box, press **[Tab]**, type your password in the Password text box, press **[Tab]**, then type the network domain name in the Domain text box, if necessary

Trouble?

If the Log On to Windows dialog box opens, type your user name, password, and domain if necessary, then click OK.

5. Click **Connect**

   The desktop for the remote computer appears on your screen.

6. Click the **Start button** on the taskbar

   The Start menu for the remote computer appears on your screen, as shown in Figure AP-18.

7. Click **Disconnect** on the Start menu

   The Disconnect Windows dialog box opens.

8. Click **Disconnect**

   The Remote Desktop Connection is disconnected.

FIGURE AP-17: Remote Desktop Connection dialog box

Click tabs to set additional remote connection options

Type remote desktop connection information here

Click button to save connection settings for another computer

FIGURE AP-18: Remote computer desktop

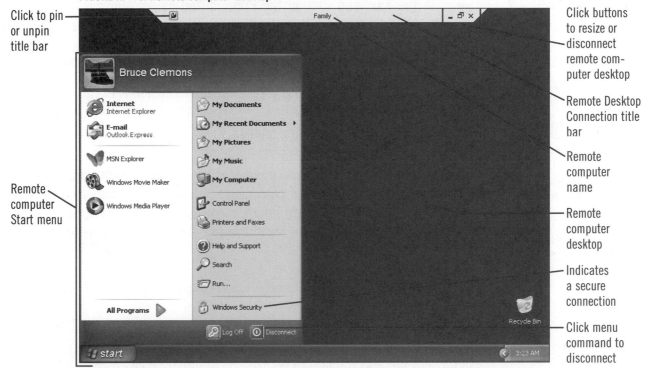

Click to pin or unpin title bar

Remote computer Start menu

Click buttons to resize or disconnect remote computer desktop

Remote Desktop Connection title bar

Remote computer name

Remote computer desktop

Indicates a secure connection

Click menu command to disconnect

TABLE AP-3: Remote Desktop Connection dialog box tabs

tab	allows you to
General	Specify logon settings and save connection information for future use
Display	Change the remote desktop size and screen resolution
Local Resources	Set a remote computer sound, change keyboard options, and connect to disk drives and printers
Programs	Automatically start programs on the remote computer upon connecting through Remote Desktop
Experience	Optimize performance and set user interface options

App

Windows XP

Sending and Receiving a Fax

Windows XP provides you with the capability to send and receive faxes with a fax device connected to your computer or with a remote fax device located on a network. You can customize fax send and receive settings with the Fax Configuration Wizard, create and modify a fax cover with the Fax Cover Page Editor program, send standard faxes using the Send Fax Wizard, track and monitor fax activity, and manage previously sent or received faxes with the Fax Console program. Before you can use Windows XP fax services, you need to make sure the component and a modem are installed on your computer. For Windows XP Professional, the component is installed by default; for Windows XP Home, you need to install the Fax Services component in the Printers and Faxes window using Set up faxing in the task pane or in Add/Remove Windows Components using the Add or Remove Programs utility in the Control Panel.

Steps

Trouble?

If you are not logged on with a Computer Administrator account, you cannot install a local fax printer. You need to log off your computer and log on again with a Computer Administrator account. If the Fax icon is available, continue with Step 2.

QuickTip

You can also click Send a fax in the task pane of the Printers and Faxes window or click the Start button, point to All Programs, point to Accessories, point to System Tools, point to Fax, then click Send a Fax.

QuickTip

To create and edit fax cover pages, click Tools on the menu bar, click Personal Cover Pages, click New to create a page or double-click the page you want to edit, then make and save changes in the Fax Cover Page Editor.

1. Click the **Start button** on the taskbar, click **Printers and Faxes**, then click **Install a local fax printer** in the task pane if available or click Set up faxing in the task pane and insert the Windows XP Home installation CD if necessary
   The Printers and Faxes window opens, displaying a fax printer and other available printers.

2. Double-click the **Fax icon** 📠 in the Printers and Faxes window, then if the Fax Configuration Wizard starts, follow the dialog box steps, entering the sender information as appropriate
   The Fax Console window, shown in Figure AP-19, works like the Outlook Express window, with Local Folders in the left pane and fax messages in the right pane. You can use the Fax Console toolbar to send and receive faxes; view faxes in the Windows Picture and Fax Viewer window; print, save, and delete faxes; and view fax details and sender information.

3. Click the **New Fax button** 📄 on the toolbar
   The Send Fax Wizard dialog box opens.

4. Click **Next**, then enter the name and number of the person to whom you want to send a fax, as shown in Figure AP-20 or click **Address Book**, select one or more contacts, then click **OK** to select fax recipient information from the Address Book
   When you use the Address Book, the fax number for the contact name is added to the fax recipient list. The contacts in the Address Book are the same as in Outlook Express.

5. Click **Next** to continue
   The next dialog box asks you to select a cover page template and type a subject line and any notes you want to include with the fax.

6. Click the **Cover page template list arrow**, click **urgent**, type the subject of the fax in the Subject line text box, press **[Tab]**, type any notes as shown in Figure AP-21, then click **Next**
   The next dialog box asks you to set a priority and to specify when to send the fax.

7. Click the **Now option button**, click the **High option button**, then click **Next**
   The next dialog box asks you to review fax settings, preview the fax page, and send the fax.

8. Click **Preview Fax** to view the fax page, click the **Close button** in the Windows Picture and Fax Viewer window, then click **Finish** in the Send Fax Wizard dialog box
   The Fax Console window appears and sends the fax. A copy of the fax is placed in the Sent Items folder as a backup.

9. Click the **Sent Items folder** in the left pane to view details about the fax, then click the **Close button** on the Fax Console window and on the Printers and Faxes window

FIGURE AP-19: **Fax Console window**

Toolbar

Fax storage folders

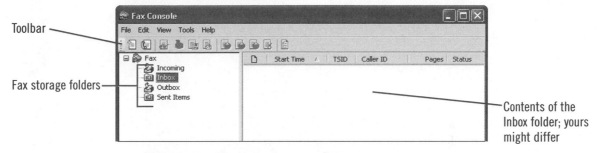

Contents of the
Inbox folder; yours
might differ

FIGURE AP-20: **Entering recipient information**

Recipient information

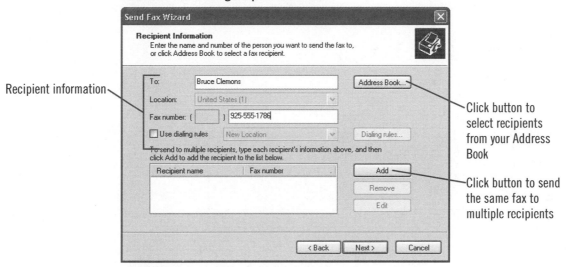

Click button to
select recipients
from your Address
Book

Click button to send
the same fax to
multiple recipients

FIGURE AP-21: **Preparing the cover page**

Fax message
information

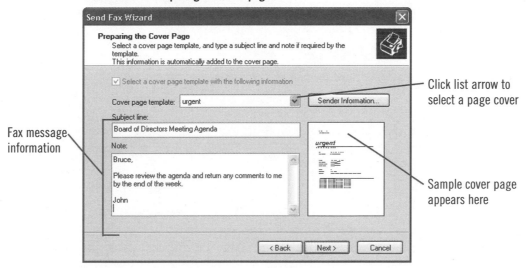

Click list arrow to
select a page cover

Sample cover page
appears here

Receiving a fax

Once your fax printer is configured, you can receive faxes automatically or manually on your computer. To configure a fax, click Tools on the Fax Console menu bar, click Configure Fax, then follow the Fax Configuration Wizard instructions to enable and set options to receive faxes. In automatic receive mode, you automatically receive a fax after a certain number of rings. In manual receive mode, click File on the Fax Console menu bar, then click Receive a fax now when the phone rings. When you receive a fax, it's stored in the Inbox archive of the Fax Console program, where you can open it.

Project Files List

Read the following information carefully!!

1. **Find out from your instructor the location of the Project Files you need and the location where you will store your files.**

   - To complete many of the units in this book, you need to use Project Files. Your instructor will either provide you with a copy of the Project Files or ask you to make your own copy.

   - If you need to make a copy of the Project Files, you will need to copy a set of files from a file server, standalone computer, or the Web to the drive and location where you will be storing your Project Files.

   - Your instructor will tell you which computer, drive letter, and folders contain the files you need, and where you will store your files.

   - You can also download the files by going to www.course.com. See the inside back cover of the book for instructions to download your files.

2. **Copy and organize your Project Files.**

   ### Floppy disk users

   - If you are using floppy disks to store your Project Files, this list shows which files you'll need to copy onto your disk(s).

   - Unless noted in the Project Files list, you will need one formatted, high-density disk for each unit. For each unit you are assigned, copy the files listed in the **Project File Supplied column** onto one disk.

   - If you complete all the exercises in some units, you might need to organize the files onto more than one floppy disk. These units are indicated by an asterisk in the Project Files List.

   - Make sure you label each disk clearly with the unit name (e.g., Windows XP Unit A).

   - When working through the unit, save all your files to this disk.

   ### Users storing files in other locations

   - If you are using a zip drive, network folder, hard drive, or other storage device, use the Project Files List to organize your files.

   - Create a subfolder for each unit in the location where you are storing your files, and name it according to the unit title (e.g., Windows XP Unit A).

   - For each unit you are assigned, copy the files listed in the **Project File Supplied column** into that unit's folder.

   - Store the files you modify or create in each unit in the unit folder.

3. **Find and keep track of your Project Files and completed files.**

   - Use the **Project File Supplied column** to make sure you have the files you need before starting the unit or exercise indicated in the **Unit and Location column**.

   - Use the **Student Saves File As column** to find out the filename you use when saving your changes to a Project File provided.

   - Use the **Student Creates File column** to find out the filename you use when saving your new file for the exercise.

Unit and Location	Project File Supplied	Student Saves File As	Student Creates File
Windows XP Unit A	No Files		
Windows XP Unit B*			
Lessons	Win B-1.rtf	Coffee Menu.rtf	
	Win B-2.bmp	Wired Coffee Logo.bmp	
	Coffee Cup.mpeg		
	AM Coffee.wav		
		Coffee Meltdown.wmv	
		Coffee Meltdown.mswmm	
Skills Review	Win B-3.rtf	Choose Coffee.rtf	
	Win B-2.bmp	Wired Coffee Logo 2.bmp	
	Better Coffee.wav		
	Coffee Cup.mpeg		
		Coffee Time.wmv	
		Coffee Time.mswmm	
Independent Challenge 1			Bestsellers List.rtf
Independent Challenge 2	Invitation Map.bmp	Invitation.rtf	
Independent Challenge 3			Stationery.rtf
			Stationery Logo.bmp
Visual Workshop	Win B-2.bmp	A Cup of Coffee.bmp	Good Time Coffee Club.rtf

*Because the files created in this unit may be large, you might need to organize the files onto two floppy disks if you are using floppies and completing all the exercises. Save the Project Files you need for each exercise you are completing on another disk, and label each disk clearly (e.g., Windows XP Unit B Skills Review).

Unit and Location	Project File Supplied	Student Saves File As	Student Creates File
Windows XP Unit C**			
Lessons	Wired Coffee folder	Wired Coffee folder	
Skills Review			
Independent Challenge 1			World Wide Books folder
			New Store Locations.rtf
			Employee App.rtf
			Employee D Quan.rtf
			Employee L Andersen.rtf
			Employee S Luoma.rtf
			Employee W Blair.rtf
Independent Challenge 2			Apex Cartons folder
			Suppliers Bid.rtf
			Manufacturing Bids.rtf
Independent Challenge 3			MO PC folder
			Customer Letter.rtf
			Business Plan.rtf

Unit and Location	Project File Supplied	Student Saves File As	Student Creates File
			MO Logo.bmp
			Shortcut to MO Logo.bmp
Independent Challenge 4			Sunrise Bakeries folder
			French Bread.rtf
			Torte.rtf
			7-Layer Chocolate.rtf
			Sweet Bread.rtf
			Shortcut to Torte.rtf

**Because the unit uses folders that contain several levels of folders with files, only the top-level folder and new files are listed.

Windows XP Unit D**			
Lessons	Wired Coffee folder	Wired Coffee folder	
Skills Review	Wired Coffee folder	Wired Coffee folder	Disk Info.rtf
Independent Challenge 1			Sewing Works folder
			Wilson Letter.rtf
			Suppliers.rtf
			Bills.rtf
Independent Challenge 2			Day Camp folder
			Camper Data.rtf
			Activities Overview.rtf
Independent Challenge 3			Summer Program folder
			2 Weeks Art.rtf
			4 Weeks Art.rtf
Independent Challenge 4			Lines folder
			Shapes folder
			Ovals.bmp
			Lines.bmp
			Curves.bmp
			Clip Art.zip

**Because the unit uses folders that contain several levels of folders with files, only the top-level folder and new files are listed.

Windows XP Unit E			
Independent Challenge 4			Company Picnic Memo.rtf
Windows XP Unit F			
Independent Challenge 1	2003 Expense Budget.rtf		
	2003 Income Projections.rtf		
Independent Challenge 3			Win Tools Training.rtf
Windows XP Unit G	No files		
Windows XP Unit H	No files		

Unit and Location	Project File Supplied	Student Saves File As	Student Creates File
Windows XP Unit I			
Lessons	JohnCasey.cer		
Skills Review	JoeJackson.cer		
Independent Challenge 2	JoeJackson.cer		
Independent Challenge 3			Point FS.txt
Windows XP Unit J**			
Lessons	Wired Coffee folder		
Skills Review	Wired Coffee folder		
Independent Challenge 2			Memos folder
			Cabral Raise.rtf
			Thielen Raise.rtf

** Because the unit uses folders that contain several levels of folders with files, only the top-level folder and new files are listed.

Unit and Location	Project File Supplied	Student Saves File As	Student Creates File
Windows XP Unit K*			
Lessons	Win K-1.rtf	Sales Promotion.rtf	
	Wired Coffee Logo.bmp		
	Win K-2.rtf	Global Coffee.rtf	
	Globe.avi		
	Coffee Cup.bmp	Coffee Cup Image.bmp	
	Win K-3.rtf	Roasting Flier.rtf	
Skills Review	Win K-4.rtf	Company Memo.rtf	
	Wired Coffee Logo.bmp		
	Globe.avi		
	Win K-5.bmp	Holiday Sale.rtf	
	Burst Sign.bmp	Burst Sign Image.bmp	
Independent Challenge 1	Win K-6.bmp	Sales Logo.bmp	
			Stamp By Me.rtf
Independent Challenge 2	Win K-7.bmp	Menu Sign.bmp	
			Hiezer Menu.rtf
Independent Challenge 3	Win K-8.bmp	Classified Collectibles Logo.bmp	
			Olympic Letter.rtf
Independent Challenge 4	Win K-9.bmp	GGRI Logo.bmp	
			LA Graffiti.rtf
Visual Workshop			Accident Report.rtf

*Because the files created in this unit may be large, you might need to organize the files onto two or more floppy disks, if you are using floppies to store your completed floppies and are completing all the exercises. Save the Project Files you need for each exercise you are completing on another disk, and label each disk clearly (e.g. Windows XP Unit B Skills Review).

Unit and Location	Project File Supplied	Student Saves File As	Student Creates File
Windows XP Unit L			
Lessons	Family Pictures folder		

Unit and Location	Project File Supplied	Student Saves File As	Student Creates File
	Family Pictures 001.jpg		
	Family Pictures 002.jpg		
	Family Pictures 003.tif		
Windows XP Unit M*			
Lessons	MM M-1.mswmm		
	MM M-2.avi		
	MM M-3.avi		
	MM M-4.avi		
	MM M-5.avi		
	MM M-6.wma		
	MM M-14.wma		
	MM M-15.wma		
	MM M-16.wma		
		Planets.mswmm	
		Space Movie.wmv	
Skills Review	MM M-7.mswmm		
	MM M-8.jpg		
	MM M-9.jpg		
	MM M-10.jpg		
	MM M-11.jpg		
	MM M-12.wma		
	MM M-13.wma		
		Wyoming.mswmm	
		Wyoming.wmv	
Independent Challenge 1	MM M-2.avi		
	MM M-3.avi		
	MM M-4.avi		
	MM M-5.avi		
			NASA.mswmm
			Education.wmv
Independent Challenge 2	Windows Movie Maker Sample File.wmv		
		Wee Folks.mswmm	
		Wee Folks Sample.wmv	
	Play1.wma		
	Play2.wma		
Independent Challenge 3	MM M-8.jpg		
	MM M-9.jpg		

Unit and Location	Project File Supplied	Student Saves File As	Student Creates File
	MM M-10.jpg		
	MM M-11.jpg		
	MM M-13.wma		
			Reunion.mswmm
			Family Reunion.wmv
Independent Challenge 4			Blythe.mswmm
			Blythe Sample.wmv
Visual Workshop			Odyssey.mswmm
			Space Odyssey.wmv

*Because the files created in this unit may be large, you might need to organize the files onto two or more floppy disks, if you are using floppies to store your completed floppies and are completing all the exercises. Save the Project Files you need for each exercise you are completing on another disk, and label each disk clearly (e.g. Windows XP Unit B Skills Review).

Unit and Location	Project File Supplied	Student Saves File As	Student Creates File
Windows XP Unit N			
Lessons	Burst Sign.bmp		
	Coffee Roast.bmp		
Skills Review	Burst Sign.bmp		
	Coffee Roast.bmp		
Independent Challenge 2			June Donor.rtf
			June State.rtf
Windows XP Unit O			
Lessons	Win O-1.rtf		
Skills Review	Win O-2.rtf		
	Win O-3.rtf		
	Win O-4.rtf		
	Win O-5.rtf		
	Wired Coffee Logo.bmp		
Independent Challenge 1			Backup Strategy.rtf
Windows XP Unit P			
Lessons			System.evt
Skills Review			Application.evt
Independent Challenge 3			Latest System.evt

Windows XP

Glossary

Accessories Built-in programs that come with Windows.

Activation A process that is required by Microsoft and ensures that each Windows product is not installed on more than the limited number of computers allowed in the software's end user license agreement (EULA).

Active Refers to the window you are currently using.

Active desktop The screen that appears when you first start Windows, providing access to your computer's programs and files and to the Internet.

Active program The program that is open. The title bar changes from light blue to a darker blue.

Address bar Displays the address of the current Web page or the contents of a local or network computer drive.

Address Book Used to store mailing addresses, phone numbers, e-mail addresses, or Web sites, along with a contact's title, street address, phone number, and personal Web page addresses.

Alert A warning that is generated automatically when a counter value exceeds or falls short of a threshold value you have specified. *See also* Counter.

Allocation unit *See* Cluster.

Annotation tools A set of buttons that allow you to draw lines and shapes, highlight areas, add text or an attached note, change annotation properties, and switch between pages in a fax.

Antivirus software A program that examines the files stored on a disk to determine whether they are infected with a virus, then destroys or disinfects them.

Applications *See* **programs.**

Archive The process of saving a copy of the logs produced by the Event Viewer.

Archive attribute A Windows marker indicating whether or not a file needs to be backed up.

Argument A part of the command syntax that gives DOS more information about what you want it to do.

Articles Another name for newsgroup messages.

Audio bar A Movie Maker work area that contains audio clips for the sound track.

Audit The ability to monitor the success or failure of security related events, such as account logon and logoff activities, user account changes, and program launches.

AutoComplete A feature that suggests possible matches with previous filename entries.

Auto-hide A feature that helps you automatically hide the taskbar.

Back up To save files to another location in case you have computer trouble and lose files.

Background The primary surface on which icons and windows appear; you can customize its appearance using the Display Properties dialog box.

Background printing *See* Spooling.

Background process The processing time that programs, such as printing or disk backup, require while you run a foreground process. *See also* Foreground process.

Backup A Windows XP program for backing up files.

Backup job *See* Backup set.

Backup medium Floppy disks, zip disks, or tape cartridges used to store computer data.

Backup set A file that Backup creates when you perform a back up. Also known as a Backup job.

Backup strategy The process in which you select a backup method by evaluating tradeoffs among safety, time, and media space.

Bad sector A portion of a disk that cannot be used because it is flawed.

Banner *See* Separator page.

Baseline chart A chart that system administrators create when the computer or network is running at a normal level, in order to compare with other charts.

Binary data Internal computer software programming code that experienced computer technicians can evaluate to better interpret the event.

Bitmapped characters Fonts that are created with small dots organized to form a letter.

Blind carbon copy (Bcc) An e-mail option to send a copy of your e-mail message to another person whose name will not appear in the e-mail message.

Bridge A hardware device that connects two LANs or two sections of the same LAN together.

Briefcase A built-in accessory that synchronizes files between two different computers.

Broadband High speed connections to the Internet that are continually turned on and connected.

Buddies A list of contacts with whom you interact regularly, transfer files, and share programs and whiteboard drawings.

Buffer A temporary memory storage area that transmits streaming media to play continuously.

Bullet mark An indicator that shows that an option is enabled, in a dialog box or menu for instance. *See also* Enable.

Burn *See* Write.

Burn in When the same display remains on the screen for extended periods of time and becomes part of the screen; this can be avoided by enabling a screen saver.

Byte A unit of storage capable of holding a single character or pixel.

Cable modems Cable television lines that provide a completely digital path from one computer to another.

Carbon copy (Cc) An e-mail option to send a copy of your e-mail message.

Cascading menu A list of commands from a menu item with an arrow next to it. Pointing to the arrow displays a submenu from which you can choose additional commands.

Case sensitive When a program makes a distinction between uppercase and lowercase letters.

Catalog An index of the backed up files that is built and stored on the backup medium.

CD or CD-ROM *See* Compact Disc-Read-Only Memory.

CD-R *See* Compact Disc-Recordable.

CD-RW *See* Compact Disc-Rewritable.

Center A paragraph alignment in which the lines of text are centered between the left and right margins.

Certificate A statement verifying the identity of a person or the security of a Web site.

Check Disk A program that comes with Windows and helps you find and repair damaged sections of a disk.

Check mark An indicator that shows a feature is enabled, in a dialog box or menu for instance. *See also* Enable.

Classic style Refers to the Windows user interface setting where you double-click icons to open them. *See also* Windows Classic.

Clean install To perform an entirely new installation.

ClearType A feature that smoothes out the edges of fonts on portable computers or flat screen monitors to look the same as fonts on the printed page.

Clicking The act of pressing a mouse button once and releasing it.

Client *See* Workstation.

Client (component) A network component that allows you to access computers and files on the network.

Client/server networking A networking configuration that enables one or more computers (the clients) to link to a central computer (the server) for accessing shared files and resources, such as a printer.

Clip A video or audio segment.

Clipboard A temporary storage space on a hard drive that contains information that has been cut or copied.

Cluster A group of sectors on a disk. Also known as an Allocation unit.

Collection A folder to store and organize media clips in Movie Maker. *See also* Windows Movie Maker.

Collections area The area in Movie Maker that displays the contents of a collection folder.

Collections pane An area in Movie Maker where you view a hierarchy of collection folders.

Command A directive that provides access to a program's features.

Command prompt The place where you type DOS commands to run different tasks.

Command syntax A strict set of rules that you must follow when entering a DOS command.

Command-line interface An interface in which you perform operations by typing commands at a command prompt.

Compact Disc (CD) *See* Compact Disc-Read-Only Memory.

Compact Disc-Read-Only Memory (CD-ROM) An optical disk on which you can stamp, or burn, up to 1 GB (typical size is 700 MB) of data in only one session (where the disc cannot be erased or burned again with additional new data).

Compact Disc-Recordable (CD-R) A type of CD-ROM on which you can burn up to 1 GB of data in multiple sessions (where the disc can be burned again with additional new data, but cannot be erased).

Compact Disc-Rewritable (CD-RW) A type of CD-ROM on which you can read, write, and erase data, just like a floppy or hard disk.

Complex password A security feature to access important areas on a computer that contains characters from at least three of the four following categories: uppercase (A through Z), lowercase (a through z), numbers (0 through 9), and nonalphanumeric (!, $, *, etc.).

Compressing Storing data in a format that requires less space than usual.

Computer Management A Windows utility that provides easy access to a specific computer's administrative tools.

Computer virus A program that attaches itself to a file, reproduces itself, and spreads to other files, usually meant to cause harm to the infected computers.

Console A Command Prompt option that enables you to change the appearance of the Command Prompt window.

Console tree The hierarchy of tools in the left pane of the Computer Management window.

Contact A person or company with whom you communicate.

Contact groups A group of contacts that you can organize together.

Container An item on the console tree to which you add objects. *See also* Console tree.

Contiguous Adjacent location on a disk.

Control Panel A central location for changing Windows settings. A window containing various programs that allow you to specify how your computer looks and performs.

Conversation thread Consists of the original message on a particular topic along with any responses that include the original message.

Cookie A file created by a Web site that stores information on your computer, such as your preferences and history when visiting that site. Also known as a first-party cookie.

Copy A command that places a copy of a selected item on the Clipboard to be pasted in another location, but the text also remains in its original place in the document.

Copy backup A Backup type that copies all selected files, like a normal backup, but does not clear the archive attribute.

Counter A performance chart item that provides specific numeric information. *See also* Performance chart.

Cross-fades A transition in which one clip slowly disappears while the next clip slowly appears, making the two clips appear on the screen at the same time.

Cut A command that removes a selected item from a file and places it on the Clipboard, usually to be pasted in another location.

Daily backup A Backup type that copies all selected files that changed on the day the backup was done.

Default The standard way of displaying information or performing a task in Windows.

Deferred printing To pause the printer so that a document sent to print waits in the print queue until the printer is unpaused.

Defragmentation A process that allows you to rewrite the files on your disk to contiguous blocks rather than in random blocks.

Delete To remove a file or folder from a disk.

Desktop The screen that appears when you first start Windows, providing access to your computer's programs and files and to the Internet.

Destination disk The disk to which you want to copy.

Destination file The file where you store a representation of a linked object.

Destination program The program where you store an embedded object.

Dialog box A window that opens when you choose a menu command that is followed by an ellipsis (...); many dialog boxes have options you must choose before Windows or a program can carry out a command.

Differential backup A Backup type that copies only selected files that have changed since the most recent normal or incremental backup.

Digital ID A certificate in some programs, such as Microsoft Outlook or the Address Book. *See also* Certificate.

Digital media Files, such as music tracks, video clips, and DVD segments.

Digital still camera A camera that stores pictures digitally rather than recording them on film.

Digital Video Disc (DVD) A type of CD-ROM that holds a minimum of 4.7 GB (gigabytes), enough for a full-length movie.

Disable To turn off a feature.

Disk defragmenter A Windows accessory that restores fragmented files in one location.

Disk label A name you assign to a hard or floppy disk using the Properties dialog box.

Display adapter A hardware device that allows a computer to communicate with its monitor.

Document A file created using a word processing program such as WordPad.

Document window The work area of the WordPad window.

Domain A collection of computers that the person managing the network creates to group computers used for the same tasks together and to simplify the set up and maintenance of the network.

Double-clicking Clicking the left mouse button twice.

Download The process of transferring files, including Web pages, from the Internet to a computer.

Drag and drop A method that allows you to move text from one location to another using the mouse and without placing the information on the Clipboard.

Dragging Moving items or text to a new location using the mouse.

Driver Software that allows a hardware device (e.g., a printer) to communicate with Windows and other software applications.

DSL lines Wires that provide a completely digital path from one computer to another.

DualView A feature that allows you to add a secondary monitor and expand the size of your desktop.

DVD *See* Digital Video Disc.

Electronic mail A system used to send and receive messages electronically. Also known as e-mail.

Ellipses In a dialog box or on a menu, indicates that you must supply more information before the program can carry out the command you selected. *See also* Dialog box.

E-mail *See* Electronic mail.

E-mail servers An Internet location where your e-mail is stored before you access it.

Embedding Inserting an object created in one program into a document created in another program.

Emoticons Graphical symbols, such as a happy face, that you can insert into an instant message to convey emotions.

Enable To turn a feature on.

Enable compression A formatting option supported only on NTFS drives that specifies whether to format the drive so that folders and files on it are compressed.

End trim point The point in a media clip where you want to trim the end, which creates a new ending point.

End User License Agreement (EULA) A contract that gives you permission regarding your use of the Windows software on your computer and imposes certain restrictions, such as against copying the software.

Extract To uncompress a file or folder.

Fault tolerance The ability of a disk to resist damage—a critical issue with disks on a network computer.

File An electronic collection of information that has a unique name, distinguishing it from other files.

File Allocation Table (FAT) The standard file system. *See also* NT File System and File System.

File extension A three letter extension at the end of a filename that refers to the program Windows uses to distinguish, create, and open files of that type.

File hierarchy A logical structure for files and folders that mimics how you would organize files and folders in a filing cabinet.

File management The process of organizing and keeping track of files and folders.

File system Management and organization system that allows a disk to work with the operating system to store, manage, and access data. Two of the most common file systems are FAT (or FAT32, which is an improvement on FAT technology) and NTFS.

Filmstrip A folder view in which image files are displayed as a filmstrip.

Filter A management feature that allows you to view only events matching specified criteria, such as all events associated with a certain user.

Firewall A security system that creates a protective barrier between a computer or network and others on the Internet.

First-line indent marker The top triangle on the ruler in WordPad that controls where the first line of the paragraph begins.

First-party cookie *See* Cookie.

Folder A collection of files and/or other folders that helps you organize your disks.

Folder template A collection of folder task links and viewing options.

Folders Explorer Bar The pane on the left side of the file management window that displays all drives and folders on the computer and connected networks.

Font The design of letters, numbers, and other characters. For example, Times New Roman.

Foreground process The processing time that the program in which you are currently working requires to start and complete tasks, such as opening a dialog box and performing a command.

Format To change the appearance of information but not the actual content.

Format bar A toolbar in WordPad that contains formatting buttons.

Fragmented file A file that is broken up and stored on different parts of a disk.

Frame A separate window within a Web page.

Free space Portions of a disk that are not yet part of a partition or filled with information.

Full format A formatting option that removes all files from any floppy disk (previously formatted or not), and also scans the disk for bad sectors.

Full permission A permission type that allows the user to edit and save changes to the file (or "write") and execute programs on server or client computers.

Gigabyte A file size measurement equal to 1,024 megabytes.

Graphical user interface (GUI) Pronounced "gooey." An environment made up of meaningful symbols, words, and windows in which you can control the basic operation of a computer and the programs that run on it.

Hanging indent marker The bottom triangle on the ruler in WordPad that controls where second and subsequent lines of the paragraph begin.

Hardware device A physical object that you plug into a computer, such as a printer, fax, or scanner.

Help and Support A book stored on your computer with additional links to the Internet, complete with a search feature, an index, and a table of contents to make finding Windows-related information easier.

Hibernation A state in which your computer first saves everything in memory on your hard disk and then shuts down.

Highlighted When an item is shaded differently, indicating that it is selected. *See also* Select.

Hits The results of an Internet search that, when clicked, open a Web page or category.

Home computer Computer that is used to connect to another computer remotely over a phone line or modem when using the Remote Desktop program with Windows XP Professional.

Home page The page that opens every time you start Internet Explorer.

Home Phoneline Network (HPN) A network configuration that uses existing phone lines and telephone cable to connect computers located in different rooms of a home together without a network hub or special cables.

Hot plugging The ability to add and remove devices to a computer while the computer is running and have the operating system automatically recognize the change.

HPN *See* Home Phoneline Network.

HTTP (Hypertext Transfer Protocol) A type of incoming e-mail server that is used for Web sites, such as Hotmail, and allows you to send and receive e-mail messages in Outlook Express or on a Web site.

Hub *See* Network hub.

Hyperlinks (links) Highlighted text or graphics in a Web page that open other Web pages when you click them.

Icons Graphical representations of computer elements, such as files and programs.

IMAP (Internet Message Access Protocol) A type of incoming e-mail server that allows you to access multiple folders.

Import The process of inserting or bringing information into a program from another program or from the Web.

Incoming network connection A network connection that enables a computer to let other computers connect to it.

Incremental backup A backup option that backs up only the files that have changed since your last backup.

Ink-jet A hardware printing device that works by spraying ionized ink onto a sheet of paper.

Insertion point A blinking vertical line that appears in the work area of the WordPad window, indicating where the next text will appear when you type.

Instant message An online type-written conversation in real-time between two or more contacts.

Internet A communications system that connects computers and computer networks located around the world using telephone lines, cables, satellites and other telecommunications media.

Internet style The Windows user interface setting where you single-click icons to open them. Also known as Web style.

Internet account A set of connection information provided by an Internet Service Provider (ISP) or Local Area Network (LAN) administrator that allows you to access the Internet, and send and receive e-mail.

Internet Explorer A program that helps you access the World Wide Web.

Internet Service Provider (ISP) A company that provides Internet access.

Interrupt Request Line (IRQ) A software setting that allows a hardware device to communicate with your computer's software.

ISDN lines Wires that provide a completely digital path from one computer to another.

Keyword A word or phrase you submit to a search engine to find various Web sites on the Internet. *See also* Search engine.

Kilobyte A file size measurement equal to 1,024 bytes.

LAN *See* Local Area Network.

Laser printer A hardware printing device that utilizes a laser beam to produce an image on a drum, which is rolled through a reservoir of toner and transferred to the paper through a combination of heat and pressure.

Left indent marker The small square under the bottom triangle on the ruler in WordPad that allows you to move the first-line indent marker and the left indent marker simultaneously, which indents the entire paragraph at once.

Legacy hardware Any hardware device that is not designed for Windows Plug and Play.

Linking Connecting an object created in one program to a document created in another program so that changes made will be reflected in both.

Links *See* Hyperlinks.

Local Area Network (LAN) A network where the workstation computers are close together in a single building or group of buildings.

Local printer A printer connected directly to a computer.

Loop An option that repeatedly plays a media clip until you stop it.

Mapping A network feature that enables a user to create a direct connection to a network drive for quick and easy access.

Maximize A button located in the upper-right corner of the window that enlarges a window so it fills the entire screen.

Megabyte A file size measurement equal to 1,048,576 bytes, which is equal to 1,024 kilobytes.

Menu A list of available commands in a program. *See also* Menu bar.

Menu bar A bar at the top of a window that organizes commands into groups of related operations. *See also* Menu.

Message flags An icon associated with an e-mail message that helps you determine the status or priority of the message.

Minimize A button located in the upper-right corner of the window that reduces the size of a window.

Monitor *See* Audit.

Monitor A hardware device that displays the computer screen.

Monitor bar A toolbar that contains buttons to control the playback and navigation of a movie in Windows Media Player.

Mouse A hand-held input device that you roll across a flat surface (such as a desk or a mouse pad). *See also* Mouse pointer.

Mouse buttons The two buttons (right and left) on the mouse used to make selections and commands.

Mouse pointer The arrow-shaped cursor on the screen that follows the movement of the mouse. The shape changes depending on the program and the task being executed. *See also* Mouse.

Multitasking Working with more than one Windows program at the same time.

My Computer A built-in file management accessory that uses a task pane to help you organize your files and folders.

My Network Places A powerful Windows XP tool for managing files and folders across a network.

Network A system of two or more computers connected together to share resources.

Network connections A Windows XP feature that enables you to access network and Internet resources, whether you are physically connected using a direct cable or connected remotely using a dial-up or cable modem.

Network hub A hardware device that connects multiple computers to a central location.

Network Interface Card (NIC) A hardware device that allows a computer to communicate with a network.

Network printer A printer connected to a network and shared by those with access to the network.

News server A computer located on the Internet that stores newsgroup messages.

Newsgroups Online discussion groups about a particular topic, usually in an e-mail format.

NIC *See* Network Interface Card.

Node A category of tools in the left pane of the Computer Management window. *See also* Console tree.

Normal backup A Backup type that backs up all selected files, regardless of when the files were last changed.

Notepad A Windows text editing program that comes as a built-in accessory.

Notification area Located on the right side of the taskbar and used to display the time and icons for current running programs and related processes.

NT File System (NTFS) An advanced file system that provides additional performance, security, and reliability.

Object A picture, chart, video clip, text, or almost anything you can create on a computer.

Object Linking and Embedding (OLE) The process of placing and working with common objects in different programs.

Open Type font A font type based on a mathematical equation that creates letters with smooth curves and sharp corners.

Operating system A computer program that controls the basic operation of your computer and the programs you run on it. Windows XP is an example of an operating system.

Optimization The procedure of rearranging fragmented files into one location on a disk.

Outlook Express Start Page Displays tools that you can use to read e-mail, set up a newsgroup account, read newsgroup messages, compose e-mail messages, enter and edit Address Book information, and find people on the Internet.

Output The results of a DOS command.

Owner The person who can make changes to a file in a shared or network environment.

Pane Refers to a part of a window that is divided into two or more sections.

Parallel port A hardware connection that sends information more than one byte simultaneously.

Paste A command that copies the last item placed on the Clipboard and inserts it in the document.

Peer-to-peer networking A networking configuration that enables two or more computers to link together without designating a central server.

Performance chart A chart that system administrators use to observe how a computer's processes are behaving over time.

Permissions Settings that designate what each user can and cannot do to each file.

Personal folders A storage area designed for managing business and personal files and folders; for example, My Documents.

Pinned Refers to putting items on the Start menu, where they will be easily accessed. Pinned items remain on the Start menu until they are unpinned, or removed.

Pixel A single point on your monitor's screen. *See also* Screen resolution.

Places bar An area on the left side of the Open and Save dialog boxes that helps navigate to common locations or recently used files and folders on your computer or network.

Playlist A customized list or sequence of digital media.

Plug and Play Hardware designed for quick and easy installation with Windows XP.

Point A unit of measurement (1/72nd inch) used to specify the size of text.

Pointing Positioning the mouse pointer over an icon or over any specific item on the screen.

POP3 (Post Office Protocol) A type of incoming e-mail server that allows you to access e-mail messages from a single Inbox folder.

Port The location on the back of your computer where you connect the hardware, such as a printer cable.

Portable device Hardware, such as a small handheld piece of hardware equipment that combines computing, telephone/fax, Internet/e-mail, and networking, such as Pocket PCs and Personal Digital Assistants (PDA).

Power scheme A predefined collection of power usage settings.

Print Preview A feature that shows the layout and formatting of a document as it would appear when printed.

Print queue The order in which a printer prints documents.

Printing A process to create a printout. *See also* Printout.

Printout A paper document that you can share with others or review as a work in progress.

Privileged system components Windows operating system processes or tasks in progress.

Program button A button on the taskbar that represents an open program, program group, or file.

Programs Task-oriented software you use to accomplish specific tasks, such as word processing, managing files on your computer, and performing calculations. Also known as applications.

Project file The working copy of your movie in Movie Maker.

Properties The characteristics of a specific element (such as the mouse, keyboard, or desktop) that you can customize.

Protocol (component) The language that the computer uses to communicate with other computers on the network.

Quick Format The fastest way to format a previously formatted floppy disk by simply removing all of the files from it.

Quick Launch toolbar A toolbar that may be located next to the Start button on the taskbar that contains buttons to start Internet-related programs and show the desktop.

Random Access Memory (RAM) A temporary storage space whose contents are erased when you turn off the computer.

Read permission A permission type that allows the user to open and view the file but not make changes that can be saved in the file.

Recycle Bin A temporary storage area for deleted files that is located on your desktop.

Registration The process of providing contact information that ensures you receive product updates and support information from Microsoft. Registration is not required.

Remote computer Computer that is accessed by another computer remotely over a phone line or modem using the Remote Desktop program with Windows XP Professional.

Restore Down A button located in the upper-right corner of the window that returns a window to its previous size.

Restore point An earlier time before the changes were made to your computer to which System Restore returns your computer system.

Rich Text Format A standard text format that includes formatting information and provides flexibility when working with other programs.

Right-clicking Clicking the right mouse button to open a shortcut menu that lists task-specific commands.

Router A hardware device that connects any number of LANs together.

Scanner A device like a photocopy machine, on which you can lay photographs, books, and other documents that you want to save in digital format on your computer.

Scheme A predefined combination of settings that assures visual coordination of all items.

Screen font A font that consists of bitmapped characters. *See also* Bitmapped characters.

Screen resolution The number of pixels on the entire screen, which determines the amount of information your monitor displays.

Screen saver A moving pattern that fills your screen after your computer has not been used for a specified amount of time. *See also* Burn in.

Screen tip A description of a toolbar button that appears on your screen when you position the mouse pointer over the button.

Scroll bar A bar that appears at the bottom and/or right edge of a window whose contents are not entirely visible. Each scroll bar contains a scroll box and two scroll arrows. You click the arrows or drag the box in the scroll bar in the direction you want the window display to move.

Scroll box A box located in the vertical and horizontal scroll bars that indicates your relative position in a window. *See also* Scroll bar.

Search engine A program you access through a Web site and use to search through a collection of information found on the Internet.

Sector The smallest unit that can be accessed on a disk.

Select To click an item, such as an icon, indicating that you want to perform some future operation on it.

Separator page A page that lists the name, owner, date, and time of a print job and that prints before each document. Also known as a banner.

Serial port A hardware connection that sends information one byte at a time.

Server A single computer on the network designated to store these resources.

Service (component) A network component that allows you to share your computer resources, such as files and printers, with other networked computers.

Share name The name network users see on the network in My Network Places.

Shared printer A printer made available to computers on a network from a client computer.

Shortcut A link that you can place in any location that gives you instant access to a particular file, folder, or program on your hard disk or on a network.

Shortcut menu A menu that you display by right-clicking an item on the desktop. *See also* Right-clicking.

Shut down The action you perform when you are finished working with Windows to make it safe to turn off your computer.

Skin The Windows Media Player's appearance.

SMTP (Simple Mail Transfer Protocol) An outgoing e-mail server that is generally used to send messages between e-mail servers.

Snap-in A tool that you add to a container in the Computer Management window. *See also* Container.

Source disk The disk from which you want to copy.

Source file The file where a linked object is stored.

Source material Media such as audio, video, and still images used to create a movie in Movie Maker.

Source program The program where you create or insert an object.

Spooling The process of storing a temporary copy of a file on the hard disk and then sending the file to the print device. Also known as background printing.

Standby A state in which your monitor and hard disks turn off after being idle for a set time.

Start button Located on the taskbar and used to start programs, find and open files, access the Windows Help and Support Center and more.

Start menu A list of commands that allows you to start a program, open a document, change a Windows setting, find a file, or display Help and support information.

Start trim point The point in a media clip where you want to trim the beginning, which creates a new starting point.

Storyboard view A Movie Maker view that shows the order of your clips and allows you to rearrange them.

Straight cut A transition in which one clip ends and the next one starts immediately without overlapping.

Streaming media A technique for transferring media so that it can be processed as a steady and continuous stream. The Windows Media Player delivers streaming video, live broadcasts, sound, and music playback over the Internet.

Stretch A display properties option that displays the wallpaper picture or pattern enlarged across the desktop screen.

Subfolder A folder within a folder.

Submenu A menu that opens when you select an item with an arrow next to it from another menu. *See also* Menu.

Synchronize To update a file or Web page stored on one computer with the latest version of the same file or Web page on another computer.

System restore A program installed with Windows XP Professional used to undo harmful changes to your computer and restore its settings. *See also* Restore point.

System state data A collection of system-specific data, such as the registry and boot files, that can be backed up and restored.

Tab stop A predefined stopping point along the document's typing line.

Tabs A user interface at the top of dialog boxes that organizes options into related categories. *See also* Dialog box.

Tape drive A hardware device that reads data from and writes data onto a tape

Task Scheduler A tool that enables you to schedule tasks to run at a time convenient for you.

Taskbar Located at the bottom of the screen, and may contain the Start button, the Quick Launch toolbar, the notification area, and program buttons, for example.

Theme A set of visual elements, such as desktop background, screen saver, mouse pointers, sounds, icons, and fonts that provide a consistent look for Windows.

Third-party cookie A file created by a Web site you are not currently viewing, such as a banner ad on the current Web site you are viewing, that stores information on your computer, such as your preferences and history while visiting the current site.

Thumbnails A folder view in which files are displayed as miniature images.

Tile To display the background picture repeatedly in rows and columns across the desktop.

Timeline view A Movie Maker view that shows the duration of each clip and the types of transitions between them as well as the sound track.

Title bar Located at the top of the window and displays the name of the program and the file name.

Toggle A button or option that acts as an on/off switch.

Toolbar Used in a program to display buttons for easy access to the most commonly used commands.

Track A ring around the circumference of a hard or floppy disk.

Transition The way movie clips change from one to the next.

Trim A movie production process that deletes portions of clips you don't want to use.

Trim handles Small triangles above the selected clip that are used to change the frame size in a movie.

TrueType font A font type based on a mathematical equation that creates letters with smooth curves and sharp corners.

Uniform Resource Locator (URL) A Web page's address.

Upload To transfer a file to a Web site.

USB (Universal Serial Bus) port An external hardware interface on the computer that allows you to connect up to 127 peripheral devices, such as mice, modems, scanners, cameras, and keyboards, using plug-and-play technology and transfer data at high speed.

Virtual memory A process by which Windows uses hard disk drive space to simulate system RAM.

Virtual Private Network (VPN) A network connection that enables a computer to securely connect to a network over the Internet.

Volume A designated storage area that can span part of one or more disks.

Volume shadow copy A backup feature that backs up files even though they are in the process of being written to.

VPN *See* Virtual Private Network.

Wallet A .NET Passport service that stores personal financial information, such as your credit card number, in one location on their secure Web site, which you can use to make online purchases at participating .NET Passport Wallet Web sites without re-entering information each time.

WAN *See* Wide Area Network.

Web address A unique address on the Internet where you can locate a Web page. *See also* URL.

Web browser A software program that you use to "browse the Web," or access and display Web pages.

Web items Elements you can place on the desktop to access or display information from the Internet.

Web pages Documents that contain highlighted words, phrases, and graphics that open other Web pages when you click them.

Web site A location on the World Wide Web that contains Web pages linked together.

Web style *See* Internet style.

Whiteboard A program in Windows Messenger that you can use to display, share, and modify graphical content with others.

Wide Area Network (WAN) A network where the workstation computers are spread over a large area across town or the entire country, or internationally, using dial-up or wireless connections.

Window Rectangular frame on your screen that can contain several icons, the contents of a file, or other usable data.

Windows Classic The look and feel of the Windows 95, 98, and Windows Me desktop display. *See also* Classic style.

Windows Explorer A Windows file management accessory that uses two panes to help you organize your files and folders.

Windows Media Player A Windows accessory that allows you to play video, sound, and mixed-media files.

Windows Movie Maker A Windows accessory that allows you to create your own movies from a variety of sources.

Windows program Software designed to run on computers using the Windows operating system.

Word wrap A feature that automatically places text that won't fit on one line onto the next line.

WordPad A Windows word processing program that comes as a built-in accessory.

Workgroup A group of computers that perform common tasks or belong to users who share common duties and interests.

Workstation Computers on a network that access resources on a server instead of having to store them. Also known as clients.

World Wide Web Part of the Internet that consists of Web sites located on computers around the world connected through the Internet.

Write The process of copying files and folders to a compact disc. Also known as burning.

Index

Index

Index

Index